THE GREAT MUGHALS AND THEIR INDIA

THE GREAT MUGHALS AND THEIR INDIA

REVISED EDITION

DIRK COLLIER

HAY HOUSE INDIA
New Delhi • London • Sydney
Carlsbad, California • New York City

Hay House Publishers (India) Pvt Ltd
Muskaan Complex, Plot No. 3, B-2, Vasant Kunj, New Delhi – 110070, India

Hay House LLC, P.O. Box 5100, Carlsbad, CA 92018-5100, USA
Hay House UK Ltd, 1st Floor, Crawford Corner, 91-93 Baker Street, London W1U 6QQ, UK
Hay House Australia Publishing Pty Ltd, 18/36 Ralph St., Alexandria NSW 2015, Australia

Email: contact@hayhouse.co.in
Website: www.hayhouse.co.in

Front cover photograph: 'Tomb of the Mughal Emperor Humayun' by Amit Nimade, Wikimedia Commons, licensed under CC BY-SA 4.0. Changes were made to the original.

First published by Hay House India, 2016
Revised edition, 2025
22 21 20 19 18 17 16 15 14 13

ISBN 978-93-85827-61-7

Printed Repro India Ltd

MIX
Paper from responsible sources
FSC® C047271

Hay House is committed to a sustainable future for our business, our readers and our planet. This book is made from Forest Stewardship Council® certified paper.

To

Anne

Bart, Kelly & Juliette

Johan, Ellen, Alix & Jim

Since wars begin in the minds of men, it is in the minds of men that the defences of peace must be constructed.

UNESCO Constitution, 16 November 1945

Those who cannot remember the past are condemned to repeat it.

George Santayana, *The Life of Reason*

For the truth, my son, is like a beautifully shaped diamond. It is one, yet, it has thousands upon thousands of facets, colours, aspects and reflections. Every person who honestly seeks the truth will have something important to say to you, but remember that no one will ever possess it entirely.

Dirk Collier, *Akbar's Farewell*

Contents

Preface

Back in 1956 – the year of my birth – S. Chand & Co. (Delhi-based publishers) released *Mughal Rule in India*, a rather compact history book written by S. M. Edwardes and H. L. O. Garrett, two former Indian civil servants.

The preface of this otherwise unremarkable publication begins with the following observation:

> *Of the making of books concerning the Mughal period of Indian history there is no end, and many volumes dealing with the lives of the emperors and with various aspects of Mughal administrative activity testify to the spell exercised upon the minds of men by the story of the Timurids of Delhi* [emphasis added].

It was true back then, and it always will be: the Mughal dynasty and its cultural legacy – the world-famous *Taj Mahal* being the most prominent among countless examples – is an inexhaustible source of inspiration to historians, writers, moviemakers, artists and ordinary mortals alike.

Why is this? Whence this widespread fascination with a few generations of in-fighting, decadent spendthrifts who, more often than not, shamelessly bled their own people dry to finance their own extravagance, and whose true military might barely lasted a century and a half?

The reason for this, in my opinion, is twofold.

First and foremost, the history of the Mughal dynasty just happens to be a *great story*. Humankind has always been fascinated by grandiose and tragic stories – both mythical and true. That is why there will always be an audience for the plays of William Shakespeare and Sophocles; that is why the Mahabharata and Homer's Iliad and Odyssey are as alive today as they were over 2500 years ago; and that is why there will always be books and motion pictures about Achilles, Alexander the Great or Queen Cleopatra, to name but a few random examples.

Mughal history abounds with all the ingredients of classical drama: ambition and frustration, triumph and despair, grandeur and decline, love and hate, loyalty and betrayal. In other words: it is fun to read, and offers ample food for thought and reflection on the human condition.

Secondly, and much more importantly, Mughal history *deserves* to be widely read and reflected upon, because of its lasting cultural and political relevance to today's world – to the Indian subcontinent in particular and to the world at large.

India's cultural identity would be mauled beyond recognition if we were to try and 'purge' the Mughal influence from it. Indian food, architecture, art (including literature, calligraphy and painting), popular music and even the Hindustani/Urdu/Hindi language itself (the very words 'Hindi and Urdu' in the first place) would be impoverished beyond recognition; they would become a mere shadow of the cultural treasure they are bringing to the world today. The same, incidentally, is true the other way round: the Mughal or Indian Muslim culture would be unthinkable without the influence of the millenary Hindu civilization.

Mughal history, first and foremost, is the history of *Majma-ul-Bahrain*, 'the confluence of two oceans', as Shah Jahan's eldest son Dara Shikoh used to call the fateful encounter of Islam with the ancient Hindu civilization.

The result is a thousand years of common history, tainted by terrible bloodshed and hatred, but, at the same time, marked by cultural exchanges and even interpenetration and syncretism, leading to mutual appreciation and even genuine friendship and brotherhood.

In this sense, Mughal history remains unfinished, a constant source of inspiration and reflection for generations to come.

***

History books, in my view, should be accurate, informative and fun to read. These were the three goals I had in mind:

- to write an entertaining book, concise enough to appeal to the ordinary reader, who neither has the leisure nor the inclination to delve into every detail;

- yet detailed and nuanced enough to provide that same reader with an accurate and complete enough picture;
- and offering her or him food for thought and reflection on today's world.

For, whether we like it or not, the Mughals have left us with a legacy that cannot be erased. Where did they succeed? Where did they fail? And more importantly, what should we learn from their experiences?

Dirk Collier

Prologue

The Central Asian 'Mughals' and the Subcontinent They Made Their Home

Mughal: The Misnomer That Stuck

Let us make one thing clear, right at the start: the early Mughal emperors never referred to or described themselves as *Mughal* or *Moghol* (i.e., the Persian word for Mongol). For one very simple and very good reason: they were not.

Zahir-ud Din Muhammad Babur (1483–1530), the Central Asian prince who was to become – entirely unplanned, quite coincidentally and almost inadvertently – the much-acclaimed founder of India's most famous dynasty, was born in the faraway valley of Fergana, a fertile region straddling the borders of present-day Uzbekistan, Tajikistan and Kyrgyzstan. Priding himself on his glorious ancestry as a direct descendant of Timur/Tamerlane (1336–1405) through his father, and of Genghis (Chingiz) Khan (*c.* 1162–1227) through his mother, Babur's ambition was to rule over Samarqand (now in Uzbekistan), Timur's magnificent capital city, and over as much land as he would be able to hold on to.

Genetically speaking, like most other people in that part of the world, he must have been an approximately even mixture of Caucasian and East Asian ('Mongol') blood. Ethnically and culturally, however, he was, from head to toe, a Turk. A typical fifteenth-century Central Asian Turk, to be precise: he was steeped in the Turko-Persian-Islamic civilization of the Silk Road. Babur did not *feel* Mongol at all: he did not consider himself to be one, and, in fact, he very much distrusted and despised them, declaring, for instance: '*Mischief and devastation must always be expected from the Mongol horde*'[1] and '... *were the Mongols a race of angels, it [sic] would still be a vile nation*'.[2]

So, while the term *Mughal* or *Moghol* may have been used quite commonly by Iranians and other neighbouring nations when referring to people from Central Asia, that does not make it any less wrong, or highly misleading at best.

Genghis Khan's conquering hordes were far from ethnically homogeneous: they consisted of a coalition of several neighbouring Mongol and Turkic nomadic tribes. The ethnic Mongols, properly speaking, are actually believed to have been a minority in their own army. In any case, soon after their spectacular conquest of Asia, they blended in with the local peoples, and soon adopted the local language, religion and culture (i.e., Manchu, Chinese, Buddhist and Daoist in the East; Turko-Persian and Muslim in the West).

***

The *Chagatai Turki* language[3] in which Babur wrote his famous memoirs was highly Persianized in its vocabulary, expressions and sentence structure. And while he did choose to write these memoirs in his own native *Turki*, Babur was, as we shall see, an accomplished poet in Persian as well.

***

The foregoing discussion clearly illustrates the essentially bilingual character of the Central Asian civilization along the Silk Road where Babur grew up. Countryside nomads, kings and army leaders like himself invariably spoke the local Turkic dialect, while the city-dwelling Muslim clerics, jurists and administrators in Samarqand, Tashkent, Bukhara and other cities were *Tajiks* – i.e., Persian-speaking people. However, a great many of both communities were fluent or at least conversant in both languages. Even today, in spite of decades of consistent attempts by the local authorities to 'homogenize' the population,[4] many inhabitants of the region still understand and speak Turkish, Persian and Russian, in varying degrees of fluency.

Compared to other tongues, Persian was always the more prestigious *lingua franca*, the common language of government, commerce, science, poetry and literature. It is therefore no surprise that the Mughal emperors continued to favour it as their official language of government, even if the first few generations (at least up to and including Jahangir:

1569–1627) continued to be conversant in their ancestral *Turki* as well, occasionally speaking it with their family members, usually when discussing confidential matters.

Sons of Timur

The Mughals actually called themselves *Silsila-i-Gurkaniyya*, the Gurkanid dynasty, in reference to their glorious – if infamously cruel – ancestor, the much-dreaded Amīr Temür. Temür (nicknamed Timur-i-Lang or Timur the Lame by his adversaries, a nickname which in turn got corrupted to Tamerlane,[5] as he is known in the West) had adopted the honorary title of *Gurkan* (meaning son-in-law, from the Mongolian word *gürägän* or *kürägän*), a name given to all those who had married a princess of Genghis Khan's blood, as he had done.

In this *political* sense, and in this political sense only, the name *Mughal* appears justified, because ultimately, throughout the history of Central Asia, any political pretence to sovereignty was ultimately based on claims of patrilineal descent from Timur and/or Genghis Khan.

Before the advent of the nineteenth-century Russian tsars, Genghis Khan had indeed been the first – and the last – ruler to have been able to unite all of Central Asia.

Several years before his death in 1227, amidst disturbing family quarrels, Genghis Khan had divided his empire among his sons into several Khanates. These were originally designed as subterritories: the Khans were expected to follow the so-called Great Khan (Genghis Khan's third and favourite son Ögedei), who ruled directly over most of Eastern Asia. Shortly after Genghis Khan's death, however, the four Khanates became effectively independent and separate empires: the Golden Horde Khanate in the northwest; the Il-Khanate in the southwest; the Yuan dynasty in the east; and the Chagatai Khanate (named after Genghis Khan's second son Chagatai) in northern Iran and Central Asia – the latter being the homeland of Babur and his ancestors.

The detailed history of these separate Khanates is of little interest here; suffice to say that, over time and for a variety of reasons, they, too, disintegrated into many smaller entities. The only one to have been able to reunite a sizeable part of Genghis Khan's empire – and add a few new territories, including Delhi – was Timur (1336–1405).

***

Timur was a military genius and a patron of the arts. Those are just about the only two nice things to be said about this absolute horror of a man, who won his empire in a series of genocidal wars, the cruelty of which defies the most morbid imagination. In proportion to the total population of the territories conquered, the scale of Timur's wholesale slaughter is absolutely unique in human history, and makes even Adolf Hitler look like an amateur. Literally millions of people,[6] the populations of entire regions, were slaughtered, systematically, to the very last man, woman, child and infant– with the exception of a few renowned artists and craftsmen, rounded up and marched off to Samarqand to embellish the conqueror's capital.

Success, however horribly attained, tends to breed respect. Timur's spectacular conquests and keen sense of grandeur and magnificence have appealed to the imagination of many a would-be king. But history has, for once, been just: Other than a few grandiose buildings and a depressing reputation as the worst mass murderer of all time, he left nothing of lasting value. After his death in 1405, his family was enmeshed in bitter disputes and civil wars, and the great empire quickly disintegrated.

Five generations later, when Timur's great-great-great-grandson Babur was born in 1483, the entire region was fragmented into a series of provinces and fiefdoms, governed by dozens of competing brothers, cousins, uncles and nephews, of varying degrees of remoteness, all priding themselves on their Timurid ancestry, the grandiosity of their pompous titles inversely proportional to their real power.

As historian Bamber Gascoigne phrased it, all these princes '*were united only in the conviction that in each of its many small and fluctuating kingdoms, a Timurid prince should occupy the throne. The question of which prince should sit on which thrones was a matter of constant warfare among themselves. Birth gave each a general claim; only possession could establish it*'.[7]

This was to be the curse of the Timurids, as it has been the plague of the Romans, the Ottomans and so many others: There was no generally accepted, orderly succession law. First-born sons theoretically were supposed to have precedence over the others; in practice, however, every prince of Timurid blood could have a go at the throne. Throughout the dynasty's history, right from the beginning until the bitter end, periods of relative calm would be interspersed with bouts of fratricidal civil war and murder.

Sons of India

Genetically speaking, the Mughals drifted away from their Turkish origins quite soon after their arrival in India.

If Babur and his son Humayun were still full-blooded Central Asian Turks, Akbar through his mother (Hamida Banu Begum) was half Persian and Akbar's son Jahangir (through his mother, the princess of Amber) was therefore 25 per cent Turk, 25 per cent Persian and 50 per cent Rajput. Shah Jahan (the Mughal par excellence), Jahangir's son, was 75 per cent Rajput: both his mother (Rajkumari Shri Manavati Baiji Lall Sahiba alias Taj Bibi Bilqis Makani) and his paternal grandmother were Rajput princesses.

From Shah Jahan onwards, the only genetic constant in the family was its mixed descent with a continuous ebbing and flowing of Persian and Rajput blood and an ever-diminishing Turkic component.

Shah Jahan's son Aurangzeb (through his mother, the famous Mumtaz Mahal) was more than half Persian – 56.25 per cent, to be exact. Through his father's side, he was still 37.5 per cent Rajput and 6.25 per cent Turkish. This, in turn, makes his son and first successor Muhammad Azam (also born from a Persian mother, Dilras Banu Begum) 78.125 per cent Persian, 18.75 per cent Rajput, and a mere 3.125 per cent Turkish. Azam lasted less than three months on the throne (details given in Chapter 7). His half-brother, usurper and successor, Bahadur Shah I, in contrast, was half Kashmiri (through his mother Begum Nawab Bai, Aurangzeb's second wife), 28.125 per cent Persian, 18.75 per cent Rajput and only 3.125 per cent Central Asian Turkish.

***

The foregoing discussion clearly shows that the 'purity' of the maternal line was of little or no political consequence in the Mughal dynasty. Strange as it may seem, there are, in fact, many examples of Mughal princes whose mothers will forever remain unknown, as their names were not even properly recorded.

It seems becoming to note, however, that Bahadur Shah II (1775–1862; also known as Bahadur Shah Zafar), the very last emperor on the Mughal throne, son of Akbar Shah II and Lal Bai, a Hindu Rajput princess, was, once again, more than half Rajput.

For indeed, Bahadur Shah II, a devout, gentle and moderate-minded Sufi Muslim, was a true Indian. And so had been his ancestors, ever since Akbar the Great. Far more important than the ancestral blood in a person's veins – in the end, aren't we all related? – is his or her *culture*, the environment he or she feels at home in and identifies with.

In that sense, Babur, the founder of the dynasty, was still very much a foreigner to India. Babur profoundly disliked India. He did not care at all for its climate, its food or its people. More often than not, he felt dreadfully homesick, filled with nostalgia for Kabul and the lost territories in Central Asia.

In contrast, Babur's famous grandson Akbar the Great, the first Mughal emperor to be born on Indian soil, was a true son of India. He was born in 1556 in Umarkot (now in Sindh, Pakistan). He cared precious little – if at all – for the ancestral lands in Central Asia. Once he could rest assured that his north-western borders were secure (with Kabul, Qandahar and Kashmir firmly under control) he resolutely turned southwards. Next on his agenda was not Timur's capital in Central Asia, but the Deccan and beyond: Akbar's ultimate ambition was to rule over the subcontinent in which he was born, had spent his entire life, felt at home in and identified with. Akbar did indeed not think of himself as a 'foreign' occupier. On the contrary, his entire career was a grandiose – if largely failed – attempt to 'blend in' with India, to blot out the difference between his Hindu and Muslim subjects, to underscore their common Indian identity and to unite them under his banner. In that sense, he was the true forerunner of today's secular Indian leaders.

With his rather unorthodox views on religion – from an Islamist point of view, anyway – Akbar was, admittedly, an exception among the members of his dynasty. His predecessors and successors, indeed, were 'normal' Sunni Muslims, with all the shades of grey that can be found behind that term, ranging from free-thinking sceptics like Jahangir, via pragmatists like Babur, to gentle-minded Sufis like Bahadur Shah II, or bigoted fanatics like Aurangzeb. But each and every one of them, with the exception of Babur, was an *Indian* Muslim, in every sense of the word.

***

Linguistically, culturally as well as ethnically, the Mughals who came after Babur no longer resembled their Central Asian ancestors: India had forever changed their faces, hearts and souls. Just like, whether one likes it or not, they have forever changed the face, heart and soul of India.

INDIAN HISTORY: A GENERAL OVERVIEW

Homo sapiens in India: Around 75,000 years ago.
IndusValley (Harappa) Civilization: c. 3300–1300 BCE.
Vedic civilization: c. 1500–500 BCE.
Spread of Buddhism and Jainism: 500–200 BCE.
Maurya Empire: 297–250 BCE.
Ashoka the Great: 304–232 BCE.
Hindu revival and classical Hindu civilization: 200 BCE–CE 1100.
Epic plus Puranic period/pre-classical period: 200 BCE–CE 300.
Gupta Empire/golden age of Hinduism: CE 320–550.
Late classical civilization: CE 650–1100.

The Hindu-Islamic Period

Early sultanates plus trading colonies: 1100–1857.
Mughal Empire: 1526–1857.
Great Mughals: 1526–1707.
- **Babur:** 1526–1530.
- **Humayun:** (1530–1540; 1555–1556).
- **Akbar the Great:** 1556–1605.
- **Jahangir:** 1605–1627.
- **Shah Jahan:** 1627–1658.
- **Aurangzeb:** 1658–1707.

The 'Lesser Mughals': 1707–1857.
Their rivals and successors
- **Maratha Empire:** 1713–1818.
- **Sikh Empire:** 1799–1849.
- **Afghan (Durrani) Empire:** 1747–1862.
- **British East India Company:** 1757–1858.
- **British Raj:** 1858–1947.
- **Indian Princely States:** 1721–1949.

Independence, partition and beyond: August 1947 to the present.

In 1525,[8] the year before Babur crossed the Khyber Pass – then and now, the most important mountain pass from northern Persia and Afghanistan into the Indian subcontinent – on his way to conquer the throne of Delhi, two features were crucial:

- India was highly *fragmented* and politically unstable, i.e., divided into many rival principalities with unsteady, fluctuating borders;
- and quite remarkably, even though Muslims made up only a small percentage of the population, the majority of these principalities was ruled by *Muslim* dynasties of *foreign* – predominantly Afghan – extraction.

Let us, before turning to the story of Babur's adventurous and eventful life, examine these two important features a bit more closely.

One Continent, Many Borders

When we speak about the Indian subcontinent or 'Greater India', what exactly do we mean? Where exactly does that subcontinent begin or end? If it is supposed to be 'Indian', what exactly does that mean? Where does 'Indianness' begin and where does it end?

The sobering and rather disconcerting answer is that – leaving aside the thorny issue of unresolved Sino–Indian border disputes[9] – there is no single, coherent, generally accepted demarcation of territories and ethnic groups to be included in the definition. Even the name itself appears to have become rather sensitive, many people living outside the current Republic of India preferring the arguably more neutral – if nondescript, noncommittal and ultimately meaningless – geographical term 'South Asian' over 'Indian'. Demarcations will vary according to the historical, cultural, ethnic, linguistic, religious, military or geopolitical context; but every definition and delineation will inevitably entail a number of rather sensitive political connotations.

A few examples:

- Akbar the Great would have argued, that Kabul and Qandahar (in present-day Afghanistan) are part and parcel of India: historically, his grandfather Babur had been the lawful king of Kabul many years before conquering Hindustan; politically, as a prominent descendant of Timur and Genghis Khan, he had, in his own eyes at least, a legitimate claim on the throne of any region that once belonged to his glorious ancestors; and last but not least, from a military point of view, he would have argued that any Indian king, worthy of that name, should realize how important it was to keep Kabul and Qandahar, once India's two western entrance gates, tightly under control.

- Others – including the vast majority of present-day Afghan leaders and many people in West Pakistan – would argue that Pakistan's (and British India's) 2640 km western border with Afghanistan (the so-called Durand Line of 1893, named after Sir Mortimer Durand, a British diplomat) is entirely arbitrary. Cutting through the homeland of Baluchis and Pashtuns, it was imposed upon the local Afghans by the British colonialists for their own geopolitical reasons, without any consideration for local realities and sensitivities. From this point of view, the western border of 'India' – historically, linguistically, culturally and ethnically – is the Indus Valley, roughly coinciding with the current Pakistani provinces of Sindh and Punjab. Indeed, it should be remembered that Sindhi, Urdu and Punjabi are *Indo-Aryan* languages,[10] while Baluchi and Pashto belong to the – closely related, but distinct – *Iranian* language group.[11]

  Historically, the Persian word 'Hindustan', meaning 'land of the Indus' refers to the areas around and beyond the Indus, or, by extension, to the historical heartlands of the Vedic or 'Hindu' civilization(s), i.e., all the lands where the 'Hindus' (the heirs of that Vedic civilization) used to live, before Hinduism and Buddhism spread northwards and eastwards to Central Asia, China and South-east Asia. The word thus refers to (i) either the Indo-Gangetic plains in the north or to (ii) the entire landmass bordered by the Indus valley in the west, the Himalayas in the north, the Ganges*/Brahmaputra delta in the east, and the surrounding ocean – roughly four million km² in total.[12]

'Greater India' thus historically includes:

- the eastern provinces of present-day Pakistan, up to, and including, the Indus Valley and Pakistan-controlled Kashmir;

*Also known as Ganga.

- the Republic of India, including the Indian part of Kashmir in the north-west and (at least the greater part of) the Indian north-eastern states with the lower reaches of the Brahmaputra River in the east;
- the predominantly Hindu and Buddhist countries of Nepal and Bhutan in the north;
- the Republic of Bangladesh; and
- the island of Sri Lanka.

By the above definition, students of Indian history will find themselves confronted with a sobering, rather disconcerting, fact: throughout its 7000 years of history, *Greater India has hardly ever, and never entirely, been united* – a state of affairs that makes Indian historiography a rather challenging endeavour, for it is well-nigh impossible to give a coherent overview of all the simultaneous developments in every region, without losing one's readers in the process.

Arguably, a few dynasties and individual rulers have come quite close to uniting the subcontinent; from a broader historical perspective, however, any real examples have been few, far between, and short-lived:

- The empires of the great Hindu dynasties of old (Mauryas, Guptas and so on) – with the important, if short-lived, and single exception of Ashoka the Great's empire, of which we know relatively little[13] – never covered more than approximately 60 per cent of the subcontinent.[14]
- Sultan Muhammad bin Tughlaq, ruler of the Delhi sultanate from 1325 until his death in 1351, briefly managed to expand his dominions all the way down south to the Kaveri river (in present-day Karnataka and Tamil Nadu). It can, however, hardly be stated that he truly managed to *unite* this vast empire under his victorious banner: the hold he had on it was precarious at best, never undisputed, and barely lasted longer than a few years. He lived to see it all fall apart, one principality after the other breaking away and declaring independence.
- Around 250 years later, Akbar the Great (1542–1605) became the unbeaten and unbeatable ruler of a vast and tightly organized Indian empire – roughly one hundred million inhabitants, close to one fifth of the total world population at that time. The military and administrative structures he left behind after

a lifetime of wars and conquests proved to be solid and stable enough to last through the reigns of three more so-called Great Mughals, i.e., his son Jahangir, his grandson Shah Jahan, and his great-grandson Aurangzeb (d. 1707). Akbar undoubtedly was a great Indian ruler, but, due to circumstances explained later, never managed to unite *all* of India. His empire, while vast by any standards, never covered more than approximately 60 per cent of the subcontinent.

- Aurangzeb, in contrast, did manage to push his empire's borders further southwards. Towards the end of his life, however, it was painfully obvious that he had ruined it in the process: his vast empire had become little more than a tired, dying giant with feet of clay. Expansion attempts in the north had failed miserably; Qandahar had been lost forever; and more importantly, the Mughal throne had lost much of its authority and legitimacy. Dangerous revolts of Jats, Sikhs, Rajputs and Marathas could barely be kept in check. Chaos and disintegration were threatening everywhere; and soon after Aurangzeb's death, they proved to be inevitable.
- Local Indian powers (the so-called 'Lesser Mughals' and their Maratha and Sikh rivals) were unable to fill the gap: their short-lived empires never covered more than half of the territory ruled by their predecessors.
- And then, barely one century after Aurangzeb's death, the British had muscled themselves in, set to take full control over virtually the entire subcontinent by the mid-nineteenth century.

***

India, so it would seem, is much too large and diverse to remain united under a single central government for long; yet, its undeniable cultural unity-in-diversity is far too strong for any division or partition to be stable, undisputed or permanent.

Indeed, Greater India's post-partition woes and current disunion do not need to be everlasting. The common culture and history shared by its people are much more significant than the fears and prejudices dividing them. One can only hope that someday soon, Indians, Pakistanis, Bangladeshis, Nepalese, Bhutanese and Sri Lankans will reunite in friendship and peace, as free and sovereign members of a strong, peaceful and prosperous South Asian Union. What their distant German and French cousins have been able to do, after centuries of ruinous infighting, they can do too.

It is rather ironic to see India achieve its greatest territorial expansion *and* strongest national unity under a foreign power. Never before, and regrettably, never since, have the Indians – Muslims and Hindus, Aryans and Dravidians, from the Khyber Pass to the shores of Tamil Nadu – felt closer to each other than when they found themselves united in their struggle to cast off the colonial yoke. And right until this day, the British legacy continues to be the strongest unifying factor on the subcontinent. In particular, the widespread and growing use of the English language proves to be a powerful competitive asset in international commerce as well as an extremely convenient internal communication tool, a well-accepted and neutral bridge between the subcontinent's many ethnic and linguistic groups.

1300 YEARS OF MUSLIM PRESENCE IN INDIA AT A GLANCE

c. CE 640: South-west India
Arab traders, who were established on the Malabar coast since pre-Islamic times, convert to Islam. Intermarriage and gradual conversion, mostly of lower-caste Hindus, gives rise to a strong indigenous (Malayalam-speaking) Muslim minority.[15]

712: First incursions and conquests; first religious contacts
Arab conquest of Sindh and Multan (both now in Pakistan) under Muhammad bin Qaṣim. Further expansion halted in the Battle of Rajasthan (738).

1001–1024
Violent looting raids into northern India under Mahmud of Ghazni (971–1030).

c. 1180
Khwaja Muin-ud Din Muhammad Chishti,[16] the saintly founder of India's most influential Sufi order, settles in Ajmer (now in Rajasthan).

1192–1526: Delhi Sultanate
Afghan Sultan Shihab-ud Din Muhammad Ghauri (1149–1206) conquers northern India and appoints his army leader Qutub-ud Din Aibak as governor. When the sultan is assassinated in 1206, Aibak becomes the first ruler of the so-called Delhi Sultanate, the collective name of five short-lived dynasties, i.e., the Mamluk (1206–1290), Khilji (1290–1320), Tughlaq (1320–1414), Sayyid (1414–1451) and Lodi (1451–1526). The sultanate briefly reaches its territorial apogee around 1340 and then rapidly disintegrates into several smaller principalities.[17]

1526
The sultanate comes to a sudden and violent end, when Sultan Ibrahim Lodi is defeated and killed by the invading Timurid Prince Zahir-ud Din Muhammad Babur, king of Kabul. The era of the Great Mughals of India has begun.

1526–c. 1857: The Mughal Empire
1526–1707: The Great Mughals: Babur, Humayun, Akbar, Jahangir, Shah Jahan and Aurangzeb.
1707–1857: End of Mughal supremacy; Marathas, Afghans, Sikhs and European colonialists fight over the spoils.

1858–1947: The British Raj.
1858–1949: Indian Princely States (under British primacy).
1947 onwards: Independence and partition.

Meeting of Two Oceans: The Advent of Islam

The other salient feature we need to examine more closely is the surprising predominance of *Muslim* principalities in a *Hindu* country. Indeed, India's population at the time of Babur's invasion must have been 90 per cent Hindu, at least; yet, native Hindu kings barely controlled 20 per cent of its territory.

***

Literally tens – if not hundreds – of thousands of pages have been written about the Muslim presence in India. Today, more than a thousand years after the arrival of the first Muslim merchants and conquerors, the issue remains a highly sensitive one. And even though it clearly is irreversible – India would change beyond recognition if one were to try and 'purge' it from its Muslim past – and in spite of the many inspiring and magnificent examples of mutual enrichment at all levels, the fateful encounter of Islam with the millenary Hindu civilization has been and remains traumatic and, to a large extent, undigested.

Like most other human histories, the history of the Muslim presence in India has been a mixed one: of love and hate, joy and tears, brotherhood and bloodshed. It has evoked, and continues to do so, considerable controversy, both in scholarly writings and in public opinion.

Under such circumstances, a truly objective, detached and balanced historiography tends to become extremely difficult, if not impossible. Was Akbar the Great a political genius, a vulgar imperialist, a religious visionary or a traitor to Islam? Was Aurangzeb a narrow-minded, murdering bigot or a misunderstood idealist who tried to live his life as a pious Muslim? All the above? None of the above? The answers tend to vary considerably, depending upon the communal and political affiliation of the people giving them.

Generally speaking, Hindu nationalists will tend to describe the advent of Islam as the result of a series of brutal, genocidal invasions, whereas Muslim historians will emphasize the gradual and generally peaceful character of the conversion process.

Reminding ourselves of Oscar Wilde's famous bon mot that the pure and simple truth is rarely pure and never simple,[18] let us briefly discuss the various hypotheses that have been put forward to explain the Islamization process, and ask ourselves two questions:

- From a *military* perspective, how is it possible that a handful of invaders with little more than a few tens of thousands of men managed to conquer a country of so many millions?
- Historically and sociologically, how is it to be explained that the Muslim population of the subcontinent grew from zero to more than 30 per cent in barely a few centuries? And conversely, how come it grew to 30 per cent *only*? And why was Islam so spectacularly successful in some areas (rural East Bengal, for

example, or Sindh and West Punjab) and relatively *un*successful in so many others, even in regions where Muslim dynasties had been ruling supreme for centuries – the Deccan, for example, or the urban centres of West Bengal, or the heartlands of Hindustan itself?

Military Aspects

As I lay awake in the night, I pondered over our conversation, and in particular, on the cleverness and perspicacity of Mān Singh, Todar Mal** and Bīrbal.† I could not help wondering – it was not the first time, nor would it be the last – how it had been possible, that so smart and competent a race like the Hindūs had been overrun so easily by a handful of Muslim invaders.*

The only plausible answer I could and can come up with – other than divine intervention, of course – is that the Hindūs were defeated because they had allowed themselves to be divided. Had there been a Hindū Akbar at the time, the invaders would never have stood a chance – the few survivors would have brought back tales of such horror, that no foreigner would ever again have dared to invade Hindustān! It is our task, my son, to see to it that such an invasion will, indeed, never happen again.

The above quote from my historical novel *Akbar's Farewell/The Emperor's Writings*†† probably summarizes the main reason for the invaders' military successes: they did not have to face a united and determined opponent. Had they invaded an empire like Ashoka's, who ruled from 269 to 232 BCE, they would more than likely have been crushed. But India was not an empire when Babur invaded it, and had not been one for centuries: it had disintegrated into a complex patchwork of small, rival principalities without any central government or authority. Moreover, there was no such thing as a nationalist feeling,

*Man Singh (1550–1614) was the raja of Amber. He was a trusted general of Akbar, who included him among the Navratnas, or the nine gems, of the royal court.

**Raja Todar Mal (d. 1589) was born in Laharpur (now in Uttar Pradesh) and rose to become the finance minister in Akbar's darbar.

†Raja Birbal (born Mahesh Das; 1528–1586), was an adviser in Akbar's darbar. He too was one of the Navratnas and was known for his clever wit and humour.

††Published by Amaryllis, New Delhi, 2011/2024.

no Hindu or Indian sense of identity or solidarity; nor would such sentiments develop until many centuries later.

Two examples – out of many more – should suffice to illustrate this point:

- The kings of the Vijayanagar Empire in South India (1336–1646) did portray themselves as the leaders of the last Hindu bastion against the Muslim onslaught. Reality shows, however, that this claim was more rhetorical (i.e., political or ideological) than real. Throughout its existence, Vijayanagar entered into many, often shifting, political and military alliances with the neighbouring sultanates of the Deccan; and its armies – just like the ones of its adversaries – were a mix of local troops and foreign, mostly Muslim, mercenaries. The vast majority of the population in the neighbouring sultanates was and remained Hindu, but never did those Hindu masses turn against their rulers to join forces with Vijayanagar in a 'war of national liberation'. In other words, the wars that the Vijayanagar kings waged against their neighbouring adversaries were 'ordinary', imperialist wars – wars for riches and territory, between rival *states*. Army leaders may have used religious rhetoric (chasing the impure *mlecchas* [foreigners; Muslims in particular] or jihad against the infidel idol worshippers) from time to time, when it best suited them to rally the troops; but the conflict in the south never came to be a truly *religious* war of one religious community against the other.
- The Marathas under the *peshwas** (1713–1818), in their struggle against the Mughals, the Afghans and the British, never were able to mobilize the Hindu chiefs of northern India (Jats and Rajputs) to side with them in their eminently 'national' Hindu war against foreign powers.

Apart from their sad lack of political union, the military tactics of most Hindu kings proved to be less effective than those of their Muslim adversaries. Even on those rare occasions when some of them agreed to join forces against the invaders, there was no unity of command, and coordination proved to be extremely difficult. Moreover, the Hindu

*Peshwa: Equivalent to the modern-day prime minister.

army leaders tended to rely on massive but rather unwieldy hosts of conscript infantry, usually supported by war elephants. While quite impressive to behold, these armies were less reliable than the much more mobile, professional and disciplined Muslim cavalry forces: conscripts are less experienced, less orderly and more prone to panic; more often than not, wounded elephants are more dangerous to their own army than that of their adversaries.

Paths to Conversion: Explanations of the Islamization Process

At least five different theories have been proposed to explain the spread of Islam in the Indian subcontinent: migration; conversion 'by the sword'; voluntary conversion as the result of preaching and social contacts; 'pragmatic' conversion for reasons of social mobility; and peripheral growth in less developed regions. Taken in isolation, none of these theories is entirely adequate. Taken together, not as competing and mutually exclusive hypotheses but as complementary explanations, they do provide a valuable insight into the societal forces at work.

Migration

While it is a well-known fact that over the centuries, hundreds of thousands of Muslim soldiers, artisans, clerics and others from Afghanistan, Central Asia, Iran and the Middle East have found their way to the subcontinent, it is clear that these migrants never constituted more than a small percentage of the total population. In other words: the vast majority of today's 500 million Muslims on the subcontinent are the descendants of *native* converts. The question therefore remains: how did this conversion come about?

Conversion 'by the Sword'

Many historians, Muslims and others, have rightfully pointed out that, contrary to what many people still believe (or choose to believe for political reasons), forced conversion has been the *exception* rather than the rule during the Muslim conquests. Out of the many thousands of possible examples, let me just quote a fragment from a famous open letter to Pope Benedict XVI, written in 2006 by thirty-eight leading Islamic scholars:[19]

> *The notion that Muslims are commanded to spread their faith 'by the sword' or that Islam in fact was largely spread 'by the sword' does not*

> *hold up to scrutiny. Indeed, as a political entity Islam spread partly as a result of conquest, but the greater part of its expansion came as a result of preaching and missionary activity. Islamic teaching did not prescribe that the conquered populations be forced or coerced into converting. Indeed, many of the first areas conquered by the Muslims remained predominantly non-Muslim for centuries. Had Muslims desired to convert all others by force, there would not be a single church or synagogue left anywhere in the Islamic world. The command 'There is no compulsion in religion' means now what it meant then. The mere fact of a person being non-Muslim has never been a legitimate casus belli in Islamic law or belief. As with the rules of war, history shows that some Muslims have violated Islamic tenets concerning forced conversion and the treatment of other religious communities, but history also shows that these are by far the exception which proves the rule. We emphatically agree that forcing others to believe – if such a thing be truly possible at all – is not pleasing to God and that God is not pleased by blood. Indeed, we believe, and Muslims have always believed, that 'Whosoever slays a soul not to retaliate for a soul slain, nor for corruption done in the land, it shall be as if he had slain mankind altogether'* (Quran, al-Ma'idah, 5:32).

Thankfully, the above statement holds true for most wars fought on the Indian subcontinent. It is undeniable that many Muslim campaigns – the early ones in particular – have been accompanied by terrible bloodshed and destruction of temples, but 'conversion by the sword' has definitely been the exception rather than the rule.

This has to do with two important facts.

First, *most rulers were motivated by power, not religion*. The vast majority of India's Muslim conquerors and subsequent rulers were exactly that: power-hungry conquerors and rulers, who happened to be Muslim. Their main goal was not religion, but military glory, political power and spoils. As stated above, Muslim army leaders may have been using religious rhetoric (jihad against the infidels, and so on) whenever it suited them to rally the foreign troops and/or to justify their own imperialist designs; they may have sacked Hindu temples as an important political statement and a symbol of sovereignty, but their motives always were imperialist, much more than religious. It is rather misleading to portray the entire Indo-Islamic period as an era where Hindu leaders were desperately trying to fend off foreign Muslim invaders. It was a chaotic period in which rivalling principalities, ruled by Muslim or Hindu kings, fought against their Muslim or Hindu neighbours and rivals; but only very rarely was it a matter of one religious community fighting another. For example, the vast majority of Akbar the Great's many wars were fought against *Muslim* rivals, and not a single one of them was religiously motivated – quite the contrary. Akbar's military power was based on a highly effective coalition of mainly foreign Muslim troops (Turkmen, Uzbeks and Persians) with Hindu (Rajput) forces; some of his most talented, loyal and prominent administrators and army leaders were practising Hindus. As we shall discuss in much more detail later, Akbar consciously tried to blot out the difference between his subjects. And while his outlook on religious pluralism and tolerance may have been exceptional, his reliance on Hindu talent was not: many Muslim kings before and after him – even his bigoted great-grandson Aurangzeb – have relied extensively on non-Muslims.

Second, *Muslim rulers demanded submission and obedience, not conversion*. Muslim rulers in general – even the bigoted ones – had little interest in conversion or proselytization. They did not demand – and often did not even encourage – their subjects to change their religion. As pointed out above, they were under no religious obligation to do so: they merely expected and demanded obedience and the payment of taxes, which, for non-Muslims exempt from military duty, included the so-called *jizya* or Islamic poll tax. In other words: non-Muslims were coerced into obedience to their Indo-Muslim *ruler*, into submission to the Indo-Muslim *state* in which they lived, but not to the Muslim *religion*.

The above is corroborated by the observable facts: more often than not, Islam was rather *un*successful in converting the Hindu masses, even – and in particular – in those areas where Muslim dynasties ruled supreme for centuries. The phenomenon has been described and argued most eloquently by the US historian Richard M. Eaton, among others, in his most illuminating and erudite study: *The Rise of Islam and the Bengal Frontier, 1204–1760*:[20]

> *If Islamization had ever been a function of military or political force, one would expect that those areas exposed most intensively and over the longest period to Muslim dynasties – that is, those that were most fully exposed to the 'sword' – would today contain the greatest*

numbers of Muslims. Yet the opposite is the case, as those regions where the most dramatic Islamization occurred, such as eastern Bengal or western Punjab, lay on the fringes of Indo-Muslim rule, where the 'sword' was [the] *weakest, and where brute force could have exerted the least influence. In such regions the first accurate census reports put the Muslim population at between 70 and 90 per cent of the total, whereas in the heartland of Muslim rule in the Indo-Gangetic Plain – the domain of the Delhi* [Red] *Fort and the Taj Mahal, where the Muslim regimes had ruled the most intensively and for the longest period of time – the Muslim population ranged from only 10 to 15 per cent. In other words, in the subcontinent as a whole there is an* inverse *relationship between the degree of Muslim political penetration and the degree of Islamization.*

We will come back to this remarkable phenomenon of 'growth on the fringes' a bit later.

Duress

The above should not blind us to the fact that conquest, in those days even more than today, inevitably involved considerable bloodshed and injustice. Examples abound of incidents where prisoners of war, defending soldiers as well as civilians were routinely put to the sword or sold into slavery. There can be little doubt that the fear of reprisals must have been a factor of considerable importance with the survivors in those turbulent times; conversion as an attempt to appease the rulers and keep out of harm's way must have played a significant role. Moreover, it cannot be denied that there are several instances – in the earlier dynasties in particular – of Muslim kings behaving as religious fanatics and bigoted brutes, subjecting their Hindu subjects to outrageous discrimination and ill-treatment. Two examples from the Delhi sultanate should suffice to illustrate the point:

- Sultan Alauddin Khilji (reign: 1296–1316) is on record[21] as having stated: '*I am an unlettered man, but I have seen a great deal. Be assured then that the Hindus will never become submissive and obedient till they are reduced to poverty. I have therefore given orders that just sufficient shall be left (for them) from year to year of corn, milk and curds, but that they shall not be allowed to accumulate hoards and property.*'

- Sultan Sikandar Lodi (reign: 1489–1517), even more notorious for his bigotry and cruelty, is said to have burnt alive a Hindu sage for having simply said that Hinduism and Islam are equally pleasing to God, provided they are followed with sincerity. Sikandar Lodi desecrated many Hindu temples, forbade the Hindus to bathe in the holy river Yamuna and coerced many people to convert, through both violence and incentives.

Apart from the actions of individual rulers, there is also a certain 'snowball' effect in regions that have become strongly Islamized, whereby the remaining non-Muslim minorities have either converted, or left, or were driven from, their ancestral lands. Majorities tend to oppress minorities, as is painfully obvious in present-day Pakistan, Bangladesh and Kashmir, where the dwindling Hindu minorities have emigrated or are under considerable pressure to do so.

Peaceful Contacts, Trade and Intermarriage

While instances of forced conversion and/or ethnic cleansing under duress are undeniable, it is equally true that the success of Islam in certain other regions – the Malabar coast (along present-day Kerala and parts of Karnataka) and other parts of Kerala in particular – had absolutely nothing to do with coercion or Muslim military or political supremacy.

It is a well-known fact that Arab traders had settled on the Malabar coast even before the advent of Islam. Those traders respected the political authority of local rulers, who, in turn, allowed them to build settlements while maintaining their own religious beliefs and practices. It is highly probable that they must have intermarried with local – usually lower-caste – women, right from the start. After the advent of Islam, when the whole of the Arabian Peninsula quickly converted to the new monotheist religion, the Malabar traders became Muslims as well. The new religion, with its simple creed and powerful, egalitarian message, combined with the success and personal wealth of the traders, must have had a powerful attraction for the local population, the lower castes in particular.

Patronage and Social Mobility

The influence of social and political superiors upon subordinate social groups is bound to play a significant role in any society. In the case of India, conversion has certainly played such a role in both the 'top' and 'bottom' layers of society: on the one hand, thousands of courtiers, civil servants, local governors and large landowners were eager to associate themselves and their families with the ruling Muslim dynasties, either directly or via intermarriage. On the other side of the spectrum, members of the very lowest, 'polluting' castes must have had strong motives to escape an oppressive and humiliating caste system by converting to Islam – or, for that matter, to Christianity – in regions where that religion was firmly established.

Genuine Change of Heart as a Result of Sufi Preaching

Many historians, Muslims in particular, have surmised that most Indian converts to Islam have done so voluntarily, attracted by the simple, saintly way of life of Sufi sages, their openness to people from all walks of life, their unfeigned devotion to God and the attractive theological simplicity of their creed. Sufi saints certainly have played a significant role in society, in certain regions in particular, but scholars have contested the importance of this societal role in the conversion process, certainly in those regions where Hinduism was already firmly established.

The reason for this is twofold: first, as mentioned above, Muslim conversion attempts were much less widespread and systematic than many people have assumed. Secondly, and more importantly, it should not be forgotten that Hindus in general do not feel the need to *convert* to another religion in order to fully recognize and appreciate its saintliness.

The pressing need to convert to the one and only 'true religion', rejecting all others, is a typically *Western* concept. 'Western' religions (i.e., Judaism, Christianity and Islam) tend to be quite *exclusive*, and extremely preoccupied with *orthodoxy*: there is one almighty God, Lord and Creator of the Universe; this God will reward the good and punish the evil; and human beings, if they are to avoid damnation, must follow God's commands. Those commands, in turn, have been revealed to humankind by God Himself, speaking through one or more prophets and through the holy scriptures. Infidels, heretics and apostates, all those who fail to embrace this one true faith and do not follow its precepts, will suffer the eternal torments of hell.

The *Sanātana* (eternal) *Dharma*, or what is generally called the 'Hindu faith', is quite different: it is much more preoccupied with attainment of *freedom* or *liberation* through *reunification with the*

Divine, than with any particular set of beliefs. In fact, true Hinduism is unencumbered by thoughts of apostasy, heresy, blasphemy and any other such destructive ideas, which have plagued 'Western' religions for so many centuries.

In the Hindu mind, all religions are ultimately the same: they are different paths towards the same mountain top; different rivers flowing into the same ocean; or separate pools of water, all reflecting the light of the same moon. The study of other religions is not only *allowed* in Hinduism: it actually is *encouraged*.

To a Hindu, every person – and indeed, every animal and plant and everything that exists – is part of God, just like a spark is part of the fire, just like a tiny drop of water is part of the ocean. Eventually, everything and everybody is destined to be reunited with its or his or her Divine origin.

Ideally, a Hindu will therefore never despise any other living creature, much less any other human being.

Hinduism readily acknowledges that wisdom can be found everywhere. Consequently, it does not claim that there is one single orthodox point of view leading to salvation. As it is proclaimed in the Vedic scriptures: '*Ekam Sat, viprah bahudha vadanti*' (there is One Truth, only men describe it in different ways). Hinduism has no central authority, and it allows hundreds of contradictory opinions and practices to coexist. In fact, there is no such thing as *the* Hindu religion or philosophy – there are so many different beliefs and systems of thought in Hinduism, that one could never study them all in depth in a single lifetime! Perhaps the only common feature of all these beliefs, traditions and convictions is their preoccupation with *moksha*, liberation, which can and will be achieved through wisdom or enlightenment.[22]

The above implies and explains why Hindus, even today, will pray with deep reverence at the tombs of Muslim saints, or in churches, without in the least feeling the need to abandon their own insights and ways of worshiping.

Islamization 'on the Fringes'

Looking at pre- and post-partition Greater India, it is important to keep in mind Professor Eaton's important observation that the Islamization of the Indian subcontinent was by far the strongest in the *periphery* of the subcontinent, not in the central Hindustani and Deccan heartlands where Muslim political power and dominance had been established for centuries. This remarkable phenomenon of 'Islamization on the fringes' appears to be linked not to the strength of the local Muslim authority, but to the relative weakness or absence of pre-existing Hindu social structures. According to Professor Eaton:

> *In 1872, when the earliest reliable census was taken, the highest concentrations of Muslims were found in eastern Bengal, western Punjab, the North-west Frontier region, and Baluchistan. What is striking about those areas is not only that they lay far from the center of Muslim political power but* [also] *that their indigenous populations had not yet, at the time of their contact with Islam, been fully integrated into either the Hindu or the Buddhist social system. In Bengal, Muslim converts were drawn mainly from Rajbansi, Pod, Chandal, Kuch, and other indigenous groups that had been only lightly exposed to Brahmanic culture, and in the Punjab the same was true of the various Jat clans that eventually formed the bulk of the Muslim community.*[23]

In Bengal in particular, Islamization was very much a rural 'frontier' phenomenon, rather than an urban one. As Professor Eaton has shown quite convincingly, the spreading of Islam in eastern Bengal was the result of the settling and cultivating, from the second half of the sixteenth century onwards, of previously forested and sparsely populated areas. The duty of the local Mughal governors was to enhance the agricultural productivity (and hence, the taxable basis) of the land entrusted to their care; favourable grants and concessions were given to enterprising individuals, who would settle the land and provide it with an adequate infrastructure, including temples and/or mosques. As most of the early settlers happened to be Muslim and the majority of the inhabitants of the new settlements came from areas that had only weak ties with the Brahmanic religion of Bengal's urban centres, Bengal's eastern frontier became Islamic, as opposed to the more urbanized West Bengal, which was and remained predominantly Hindu, even after centuries under Muslim rulers.

Many Rivers, One Ocean

India's post-partition woes and communal problems have been given much attention by historians and lay commentators alike. While this is of course understandable and necessary, it should not make us lose sight of a much more important fact: the history of Hindus and Muslims is not only one of distrust, fear, anger and strife, but also one of mutual appreciation, friendship and brotherhood.

The 'real' India is the country of Kabir (*c.* 1440 to *c.* 1518), the great mystical poet, the Muslim weaver's son who became a Hindu guru's apprentice and a Sufi saint, and moved Hindus and Muslims alike with his love-struck devotional poetry and teachings (mostly in the form of pithy *dohas* or couplets). Kabir showed his many followers, past and present, that God is more interested in the goodness of people's hearts than the communities they belong to or the formal creeds they adhere to. Such was his wisdom that both Hindus and Muslims claimed him as theirs and that the followers of a third religion, the Sikhs, included the major part of his work in their most sacred text, the Guru Granth Sahib. As the poet has declared:

Hindūs call Him Rām, Muslims Khudā
Kabīr says: whoever lives should not bother about this:
Ka'bah becomes Kashi, Rām becomes Rahīm.[24]

The 'real' India is the country of Guru Nanak (1469–1539), the founder of the Sikh religion, who travelled far and wide, preaching about the one God who dwells in each and everyone and everything, and wants us to lead our lives in righteousness and brotherly love.

The 'real' India is the country of Abu'l Fazl Allamī (1551–1602), Akbar the Great's shrewd, wise and competent minister, who, profoundly convinced that all religions found favour in the eyes of the Creator, wrote the following verses:[25]

O God, in every temple I see people that are seeking You, and in every language I hear, people are praising You!
Polytheism and Islām feel after [sic] *You, each religion says, 'You are One, without equal!'*
If it be a mosque, people murmur the holy prayer, and if it be a Christian church, people ring the bell out of love to You.
Sometimes I frequent the Christian cloister, and sometimes the mosque, but it is You whom I search, from temple to temple.

The 'real' India begins where the boundaries of communalism are transcended, where Muslims celebrate Holi and Diwali with their Hindu neighbours, where Hindus pray at Muslim tombs, where sages and saints of both religions unite in peaceful worship of the one Deity. For, in the immortal words of Mahatma Gandhi: God has no religion.

Notes and References

1. R. Nath, *India as Seen by Babur (A.D. 1504–1530)*, MD Publications, Delhi, 1996, Introduction, p. 3.
2. Abraham Eraly, *The Mughal Throne: The Saga of India's Great Emperors*, Viking (an imprint of Penguin Books India and Penguin Books UK), New Delhi and London, 1997 and 2000, p. 5.
3. An idiom quite close to present-day Uzbek, Uygur, Kyrgyz and Kazakh – all of which, arguably, are not really distinct languages, but closely related dialects of one another.
4. Russification and Uzbekization policies.
5. Timur-i-Lang means Timur the Lame, a nickname he got ever since his right arm and leg had been partly incapacitated as a result of arrow wounds sustained during a raid early in his life.
6. Estimated at 17 million people, approximately 5 per cent of the total world population.
7. Bamber Gascoigne, *A Brief History of the Great Moguls,* Carroll & Graf Publishers, New York, 2002, p. 4.
8. Charles Joppen S. J., *Historical Atlas of India*, Longmans, Green & Co., London, 1907–1914.
9. Involving two large and several smaller territories along the borders between China, India and Pakistan-controlled northern Kashmir (known in India as 'Pakistan-occupied Kashmir or POK), covering – from east to west – the Indian state of Arunachal Pradesh, the northern tip of Sikkim and the north-eastern border of Kashmir, including the territory of Aksai Chin, administered by China since the 1962 Sino–Indian War.
10. Related to other Indian languages including standard Hindi, Rajasthani, Bihari, Bengali, Assamiya (Assamese), Oriya, Gujarati, Marathi, Konkani and even Sinhalese, spoken in the island of Sri Lanka. Taken together, the Indo-Aryan and Iranian language families are referred to as Indo-Iranian, i.e., the south-eastern group of the Indo-European languages.
11. To which others might object that Balochistan needs to be considered as part of Greater India, since the Brahui language, spoken in the central part of Pakistani Balochistan and neighbouring regions in Afghanistan, is actually a *Dravidian* (South Indian) language, possibly a remnant of pre-Aryan times.
12. The combined surface area of India, Pakistan and Bangladesh is approximately 4.23 million km^2; adding Nepal, Bhutan and Sri Lanka brings that total area

to 4.48 million km^2; without the Iranian-language territories of Balochistan, the North-West Frontier Province and Federally Administered Tribal Areas or FATA (all three now in Pakistan), it is about 4.036 million km^2.

13. 268–232 BCE.
14. See, for example, John Keay, *India: A History*, Grove Press, New York, 2000, pp. xxii–xxiii.
15. Currently close to 30 per cent of Kerala's population.
16. Khwaja Muin-ud Din Chishti (1142–1236): one of the greatest Muslim saints in Indian history. The founder of the Chishtiya Sufi order in India, he came to Ajmer from Persia in 1192. Even today, his tomb in Ajmer is a very important place of pilgrimage for Muslims and Hindus alike.
17. Including the Hindu Vijayanagar Empire.
18. Oscar Wilde, *The Importance of Being Earnest* (original play written in 1895), Act I, Leonard Smithers and Company, London, 1899.
19. http://islamicamagazine.com/online-analysis/open-letter-to-his-holiness-pope-benedict-xvi.html/; quoted in my book, *Paths to Peace: Religion, Ethics and Tolerance in a Globalizing World*, Vakils, Feffer & Simons, Mumbai, 2013 (Foreword by European Union President Herman Van Rompuy), pp. 137–138.
20. The University of California Press, Berkeley, 1993, p. 115. See also Rowena Robinson and Sathianathan Clarke (eds.), *Religious Conversion in India: Modes, Motivations, and Meanings*, Oxford University Press, Delhi, 2003: in particular the papers on pp. 23–28 (by Rowena Robinson); pp. 54–74 (by Stephen F. Dale); and pp. 75–97 (by Richard Eaton).
21. Dilip Hiro, *History of India, Rough Guide Chronicle*, Penguin Books, London, 2002, p. 142.
22. *Paths to Peace*, op. cit., pp. 149–150.
23. Richard M. Eaton, *The Rise of Islam and the Bengal Frontier, 1204–1760*, University of California Press, Berkeley, 1993, p. 118.
24. *Khuda*: the Persian word for 'God' (etymologically related to the word 'God' or 'Gott' in Germanic languages). Ka'bah: the central shrine at the centre of Islam's most sacred mosque, Al-Masjid al-Haram, in Mecca. Kashi: the old name for the holy city of Varanasi/Benares (now in Uttar Pradesh), one of the most sacred places of pilgrimage in Hinduism.
25. Fragment of an inscription on a temple in Kashmir, quoted in the introduction to the *Ā'īn-ī-Akbarī*, pp. liv–lv. See Abu'l Fazl Allamī, *The Akbar Nāmā*, translated from the Persian by H. Beveridge, 1902–39 (in three volumes), Low Price Publishers, Delhi, reprinted 1989, Vol. I, pp. 642–651.

Chapter 1

Babur the Tiger: Coincidental Emperor, Accidental Indian

'In the month of Ramadan of the year 899, in the province of Fergana, in my twelfth year, I became king.'

Thus begins, with characteristic matter-of-factness, the *Baburnama* or *Tuzuk-i-Baburi*, Babur's famous autobiography, deservedly renowned for its originality and unusual frankness.

That nickname *Babur*, incidentally, is somewhat of a mystery. Most authors seem to agree that he got it from 'the rustics of Fergana', who must have found his official Arabic name (Zahir-ud Din, 'protector of religion') rather difficult to pronounce. Popular tradition as well as most historians will also point out that *babr* (ببر) means 'tiger' in Persian.

Harvard professor emeritus, Wheeler M. Thackston (the eminent Orientalist who translated, among others, the *Baburnama* and the *Jahangirnama* into English), however, strongly disagrees with this interpretation:[1]

> *Babur's name has also appeared as Baber and Babar. There is not the slightest doubt, however, that the name is Babur (BAH-boor), which is ultimately derived from the Indo-European word for beaver. Although it has often been suggested that Babur means tiger, it has, in fact, nothing to do with the Persian word* babr, *'tiger'.*

While I am, of course, in no position to contradict as distinguished a scholar as Professor Thackston, I would venture to postulate that Babur himself, quite fluent in both spoken and written Persian, must have been aware of the popular association of his name with the magnificent king of the jungle and did not at all object to it; in any case, he must have preferred it over the association with an innocuous rodent. Possibly, the name Bābur (بابر), with a long *alif* (the first letter of the Persian/Arabic alphabet), is merely a corruption or misspelling of *babr* (ببر), with a short a? We will, most probably, never know.

The Boy King

Coming back to Babur's memoirs, historical accuracy appears to have been the sole motivation for writing them. He states:

> *I have simply written the truth. I do not intend by what I have written to compliment myself: I have simply set down exactly what happened … as a consequence, I have reported every good and evil I have seen of father and brother, and set down the actuality of every fault and virtue of relative and stranger. May the reader excuse me; may the listener take me not to task.*[2]

Rather than telling his readers right away how and why a eleven-year-old boy suddenly found himself on the rather shaky throne of a small Central Asian principality, he goes on for another five pages[3] with a businesslike description of his home country:

> *The province of Fergana is in the fifth clime, situated on the edge of the civilized world …. To the north, although formerly there were cities … because the Mongols and Uzbeks passed there, there is no longer any civilization …. It is a smallish province. Grain and fruit are plentiful. All around are mountains, except on the western side, that is, in Samarqand and Khodzhent, where there are none. So, aside from that direction, foreign enemies cannot penetrate. …. The income of Fergana Province, if justly managed, will maintain three to four thousand men …*

He then proceeds to talk about his father,[4] Umar Shaykh Mirza, '*a Padshah* [emperor] *of exalted ambition with great claims, always bent on territorial expansion*' – an ambition, which, understandably, had earned him his fair share of enemies. '*On account of his urge to expand his territory,*' Babur notes, '*he turned many a truce into battle and many a friend into a foe.*'

True to his promise to accurately record the faults and virtues of friend and foe alike, he candidly describes his father's physical appearance, habits and character, warts and all:

> *He was short in stature, with a round beard and a fleshy face, and was fat. He wore his tunic so tight that to fasten the ties, he had to hold in his stomach; if he let himself go, it often happened that the ties broke. He was unceremonious in both dress and speech.*

Umar Shaykh Mirza's lack of worldly sophistication was also apparent in a sad lack of any literary achievements worthy of mention: although, according to Babur, he was '*well read and literate*' and '*had some poetic talent*', he '*paid no attention to composing poetry*' – a deficiency that his son, himself an enthusiastic and quite a talented poet, found hard to understand.

Like many of his contemporaries, Umar Shaykh Mirza led a rather loose life with little concern for either morals or manners. In addition to a particular fondness of women, gambling and opium, he drank a lot, a vice that proved to be hereditary, as many of his descendants – Babur included – were heavy drinkers, if not outright alcoholics. Under the influence of liquor, he, as Babur put it, '*was of a scrappy temperament, and had many scars and brands to show for it*'.

That being said, he was, in Babur's view, '*orthodox of belief* [and] *never neglected the five prayer times. Throughout his lifetime, he always made up for missed prayers and often recited the Quran*'. He also had a great sense of justice and honesty, was '*good-natured, talkative, eloquent and well-spoken*', in addition to being '*brave and valiant*'.

As an army leader, however, his track record was mixed at best: two of the three main battles he fought in his life ended in defeat; and, more importantly, he lost the important regions of Tashkent (now in Uzbekistan), Sayram (now in southern Kazakhstan) and Shahrukhiyya (now in Uzbekistan), which had been under his control for some time. As an individual warrior, he was but '*a middling shot*', but '*packed quite a punch*'. As Babur declares: '*No one was ever hit by* [him] *who did not bite the dust.*'

***

On the fateful day of his untimely, accidental death, finding himself under attack by a coalition of his elder brother Sultan Ahmad Mirza, ruler of Samarqand (one of Babur's paternal uncles) and one of his brothers-in-law (one of Babur's maternal uncles), Umar Shaykh Mirza was staying at Akhsi, a fort in the northern mountains of Fergana, surrounded by steep ravines. A great pigeon enthusiast, he was tending to his feathered friends, when, as Babur observes laconically, '*a strange event occurred. It has been mentioned that the Akhsi fortress is situated atop a high ravine, with the buildings at its edge. On Monday the fourth of Ramadan of this year* [899, i.e., 8 June 1494[5]], *Umar Shaykh Mirza toppled into the ravine with his doves and their dovecot, and became a falcon. He was thirty-nine years old*'.

At the time of the accident, Babur was spending some time in the *chārbāgh*[6] garden outside Fergana's capital Andizhan – gardening would always be among his favourite pastimes.

Typically, he wastes little time in describing his emotions upon hearing the sad news; he merely states that he '*mounted in consternation and set out for the fortress with the retainers and servants who were there with* [him]': a Timurid prince born and bred, his first thought went to the throne. For a number of tense hours, the young boy's fate hung by a thread, as the *begs* or *baigs* (nobles) kept arguing among themselves: should they enthrone the young prince, or turn him over to his powerful uncles? At long last, it was decided to make a stand and hold the fort. It had, to put it mildly, not been an easy discussion: one of the dissidents had to be executed '*for unseemly speech*', but '*after this example, all the people came into line*', Babur notes with wry phlegm.

Fortunately, '*God ... effected a few events*' that caused his invading uncles '*not merely to change their minds about coming, but actually regret having set out*' relates Babur. His powerful, but rather mild-mannered paternal uncle headed back to Samarqand when an epidemic broke out among his horses; his ally, Babur's maternal uncle, decided to call it a day when he fell ill after the first few skirmishes. Divine intervention or not, Babur was safe – for the time being.

But Zahir-ud Din Muhammad Babur was not cut out for the tranquil life of a petty king or country squire. Was he not, through his father, a direct descendant of the mighty Amīr Temür (i.e., Timur or Tamerlane)? Was not his maternal grandfather a direct descendant of the great Genghis Khan? Was it not his God-given right – nay, his duty – to follow in his glorious ancestors' footsteps?

Babur's dream, one that would haunt him for most of his adult life, was to capture the throne of Samarqand, Timur's glorious capital city with its magnificent, azure-tiled monuments.

A Hundred Days at Samarqand

That opportunity soon arose: on his way back from Fergana, his mild-mannered and capable uncle Sultan Ahmad Mirza, the king of Samarqand, developed a raging fever and died (or, in Babur's words, '*bade farewell to the mortal world*'). The vacant throne was seized by another one of Babur's paternal uncles, Sultan Mahmud Mirza, a man whom Babur describes as being '*addicted to vice and debauchery*'. In addition to being a perpetual drunk, writes Babur, '*he kept a lot of catamites. In his realm wherever there was a comely, beardless youth, he did everything he could to turn him into a catamite .... The young sons of civilians, merchants, even the sons of Turks and soldiers, could not leave their houses for fear of being turned into catamites. The people of Samarqand, who had lived in ease and comfort for twenty or twenty-five years under Sultan Ahmad Mirza ... were scandalized and outraged by such tyranny and vice. Lowborn and noble, poor and rich, all opened their mouths with curses and raised their hands in supplication*'.

Much to everyone's relief, Heaven appeared to have heard those supplications, for, in the course of the month of January 1495, barely six months after he had seized the throne, Sultan Mahmud Mirza was stricken with a severe illness and died. '*That day became a great moment of rejoicing for the people of Samarqand*', Babur writes. The moment of rejoicing, however, was disappointingly brief, for, as could be expected, Sultan Mahmud Mirza's death was merely the starting signal for yet another war of succession.

In the ensuing chaos, with several Timurid princes fighting over the throne, Babur rushed into the fray in mid-1496, just thirteen years old. Arriving at the gates of the city, he found it beleaguered by two of his cousins. He joined forces with them, but, at the onset of winter, since the city had not yet fallen, he was forced to retreat to Fergana, returning the following year, not in the least discouraged. After a siege of seven months, he finally managed to wrestle the much-coveted city from the hands of Baysunghur Mirza, one of his cousins.

The young monarch was ecstatic. '*Few cities in the civilized world are as pleasant as Samarqand*', he affirms, and goes on for about seven pages describing the city's many charms and attractions: its superb buildings, including Timur's magnificent tomb, the famous astronomical observatory built by Ulugh Beg, Timur's grandson, and the elaborately tiled centre of Islamic studies. Not surprisingly, a lot of Babur's attention goes to the nine gardens outside the city walls, the fertile fields and orchards and the succulent grapes, melons, apples, pomegranates and other fruits and vegetables that were (and are) grown there. Such is the city's opulence, that Turks and Mongols alike have called it *Semizkand*, the fat city.

His enthusiasm, alas, was short-lived. Poor Samarqand had been bled dry in the past months of civil war; and the bulk of Babur's troops, disappointed by the lack of plunder, began deserting him, '*one by one and two by two*', in a matter of days. To make matters much worse, courtiers back in Fergana were conspiring against him, putting his younger half-brother Jahangir on the throne. Barely three months – 100 days – after winning Samarqand, he found himself forced to abandon it and march back to Fergana to try and redress the situation. But it was too late: both Samarqand and Fergana were lost to him. The ambitious young king had become a hapless wanderer, a robber warlord with a retinue of barely two to three hundred lawless brigands. '*I could not help crying a good deal,*' Babur confesses.

Throneless, but Not Beaten

But he refused to give up. '*When one has pretensions to rule and a desire for conquest, one cannot sit back and just watch if events don't go right once or twice*', he advises. Slowly but surely, bit by bit, he managed to win back some territory from his younger brother, enough for his mother and grandmother and the families of his followers to join them: even in times of civil war, Timurid ladies were usually left undisturbed and free to follow their husbands and sons whenever they wanted.

Among the ladies joining Babur was his first wife, Ayisha Sultan Begam, one of his cousins, daughter of the late Sultan Ahmad Mirza. Pressed by his mother, he married her in the town of Khodzhent, in the month of Shaban of the year 905 (March 1500). The marriage can hardly be called a success. '*In the early days of the wedding,*' says Babur, '*since it was my first marriage and I was bashful, I went to her only once every ten, fifteen, or twenty days. Later on, I lost my fondness of her altogether, and I was still shy. Once every month or forty days my mother the* khanïm [a woman of rank or position] *drove me to her with all the severity of a quartermaster.*'

What was the reason behind this remarkable lack of interest in a newly wedded wife? Babur reveals it in the next sentence,[7] with an unashamed, disarming frankness that would be remarkable even in today's free-and-easy Western world: he had become infatuated with a shapely boy from the camp market. '*I developed a strange inclination for him*', he confesses. '*Before this experience, I had never felt a desire for anyone, nor did I listen to talk of love and affection or speak of such things.*' The whole affair, however, appears to have remained limited to platonic adoration: '*I was so bashful that I could not look him in the face, much less converse freely with him. In my excitement and agitation, I could not thank him for coming, much less complain of his leaving .... One day ... all at once I found myself face-to-face with the boy, and I was so ashamed I almost went to pieces. There was no possibility of looking straight at him or of speaking coherently. With a hundred embarrassments and difficulties I got past him.*'

Babur's marriage to Ayisha was not a happy one. '*She came to Khodzhent and I married her* [i.e., in March 1500]. *The second time I took Samarqand* [i.e., between November 1500 and May 1501] *she had a little girl who died within several days. Shortly before the debacle of Tashkent* [i.e., somewhere between late 1501 and early 1503; mentioned later in this chapter] *she left me at her elder sister's instigation,*' Babur states with cold matter-of-factness.[8]

He was not much of a ladies' man, anyway. In due course, as it behooved a man of royal blood, he would marry several other women and father four sons, but there is no trace in his memoirs of the kind of romantic love that, four generations later, would cause the incomparable Taj Mahal to be built.

***

By early 1500, Babur had managed to recover so much territory that his younger half-brother felt compelled to offer him a truce: for the time being, Fergana would be split in two; the two brothers would join forces to recover Samarqand, after which, Babur would be king of Samarqand, and Jahangir would keep Fergana.

Meanwhile, Samarqand no longer was in Timurid hands; it had fallen to a formidable conqueror from the north: Shaybani Khan, king of the Uzbeks. Priding himself on a glorious ancestry all the way up to Genghis Khan, he had made it his goal in life to rid Central Asia of the Timurids – an endeavour in which he would succeed with brutal efficiency. This time, much more was at stake than Babur's personal aspirations: Samarqand had become a matter of honour for the entire Timurid family.

Samarqand, Again

For once, Lady Luck was on his side. Sometime in July 1500, arriving in the dead of the night, he found Shaybani Khan's army encamped and sound asleep in one of the gardens outside the city walls. 'If I manage to get inside the ramparts, the people will rally behind me,' Babur figured, correctly assuming that the inhabitants had little love lost for their rough new masters. Around seventy of Babur's best men stealthily climbed the city wall, killed the sentries at the gate, and he sneaked in unhindered with the rest of his fighting force. As he had hoped, Samarqand's riffraff readily joined him in the ensuing 'purging' process: every single one of the approximately five hundred Uzbeks inside the city ramparts was butchered in his sleep or hunted down and lynched. By the time Shaybani Khan realized what had happened, Samarqand's gates were safely barricaded against him. Seething with anger and vowing bloody revenge, the Uzbek had no alternative but to slink off.

Throughout the winter months in 1500, Babur was safely enjoying his much coveted throne. In the spring of 1501, however, Shaybani Khan was back – in force. Babur's men did manage to repulse the first frontal attacks on the gates and ramparts, but the protracted hardships of the ensuing siege were too much for them. Slowly but surely, Samarqand was starved into submission. When all the pack animals had been slaughtered and eaten, the beleaguered even had to resort to eating dogs – a repulsive idea in the mind of any right-minded Muslim. With his men deserting in droves, night after night, Babur's army had melted away like snow in summer; the situation had become untenable. In an effort to placate his enemy, Babur suffered the affront of having to offer him his elder sister in marriage, in exchange for guarantees of safe passage; then one night in May 1501, he stealthily sneaked out of the city, with his mother and a handful of followers. Barely eighteen years of age, Babur had twice been king of Samarqand, and twice, he had lost it in a matter of months.

***

Once again, his life was in ruins. Desperate and destitute, he sought asylum with his uncles in Tashkent, but found little else than poverty and humiliation. There was a faint glimmer of hope when he did manage to recuperate a small part of Fergana with the help of a few men his uncles had put at his disposal; very soon, however, things started to go downhill again. The dreaded Uzbeks were everywhere, and Babur's own retinue had dwindled to barely two hundred ragged men, most of them on foot and poorly equipped.

Kabul

Then suddenly, fortune again smiled on him: about 700 km south of Fergana, across the arduous mountain passes of the Hindu Kush, the throne of Kabul had fallen vacant. Until 1501, the small kingdom had been in the hands of one of his uncles, but that uncle having passed away with an infant as his sole heir, the throne had been usurped by the non-Timurid ruler, Muhammad Muqim Arghun of Qandahar. This was all Babur needed: a legal claim on a Timurid throne, at a safe distance from Shaybani Khan's hordes. He again managed to raise himself a decent army – with the prospect of plunder, any Timurid prince could find himself plenty of followers – and crossed the mountains in 1504. For once, things went off rather smoothly: after a brief, token resistance, the usurper headed back to Qandahar, tail between his legs.

From Babur's perspective, Kabul was a mere consolation prize, a refuge he had run to for want of anything better, but it turned out to be a godsend. Pleasantly located in a verdant valley, cold in winter, but pleasingly warm and not too humid in summer, its soil fertile, with lush pastures for horses and livestock, excellent fruits and vegetables and plenty of tasty honey, the city was easily defensible, guarded by a powerfully fortified mountain ridge. It was an important trading centre for horses, textiles, sugar and spices, with at least twelve languages spoken all year round: not only the local Pashto but also Persian, Arabic, Hindi, Turkish, Mongol and a number of mountain dialects. Babur had finally found himself a home.

***

Meanwhile however, up north, the unstoppable Uzbek tidal wave had swept away every single obstacle in its way. Soon, Kabul and Herat, south of the Hindu Kush in present-day Afghanistan, were the last two cities to be ruled by Timurids; but even there, doom was looming on the horizon, as the insatiable Shaybani Khan was casting his covetous eyes southwards.

At the invitation of his worried cousins, Babur spent a pleasant few weeks in Herat, discussing a joint defence against the invader. For a while, he and his hosts deluded themselves in grandiose plans of revenge, conquest and glory, but Babur was smart enough a judge of character to realize that his effeminate cousins would be no match for the ruthless Uzbek. '*Although these Mirzas were outstanding in the social graces, they were strangers to the reality of military command and the rough and tumble of battle,*' he notes. Prudently, '*on the pretext of finding winter quarters*', he headed back to Kabul in 1506, in spite of the brutal Afghan winter. '*I became a snow trampler,*' he notes wryly; and adds, '*every time we put our foot down we would sink in to the waist or chest*'. Further developments, however, soon proved him right: barely a few months later, in the spring of 1507, Herat fell to the Uzbeks.

Babur now found himself, as Bamber Gascoigne aptly phrases it,[9] '*in the distinguished but alarming position*' of being the only Timurid prince still sitting on a respectable throne. As the de facto leader of his erstwhile glorious clan, he assumed the superlative royal title of Pādshāh or Pād-i-Shāh, a Persian compound word meaning 'master king', 'great king', or, in Western parlance, 'emperor'.

Lofty titles, however, are of little avail on the battlefield, and Babur was painfully aware of this reality: It was only a matter of time before the Uzbeks would take Qandahar, and then, march on Kabul itself. Safe rather than sorry, he started making plans to flee, back across the mountains to Badakhshan,[10] or eastwards, to Hindustan. '*A foreign people like the Uzbeks and an old enemy like Wormwood Khan* [Babur's preferred term of abuse for Shaybani Khan] *had overrun the territory held by Temür Beg's descendants. Turk and Chagatai, in every nook and cranny where they were left, had joined the Uzbeks, some willingly and others unwillingly. Only I was left in Kabul. The foe was powerful, and we were weak. There was neither any possibility for coming to terms nor any hope for resisting. Such potency and strength did not allow us to think of any territory for ourselves, and at this juncture there was no way we could get far enough from such a mighty foe. We would either have to go to Badakhshan or to Hindustan*',[11] Babur admits with his usual frankness.

An Unexpected Ally

Once again, however, Lady Luck came to the rescue, in the guise this time of Shah Ismail of Persia, who had been watching the rapid expansion of the Uzbeks near his borders with increasing displeasure. Bones of contention were sought and found, insults were exchanged, and Shaybani Khan, foolish enough to antagonize the young Persian monarch, found himself at war with what soon would be known as the mighty Safavid Empire.

He may have been quite young still, but Shah Ismail really was not to be underestimated. Merely twenty-three years old in 1510, he was a battle-hardened veteran, and a highly successful one at that.

The start of his remarkable career had been extremely difficult: in 1488, when Ismail was a barely one-year-old infant, his father was killed in battle, and the young orphan, nominally the last-in-line leader of the Safaviyya, a militant Twelver Shia Sufi order, was raised in hiding, getting a bilingual education in both Azeri Turkish and Persian. Barely twelve years old, he came out of hiding to lead his fanatical Qizilbash[12] Turkoman horsemen into battle, with spectacular success: by his fourteenth birthday in July 1501, he was enthroned as Shah of all of Azerbaijan. Nine years later, he had conquered and unified all of Iran, Azerbaijan, eastern Anatolia and Iraq (including the eternal city of Baghdad), thus becoming the founder of the powerful Safavid dynasty, destined to hold sway over Greater Persia for over two centuries. Unbridledly ambitious, fanatical, cunning and utterly ruthless, he ruled supreme, devoting all his efforts to imposing Shia Islam in his dominions. Right until today, the mass conversion of Iran to Shiism under Ismail and his Safavid dynasty is of important geopolitical significance.[13]

It will be clear from the above that Shaybani Khan had chosen to antagonize a fearsome adversary. This time, the ambitious Uzbek had bitten off more than he could chew. On 2 December 1510, near the city of Merv in present-day Turkmenistan, he and his army of 28,000 men were ambushed and crushingly defeated by Shah Ismail's 17,000-strong fighting force. The Uzbek tried to flee, but was apprehended and executed on the spot. Shah Ismail, evidently a sophisticated amateur of gruesome souvenirs, ordered the body hacked to pieces and the scattered limbs put on display in the four corners of his empire. The head was put to more practical household use: after the flesh had been boiled off, the remaining skull, set in gold, was turned into a bejewelled drinking goblet, which, history reports, the Shah was extremely fond of using.

***

Once more, the tables were turned. Babur's archenemy was dead, and he appeared to have found himself a powerful new ally. The Shah was kind enough to have Babur's elder sister – who, as mentioned above, had been given in marriage to Shaybani Khan at the time of Babur's second Samarqand debacle – escorted back to Kabul, laden with lavish gifts. It was Babur's first diplomatic contact with mighty Persia, and he did not fail to seize the opportunity: this was his long-awaited chance to seize the throne of Samarqand, and fulfil, as the nineteenth-century Americans would later phrase it, his *manifest destiny*.

The powerful Shah agreed to help him, on two conditions: first, he was to convert to – or at least adopt the dress and customs of – Shia Islam, and secondly, once Samarqand had been recovered, the *khutba* (the formal Friday sermon, including a prayer for the ruling monarch) was to be read and coins were to be struck in Shah Ismail's name. In other words: Babur was to officially recognize Persian suzerainty. A rather steep price to pay, but beggars can't be choosers; besides, since the *khutba* back in Kabul would still be read in Babur's name, he had, so it seemed, little to lose and much to gain.

At the head of his army, reinforced by a Persian expeditionary corps, Babur marched north and took Bukhara; meanwhile, one of his cousins had driven the Uzbeks from Fergana. The road to Samarqand was open, at last. In October 1511, after an absence of ten years, Babur triumphantly entered the city, acclaimed by the entire population.

Popular enthusiasm, however, quickly subsided to give way to scorn and scepticism: the returning Timurid monarch insisted on wearing Shia clothes – nothing less than blasphemous in a Sunni city. Babur had gotten himself into an impossible position: in the eyes of his staunchly Sunni subjects, he had become a despicable heretic, while in the eyes of the Shah, his failure to persecute the city's Sunni clerics and actively impose Shiism had made him an unreliable – if not outright disloyal – vassal.

Kabul, *Faute de Mieux*

Meanwhile, the dreaded Uzbeks were back, and this time, they were there to stay. Taking advantage of the absence of the Shah in faraway Azerbaijan, they retook Bukhara under the leadership of Abaidullah Khan, nephew of the late Shaybani Khan.

History soon repeated itself: Babur left Samarqand posthaste in an attempt to save another of his possessions, and in the process, lost both. Riding out to relieve Bukhara in May 1512, he was badly defeated outside the city gates, at Kul-i-Malik. Samarqand being lost as well, he had no alternative but to retire to Hisar in Badakhshan.

Once again, the Shah had to come to the rescue. Later in 1512, he sent Babur an auxiliary army headed by Najm Beg, one of his generals. Babur and his Persian allies rode against Bukhara, only to find the Uzbek enemy well entrenched in a strong fortress. By this time winter had set in. Badly suffering from the cold and lack of adequate provisions, the Persians decided to raise the siege, and, during their retreat, were taken by surprise by a massive Uzbek counterattack, in which the Persian general perished, along with many of his men. Babur, who headed the rearguard, did little or nothing to help his unfortunate Persian allies, and fled. Persian history, understandably so, would forever consider him a coward and a traitor.

Babur planned to retreat to Badakhshan, but found that Hisar had rebelled against him. There was no alternative but to recross the Hindu Kush and head back to Kabul. He did not fully realize it at the time, but this was the final point of no return: he would never set eyes again on his native country.

***

Any hope he may have still entertained of regaining power was rudely shattered, when, in 1514, his Persian allies suffered, entirely unexpectedly, a crushing defeat against an invading Ottoman army in the west of Iran. At the Battle of Chaldiran (a town in present-day Turkish Kurdistan near the Iranian border) in August 1514, the gallant and erstwhile invincible Persian cavalry was cruelly decimated by the murderous fire of the Ottoman cannons and matchlock muskets. Shah Ismail would spend the rest of his short life – he died in May 1524, two months before his thirty-seventh birthday – recovering the lost territory and modernizing his army after the Ottoman model.

Babur realized that, under the circumstances, Samarqand and Central Asia were lost to him: there was no hope for a renewed Safavid–Timurid alliance against the Uzbeks. Whether he liked it or not, henceforth, his future would lie in the Indian subcontinent.

***

The next eleven years in Kabul, from 1514 to 1525, were a time of relative peace and tranquillity insofar as the life of a medieval prince can be peaceful. There still was a good deal of fighting to be done – rebellious nobles to be brought in line, recalcitrant hill tribes to be chastised and neighbouring regions to be raided, but, by and large, Babur now found ample time to busy himself with more peaceful endeavours: gardening, poetry and the arts, and the education of his four sons: Humayun, the eldest, born in 1508, and the three younger brothers, Kamran (b. 1509), Askari (b. 1516), and Hindal (b. 1519).[14] Babur also began to devote quite some time to much less refined pastimes: opium, and more importantly, drinking. Only now, well in his thirties, did he discover the joys of wine and hard liquor, but, as Abraham Eraly observes,[15] he briskly made up for the lost time.

Onward to Hindustan

Babur loved and enjoyed Kabul, but it was much too small a kingdom for a man of his grandiose ambitions. Pillaging forays beyond the Khyber Pass may have satisfied the greed of his men, but Babur wanted more, much more: he wanted all of Hindustan. After all, was the Punjab not an integral part of Amīr Temür's empire, ever since the conquest of Delhi in 1398? After all, did not Khizr Khan – the founder of the Sayyid dynasty, which ruled the Delhi Sultanate afterwards from 1414 to 1451 – formally acknowledge Amīr Temür's suzerainty? Did Khizr Khan not strike coin in Amīr Temür's name? Did he not refuse to take up any royal title for himself? No, Hindustan lawfully belonged to the house of Timur; Hindustan was Babur's to take.

He sent an envoy to Hindustan '*for the sake of peace*', inviting the Afghan king, Sultan Ibrahim Lodi, to give '*the countries which from old* [sic] *had depended on the Turk*' back to him.[16] Was this naiveté, as some historians seem to think? Was it psychological warfare? Or was it a subtle opening move on the Indian political chessboard, a way to stand up and be counted among the sultan's many rivals? In view of the later developments, one is inclined to believe the last hypothesis.

***

Steadily and methodically, Babur began preparing his army for a major campaign. His military track record may have been far from impressive until then, but this time, he did have a stroke of genius: he started acquiring large numbers of cannons and muskets and hired a Turkish artillery expert, going by the name of Ustad (master) Ali Quli. Another smart and strategically important move on the part of Babur was the conquest of Qandahar, south-west of Kabul. It took him three successive summers of siege before the powerful citadel finally surrendered to him in 1522, but it was worth the effort: strategically located to secure

Babur's home base during his absence, this 'entrance gate to Hindustan' was of capital importance.

The preparatory work behind him, Babur was ready for action. All he needed was an opportunity to attack.

And that opportunity would arise soon enough. Ever since the death of Sultan Sikandar Lodi in 1517, the sultanate had been in turmoil, plagued by internal strife, which Ibrahim Lodi, Sikandar Lodi's youngest son and much less competent successor, was unable to quell. Amidst this quagmire, two of Ibrahim Lodi's most serious rivals – his own uncle, Alam Khan, and Daulat Khan, the aging but always rebellious governor of the Punjab – sent an envoy to Kabul, begging Babur to help them in ousting the sultan.

This was the moment Babur had been waiting for. For the sixth time since his arrival in Kabul, he crossed the Khyber Pass in late 1524; only this crossing was more than a vulgar plundering raid. This time, he was out to claim for himself a new throne. After taking Lahore (now in Pakistan), however, he was forced to abort the campaign and return to Kabul, when he and his newfound allies started bickering about the division of the province: it would have been too dangerous for him to advance deeper into Hindustan, with a potential enemy in his rear.

But all is not lost that is delayed. One year later, in November 1525, just before the winter snowfalls began, Babur was back; and this time, he was back for good. Henceforth, his future would lie in Hindustan.

***

The first task before him was to retake the Punjab from Daulat Khan, his treacherous former ally, who, in a show of defiant bravura, girded himself with two swords. Daulat Khan's men, however, were less self-assured: upon Babur's arrival, most of them ran like rabbits. Daulat Khan soon found himself bottled up in a small fortress with a handful of followers, and tamely surrendered, when his grandson, whom he had sent out to parley, was sent back to the fortress '*with some enticing promises and threats*', as Babur succinctly puts it. '*I ordered him to hang around his neck the very same two swords he had strapped to his waist to fight us .... When it was time for the interview, he was slow to kneel, so I ordered his leg pulled to make him kneel*', he further reports.[17] As Babur had promised, the old man's life was spared; he was assigned a home to live in with his wives, but the rest of his family's possessions – including an interesting library, Babur notes – were confiscated.

The next few weeks were spent mopping up the last pockets of enemy resistance. Then, it was time to go for the big prize: the throne of Hindustan itself. '*We placed our feet in the stirrup of resolve, grabbed the reins of trust in God, and directed ourselves against Sultan Ibrahim, son of Sultan Sikandar, son of Bahlul Lodi the Afghan, who controlled the capital Delhi and the realm of Hindustan at that time. He was said to have a standing army of one hundred thousand, and he and his* begs [nobles] *had nearly a thousand elephants*', notes Babur.

Panipat

The enemy's vastly superior numbers did not seem to frighten Babur. Virtually unopposed at first, he advanced through the Punjab, straight towards Delhi. Then, by the end of February 1526, near the town of Hisar-e-Firoza (in present-day Haryana, close to the Punjab border), his advance was blocked by a vanguard of Sultan Ibrahim Lodi's army.

Unimpressed, Babur sent his eldest son Humayun ahead with the right wing of the army to deal with the situation. It was the boy's maiden battle, but in spite of his relatively tender age – barely eighteen – he made quick work of the enemy. Engaging the front of the enemy forces with a small but highly mobile detachment of about 150 scouts, he surprised them in the rear with the main body of his army group. The enemy, suffering heavy casualties, was completely routed. About 200 enemy soldiers were taken prisoner; Humayun had half of them beheaded on the spot, and took the rest to his father, along with a handsome booty, including seven war elephants.

Babur was elated at his son's triumph. Humayun was awarded a royal robe of honour and a prize steed from his father's personal stables, plus one crore (ten million) in cash and the governorship of the Hisar district, estimated at another crore per year in revenue. As far as the enemy prisoners were concerned, '*Ustad Ali Quli and his matchlockmen were ordered to shoot all the captives*', Babur reports with stone-cold brevity. He neither expands on his motivation for having the prisoners killed nor on the reason why he insisted on having it done by his musketeers. '*The oddity of this early firing squad, using expensive powder where a sword was so much easier, suggests … that it was meant to be a demoralizing demonstration, word of which would certainly get back to Ibrahim's army, of the magical power of the new weapons*', Gascoigne suggests.[18] Psychological warfare may certainly have been one of Babur's main reasons; but it is equally likely that the execution was also a gruesome clinical trial, Babur wanting to test, one last time, the efficiency of his gunmen and the effect of their weapons on human flesh.

The result must have been to his liking, for he continued his advance towards Delhi, full of confidence in spite of scouting reports confirming his opponent's vast numerical superiority. On 2 April 1526, he got another moral boost, when his left wing successfully ambushed another enemy vanguard near Sarsawa on the banks of the Yamuna River (in present-day Uttar Pradesh, about 180 km north of Delhi), bringing in another seven war elephants and about eighty prisoners, most of whom were summarily executed '*as retributive justice*'.[19]

***

Ten days later, with both opposing armies approaching the town of Panipat (approximately 80 km north of Delhi; now in Haryana), the final confrontation was near.

Babur understood fully well that his much smaller army – outnumbered four or five to one – did not stand a chance, unless he found a way to make the enemy fight him on a narrow battlefront, in order to prevent them from sweeping around his flanks. But Babur came well prepared. His scouts having reconnoitered the prospective battlefield, he had held a general war council with '*all the* begs *and great warriors who knew what they were talking about*' to analyse the situation. He now knew exactly how he wanted to fight this battle. Making haste to get there well ahead of the enemy, he arrived at Panipat on 12 April, positioning his forces to the east of the town, between the town walls and the Yamuna River.

The right wing of his army had the town walls to its right, while the left flank was protected by ditches, felled trees, and artificial hedges made of thorny shrubbery, all the way to the riverbanks, to make sure that his army could not be bypassed and surrounded by the enemy. The fighting forces in the centre were positioned behind an ingenious mobile defence made of approximately 700 carts, linked together with ox-harness ropes, behind and in between which he positioned his archers and musketeers, protected by movable wooden mantlets. At regular intervals, he left openings in the front, a bit less than a bow-shot wide, through which assaults of up to 150 horsemen could be launched.

Babur's preparations were impeccable, but Sultan Ibrahim Lodi failed to take the bait. He deployed his army, but refused to give battle, and quite rightfully so: after all, time was very much on his side. He had no difficulties in procuring supplies, whereas Babur would sooner or later be forced to withdraw, or leave his entrenched position and attack.

For seven days, in the blazing heat of early summer, the opposing armies kept facing each other.

With a series of quick hit-and-run raids, Babur tried to provoke the enemy into attacking him, but Ibrahim Lodi ignored all insults and did not move. As morale in his camp was deteriorating fast, Babur then decided to launch a night attack.

About 5000 men moved stealthily to the enemy camp, but upon arrival, they were in for a very unpleasant surprise themselves: the Afghans were ready and waiting for them. Fortunately, Babur's men did not confuse bravery with foolishness – they managed to quickly disengage and withdraw without too many losses. Had they continued their attack, they would most certainly have been annihilated.

Ironically, it was this debacle that won the war for Babur. After another day of waiting, shortly after dawn on 21 April 1526, encouraged by their easy victory, the Afghans moved in for what they thought was the final kill.

The battle went exactly as Babur had planned. The mighty Afghan cavalry charge, started on too broad a front, was slowed down considerably when it had to squeeze itself through the narrow funnel created by Babur's entrenchments, its left flank pushing sideways into its own centre formation.

Babur's forces waited in silence until the Afghan front was well within reach of the artillery. Then, Babur's field cannons opened up, their projectiles penetrating deep into the enemy formation. As the large guns reloaded, deadly volleys of infantry muskets and rockets further decimated the Afghan front, the bullets and missiles easily piercing enemy shields and armour. The Afghan vanguard tried to turn around and move out of reach of the guns, but the attacking ranks behind slammed into them. Before long, the entire Afghan fighting force had turned into a compacted, disorganized mass; those caught in the middle unable to move anywhere, defenceless fodder for Babur's mortar bombs and the clouds upon clouds of arrows that kept raining down on them.

Babur did not waste any time to seize the opportunity.

The best of his cavalry – fearless, battle-hardened Turkoman archers on the swiftest horses – stormed through the openings in Babur's defences, wheeling round the Afghan flanks and effectively preventing them from manoeuvring.

The Afghans fought bravely and with honour, repeatedly charging Babur's front lines at the centre in an effort to break out of the trap, but to no avail: very few of them even managed to reach Babur's positions, and those who did, were finished off quickly.

'*The sun was one lance high when the battle began, and the fighting continued till mid-day, when the enemy was completely broken and routed, and my friends victorious and exulting. By the grace and mercy of almighty God, this arduous undertaking was made easy for me, and such a numerous army, in the space of half a day, ground into the dust*', Babur notes. All told, between 15,000 and 16,000 Afghans had been killed; Sultan Ibrahim Lodi's body was found amid the other corpses. When his head was brought to Babur, he ordered the sultan's remains to be washed, shrouded in the finest cloth and buried with honour at the spot where he and his men had fallen. Ibrahim Lodi's tomb, a simple rectangular structure on a high platform with a flight of steps, is still in that same area,[20] although the British did relocate and renovate it way back in 1866, during the construction of a road.

***

There was no time to be wasted. Babur ordered Humayun and a group of men to leave behind their baggage and '*proceed swiftly and unencumbered, to get hold of Agra* [Lodi's capital city] *and confiscate the treasury*'; another battle group was sent to Delhi with similar instructions. Babur himself proceeded to Delhi at a more leisurely pace and camped on the banks of the Yamuna, '*for the sake of the horses*'. The next day (22 April), he rode into Delhi, where, for the first time, the *khutba* was read in his name. He had become, quite officially, Padshah of Hindustan.

He spent a day inspecting the city's defences and visiting the most important monuments of the city; then, he returned to his army camp to celebrate his victory – with rivers of hard liquor.

He then headed to Agra, where Humayun presented him with the spoils, including a magnificent diamond, given to him by the royal family of Gwalior, who had taken refuge in a fort in Agra and whose safety Humayun had courteously guaranteed. Raja Vikramjit, one of

Ibrahim Lodi's allies, had fallen with the sultan on the battlefield.

Rarely, if ever, had the world seen so large a diamond; Babur estimated its value at '*two and a half days' food for the whole world*'.

Thus commenced – in all probability – the extraordinary history of the famous Koh-i-Noor (mountain of light), the centrepiece in the British crown jewels and once the largest known diamond in the world.

As per Gascoigne's[21] summary:

- Babur – reputed for his largesse – casually handed it back to Humayun;
- two decades later, Humayun, in dire straits at that time, gave it to Shah Tahmasp of Persia;
- Shah Tahmasp sent it as a present to Nizam Shah in the Deccan (in India);
- from there, it somehow found its way back to the Mughal treasure under Shah Jahan;
- barely two generations later, after the sack of Delhi in 1739 by Nadir Shah, it was again carted off to Persia along with the rest of the Mughal treasure; it was over there that it got its current nickname;
- it then passed from Nadir Shah's grandson to the reigning family in Kabul, and from them to Ranjit Singh, the Sikh ruler of the Punjab from 1801 to 1839;
- when the Punjab was annexed by the British in 1849, the diamond was gifted away by Maharaja Dulip Singh of Lahore to Her Majesty Queen Victoria, via the British chief commissioner, Sir John Lawrence, who promptly forgot about it, leaving it in his waistcoat pocket for six weeks;
- when the absent-minded commissioner finally remembered about the jewel, it was sent posthaste to Queen Victoria in London, arriving in time to become the prize exhibit in the Great Exhibition of 1851, 'and so,' writes Gascoigne, '[it went] into the Tower of London, from which nothing escapes'.

The version about the precious object lying in the commissioner's pocket may or may not be true; anyway, the diamond remains an apple of discord between India and the UK, right to this day. During Queen Elizabeth's state visit to India in August 1997 (on the occasion of the fiftieth anniversary of Indian independence), many Indians demanded, to no avail, the return of the diamond to India.

A Foreign Land ...

For a while, all Babur's troubles seemed to be a thing of the past. The enemies who had not died on the battlefield or fled the country, appeared – at least for the time being – to have resigned themselves to the new situation. Even Sultan Ibrahim Lodi's mother Buwa had meekly accepted the state pension that Babur had been gracious enough to offer her.

It soon appeared, though, that the old lady's thirst for revenge had not at all been slaked: a few months later, on 21 December 1526, she nearly succeeded in having Babur poisoned, after bribing one of his Hindustani cooks. Babur describes the incident with clinical precision and colourful detail:[22] the cook had cleverly sprinkled a dose of poison on a piece of thin bread, topped with some meat dressed in oil. Babur, however, had wolfed down, luckily for him, '*a lot of rabbit stew*' and '*quite a bit of dressed saffroned meat*' before trying '*one or two tidbits from the top of the poisoned Hindustani food*'. Soon after eating those tidbits, he became violently nauseous and rushed to the latrine, where he '*vomited a lot*'. Something was terribly wrong here, Babur thought. '*I never vomited after meals, not even when drinking. A cloud of suspicion came over my mind,*' he writes. The affair was then investigated with well-nigh scientific rigour: '*I ordered the cook to be held while the vomit was given to a dog that was watched.*' When the dog became quite sick as well, Babur knew enough. The cook, under torture, confessed in full detail; three more offenders – a taster and two female kitchen helps – were arrested, and appropriate punishments meted out. One of the women was shot to death; the other, less fortunate, was trampled to death by an elephant. The taster was hacked to pieces, and the cook, finally, was flayed alive. As far as Lady Buwa, the original culprit, was concerned: she was thrown in jail and '[would] *pay for what she* [had] *done,*' Babur promised in a letter to the home front in Kabul. With her entire property confiscated, she reportedly spent the rest of her life in captivity.

***

Another, and potentially even more dangerous, challenge Babur had to face during those first few months after the Panipat victory was the morale of his own men. Now that the country had been plundered and the spoils distributed – '*Babur gained the treasure of five kings,*' his daughter Gulbadan (literally meaning 'flowerbody') later wrote, '*and he gave it all away ...*' – why on earth should they be staying here in the sweltering heat, when they had a home in Kabul, where the air was so much more pleasant, the food so much tastier and the people so much nicer?

But Babur did not want to go home. This was not a vulgar plundering raid: he had won himself a prestigious throne and a country much larger than the petty kingdom of Kabul. He simply could not afford to go back: he needed time to consolidate his throne.

It took all of Babur's diplomatic and oratorical skills to convince at least a majority of the men to stay in Hindustan with him: '*For years we have struggled, overcome difficulties, traversed long distances .... Through God's grace we have defeated such numerous enemies and taken such vast realms. What now compels us to throw away for no reason all the realms we have taken at such cost? Shall we go back to Kabul and remain poor?*' he pleaded. In the end, he succeeded in convincing the majority and restoring at least a semblance of order, although a minority of the men still insisted on leaving. A deserter, Khwaja Kalan, one of Babur's intimates, wrote a mocking line of poetry on the wall of his quarters in Delhi:

If safely I recross the River Sind [Indus],
Black be my face, ere I wish to see Hind.

Babur was not amused, but what was he to do? He was disappointed with the defectors, but in his heart, he understood them all too well. For Babur, too, felt terribly homesick.

'*Hindustan is a country of few charms,*' he states in his memoirs. '*Its people have no good looks. Of social intercourse, paying and receiving visits, there is none; of genius and capacity none; of manners none. In handicraft and such work there is no form or symmetry, method or quality. There are no good horses, no good dogs, no grapes, musk melons or first-rate fruits, no ice or cold water, no good bread or cooked food in the bazars, no bath-houses, no colleges, no candles, torches or candlesticks ... except their large rivers and their standing waters which flow in ravines or hollows, there are no running waters, not even in their gardens and residences: they do not have the pleasure of swift currents of clear water flowing through channels into private precincts. Their residences have no charm, air, regularity or symmetry.'*

In his view, the country did have a few advantages, but even those seemed to have their own shortcomings: '*The weather is quite nice during the rainy season .... One drawback, though, is that the air becomes too humid. During the rainy season,* [composite] *bows* [from Central Asia] *cannot be used to shoot or they are ruined. Armour, books, bedding and textiles are also affected ...*'

In the end, the reason why he wanted to stay in Hindustan was twofold: money and people. '*One pleasant thing about Hindustan is that it is a large country with lots of gold and money .... Another good thing in Hindustan is that it has unnumbered and endless workmen of every kind. There is a fixed caste for every sort of work, which has done that work or that thing from father to son till now ...*'[23]

Yet, he sadly missed Kabul and the surrounding regions. '*Boundless and infinite is my desire to go to those parts,*' he writes in a letter back home. One day, when a melon from Kabul was brought to him and he smelt its aroma, '*I felt myself affected with a strong feeling of loneliness and exile from my native country, and I could not help shedding tears while eating it,*' he confesses.[24]

***

At times, Babur's poetry discloses a wistful, melancholy nature, and, at times, an inclination towards mysticism and prayerful reflection, which would reveal itself, much stronger, purer and more honest, in Akbar the Great, his brilliant grandson:

Darweshan ra garchi na az khweshanim
Lek az dil-o-jan mu'taqid ishanim
Dur ast magoyi Shahi az darweshi
Shahim wali banda-i-darweshanim.
(Though I am not related to dervishes,
I am their follower in heart and soul.
Say not: A king is far from a dervish;
I am a king, yet the slave of dervishes.)[25]

The Clash at Khanwa

However, there was a lot of work to be done, a mission to be accomplished. By Central Asian standards, Babur was ruling over an immense country, but in an Indian context, he merely occupied – for the time being, until further notice – just a few squares on a much larger chessboard. He might have won an important victory, but that was by no means final: there were still many actual and potential rivals to be reckoned with. The ousted Lodis and their allies were waiting for an opportunity to strike back; to the east, in Bihar and Bengal, there were other Afghan clans (which, a few generations earlier, had gained de facto independence from Delhi) feeling tempted to expand their dominions and challenge Babur's throne, now that the sultanate had collapsed; and last but not least, there was Rajputana (Rajasthan) to the southwest. Never conquered by any Muslim invader, the formidable Rajput clans – usually divided by internal rivalry and bloody feuds – were forming a confederation under Rana Sangram Simha – aka Rana Sanga – of Mewar (in southern Rajasthan, including the powerful fortress of Chittorgarh).

In early 1527, an attempt by the ousted Afghans to regroup under Sultan Ibrahim Lodi's brother Mahmud Lodi was swiftly crushed by a Mughal expeditionary force, brilliantly led by Humayun. Rana Sangram Simha, however, was a different kettle of fish altogether. A battle-hardened ironside, he proudly bore the marks of a belligerent life: one eye lost in a brawl with his own brother; an arm cut off in a battle against the sultan of Delhi; one leg smashed and permanently crippled by a cannonball hit; and no less than eighty other scars all over his body. The strength of his army was estimated at two hundred thousand men, twice the size of Sultan Ibrahim Lodi's forces at Panipat. And to make things worse, this formidable fighting force was reinforced by several Afghan contingents, thirsting for revenge.

With his usual optimism, Babur was tempted to underestimate the threat, but soon changed his mind when every Mughal vanguard he sent ahead was decimated by the advancing Rajputs. Morale was deteriorating fast: indigenous auxiliary troops were deserting in droves and his own men were once again begging him to go back to Kabul, instead of risking everything for a land they all hated, anyway. To make things worse, Babur's newly arrived astrologer appeared to side with the sceptics: Mars was in an unfavourable position and the stars presaged nothing but defeat and disaster, was his prediction. But Babur wouldn't budge. Stubbornly, he continued his advance, taking maximum precautions at every halt, using the same tactics that had proved so valuable at Panipat and protecting his camp with movable bulwarks of interlinked carts.

Then, in a flash of intuition, he found the way to rally the troops: *jihad*, holy war, sanctioned by Allah Himself. Indeed, this was the first time in his entire military career that he would be fighting *kafirs*, infidels. Conveniently glossing over the presence of thousands of fellow Muslim Afghans in the enemy army, he persuaded his men of the vital importance of the upcoming battle: the entire future of Islam on the subcontinent depended on them! If they won, undying glory and untold wealth would be theirs; and if, by Allah's decree, they would fall on the battlefield, the eternal rewards of paradise awaited them.

In a dramatic gesture, he ordered his entire supply of wine and arak* to be poured into the dust and all his precious gold and silver goblets, pitchers and flasks to be crushed or donated to the poor. Every single man in the army was made to swear a solemn oath, on the Holy Quran and '*by the divorce of their wives*',[26] that he would die rather than turn his back or surrender to the accursed infidels.

Morale thus restored and steeled with religious fervour, Babur continued his advance westwards, until, on 17 March 1527, the opposing armies clashed near the village of Khanwa, approximately 50 km west of Agra. The battle lasted for ten hours and was far more fiercely contested than that at Panipat, with heavy casualties on both sides. It ended as a reenactment of Panipat, with Babur's artillery and muskets winning the day against superior numbers. Wounded and badly defeated, Rana Sangram Simha withdrew to his home base in Mewar.

After this victory, Babur solemnly assumed the title of Ghazi (warrior on the path of God; slayer of the infidel) and ordered a tower of enemy heads to be built on the battlefield – the standard Mughal practice to discourage future enemies. He then publicly dismissed the astrologer who had been foolish enough to predict his defeat. '*I poured forth upon him a torrent of abuse,*' Babur confesses. Eventually, however, his generous character prevailed and he awarded him generous severance pay: '*Yet, as he was my old servant, I gave him a lakh in presents, and dismissed him, commanding him to depart from my dominions.*'

***

The die had finally been cast: Babur was the true master of Hindustan.

*A strong, anise-flavoured alcoholic spirit.

With the Rajput threat averted, he could afford to send Humayun way up north to Badakhshan with a large force to keep Kabul's northern borders secure, while he further consolidated his power in India, enjoying the sweet fruits of victory. He spent the pleasant rainy season of 1727 in Agra, building gardens and bath-houses, reading and writing poetry and working on his memoirs.

One thing, however, he profoundly regretted: the promise he had made at Khanwa. No more boozy celebrations and no more wine-soaked afternoons ... kicking a long-time habit proved to be far from easy.

There was solace in a drug called *majun*, probably a concoction of opium, which allowed him to see '*magnificent fields of flowers*', but he did miss his wine. '*Everybody repents and then gives up drinking; but I have given up drinking and now I repent,*' he writes with wistful self-mockery. In the end, the temptation would prove too strong: two years later, he quietly slipped back into his old vice. As the Bible states: '*the spirit is willing, but the flesh is weak ...*'[27]

His Last Battles

At the end of the rainy season in 1527, Babur again set out to consolidate and secure his borders with Rajputana, this time against Chanderi, a fortress in north-eastern Malwa.* Arriving at the gates on 21 January 1528, he took the stronghold in spite of the garrison's heroic resistance. It was there that the Mughals first came across the gruesome rite of *jauhar*: faced with defeat, the proud Rajput warriors, rather than risking slavery, preferred to kill their own wives and children (or have them throw themselves in the flames of a funeral pyre), upon which they either would slay each other or run towards the enemy to fight and die. The outcome, as wryly summarized by Abraham Eraly, was to be expected: the Rajputs kept their honour; Babur took the fort.[28]

In the *Baburnama*, Babur himself describes the horrible incident with characteristic matter-of-factness, and then casually goes on to describe the charms of the place he had just taken:[29]

> *They killed each other almost to the last by having one man hold a sword while the others willingly bent their necks .... A tower of infidels'*

*Chanderi is now a town in Madhya Pradesh. Malwa includes parts of present-day western Madhya Pradesh and parts of south-eastern Rajasthan.

skulls was erected on the hill on the northwest side of Chanderi ... Chanderi is a superb place. All around the area are flowing streams. The lake is renowned throughout Hindustan for its good, sweet water. It is truly a nice little lake.

***

Before being able to return to Agra, Babur found himself compelled to launch yet another campaign – this time against a coalition of rebel Afghan nobles who had occupied Lucknow (now the capital of Uttar Pradesh). His forces easily routed the enemy army at Kannauj, a village nearby; they chased the rebels all the way to Ayodhya,* forcing them to flee to Bengal. By the end of March 1528, he triumphantly returned to Agra.

***

The rest of the year 1528 went by rather leisurely, culminating in the grandest celebration of Babur's career. Soon after Panipat, Babur had sent out emissaries to Central Asia, inviting all of Timur's and Genghis Khan's descendants and all his erstwhile friends to come and join him in Hindustan, to celebrate and receive 'fitting benefits'.[30] In late 1528, a grandiose feast was organized, with hundreds of guests – Timurid princes and nobles, ambassadors of foreign nations, even including envoys of his old enemies, the Uzbeks, and also ordinary soldiers and farmers who had helped him during his throneless ordeal – receiving due recognition and lavish gifts, such as robes of honour, swords, daggers and other royal presents. The most important guests were invited to sit in a semicircle, as wide as a football field, with Babur at the centre in a pavilion built especially for the occasion. This was the apogee of Babur's career; for generations to come, people far and wide would talk about the magnificence and generosity of the great Padshah of Hindustan.

It appears, though, that he never entirely lost the ambition to reconquer Samarqand. Late in the fall of 1528, hearing the news that the young Persian Shah Tahmasp (son and successor to the untimely deceased Shah Ismail) had inflicted a crushing defeat on the Uzbeks, he immediately ordered Humayun to ride against them and reconquer

*A holy city for Hindus (in Uttar Pradesh) and the birthplace of Lord Ram, one of the avatars of Lord Vishnu.

as much territory as possible. Humayun did advance northwards and occupied Hisar, but ultimately had to abort the campaign, when Shah Tahmasp left the area to confront the Ottomans in the west. Bitterly disappointed once more, Babur had no alternative but to resign himself to the inevitable: the accursed Uzbeks would never leave his beloved Samarqand. Hindustan was a consolation prize, but it would have to do.

***

One more battle – his last – needed to be fought to secure that consolation prize. By the spring of 1529, the Afghan nobles had regrouped once again, in an ultimate attempt to oust him and reinstate the sultanate under Mahmud Lodi. Babur drove them back eastwards, all the way to Bihar. There, on 6 May 1529, at the confluence of the rivers Gogra (aka Ghaghara) and Ganga near Patna, he brilliantly and decisively defeated the rebels and the powerful Bengali–Afghan army that had come to their assistance.

At forty-six years of age, Babur could finally rest on his laurels. For the first time in his life, he had no one to fear; there was no force in all of northern India strong enough to challenge him.

Luckily for him, he did not realize how little time he had left to enjoy the pleasures of life. Babur's health never was very robust. From a tender age, he had been plagued rather frequently by a series of ailments: excessive discharge from the ears, frequent boils, backaches, fevers and, more alarmingly, spitting of blood. Early in 1530, the reports about his condition were alarming enough for Humayun to leave his station and return to Hindustan, much against his father's wishes.

Ironically, it was Humayun who was first struck with a serious illness. Tradition has it that Babur, in despair, circumambulated his son's sickbed three times, pledging his own life in exchange for that of his ailing son. That very same day, Humayun's condition started to improve, while Babur fell gravely ill from the fever that would soon take his life. Appealing though this story may be, it is, alas, not true. Babur may well have walked around his son's bed and taken the oath as described above, but several months elapsed between Humayun's recovery and his own fatal illness.

That final illness was an acutely painful disorder of the bowels, accompanied, luckily for Babur, by bouts of burning fever, which left him delirious most of the time. He kept asking for his youngest son Hindal, wanting to know how tall he had grown, lamenting that he was not there to hold his hand. But he remained clear-headed enough to think about his succession: when Humayun arrived at his bedside, he had the amirs (chieftains) called in and ordered them to acknowledge his firstborn as the rightful heir to the throne.

Utterly exhausted and emaciated, Babur passed away on 26 December 1530 at Agra, forty-seven years and ten months old. '*Black fell the day for children and kinsfolk and all,*' laments his daughter Gulbadan in her chronicle, the *Humayunnama*; she adds that '*voices were uplifted in weeping; there was utter dejection*'.[31]

Good or Bad?

Black fell the day, says Gulbadan .... Well, did it, indeed? Should history bewail the passing of this *buccaneer with royal blood in his veins*, as Gascoigne called him? All things considered: no.

In his introduction to Professor Thackston's translation of the *Baburnama*,[32] Salman Rushdie states:

> *Who, then, was Babur – scholar or barbarian, nature-loving poet or terror-inspiring warlord? The answer is to be found in the* Baburnama, *and it's an uncomfortable one: he was both .... Both Baburs are real, and perhaps the strangest thing about the* Baburnama *is that they do not seem to be at odds with each other.*

Rushdie is right, of course: like everybody else, Babur was both good *and* evil. If we are honest with ourselves, we will have to admit that the chasm between good and evil runs inside every human being. But that is not the point. Knowing that good and evil inclinations live inside every one of us, the real question is: what have we *done* with them? In which *respect* have we been good? How have we touched other people's lives?

To live a good life, says Babur, means living your life in such a way that after you're gone, people cherish your memory. '*In this world,*' he states, '*a man's actions outlive him. If he has any intelligence at all, why would he try to be ill-spoken of after death? If he is ambitious, why would he not try to act in such a way that, when he has passed away, people continue to praise him? In the honourable mention of their names, wise men find a second life.*'[33]

One can only agree with Babur's statement: the true moral value of a person's life can only be measured by the joy and the added value it has brought to other people's lives. By these standards, has he lived up to his own ideal?

Admittedly, Babur appears to have been quite pleasant company; admittedly, he was generous to those near and dear to him; admittedly, he loved nature, gardening, literature, poetry and the arts. Admittedly, he was resilient in the face of adversity, resourceful in times of need; admittedly, his victory at Panipat – after a lifetime of defeat, one should add – entitles him to a place in military history textbooks. But does that make him a good person? According to many eyewitnesses, Adolf Hitler, too, had a mesmerizing personality. Hitler, too, was kind to the people who typed his letters and dished out his food. Hitler, too, loved animals. Hitler, too, was not a bad tactician. But Hitler was and remains a monster. The world would have been a much better place if he and the likes of him had never existed.

The same, to a lesser extent, is true of Babur. What is absolutely intolerable about him is his unapologetic disdain for human life: the self-righteous egotism with which he seems to think that whatever he does to other people is right and good, provided it happens to suit his own selfish purposes.

One example out of the many dozens in the *Baburnama* is the following matter-of-fact description of one of his forays across the Khyber Pass in the year 1519:[34]

> ... *we led the army and took Bajaur* [now in Pakistan, close to the Afghan border] *by force in two or three gharis* [a *ghari* is equivalent to 24 minutes], massacred the people, *and came to Bhera* [now in the Punjab province of Pakistan]. *The people of Bhera paid ransom to keep their property from being plundered and pillaged, and we took four hundred thousand Shahrukhis* worth of cash and goods, distributed it to the army according to the number of liege men, and returned to Kabul* [emphasis added].

We massacred the people. Babur *informs* us about it, unashamedly, casually, matter-of-factly, as if he were telling us that he had mutton for supper that evening. He does not even have the decency to be apologetic about it.

*A Shahrukhi was a coin of the Mughal era; each coin weighed about 4.60 grams.

That is the hard and sad truth about him: Babur was a predator. The way he made a living was through ruthless plunder, extortion and cold-blooded massacre of defenceless civilians. He had no regard whatsoever for the sanctity of human life, much less for the sanctity of other people's property. That he also happened to be fond of gardening, architecture, poetry and music is hardly an excuse; that he thought of himself as a devoutly religious man, even less. Any which way one looks at it: the world would have been a much better place without him or the likes of him.

He does have one, if rather lame, excuse: he was very much a child of his own time and geography. He was but one of countless many robber kings and kinglets scourging Central and other parts of Asia. If he would not have done what he did, someone else would have.

That may well be; but it puts him in a distinctly lower category than many other absolutist rulers, before and after him. Trajan, Hadrian, Marcus Aurelius,* Ramses II,** Ashoka the Great and Akbar the Great: they were shameless imperialists, all of them, no doubt about it; unlike Babur, however, they also were *statesmen*. They cared about the prosperity of the regions and peoples they ruled and reflected upon their own personal duties as a king. Babur did not come even close to them. He was a shoddy administrator; he did not have an inkling of how wealth and prosperity were created or maintained. The empire he left behind would have quickly vanished into the mists of time, had it not been for a number of much more competent people – friend and foe – who came after him.

That, however, is another story.

Kabul, at Last

Babur was laid to rest in his own Garden of Eight Paradises on the banks of the Yamuna in Agra, one of the last gardens he had planned and landscaped himself, about 4 km north of the spot where, four generations later, the Taj Mahal would arise.

At some time between 1540 and 1544, his remains were transferred to Kabul and reburied in his favourite garden on the east bank of the Kabul river, appropriately called Bagh-e-Babur Shah (Babur Shah's Garden). The king of Kabul was back home, at last.

*All three emperors of ancient Rome.

**A pharaoh of ancient Egypt.

Babur would have loved it; but he would have been horrified, had he known that the one to fulfil his dying wish was not his beloved son and heir, but the Afghan usurper Sher Khan (or Shah) Suri, Humayun's mortal enemy.

CHRONOLOGY

14 February 1483: Zahir-ud Din Muhammad Babur is born in Fergana, Central Asia.

8 June 1494: Umar Shaykh Mirza (Babur's father) dies in an accident; Babur, eleven years old, succeeds to the throne.

November 1497: Babur conquers Samarqand, only to lose it again after barely 100 days, also losing Fergana in the process.

1498: Fergana recovered.

November 1500: Second conquest of Samarqand.

May 1501: Defeated by the Uzbek leader Shaybani Khan, Babur loses Samarqand and is forced to offer his eldest sister in marriage to his enemy. Throneless, he seeks asylum in Tashkent.

14 June 1504: Babur becomes king of Kabul.

May 1506: Babur goes to Herat; returns to Kabul; faces rebellion.

May 1507: Uzbek forces take Herat; Babur plans Hindustan campaign.

17 March 1508: Birth of Humayun.

10 April 1510: Shah Ismail of Persia defeats and kills Shaybani Khan; the Persians occupy Herat.

October 1511: Babur reoccupies Samarqand and Transoxania (covering parts of present-day Uzbekistan, Tajikistan, southern Kyrgyzstan and south-west Kazakhstan).

1512–1514: Defeated once again by the Uzbeks, Babur retires to Kabul.

December 1521: Conquest of Qandahar.

October 1525: Seventh and last expedition to Hindustan.

21 April 1526: First Battle of Panipat. Babur defeats Sultan Ibrahim Lodi and takes Delhi and Agra.

17 March 1527: Battle of Khanwa. Babur defeats a powerful Rajput coalition.

January 1528: Conquest of Chanderi.
6 May 1529: Battle at the Gogra river.
26 December 1530: Babur dies. Humayun ascends the Mughal throne.

Notes and References

1. *The Baburnama: Memoirs of Babur, Prince and Emperor*, translated, edited and annotated by Wheeler M. Thackston. Introduction by Salman Rushdie, Random House, New York, 1996–2006, translator's Preface, p. xvii, footnote 1.
2. Ibid., pp. xviii and 241.
3. Ibid., pp. 3–7.
4. Ibid., pp. 7–10.
5. The date appears to be mistaken: the fourth of Ramadan 899 was actually a Sunday, not a Monday.
6. Quadrilateral, Persian-style garden (in Persian, '*chār*' means 'four' and '*bāgh*' means 'garden'), divided symmetrically into four (or more) smaller parts by walkways and/or flowing water.
7. Thackston, op. cit., pp. 89–90.
8. Ibid., p. 24.
9. Bamber Gascoigne, *A Brief History of the Great Moguls,* Carroll & Graf *Publishers*, New York, 2002, p. 16.
10. Badakhshan: a region comprising parts of what is now north-eastern Afghanistan and south-eastern Tajikistan.
11. Thackston, op. cit., p. 257.
12. 'Redheads', referring to their distinctive crimson-red headwear.
13. The conflict between Sunni Islam and Shia Islam is based on a fundamental disagreement about the rightful succession of the Prophet Muhammad: the Shias believe that Ali ibn Abu Talib (known by his first name Ali), Prophet Muhammad's son-in-law and first cousin, had been divinely appointed as the first *imam*, whereas the Sunnis chose an adviser of the Prophet, Abu Bakr, as his successor.
14. Humayun: fortunate, auspicious; Kamran: lucky, successful; Askari: soldier; and Hindal: taker of India.
15. Abraham Eraly, *The Mughal Throne: The Saga of India's Great Emperors*, Viking (an imprint of Penguin Books India and Penguin Books UK), New Delhi and London, 1997 and 2000, p. 11.
16. Gascoigne, op. cit., p. 19.
17. Thackston, op. cit., p. 319.
18. Gascoigne, op. cit., p. 20.

19. Thackston, op. cit., p. 323.
20. And not, as some people mistakenly believe, in the Delhi Lodi Gardens, where several other members of the Sayyid and Lodi dynasties have found their final resting place.
21. Gascoigne, op. cit., p. 22.
22. Thackston, op. cit., pp. 373–374.
23. R. Nath, *India as Seen by Babur (A.D. 1504–1530)*, MD Publications, Delhi, 1996, pp. 57–58.
24. Eraly, op. cit., p. 22.
25. Quoted by Dr Muhammad Qamaruddin, *A Politico-Cultural Study of The Great Mughals (1526–1707)*, Adam Publishers, New Delhi, 2004, p. 7.
26. Gulbadan, *Humayunnama*; Annette S. Beveridge (trans.), Munshiram Manoharlal Publishers, Delhi, 2001 edition, p. 99.
27. Matthew, 26:41.
28. Eraly, op. cit., p. 33.
29. See Salman Rushdie's Introduction in Thackston, op. cit., p. xii.
30. Gascoigne, op. cit., p. 28.
31. Gulbadan, op. cit., p. 109.
32. Thackston, op. cit., p. x.
33. Qamaruddin, op. cit., p. 7.
34. Thackston, op. cit., p. 329.

Chapter 2

Humayun: The Savant Dilettante

A Drama in Four Acts

Humayun, twenty-two years old when he ascended the throne in December 1530, was even less of a statesman than his father. With a minimum of precautions, he could have lived the kind of life his father had always dreamed of; instead, through his own fault, most of his career was fraught with hardship, humiliation and despair.

***

The history of his reign was, as one historian[1] aptly put it, a drama in four acts.

The first act, from 1530 to 1540, is the story of how, through a series of grave strategic blunders, he lost his inheritance to Sher Khan Suri (later known as Sher Shah Suri), his erstwhile vassal. Then followed the absolute lowest ebb of his life: five years spent in bitter exile as a hapless wanderer, at times little more than a common marauder with a dwindling group of ragged followers. Next, things got better from 1545 onwards, when, with Persian help, he managed to regain control and prepare for his return to Hindustan. The fourth and final act consists of the last eleven months of his life – from 22 February 1555 to 27 January 1556 – during which he could finally call himself Padshah of Hindustan again, before losing his life in a silly accident in his library.

An Amazing Character

All of the above had to do with Humayun's – to say the least – remarkable, and in all likeliness, pathological personality. While he was brave, highly educated, witty, generous, kind and – most of the time, anyway

– merciful, he also had many dangerous defects, which altogether made him quite unsuited for the task ahead.

Humayun's essentially gentle character, and, in particular, the sentimental feelings he entertained towards his treacherous brothers, was his most endearing weak spot – if also among the most dangerous ones. Brotherly love, arguably, is an amiable trait, not always wise, but certainly adorable and hardly reprehensible; in Humayun, however, it amounted to suicidal masochism. Time and again, his brothers would betray him and even try to kill him; time and again, he would forgive them their most blatant transgressions, thereby exposing himself and his next of kin to new danger.

It was, alas, not his only weakness. He was, at times, unbelievably lazy – or, as a chronicler put it slightly more euphemistically, '*disposed to spend his time in social intercourse and pleasure*'.[2] Even in the early days when Babur sent him out to govern Badakhshan in 1727, he kept pestering his father with letters, beseeching him to allow him to 'retire' from that faraway province, which he, so it seems, did not like very much. Upon which Babur had severely reprimanded him, replying that '*retirement matches not with rule*'.

Indolence and hedonism may be exceedingly common and quite human weaknesses, but, in Humayun, they bordered on the criminally insane, making him seemingly oblivious to even the most obvious and pressing emergencies. More than once, he literally managed to snatch defeat from the jaws of victory because of this morbid preoccupation with pleasure and all kinds of weird personal hobbies; and with advancing age, the problem was much aggravated by his worsening opium addiction.

***

As if the above were not bad enough, Humayun's sound judgement and common sense were completely clouded by an incredibly superstitious nature, *to a point ludicrous even in his own age*, as Gascoigne[3] aptly summarized it. There is, indeed, little doubt that, had he been examined by a present-day psychiatrist, he would have been diagnosed with severe obsessive-compulsive disorder.

For instance, Humayun would never place his left foot first when entering a building, and anyone who did was immediately sent out to correct the faux pas; he would waste entire afternoons shooting arrows in the air, marked with his own name or that of the Persian Shah, to derive, from the respective positions and angles in which they had fallen, the future of both monarchs and their empires; strategically important decisions – such as the invasion of a country – would be based on the numerical value of the names of peasants who happened to cross his path. Never would he even consider doing anything important without the help of astrology, numerology and other methods of divination. That none of these abstruse 'methods' ever produced even the slightest reliable result did not seem to bother him in the least.

***

Whenever he found the time – provided he was not wasting it in the harem or in opium's false paradise – he would be working on some kind of contraption, feverishly drawing and calculating; or he would sit in his library, reading voraciously, adding yet another insight to his vast knowledge about the movements of celestial bodies, the properties of metals and precious stones, flowers, herbs and plants, the four elements and their relationship to the letters of the Arabic alphabet, and many other such arcane matters.

He designed and built a vast array of complicated inventions and contraptions of varying and often doubtful practical use, ranging from portable bridges to a floating palace, and a huge tent with twelve partitions, corresponding to the twelve signs of the zodiac, with lattice openings at the exact spots where the light of the corresponding stars would fall through. He also had an enormous,[4] perfectly round carpet made, with circles representing the orbits of the planets and colours symbolizing the elements. He used to play a strange game on it, whereby the courtiers present had to take their places on the carpet near the planet corresponding to them. Humayun, seated on a throne, would occupy the circle of the sun. A dice was used, with pictures of a person standing, sitting, reclining, crouching, and so on, on each of its sides. Every participant would throw the dice and assume the position indicated, inviting, of course, laughs from the others. Humayun would then comment on the astrological significance of the constellations, and link them to events past, present and future. All members of the court pretended to be very fond of the game …

Literally everything and everybody in his court and army was referring in some way or other to the stars and the planets, and to the colours, numbers, substances and attributes associated with them.[5]

He would wear different colours each day of the week, each referring to a different planet and devoted to an aspect ruled by that planet.

Monday and Wednesday, for instance, were 'days of joy' (*murad*), when he would wear green clothes, and '*old companions and chosen friends were convened, and a band of musicians and singers was called, and they were all satisfied in their wishes*'. '*The cause of appointing these days for this purpose,*' explains Abu'l Fazl, '*was that Monday is the day of the Moon, and Wednesday of Mercury; and it was therefore reasonable* [sic!] *that on these days he should keep company with young men beautiful as the moon, and hear sweet songs and delightful music.*' On Sunday (the day of the Sun, the sovereign of the sky) and Tuesday (the day of Mars, the patron of war and soldiery), he would devote himself to government affairs (i.e., to *daulat* or empire), and wear yellow and red clothes, respectively. Saturday (the day of Saturn, with black as its associated colour) and Thursday (day of Jupiter, sandalwood-brown) were devoted to religion and learning, subsumed in the overall category of *sa'adat*, auspiciousness. Friday, finally, was a day open to all matters.

Similarly, the nobles, officers, artisans and the like were divided into the same categories of 'empire', 'auspiciousness' and 'joy'. The administrators were called *Ahl-i-Daulat*, men of empire; the *Ahl-i-Sa'adat*, men of auspiciousness, were the religious scholars, literati, scientists, poets, law officers and other 'great and respectable men'; and the *Ahl-i-Murad*, or people of joy, were those who 'possessed beauty and elegance', and included virtuoso singers and musicians. Within each of the three classes were twelve orders or 'arrows', each divided into three ranks.

Records Abu'l Fazl:

> *Among the customs introduced by this King, one was that of the distribution of arrows, by means of which the distinction of ranks and stations among servants of the throne was marked .... According to the different standards of gold, the ranks of all the people composing the three classes were divided into twelve orders or arrows, and every one received a grade and rank suitable to himself. The twelfth arrow, which was made of the purest gold, was put in the auspicious quiver of this powerful King, and nobody could dare to touch it. The eleventh arrow belonged to His Majesty's relations and brethren, and all the Sultans who were in the government employ. Tenth, to the great shaykhs, sayyids and the learned and religious men. Ninth,*

to the great nobles. Eighth, to the courtiers and some of the King's personal attendants. Seventh, to the attendants in general. Sixth, to the harems and to the well-behaved female attendants. Fifth, to young maidservants. Fourth, to the treasurers and stewards. Third, to the soldiers. Second, to the menial servants. First, to the palace guards, camel drivers, and the like. Each of these arrows or orders had three grades; the highest, the middle and the lowest.

The administration itself was 'functionally' organized in departments on the basis of the four elements: Earth (agriculture and buildings); water (canals, irrigation and wine cellars); fire (army); and air, the catch-all department including such diverse matters as kitchens, the royal wardrobe, stables and the management of mules and camels.

***

As will be abundantly clear from the above, Humayun was, quite literally, obsessed with categorization and systematization, sparing neither trouble nor time to get everything 'just right'. For all its intricate complexity, the system had just one tiny flaw: virtually none of it served any practical purpose whatsoever. Not a single one of his learned observations and calculations warned him about his archrival and nemesis, Sher Khan Suri, who would drive him out of his own kingdom – or about anything else, for that matter. It did not seem to bother him in the slightest. He would, quite literally, remain faithful to his astrological delusions until his dying breath: it seems fate's ultimate irony that it had him fall to his death from the very stairs of the observatory from where he had been supposed to look into the future.

ACT ONE: PARADISE LOST

Balance of Power(s)

The most salient feature of India's feudal period was its utter *instability*. With the exception of a few decades at the apogee of the Mughal Empire, the entire history of the Muslim dynasties in India appears to be a constant ebbing and flowing of rulers and empires, a concatenation of wars and uprisings, triumph and defeat. Time and again, we see alliances formed and broken as a matter of routine; we witness the disintegration of vast and seemingly invincible empires in a matter of years, months or even weeks. The scenarios are always the same: local rulers submitting to a conqueror, only to redeclare their independence as soon as the victor has left the region; and local governors breaking away or collaborating with foreign invaders to oust their own overlords.

There are two reasons behind this phenomenon: one political and one practical. First and foremost, there was no such thing as a universally accepted source of political power among the Indian Muslims, no generally accepted hierarchy, not even anything like a strong ethnic identity or allegiance. Babur and Humayun had no *nations* behind them; their armed forces consisted of a loose alliance of individual Persian, Turkoman, and even Afghan and Uzbek warlords, whose allegiance to them was fully dependent on their own selfish interests; 'loyal' supporters in one campaign could easily turn into deadly opponents in the next.

The second and more practical explanation has to do with simple geography and lack of communication. As soon as victory is won and fiefs have been parcelled out, distance and greed can begin to do their poisonous work. The rewarded soldier becomes a governor, sets up a sumptuous court of his own, and, suddenly, the emperor seems a distant memory. How far away is he, when his messengers take several days or even weeks to reach one's province; how easy it is to siphon off part of the imperial revenues; and when those first embezzlements appear to go unpunished, how tempting it becomes to just keep everything for oneself ...

This was the kind of environment Humayun had inherited: no victory was permanent, no conquest guaranteed. He knew, from the moment he ascended the throne, that sooner or later, he would have to fight to defend it.

***

Among the neighbouring powers, the Afghans – in Bihar, Bengal and the sultanate of Gujarat – were the most redoubtable. The Rajput clans seemed to have – for the time being, anyway – abandoned their earlier expansionist ambitions. The Afghan nobles, on the other hand, while soundly defeated, had not been crushed; back in the territories under their effective control, they found ample opportunity to lick their wounds and rebuild their strength.

Humayun's potential adversaries were by no means limited to powers *outside* his dominions: throughout his life, the balance of power between him and his own relatives – his brothers Kamran, Askari and Hindal in particular – would remain extremely delicate.

At the time of his accession, in December 1530, Humayun received – as per Babur's dying instructions – the overlordship of the empire and direct control over the territories east of the River Indus. Kamran received Kabul and Qandahar; smaller fiefs went to the two younger brothers, barely eleven and fourteen years old at the time; the governorship over the distant province of Badakhshan was entrusted to one of Humayun's cousins. Kamran, however, not satisfied with his share, soon crossed the Indus, taking possession of the entire Punjab as well. This could have meant civil war; but Kamran had taken care to send reassuring messages professing continued loyalty and subservience to Humayun, and the latter, following his father's advice to always be indulgent with his brothers, chose not to react.

Din Panah

Humayun's first few months on the throne went by rather peacefully. An attempted rebellion by two of his cousins, Muhammad Zaman Mirza and Muhammad Sultan Mirza, had been easily subdued and the two culprits pardoned and reinstated in their *jagirs* (fiefs).

By late 1531, however, that period of relative calm appeared to be over. The Afghan nobles in Bihar had rallied under the nominal leadership of Sultan Mahmud Lodi (the late Ibrahim Lodi's brother) and captured Lucknow. Thanks to a lack of discipline and internal rivalry among the Afghans, Humayun won an easy victory at the Battle of Dadrah (now in Uttar Pradesh), where he routed and scattered the main force of the insurgents (1532).

There was, however, one Afghan nobleman, one Sher[6] Khan Suri, who had not participated in the fight: he had deserted the rest of the Afghans and retired to the strategic fortress of Chunar on the Ganga River, south-west of Varanasi. Humayun at first laid siege to that fort as well, but was talked into returning to Agra when Sher Khan Suri meekly submitted to him and accepted his overlordship. Little did Humayun suspect that this obsequious, lowly Afghan would, a few years later, kick him out of India.

***

Back in central Hindustan, Humayun personally laid the foundation stone, in August 1533, for an entirely new capital in Delhi, to be called

Din Panah, the 'refuge of religion', a city that would be open to scholars and clerics of all Islamic denominations and sects – in sharp contrast to the sectarian policies of the staunchly Sunni Uzbek Khans and the even more fanatically Shia Persian Shahs. The initiative, a tribute to Humayun's broadmindedness in religious matters, foreboded the far-reaching reforms his son and successor, Akbar, would be pushing through, a few decades later.

Gujarat

Humayun's newfound peace and quiet was, alas, short-lived. His next opponent was Sultan Bahadur Shah, the ambitious Afghan king of Gujarat, a relatively small but wealthy and increasingly powerful kingdom, which had by now become a place of refuge for many disgruntled Afghan warlords from all over Hindustan. After capturing several Rajput fortresses in southern Rajputana, Bahadur Shah now cast his covetous eyes on the rest of Hindustan.

Gujarati-Afghan forces even penetrated the environs of Agra, but soon found themselves on the defensive and forced to retreat. A triumphant and unusually energetic Humayun pursued the enemy all the way down to the Gujarat coast on the Arabian Sea. Bahadur Shah fled head over heels on a boat to the island of Diu, where the Portuguese – with whom, few months earlier (23 December 1534), he had been obliged to sign the treaty of Bassein, ceding them the seven islands of Bombay and the nearby strategic town of Bassein – were building a fortress to protect their local trading settlement.

Humayun – the first Timurid prince ever to lay eyes on the ocean – paused for a few weeks at the flourishing port of Cambay (Khambat). He then turned his attention to the inland fortress of Champaner, where, so people said, the immense royal treasure of Gujarat was hidden. In 1535, after a siege that lasted four months, the fort was taken in a daring, commando-style night action, whereby Humayun personally led the elite troops climbing the wall on iron spikes driven into the rocks and masonry. The spoils exceeded everyone's wildest expectations, even though Bahadur Shah had managed to remove his crown jewels and a small part of the treasure before making his escape to Diu.

After showering his men with lavish rewards, Humayun indulged in sumptuous celebrations rather than being worried about consolidating the conquest. It was the first out of a series of grave strategic errors, which eventually would cost him his throne.

It must have been quite a celebration indeed. Discipline in the victorious Mughal camp had all but disappeared. Abu'l Fazl,[7] Akbar's famous minister and chronicler, relates how a band of about four hundred low-ranking camp followers, '*book-bearers, armour-bearers, inkhorn-bearers and the like*', inspired by Timur's heroic exploits (and a copious amount of alcohol, no doubt), suddenly '*girt up their loins of courage and went forth to conquer*' the sultanates of the Deccan, no less. A thousand battle-hardened warriors were sent out to track down the overzealous amateurs, who were soon caught and dragged back to court, '*bound neck and hand*'. To their misfortune, '*it was Tuesday, a day when His Majesty wore the red vesture of Mars and sat on the Throne of Wrath and Vengeance*'. Each of the criminals, relates Abu'l Fazl, '*received sentences fitting their destiny, and the requirements of complete justice*'. Complete justice apparently required some to be '*trodden under the feet of mountain-like elephants*'; others, who had '*carried their heads beyond the line of respect, received distinction* [sic!] *by the removal of the burden of their heads from their bodies*'; those '*not distinguishing between their feet and their hands*', who '*had clapped their hands at seditious thoughts, were made handless and footless*'; those who '*had not kept their ears for the royal commands, found* [their] *ears and nose gone from their places*'; and finally, those '*who had laid the fingertip of intent on the edge of misfeasance*' had all their fingers cut off.

The punishments meted out had been remarkably harsh by Humayun's usually mild standards, but still, '*the fire of wrath was darting tongues of flame*'. At the time of the evening prayers, an imam who had been foolish enough to recite Surah Al-Fil (The Elephant, the 105th *surah* or chapter of the Quran), was trampled to death under the feet of an elephant: Humayun had taken the recitation of this particular *surah* (beginning with the verses '*Have you not seen what your Lord did with the companions of the elephant? Did he not make their plot to go astray?*') as an implied but severe criticism of the punishments meted out earlier that day and an evil presage for the campaign ahead. Later that evening, when '*the conflagration of the flames of wrath was stayed*' and Humayun realized that the poor and well-nigh illiterate imam had probably meant no harm, '*he expressed much regret and spent the whole night in sorrow and weeping*'.

***

Shortly after the Mughal conquest of Champaner in 1535, Bahadur Shah again emerged from Diu in an attempt to recover his lost dominions, only to find himself defeated once more. The Mughal army now made its triumphant entry into Ahmedabad, the capital city; it was the apogee of Humayun's military career.

But he could not afford to stay down in Gujarat: worrisome messages kept coming in from Agra, reporting rebel activity in the north. Humayun headed back north, leaving his brother Askari in charge of Gujarat. That, however, proved to be a costly mistake, for as soon as the main body of the Mughal army had marched off, Bahadur Shah calmly returned to the mainland, and Askari, instead of defending Ahmedabad as was his duty, abandoned his post and quickly rushed back to Agra, with unclear intentions, but in all likeliness, to usurp Humayun's throne. The Afghans, meanwhile, quietly retook all of Gujarat and even invaded neighbouring Malwa. In a matter of weeks, the spoils of nearly twenty-two months of victorious campaigning (from November 1534 to August 1536) had been squandered.

We do not know how bad Humayun really felt about all this. If he was enraged or desperate, he certainly did not show it. With characteristic leniency, he forgave Askari's treacherous blunder and spent the next few months in Agra, indulging, to the fullest extent possible, in the luxuries of life and his many bizarre pastimes.

It must have been some kind of consolation for Humayun to learn that Bahadur Shah never had the time to enjoy his return to fortune. Barely a few months after Humayun's retreat, Bahadur Shah fell out with the Portuguese, the newfound allies to whom he had twice owed his rescue. In February 1537, at a parley on a Portuguese ship anchored off the coast of Gujarat – during which he intended to kidnap the Portuguese viceroy, who, in turn, had plans to arrest him – he was killed and his body unceremoniously dumped into the Arabian Sea.

Bahadur Shah's cruel – if self-inflicted – fate was more than one of history's countless bloody anecdotes. It was illustrative of a whole new era, a strategic reality the land-locked Mughals did not even begin to understand the significance of: the Portuguese, then a small nation of barely one million souls, were aggressively and unashamedly taking control of India's shores.

They had arrived on new and improved ships (caravels, carracks, galleons and galleasses), with superior armament, in search of treasure and spices. And they meant business: on 3 February 1509, near the port of Diu, their small but powerful war fleet of merely eighteen ships had annihilated an Egyptian–Ottoman–Gujarati armada of two hundred and fifty, including twelve large battleships and forty galleys. And they were here to stay. For over a century, they would dominate the entire Indian Ocean and the Arabian Sea, only to be dislodged by another, more numerous and even more aggressive European nation: the British, whose advent would forever change the face of India.

The Tiger King

While Humayun was wasting his time in revelry, danger was looming in the east. With Humayun safely away in Gujarat, Sher Khan Suri had quietly built himself an empire: now, after consolidating his power in Bihar, he was aggressively expanding his dominions into Bengal.

As usual, Humayun, now back in Agra, was much too slow to react. His dilemma was: Should he act against Sher Khan? Or could he afford to recapture Gujarat first? After all, legally and formally speaking, Sher Khan had not been doing anything wrong: he still acted as Humayun's vassal; in all of Sher Khan's dominions, the *khutba* was still read in Humayun's name. After a while, however, things had become blatantly obvious, even to Humayun: it was only a matter of time before this ambitious nominal vassal of his would become a fearsome opponent. Humayun simply could not afford to let him go on.

Chunar

It took a full year before Humayun finally decided to act. In mid-July 1537, accompanied by his brothers Askari and Hindal and most of his harem, he finally set out against his opponent with a grand army on a flotilla of barges down the Yamuna and on to the Ganga.

It was all too little, too late. He had taken a full year, where he should have acted immediately; and now, when he finally had launched his campaign, he wasted his valuable time and resources on the wrong strategic objectives.

What should have been swift punitive action started as a leisurely boat excursion; it took Humayun close to five months before he finally arrived at Chunar, Sher Khan's fort on the Ganga near Varanasi. Instead of quickly bypassing the fort and chasing Sher Khan as he should have, he wasted another three months conquering the fort, which, when he finally did take it, proved of precious little use to him: Sher Khan was long gone, completing his conquest of Bengal, after having moved his treasure and harem into safety at the much more secure hill fort of Rohtas (in Bihar) on the upper reaches of the Son River, south of the Ganga.

The wily way in which he managed to capture this hill fort is telling of Sher Khan's devilish cunning and trickery. He humbly implored Raja Hari Kishen Rai, the chieftain of the Rohtas fort, to allow him to bring his harem and treasure into safety while he faced the Mughal army: if things would go wrong, he argued, his belongings would, at least, not fall into the hands of the 'accursed' Mughals. Tempted by the prospect of easy gain, the raja agreed. To his horror, however, the long and stately procession of curtained palanquins entering the fort was not carrying the gracious ladies of Sher Khan's harem, but a good number of his best and bravest soldiers. In a swift surprise attack, the occupants were overwhelmed, and the poor raja had to run for his life.

While Humayun was laying siege to the fort at Chunar, Sher Khan completed the conquest of Bengal, amassing untold amounts of treasure. There, in the capital city of Gaur, when diplomatic contacts between him and Humayun had failed to achieve a solution acceptable to both parties, he finally decided to cross the Rubicon: henceforth, he declared, he would be called Sher *Shah*. He was a king now, no longer a mere khan; and clearly, Hindustan was too small for two kings.

***

Humayun finally realized he had been wasting his time in Chunar. Leaving his brother Hindal on the banks of the Ganga with a mobile fighting force to secure his rear, he now moved into Bengal. Sher Shah made no attempt to stop him. On the contrary: leaving only Jalal Khan, one of his sons, with a rearguard at the narrow Teliyagarhi pass to slow down the Mughal advance, he carted off the captured treasure and moved the main body of his army back to Rohtas. Jalal Khan did manage to slow down the Mughals considerably, and more than that: before withdrawing from the pass, he inflicted a humiliating defeat on Humayun's advance guard. It proved to be an ominous presage.

Gaur

When Humayun, plodding through the muddy slush of Bengal in the middle of the rainy season of 1537, finally arrived at Gaur to drive off the remaining Afghans, he found the city desolate and empty, everything of value plundered. Nevertheless, he decided to stay and celebrate. After all, had he not chased the enemy away? Was Bengal, with its fairy-faced maidens, gurgling rivulets and lush greenery, not akin to paradise itself? He divided the new province among his amirs, proudly renamed its capital 'Jannatabad' (paradise city), locked himself in the harem, and, as the historians put it, 'abandoned himself to every kind of indulgence and luxury'.

While Humayun was thus wasting about nine more months of his precious time in the harem in faraway Bengal, Sher Shah got busy in his home base. Soon, all of Bihar, as well as the venerable old city of Varanasi, had fallen to him. Adding insult to injury, he laid siege to Chunar and even to Jaunpur (in Uttar Pradesh, about 55 km from Varanasi).

When Humayun finally learned about all this, it was too late: with Sher Shah's men blocking the passes between Bihar and Bengal and cutting off his lines of supply and communication, Humayun and his army found themselves bottled up in faraway Bengal. To make things much worse, they found themselves all alone: Hindal, who was supposed to cover Humayun's rear, had fled back to Agra, where he set himself up in the imperial palace. Shaykh Bahlul, a venerable old cleric to whom Humayun had always been much attached, was sent to reason with him, but Hindal had the old man executed for treason. Henceforth, the *khutba* was read in Hindal's name; he was, formally and officially, in open rebellion against his brother.

When Humayun heard about this act of treason, he finally realized how desperate his own situation had become. Leaving one of his officers in charge of Bengal with a fighting force of 5000 men, he set off on the long journey back to faraway Agra. With the heat and humidity taking their toll on his weary men and their animals, Bengal's greenery suddenly seemed like hell.

***

Meanwhile, the ever-jealous and ambitious Kamran had heard about Humayun's predicament and Hindal's rebellion. In 1539, Kamran left his court at Lahore and crossed the Sutlej into Hindustan with a well-equipped and disciplined army, ostensibly to strengthen the Mughal position, but in reality, to secure his own future. Ten years older and much shrewder than Hindal, he quickly occupied Delhi, preventing Hindal from doing the same, and then persuaded his brother – with an appropriate mixture, no doubt, of brotherly affection and veiled threats

– to give up his rebellion. Then, he made himself at home. Officially subservient to Humayun, the two brothers now calmly awaited the course of events, turning a blind eye and a deaf ear to the emissaries bringing Humayun's urgent requests for help, like vultures on a tree above a dying animal. Their beloved brother and king would have to fend for himself.

Chausa

Meanwhile, Humayun was still plodding his way back home. When Sher Shah heard about the Mughal retreat, he immediately lifted the siege of Jaunpur, crossed the Ganga and moved into south Bihar, ready for a hide-and-seek game with his agile forces pitted against the much more cumbersome Mughal army. But Humayun refused to take the bait and kept trudging westwards along the south bank of the Ganga, passing Patna and crossing the Son River, constantly trailed and occasionally harassed by Sher Shah's scouts.

Sher Shah, always on his guard, had thus far painstakingly avoided any major battle with Humayun's much larger and – theoretically – stronger army. He was a prudent and level-headed man: why gamble away, in a single battle, everything he had been working for so hard, all his life? But when his scouts described to him the sorry state the demoralized Mughal army actually was in, he moved in for the kill.

Upon reaching the town of Chausa on the banks of the Ganga approximately 120 km east of Varanasi, Humayun found, to his bewildered dismay, his passage blocked by Sher Shah's army.

A few of Humayun's generals advised him to attack immediately. After all, they argued, the Mughal army greatly outnumbered the enemy, and Sher Shah's men and animals would not have had the time to recover from what must have been a series of exhausting forced marches. Humayun, however, decided to follow the more conservative majority among his advisers: the powerful Mughal artillery, Humayun's main strategic advantage, would be useless if he attacked first. Was it not much more prudent to follow Babur's example at Panipat, and meet the enemy charge from a safely entrenched position?

For nearly three months, the enemy armies faced each other, improving their respective defences, alternating occasional skirmishes with diplomatic overtures. It has been described how Humayun's emissary, a cleric name Mullah Muhammad Barghiz, found Sher Shah, spade in hand, helping his soldiers engaged in digging fortifications in the heat of the day. On seeing the envoy, the Afghan king washed his hands, ordered an awning installed to provide a bit of shade, and sat himself down to parley. His tone was quietly defiant: 'Go and tell your emperor this from me,' he said. 'He wants war, his troops do not; and I don't want war, but my troops do.'

In the end, however, some kind of truce was patched together: Humayun would pardon Sher Shah's transgressions; Sher Shah would keep Bihar and Bengal as Humayun's vassal; and the *khutba* would be read in Humayun's name. In short: things would go back to the way they had been before the confrontation. It was a rather meagre outcome for such an arduous campaign, and Humayun therefore insisted on another, rather symbolic, kind of gratification: his troops would advance on Sher Shah's lines and the latter would hastily retreat in ostensible awe and submission. The agreed upon date was 25 June 1539.

As Gascoigne pertinently observes,[8] it was quite typical of Humayun to insist on this kind of childish gratification and it was equally typical of Sher Shah that he agreed to play along in the charade – and shamelessly use it to his own advantage. He meekly withdrew a few kilometres, only to return stealthily in the middle of the night. Finding, as he had hoped, the Mughal camp sound asleep and barely guarded, he pounced on it like a cobra on a rat's nest.

The result was devastating. The survivors of the initial massacre were driven into the Ganga, where most of them drowned miserably. Humayun himself narrowly escaped the same fate, when he fell of his horse in mid-stream; luckily, a water-bearer named Nizam gave him an inflated leather water bag and helped him to swim across. It is again typical of Humayun's sentimental naiveté that, on reaching the left bank of the Ganga, he promised the bewildered servant that upon their return to Delhi, he would have him sit on the imperial throne; and it is even more typical, that he later insisted on keeping his promise.

The battle of Chausa – the massacre of Chausa would be a more appropriate name, for the Mughal army did very little fighting – was a horrible disaster for Humayun. From a military point of view, he lost over 8000 of his best men and all of his heavy weapons; even more distressing, and quite illustrative of the magnitude of the cataclysm, was that several ladies of the imperial harem, and even one of Humayun's young daughters, had perished in the waters as well.

Sher Shah, for his part, showed himself to be a noble and dignified victor. Entering the imperial tented camp, where most of Humayun's harem and families of the Mughal officers tremblingly awaited their fate, he prostrated himself at the durbar tent in grateful prayer, and gave orders to take the Mughal women and children in safety to Rohtas, where they were treated with every courtesy and later escorted back to Humayun in Agra.

Cautious and methodical as always, he did not immediately pursue Humayun to Agra, but returned to Bengal instead, where he expelled the remaining Mughal governor and solemnly ascended the royal throne, assuming a royal title that would be the theme of his reign: *Sultan-ul Adil*, the just ruler. It was an ambitious promise, and he would make every effort to live up to it.

***

When the festivities were over, Sher Shah returned to Bihar to organize his administration and firmly consolidate his hold on the region, before calmly proceeding westward – to Agra.

He was now in his early fifties. The dream he had been fantasizing about since early puberty was, at last, about to come true: he would throw the accursed Mughals out of India.

Kannauj*

Meanwhile, Humayun had limped back to Agra, where he tearfully reunited with his brothers. With the ominous prospect of another battle with Sher Shah looming large, this was no time for revenge or recriminations. The brothers, however, failed to agree on the best course of action. Kamran, eager to assume the effective leadership of the family, offered to take his 12,000 well-equipped horsemen from Kabul and ride against Sher Shah. Humayun refused categorically, insisting that a much larger army had to be formed under his personal leadership. 'I want to have my revenge,' he insisted. For all his naiveté, he must have realized full well that a victorious Kamran would nearly be as dangerous to his throne as Sher Shah himself.

It was in this tense atmosphere that Humayun suddenly insisted – out of superstition, probably even more than out of gratitude – on keeping his promise to Nizam, the water-bearer who had saved his life at Chausa. The poor man found himself solemnly seated 'on the throne

*A town in central Uttar Pradesh.

of the world' and invited to issue his august imperial orders. We do not know exactly for how long this embarrassing spectacle lasted: at least two full hours, according to some sources; but Humayun's sister Gulbadan grudgingly affirms that '*for as much as* two days *the Emperor gave royal power to that menial*'. No real harm was done – the water-bearer was wise enough not to issue any orders contrary to the interests of anyone important – but it can be no surprise that the incident did very little to restore Humayun's already much tarnished reputation as a king and army leader, and one can hardly blame Kamran for snapping indignantly: '*At a time when Sher Khan is near, is this a matter for Your Majesty to be concerned with*?'

***

For seven months and in an increasingly tense atmosphere, the two elder brothers kept bickering about the appropriate strategy – Humayun insisting that Kamran's horsemen be integrated in the larger imperial army under his own command and Kamran finding excuses not to comply with the request. Agra's climate did not agree with him, he pleaded; he wanted to take his soldiers back to Kabul to secure the Mughal home base. Humayun refused to let him go, but when Kamran suddenly fell seriously ill, suspecting that someone had tried to poison him on Humayun's order, his mind was made up: sick as he was, he returned to Lahore with most of his men. Humayun, Hindal and Askari were on their own.

***

Meanwhile, unhurriedly but steadily, ominously, Sher Shah was advancing westwards along the banks of the Ganga. Emboldened by what his spies were telling him about the tensions in the Mughal camp, he even at one point – for the first and last time in his career – got reckless, sending off his youngest son, Qutub Khan, with an advance guard across Mughal territory towards Malwa. The Afghan detachment, however, was soundly defeated at Kalpi (in southern Uttar Pradesh) by a Mughal force under Kasim Husain Sultan Uzbek, one of Humayun's generals. Qutub Khan was slain in the battle, and his severed head, along with those of many of his men, was sent to Agra as a gruesome trophy.

Remarkably enough, the victory, though spectacular, did very little to rouse the spirits in Humayun's camp. Yes, a victory had been won, but they still were up against a hitherto invincible enemy, who would now be thirsting after bloody revenge; and yes, thousands of new troops from all over the empire had been flocking to Agra, but they were an untrained, ill-led bunch of green recruits, who could not even begin to make up for the loss of so many Mughal veterans fallen at Chausa. It was at the head of a large and well-equipped, but deeply demoralized and frightened army that Humayun and his two youngest brothers marched eastwards to confront the enemy.

For about a month, the adversaries faced each other near the town of Kannauj on the Ganga, 210 km east of Agra.

It must have been a nerve-wracking month for Humayun, with massive desertions on a daily basis foreboding inevitable disaster. Sher Shah, however, did not move, quietly biding his time, watching in ominous silence as the great Mughal army disintegrated before his very eyes. Finally, it was the unseasonably early monsoon that year to put Humayun out of his misery. At noon on Monday, 17 May 1540, as unexpected heavy rains were flooding the imperial camp and the Mughals were manoeuvring to shift to higher ground, Sher Shah suddenly attacked.

It was not much of a battle, testifies Haidar Mirza Doghlat, one of Babur's cousins who witnessed the events.[9]

> *On the right Sher Khan advanced in battle array; but before an arrow was discharged, the camp followers* [of Humayun] *fled like chaff before the wind, and breaking the line they all pressed towards the center .... While the center was thus thrown into disorder, all the fugitives from the right bore down upon it. So before the enemy had discharged an arrow, the whole army was scattered and defeated. I had estimated the Chaghatái army as numbering 40,000 men, excluding the camp followers* (ghulám) *and workmen* (shágird-pesha). *They fled before 10,000 men, and Sher Khan gained a victory, and the Chaghatáis were defeated in this battlefield where not a man, either friend or foe, was wounded. Not a gun was fired, and the chariots* (gardún) *were useless.*

Once again, those who survived the ensuing massacre threw themselves into the Ganga in a desperate attempt to escape the Afghan onslaught, only to perish by the thousands in the swirling waters

– or, in Abu'l Fazl's flowery language, they '*sank in the whirlpool of disappointment, giving the vessels of their lives to the boisterous waters of annihilation*'.[10] Humayun made it across the river, slightly more comfortably than at Chausa, on the back of an old elephant this time. On the other side, he was so upset and exhausted that he did not have the strength to clamber up the steep and slippery river bank; a few of his men tied their turbans together to drag him up and save him.

In utter panic, a bareheaded, barefoot and mud-stained fugitive, Humayun rushed back to Agra as fast as the crippled packhorse his men had given him could move. Hours earlier, he had been in command of a seemingly invincible army of forty thousand iron-clad horsemen on the best Central Asian mounts, supported by twenty-one heavy cannons, seven hundred swivel guns and five thousand muskets; now, he had to suffer the affront of a band of mere villagers harassing him.

***

He did not stay a minute longer than necessary in Agra – just the time to gather up his family and the treasure – and then pressed on, in the pouring monsoon rains, towards Delhi and on to Lahore. Total chaos reigned everywhere. '*No one attempted to assist another; the son paid no attention to the father, nor the father to the son, but each person attempted to conceal whatever valuables he had, and to make his escape,*' affirms Jauhar, Humayun's personal attendant who was with him on that journey, in his personal memoirs.[11] A semblance of order only returned when it became clear that Sher Shah was not on their heels in hot pursuit, as they all feared, but was calmly taking possession of his new conquest. Humayun allowed himself a few days in Delhi to scrape together whatever valuables he could lay his hands on and then fled to Lahore.

Sher Shah continued behind him, occupying his new dominions, calmly and orderly, city by city. By the middle of June 1540, he entered Delhi, where the *khutba* was read in his name.

Gone were the arrogant, bungling Mughals and their so-called empire; it was time for a whole new era.

ACT TWO: HELL

Lahore

It was early July 1540 when Humayun and his retinue reached the – relative and provisional – safety of Lahore. Barely nine-and-a-half years had elapsed since he had ascended Babur's throne; he was now a homeless fugitive.

Just like the year before, the four brothers reunited in tearful embrace. Manful words were spoken, bloody revenge was vowed and solemn oaths sworn – after which, just like the last time, nothing happened.

Five more months were wasted in futile bickering about the best course of action: Kamran offered to take the royal families to safety in Kabul and then return with reinforcements to defend the Punjab; Hindal wanted to reconquer Gujarat (via Sindh), and from there, attack Hindustan; a few generals recommended heading north and conquering Kashmir … but none of the alternatives seemed ideal, and the brothers failed to settle on any single one of them – or, as Abu'l Fazl put it, they '*did not bind the girdle of sincerity on the waist of resolve*'.[12]

More than with military strategy, the doubts and disagreements had, of course, everything to do with the unspoken, but patently obvious rivalry between the two elder brothers: Kamran had no intention of sharing his own inheritance, Kabul and the Punjab, with anyone – least of all with Humayun, his nominal overlord.

The internal squabbling stopped abruptly when the news arrived that Sher Shah and his army had now reached the town of Sirhind (or Sar-i-Hind, frontier of Hindustan; now in Indian Punjab) near the Sutlej River. Humayun sent him an emissary with a message pleading for peace: '*I have left you the whole of Hindustan. Leave Lahore alone, and let Sirhind be the border between you and me.*' To which, Sher Shah curtly replied: '*I have left you Kabul. You should go there.*'

That, of course, was the one place on earth Humayun could not possibly go to, because, as stated earlier, Kamran had no intention of sharing Kabul with his brother. For days on end, he kept pacing up and down in the palace at Lahore, wringing his hands in despair, '*not knowing what to do, or where to go*', affirms Jauhar.

To add insult to injury, Kamran now secretly sent one of his courtiers to Sher Shah,[13] offering his support in return for the Punjab. Sher Shah was neither impressed nor interested. He needed no one's support, least of all that of a Mughal.

Sindh

With Sher Shah now advancing ominously on Lahore, the Mughal princes and their generals ran like rabbits. Humayun, as usual, could not make up his mind where to go to. He first decided on Badakhshan, the province he had governed in his early years under Babur, but Kamran wanted none of that: the way to Badakhshan goes via Kabul, and Kamran would not have his brother staying there.

With Sher Shah's dreaded general, Khavass Khan, breathing down their necks, it was then decided to follow Hindal's plan: heading southwards to Sindh, and from there, God willing, invade Gujarat. The newfound solidarity was, however, short-lived. Barely 220 km further west from Lahore, near the town of Khushab on the west bank of the Jhelum river, after an angry quarrel over precedence in entering a defile, Kamran no longer found it necessary to keep up appearances: he and Askari left for Kabul, while Humayun and Hindal continued their arduous journey along the Indus, constantly harassed by hostile Baluchi tribesmen. On 26 January 1541, they at last reached the fortress of Bhukkur (later called Sukkur) opposite the town of Rohri in northern Sindh, about 420 km north of the capital Thatta. Humayun sent envoys asking for assistance from the ruler of Sindh, Shah Hussain Mirza, a distant relative and nominally his vassal, but in reality, an independent king with little love lost for the Mughals – Babur had ousted his father from Qandahar – and much too smart to do anything that could offend Sher Shah. With a series of deliberately belated and evasive promises, he kept Humayun waiting.

***

In an attempt to strengthen his bargaining position, Humayun then laid siege to Bhukkur and sent Hindal southwards along the Indus to take Shah Hussain Mirza's other fort at nearby Sehwan. Predictably, both attempts failed miserably. After the siege of Bhukkur had continued for six months without any effect, Humayun grew suspicious of Hindal's movements and headed south to join him; the two reunited at Pat, a hamlet about 150 km south of Rohri.

So far, Humayun's sojourn in Sindh had been, as usual, an utter failure. This, however, was about to change, for it was then and there that he met the girl who was to become his pre-eminent spouse: Hamida Banu Begam, the lovely daughter of Shaykh Ali Akbar, a Persian Shia scholar and Hindal's teacher and adviser. From the moment he laid eyes on her, he decided that she would become his wife. The feeling was, to say the least, not mutual. For no less than forty days, she stubbornly refused to marry him, in spite of her young age – she was only fourteen at the time – and in spite of her parents' embarrassed insistence. The reason for her reluctance is not entirely clear: most probably, she was far from impressed by this pompous yet destitute would-be emperor, more than twice her age – '*he may well not have seemed much of a catch at the time*', observes Gascoigne. Equally probably, she and twenty-five-year old Hindal had been in love for some time. One thing, in any case, is certain: Humayun's amorous plans led to an angry break-up between the two brothers, with Hindal marching off spitefully to Qandahar.

But in the end, Humayun got his way: Hamida gave in to the combined pressure of her family and finally agreed to the marriage. Not surprisingly, Humayun now '*took the astrolabe in his own blessed hand*', as Gulbadan admiringly put it, to calculate the most propitious hour for the ceremony. It turned out to be high noon on Monday, 21 August 1541.

Auspicious though the hour may have been, the good times did not last: the following two years turned out to be the darkest in Humayun's entire life. Constantly harassed by Shah Hussain Mirza, now thoroughly fed up with his uninvited visitor, he was now little more than a vulgar bandit, living off whatever he could lay his hands on – which, more often than not, was very little indeed: hunger had become a grim daily reality. His position was utterly hopeless, and his men knew it, and deserted him in droves – even such loyal veterans who had been with him for so many years. In Abu'l Fazl's flowery language: '*the base and dishonest began to desert and even the feet of great men, whose notions of rectitude had departed, came to slide from their places*.'[14] Jauhar recounts a particularly embarrassing incident, when two senior generals, Munim Khan and Tardi Beg, mounted their horses to leave, and Humayun ran after them, and only with great difficulty managed to persuade them to stay.[15]

***

At this stage, his position utterly untenable, Humayun jumped at an unexpected invitation by Raja Maldeo Rathore of Marwar (Jodhpur in Rajasthan), who promised him assistance. After a – quite literally – murderous journey in the sweltering heat of the Rajasthan desert, where the horses kept sinking to the knees in the sand, and men fought and killed for every drop of water, Humayun reached the vicinity of Bikaner (about 250 km from Jodhpur), where, to his utter dismay and horror, he found himself in grave danger. We do not know whether the raja changed his mind when he saw the sorry state Humayun's feeble forces were in, or whether it had always been his plan to turn Humayun over to Sher Shah; but before long, Humayun was on the run for his life, ploughing through the same 250 km of sandy inferno to escape Maldeo Rathore's clutches. To make things worse, the Rajputs had filled up every single one of the few wells on the way back, because Humayun's men had been stupid and insolent enough to kill a cow for food in a Hindu province.

Morale was so low at this time, that Humayun's authority had all but disappeared. His retinue had dwindled to a mere handful of ragged men, and those who remained had little regard left for their king. At one time, Tardi Beg flatly refused to lend one of his horses to the eight months' pregnant Hamida; Humayun then had to give her his own steed and suffer the affront of having to ride on the back of a camel – considered a vulgar pack animal, never a mount for a nobleman, let alone a king – for about half an hour before one of his men finally offered him his own mount.

***

There was one stroke of unexpected good fortune – enough to rekindle the hopes of a superstitious man like Humayun – when the heavily pregnant Hamida suddenly developed a craving for a pomegranate – hardly the kind of food one would expect to find in the middle of the desert. Soon after, however, they crossed paths with a merchant of animal fodder, who happened to carry a pomegranate in his bag. Could this be a sign? Was divine favour coming back, at last?

So it seemed, for when the weary caravan arrived at Umarkot, a small fortified town on the edge of the desert in Sindh in present-day southern Pakistan, the local ruler, Rana Prasad, a Sodha Rajput nobleman, bade them a hearty welcome, offering them hospitality and even military assistance against Shah Hussain Mirza. The Rana, so it turned out, was thirsting for revenge against the Mirza who, years before, had killed his father.

***

It was thus, in the relative comfort of the Umarkot fortress, that on Sunday,[16] 15 October 1542, Hamida Banu Begam, fifteen years old, gave birth to a healthy young boy: Jalal-ud Din (splendour of religion) Muhammad Akbar,[17] a name, affirmed Humayun, that had been revealed to him in a dream, back in Lahore.

Needless to say that Humayun personally cast the infant's personal horoscope; and, again, needless to say that it was exceptionally promising.[18]

For once, Humayun's predictions would be proven right, for this baby boy, born in a forlorn desert outpost as the son of a destitute fugitive, would grow up to be one of the greatest and the most remarkable monarchs in Indian – and indeed, world – history.

For a brief while, everything seemed to be going Humayun's way again. The good Rana of Umarkot set out with him to conquer Shah Hussain Mirza's dominions, their fighting force of approximately three thousand men quickly growing to over ten thousand, with the support of local tribesmen loyal to the Rana. They quickly conquered the nearby town of Jun with its beautiful mirror garden – according to Gulbadan, a very enjoyable place, '*where the Emperor alighted*'. It was only a six-day journey from Jun to Hussain Mirza's capital Thatta, but Humayun now happily frittered away his time, staying in Jun for nearly nine months, after which, not surprisingly, his luck ran out on him.

After an angry quarrel with one of Humayun's generals, the Rana, followed by his militia, marched off, back to Umarkot. After a few skirmishes with Hussain Mirza's forces, in which Humayun lost a few of his most trusted allies, his army was now plagued by internal strife and daily desertions. One of his officers, Khalid Beg, went over to Hussain Mirza with all his men; Munim Khan deserted and went off to Qandahar after a violent row with Tardi Beg. Once again, Humayun found himself on his own.

***

God only knows what would have happened next, had it not been for an unexpected stroke of luck: in this dark hour, Humayun was joined by Muhammad Bairam Khan, one of his army's best officers, who had become separated from him after the disastrous battle at Kannauj and had made an adventurous escape from Sher Shah's clutches.

Bairam Khan, a Shia Turkoman, belonged to the Baharlu clan of the Qara Qoyunlu (or 'Black Sheep') tribe;[19] his father and grandfather had always been loyal allies in Babur's service. As will become clear from further developments, he was an erudite, brave, trustworthy, and above all, highly capable army leader; it is by no means an exaggeration to state that Humayun, young Akbar and the entire Mughal Empire owe their survival to the loyalty and competence of this exceptional man.

On Bairam Khan's sound advice, Humayun now proved himself smart enough – for once – to quit while still ahead. He patched up a peace treaty with Shah Hussain Mirza, who was so relieved to see him go, that he provided him with two thousand loads of fodder on three hundred camels and built a pontoon bridge across the Indus to speed him on his way westwards.

***

The die was cast. On Wednesday, 11 July 1543, Humayun crossed the Indus and headed for Quetta (in Baluchistan, Pakistan), on his way to Qandahar. It was – or so it seemed – the end of an era. Twelve years and six months after Babur's passing, the last of his sons had been kicked out of India.

ACT THREE: PURGATORY

Qandahar

Humayun was headed towards Qandahar, where Hindal and so many other Mughal leaders had fled to before. It seemed like a perfectly rational plan, but it almost got him killed.

While Humayun had been frittering away his time in Sindh, Kamran had firmly established himself in eastern Afghanistan. Hindal, who refused to pledge allegiance to him, had been put under house arrest; Askari had been appointed as the new governor in Qandahar. There was no room for two kings in the Afghan borderlands; Humayun was no longer welcome.

Forewarned that Askari was on his way to 'greet' him at the head of a large and heavily armed fighting force, Humayun made his escape just in time to avoid capture, but found himself compelled to leave little Akbar, fourteen months old at that time, in the care of a few trusted servants – and at the mercy of his brother.

Fortunately, he was not disappointed in his hopes. Askari affectionately cradled the little boy in his arms and took him to

Qandahar, where he was cared for with the greatest tenderness by Askari's own wife and several wet nurses. Such, apparently, were the unspoken rules of combat among the Timurids: no rival was safe – but family remained sacred at all times.

Herat

As 1543 went by, in the bitter cold of winter, with only his forty closest supporters, plus Hamida and just one of her companion ladies, Humayun, '*planting his foot in the valley of resignation and taking the path of the perilous wilderness*',[20] now headed westwards to Persia, where, so he hoped, he would, at last, be safe. He sent a grovelling letter to Shah Tahmasp, informing him about his plight, and stating that '*the bird of desire was spreading his wings in order that he might be rewarded by beholding the Sun of Greatness and Glory* [i.e., the Shah]'.[21] If Shah Tahmasp would be able to help, so much the better; if not, he would resign himself to the will of the Almighty and depart on the sacred Hajj to Mecca, wrote Humayun.

An arduous journey still lay ahead, with scant provisions, even fewer utensils and no domestic help: when a horse was slaughtered for food, some of the meat had to be boiled in a helmet for want of a kettle; the rest was roasted over an open fire and even '*the Emperor with his own blessed hand roasted some meat which he ate*'. '*It was so cold, that even my head was frozen*,' Humayun testified.

It proved to be the darkest hour just before dawn, for, as soon as he had crossed the Helmand River (now in Afghanistan) into Persia, fortune, at last, knocked at his door.

Shah Tahmasp, clearly of the opinion that the visit of the high-born refugee added to his own prestige, literally received his unexpected guest like a king.

The text of the Shah's *firman* (imperial order), addressed to the governor of Herat and tutor of Sultan Muhammad Mirza, the Shah's eldest son, is quoted in its entirety by Abu'l Fazl[22] and contains fourteen (*sic*!) pages of detailed instructions in small print.

Humayun is first described – without a trace of mockery – as '*the sphere-rider, sun-cupola, pearl of success and sovereignty's ocean, goodly tree ornamenting the garden of government and world sway, world-illuminating light of the portico of sovereignty and glory, soaring cypress of stream of auspiciousness and fortune, aromatic tree of glory and majesty's rose garden … world-warming sun of felicity's heaven, exalted full moon of the zenith of the khalifate and world rule, altar and exemplar of just princes ... lord of majesty, high-born sovereign of supremacy's throne, exalted king of the kingdom of the dispensation of justice ... glorious potentate, enthroned Solomon, lord of guidance and assurance*', and so on.

The Shah then proceeded to instruct the governor – warning him that '*there be no remissness concerning these paramount instructions* [sic!]'. There was an advance party to be sent of '*five hundred prudent and experienced men, each of whom shall have a led horse, a riding mule, and the necessary accoutrements*'. They were to take with them '*three*[23] *swift horses sent from the Sublime Court* [for Humayun's personal use], *together with golden saddles*'. The governor was to add '*from his own stable six swift horses, quiet, of good colour and strong ...*' and he was '*to place on them azure and embroidered saddles, with housings of gold brocade and gold thread*'. The welcome party was to present the honoured guest with a number of other presents, including an exquisitely bejewelled dagger that once belonged to the great Shah Ismail and a golden-hilted scimitar with a bejewelled girdle.

The Shah had also sent '*four hundred pieces of velvet and satin from Europe and Yazd*',[24] so that '*one hundred and twenty coats may be made for the king's special use, and the remainder may be for the servants attached to the victorious stirrup* [sic]', besides several loads of gold-brocaded velvet and silk carpets, and '*twelve tents, crimson, green and white*'.

The Shah then went on to give detailed instructions on how Humayun's further journey was to be managed:

> *Let arrangements be made day by day for sweet and pleasant drinks, with white loaves kneaded with milk and butter and seasoned with fennel seeds and poppy seeds .... Be it also arranged that at the places where His Majesty will halt, there be arranged and pitched, on the previous day, cleansed, pleasant, white, embroidered tents and awnings of silk and velvet, and also pantries and kitchens .... When he, in his glory and fortune, shall direct a halt, let rosewater sherbet and wholesome lemon juice be prepared and poured out, after having been cooled with snow and ice. After the sherbet, let conserves of Maskan apples, watermelons, grapes, etc., with white loaves as already directed, be tendered; and let care be taken that all beverages be examined ... and that rosewater and grey ambergris be added to*

them. Each day let five hundred dishes of varied food be presented, together with the beverages.

These are, of course, preliminary arrangements only. Three days after the welcoming party of five hundred greeted Humayun and his retinue, the son and grandson of the governor were to ride out with one thousand chosen men, who were to be given *tipchaq* and Arab horse, '*for there is no finer decoration for a soldier than a good horse; and let the uniforms of the one thousand be coloured and smart*'. The officers were to serve Humayun '*in the manner that one would serve one's own king*'; they were to '*adopt and bring into practice the utmost attentiveness*'.

Entertainments should '*be so conducted that the total of the food, sweetmeats and liquids be not less than 1500 dishes .... After food has been partaken of, let sweetmeats and comfits prepared from candy* (qand) *and refined sugar* (nabat), *and various conserves, and* risha-i-khatai *(Chinese threads), which shall have been perfumed with rosewater, musk and ambergris be brought in*'. Each officer, on the day that he was to be the host, is to '*tender a present of nine horses, three of which will be for the king's special use, one for the chief amir, Muhammad Bairam Khan, and the five others for such of the select officers as may be fitting*'.

When Humayun's caravan would have arrived at 12 *farsakhs* (about 80 km) from the city of Herat, the governor himself was to leave the Shah's son to the care of one of his officers, and to ride forth to greet Humayun at the head of a cavalry force of thirty thousand, '*which number must be exact*', specified the Shah. There were many more instructions in a similar vein.

Shah Tahmasp

Travelling via Mashad, Sufiabad and Bastam (all in north-east Iran), Humayun took his time, as usual, meeting and greeting local grandees and scholars and visiting dozens of famous mosques, shrines and palaces on his way. By the time he arrived in Qazvin, the Shah had already moved to his summer retreat in the hills between Abhar and Soltaniyeh, another 140 km further west.

It was late July or early August 1544, when the two monarchs finally met. The reception, as could be expected, was cordial – '*the meeting of two eyebrows*', as one poet put it[25] – with the Shah walking all the way to the edge of his carpet to greet Humayun, and showering him, once more, with lavish presents. It was now time for Humayun to return the favour: from the green velvet purse he had kept hidden under his clothing all this time, he presented to the Shah '*two hundred and fifty Badakhshan rubies, plus a diamond of great value, worth the revenues of countries and climes*', affirms Abu'l Fazl;[26] no doubt, it was Babur's famous diamond – which, as we have seen, was probably the world-famous Koh-i-Noor. Abu'l Fazl hastens to add that '*without a doubt, all the expenditures which the Shah, whether from his privy purse or through his officers, incurred on account of* [Humayun] *from the time of his entering the country to his exit therefrom was hereby repaid more than four times*'.

Abu'l Fazl's remark is hardly a coincidence. Behind the extravagant festivities and declarations of eternal friendship and brotherhood, serious tensions were looming. The Shah's extravagant hospitality was, of course, a studied display of superiority, a way to pressurize his guest: if Humayun wanted help, he would have to prove himself a faithful ally. First and foremost, he would have to convert to Shia Islam – Shah Tahmasp was just as fanatic about it as his father. Humayun, vexed by the Shah's vehemence, resisted at first, but in the end, thought it wiser to conform: he had his hair cut in the Persian style and started wearing, for the time being at least, the typical Shia *taj*, a high conical cap of red silk. When in Persia, do as the Persians do, he must have thought.

The monarchs proceeded to talk strategy and logistics. Humayun would be provided with twelve thousand Persian cavalrymen, plus three hundred heavily armoured elite soldiers from the Shah's personal guard. With their help, Humayun would then take Kabul and Qandahar, and cede the latter city and its province to Persia; the Shah's infant third son, Murad – some sources affirm that he was still a mere suckling, others say he was about three years old at the time – would accompany the army and, when Qandahar had been conquered, formally be installed as its governor.

***

It is interesting to note that at this stage, unbeknownst to Humayun, his loving brother Kamran had sent a message to the Shah, offering Qandahar in exchange for Humayun's extradition. We do not know exactly what motivated Shah Tahmasp to turn down the offer. It is reported that his sister was rather fond of Humayun's erudition and mild manners; equally probable is that he did not want to lose face by turning against a guest whom he had just received with such extravagant pomp and circumstance; and even more probable is that the shrewd Shah thought it more prudent to do business with a naïve, but altogether honourable, man whom he controlled, rather than with his obviously treacherous and faraway brother; after all, one bird in the hand is worth two in the bush ...

With the deal being concluded and the promised Persian expeditionary force readying itself near the eastern border, it was time for Humayun to take his leave from the Shah and march on Qandahar. As usual, however, he was not in a hurry, and first went on a relaxed sightseeing tour to the ancient city of Tabriz – another 350 km further northwest, where the biblical Garden of Eden is supposed to have been located – and to several pleasant locations on the shores of the Caspian Sea. When the Shah returned from his summer retreat to Qazvin, he was most unpleasantly surprised to find Humayun still encamped in the area. Urged on by an irritated message from his host, Humayun finally set out eastwards, to his army and on to his homeland.

Qandahar and Kabul

Around February 1545, Humayun crossed the Persian border into the province of Qandahar. Upon hearing the news of his approach, Askari – who was holding Qandahar on Kamran's behalf – ordered the young prince, Akbar, two and a half years old at the time, to be brought over to Kabul, no doubt as a strategic precaution. Accompanying the young prince – the '*Nursling of Divine Light*', as Abu'l Fazl calls him – on his journey through the ice-cold Afghan winter were his two favourite nurses, Maham Anaga and her own little boy Adham Khan, and Jiji Anaga with her husband Shams-ud Din Atga Khan and their son Mirza Aziz Koka – the words '*atga*' and '*koka*' meaning 'foster father' and 'foster brother', respectively. The position of a wet nurse and her family at the Mughal court was an extremely important one, united, as they were, '*by a river of milk*'. As will be related in due course, these four people would indeed play an extremely important – if not always positive – role in Akbar's early career.

With characteristic grovelling adoration, Abu'l Fazl recounts how, at this stage, '*notes of greatness*' were clearly visible in the young prince. In a refuge near Ghazni (in Afghanistan), the lamp went out, and the little prince; '*fell a-weeping from horror of the darkness*' and remained inconsolable until people brought in a new lamp. This, states Abu'l

Fazl, '*was a clear proof of light-augmenting and darkness-dispelling, both internally and externally*'. A slightly more impressive incident occurred upon arrival at Kabul, where Kamran's own son Ibrahim, a few months older than Akbar, was playing with a small kettledrum. This gave rise to a typical toddler conflict, as can be witnessed in kindergartens all over the world: young Akbar wanted the toy, and young Ibrahim refused to give it up. Kamran, unfamiliar with more enlightened parenting principles, ordered the boys to fight it out: whoever won the wrestling match would have the drum. To everybody's surprise, Akbar won. In Abu'l Fazl's words: '*Despite his tender years, which made such actions very surprising, he, by Divine inspiration and celestial teaching, without hesitation girt up his loins and rolled up his sleeves, and with strong arm, which was strengthened by eternal power* [sic!], *stepped bravely forward*'. He grappled with his adversary '*according to the canons of the skilful and of the masters of wrestling*', and '*flung him on the ground*'; upon which, he '*beat the drum which he had gained by the strength of his arm*'. Kamran took it as an extremely bad omen, Abu'l Fazl affirms. For once, the omens were right.

***

On 21 March 1545 – close to a year and a half since his flight to Persia – Humayun and his army arrived at the gates of Qandahar and laid siege to the city. Gradually, slowly but surely, Askari's situation became untenable, as his men deserted in droves, or, as Abu'l Fazl put it, '*seizing the collar of supplication with the hand of contrition … fell at the holy feet of His Majesty* [Humayun]'. After five months of siege, on 3 September, Askari surrendered; and as could be expected, naïve as always, Humayun forgave him.

As agreed with the Shah, Qandahar was now made over to the Persians. A few months later, however, the Shah's infant son died, and Humayun reoccupied the fort, dismissing the Persian commander for 'dereliction of duty', although he was smart enough to keep holding the city in the name of the Shah, for some time anyway. It was the beginning of a border dispute between Persia and the Mughal Empire, a dispute that would last for more than a century, with the city changing hands several times, until, in 1649, under the reign of Shah Jahan, it finally fell to the Persians. The conquest of Qandahar was the final turning point in Humayun's career. Several senior army leaders – opportunistic as always and more than fed up with Kamran's brutal reign – now deserted and flocked towards Qandahar. For the first time since his short-lived conquest of Gujarat, Humayun was a winner again.

He set out for Kabul, joined on the way by his brother Hindal and several others. Kamran, who in Abu'l Fazl's words had neither the strength to resist nor the grace to submit, now hastily abandoned Kabul, escaping to Sindh via Ghazni and Baluchistan. On 18 November 1545, Humayun entered Kabul, where, for the first time in two years, he saw little Akbar back, now a cheerful, healthy boy of three, brought up in the loving care of his foster mothers and his great-aunt, Babur's elder sister Khanzada Begum.

It was, understandably, a time of celebration, culminating, in the spring of 1546, with young Akbar's circumcision ceremony. The event must have made an indelible – and rather negative – impression on the child: later in life, Akbar reportedly issued regulations forbidding circumcision before the age of fifteen, an age when a boy was old enough to decide for himself.

But it was not over: the struggle with Kamran would continue for another eight years. In the winter of 1546, while Humayun was campaigning in Badakhshan, Kamran returned from Sindh and managed to occupy Ghazni and Kabul, where he began a reign of terror, brutally executing many of Humayun's supporters. Humayun had to rush back and lay siege to the city. Kamran resisted for several months – at one time even exposing young Akbar on the battlements to force the assailants to withdraw – but in the end, his situation became untenable, and on 27 April 1547, he escaped through a hole in the wall. He then fled north, approached the Uzbek chief of Balkh, and with his help, conquered much of Badakhshan.

***

The usual scenario kept repeating itself, with Humayun winning the campaign and forgiving Kamran, only to find himself betrayed again. In the middle of 1550, he almost paid for his generosity with his life, when he was ambushed in the Qibchaq defile, about 60 km north of Kabul. Many of Humayun's men were killed, and he was badly wounded – so severely, writes Jauhar, '*that he became weak from loss of blood, and therefore threw off his jabba* [quilted coat], *and gave it in charge of an Abyssinian servant; but his servant being obliged to make his escape from the battle, threw away the jabba, which having been found by some of Kámrán's followers, was brought to the Prince* [i.e., Kamran], *who immediately proclaimed that the King was killed*'.

Kamran now made a hurried march to Kabul, where, under the pretext that Humayun was dead, he was allowed to enter the fort and proclaim himself king. But not for long: three months later, Humayun, recovered from his wounds, kicked him out again. Kamran managed to escape, but Askari, who had once again turned against Humayun, was captured, put in chains, and, after a considerable period of captivity, exiled – i.e., ordered to go on the sacred pilgrimage to Mecca. He died on the journey, in the desert outside Damascus.[27]

***

It would take another two years before Humayun finally got rid of Kamran too. Kamran at first waged a kind of guerilla war in the borderlands between Kabul and the Indus, stirring up strife among the local Pashtun (Afghan) tribes. In one of the ensuing skirmishes, on 20 November 1551, although Humayun's men carried the day, Hindal was killed in action.

Pursued by Humayun, Kamran now fled across the Indus, seeking a treacherous alliance with Islam Shah, son and heir of Sher Shah (who, as will be related later, had died in May 1545). Then and there, however, his luck finally ran out on him. Islam Shah, though impressed by Kamran's knowledge of poetry, soon made it abundantly clear that he did not wish to associate himself with the Mughal renegade. Kamran, now fearing for his life, escaped from Islam Shah's court and fled posthaste through the Punjab, disguised at one time as a woman, to take refuge with a local ruler, Sultan Adam Gakkhar, who, after some hesitation, decided to extradite him to Kabul where Humayun was.

According to Abu'l Fazl, Humayun now organized a lavish feast, where, to everyone's astonishment, Kamran was again treated kindly. This time, however, the amirs insisted that Kamran should get what he deserved: death. '*It was advisable for him and for all that he should become a traveller to the world of non-existence*', recounts Abu'l Fazl, '*so that the dust of wickedness might be wiped from the face of men's safety*'.[28] Gulbadan quotes some of the pertinent arguments used: '*Brotherly custom has nothing to do with ruling and reigning. If you wish to act as a brother, abandon the throne. If you wish to be king, put aside brotherly sentiment! It was this same Kamran who had you severely wounded at the Qibchaq defile; it was he who conspired with the Afghans and killed*

Mirza Hindal. Many a Chaghatai has perished through him; women and children have been made captive and lost honor .... This is no brother! This is Your Majesty's foe!' Humayun was still not convinced: '*Though my head inclines to your words, my heart does not.*' In the end, as the amirs kept insisting, he asked them to attest their advice in writing. So they did, ending with the words: '*It is well to lower the head of the breacher of the kingdom.*' This time, Humayun gave in, though he still refused to have Kamran killed: he was to be blinded in both eyes – which in those days, was an equally effective way to eliminate a rival.

Jauhar provides a full and vivid, if gruesome account of the event:

> *After receiving this command, we returned to the Prince* [i.e., Kamran], *and Ghulám Alí represented to him, in a respectful and condoling manner, that he had received positive orders to blind him. The Prince replied: 'I would rather you would at once kill me.' Ghulám Alí said: 'We dare not exceed our orders.' He then twisted a handkerchief up as a ball for thrusting into the mouth and seizing the Prince by the hands, pulled him out of the tent, laid him down, and thrust a lancet into his eyes (such was the will of God). This they repeated at least fifty times; but he bore the torture in a manly manner, and did not utter a single groan, except when one of the men who was sitting on his knees pressed him. He then said: 'Why do you sit upon my knees? What is the use of adding to my pain?' This was all he said, and he acted with great courage, till they squeezed some (lemon) juice and salt into the sockets of his eyes. He then could not forbear, and called out: 'O Lord, O Lord, my God, whatever sins I may have committed have been amply punished in this world, have compassion upon me in the next!' ... The author of these pages, seeing the Prince in such pain and distress, could no longer remain with him. I therefore went to my own tent, and sat down in a very melancholy mood.*

Humayun however seemed to have gotten over his emotions rather quickly: '*The King having seen me,*' recounts Jauhar, '*sent* [his librarian] *to ask me if the business I had been employed on was finished, and why I had returned without orders.* [I] *answered that the business I had been sent on was quite completed. His Majesty then said: "He need not go back, let him get the water ready for me to bathe."*'

Kamran would not bother Humayun again. He asked and got permission to leave on the Hajj to Mecca, where he died, four years later, in October 1557.

***

With Hindal killed, and Kamran and Askari out of the way, Humayun was now the undisputed king of Kabul, Qandahar and Ghazni. Thanks to Bairam Khan's military and administrative prowess, the erstwhile unruly territory was prosperous and well under control.

Then, encouraging news came in from Hindustan: Islam Shah, Sher Khan's son and successor, was dead, and civil war had broken out among the various pretenders to the throne. After fifteen years of exile, it was time to reclaim Babur's heritage.

INTERLUDE: THE SURI DYNASTY

Self-made Man

If Niccolò Machiavelli (1469–1527) had been a mid-sixteenth century Bengali or Delhiite, his famous political essay – *Il Principe* (*The Prince/The Ruler*) – would, most probably, have been dedicated to Sher Shah.[29] Very few characters in history so perfectly match Machiavelli's ideal of the absolute ruler, to whom any means, fair and foul, are justified in order to achieve and maintain absolute power. His entire life story is one of relentless striving and toiling to get to the throne; and his method, a truly Machiavellian mix of caution, treachery and brutality.

What makes him special, though, is not that he managed to rise from humble beginnings to absolute power, nor that he did not shrink from anything, no matter how immoral or cruel, to get what he wanted. What makes his career truly exceptional and worthy of remembrance is that, after a reign of barely five years, he managed to leave behind a well-organized administration and government principles that would benefit and influence his successors – including the Mughals and even the British Raj – for generations to come. Sher Shah was one of the very first monarchs in Indian medieval history who consciously and methodically occupied himself with the essence of government, i.e., the establishment of justice, law and order, and the furtherance of prosperity for the entire population. It is by no means a coincidence that he chose *Sultan-ul Adil* (the just king), as his royal title: that was a promise, a commitment, and one he would, to the best of his abilities, live up to.

In 1540, at the time he kicked the Mughals out of India, Sher Shah was about fifty-four years of age, a lifetime of experience and a remarkable career behind him. At the time of his birth, no one would ever have guessed that this son of a low-ranking Afghan officer would get this far.

Farid Khan, as was his original name, was the grandson of one Ibrahim Suri, an obscure Afghan horse dealer who had migrated to India and enlisted in the army to improve his fortune. He, however, only made it to the rather modest rank of 'commander of forty horses', responsible for a few poor villages near the town of Narnaul (now in Haryana), about 140 km southwest of Delhi. Hasan, his son and successor, gradually rose to the much higher rank of 'commander of five hundred', with a larger and more prosperous *jagir* (fief) near Sasaram in western Bihar.

Farid's boyhood was far from happy. He and his brother Nizam were born of Hasan's first wife, an Afghan lady, while his two younger half-brothers were the sons of his youngest wife, originally a Hindu slave. The unkindness of Hasan towards Farid's mother and the hateful jealousy of his stepmother became so unbearable that young Farid decided to leave home and go to study at one of the Muslim madrasas in Jaunpur, where he got free board and lodging, and had the opportunity to read a good number of history books on the lives of Alexander the Great and the Persian kings of old. No doubt, these books constituted a well of inspiration to the ambitious young man.

Reconciliation with his father was brought about through the mediation of other family members, and the young man was given responsibility, as his father's deputy, for the administration of the *jagir*. It proved to be an excellent training experience. Fully aware that agriculture was the principal source of wealth, he encouraged cultivation in every possible way and took drastic and, at times, draconian measures to protect the humble peasantry from oppression and exploitation by greedy tax collectors, local zamindars (landowners) and village headmen. '*If it reaches my ears that anyone has forcibly taken even a blade of grass,*' he is reported to have said, '*I shall inflict such punishment that others will take a lesson from it.*' And he meant business. Defiant chieftains were executed without further ado; the villages harbouring them were brutally sacked, the men butchered and the women and children sold into slavery. On the other hand, in the areas that submitted to his rule, he diligently applied himself to the administration of justice, personally investigating the complaints of even the lowliest farmer or soldier. The results were impressive. In a matter of just a few years, through a judicious and effective – if rather immoral – mix of kindness and brutal violence, his father's *jagir* had become more prosperous and orderly than ever before.

Unfortunately, Farid's conspicuous success roused the jealousy of his stepmother, who saw in him a threat to the chances of her own two sons. Day and night, she kept nagging and pestering her husband, until he finally gave in and dismissed Farid.

The following years, Farid's fortunes continued to ebb and flow. Under the local king Bahar Khan Lohani, he not only won Sasaram back after his father's death, but even made it to the rank of *vakil* (vice-governor, prime minister) of south Bihar and *ataliq* (guardian) of the king's young son. Farid worked day and night, and his master was pleased with him. When he also demonstrated his valour and prowess on a hunting excursion by killing a tiger single-handed, the king bestowed the honorary title of Sher Khan on him. Not only would he wear it with pride; he would, in every sense of the word, live up to it.

***

These, however, were times of trouble in Hindustan; times of constantly shifting alliances and widespread distrust. With the advent of the Mughals and with Sultan Ibrahim Lodi's death, the east was now swarming with Lodis and other Afghan warlords, constantly rebelling against – and then submitting again to – Babur or to one or other of the Afghan pretenders. When Farid – now Sher Khan – temporarily lost his king's favour, he went to Agra (in 1527), offering his services to Babur, the new ruler, and once again recovered Sasaram, this time with Mughal support.

King of Bihar, in All but Name

Upon the king's (Bahar Khan Lohani) death in 1528, his minor son Jalal was installed in his place, with the boy's mother as regent. As it was not possible for her to manage all the duties incumbent on her, Sher Khan, who had already proved his considerable ability, was appointed as deputy *(naib)*. All the powers of state were now effectively in his hands, and with the queen's passing in the beginning of 1530, he had become the true king of Bihar in all but name.

That same fateful year 1530 – the year of Babur's unexpected death and Humayun's accession to the throne – he further strengthened his position through two strategic marriages, both with rich and childless widows. By his marriage with Lad Malka, the widow of Taj Khan, commander of the important fortress of Chunar, located on the southern bank of the Ganga near Varanasi, he gained control over this strategic region. Through the second marriage, with a lady named Gauhar Gossain, the widow of Nasir Khan Lohani of Ghazipur (in eastern Uttar Pradesh), he acquired an enormous fortune in gold; he was now, in his own right, a force to be reckoned with.

His hierarchic position suffered a major – if only temporary – setback when Mahmud Lodi – Sultan Ibrahim Lodi's brother and legitimate heir – took control of Bihar. Sher Khan feigned loyalty, but secretly approached Humayun, offering his support in the imminent clash between Mahmud Lodi and the Mughals. As has been related earlier, Humayun did win an easy victory against Mahmud Lodi at Dadrah, thanks to a considerable extent, to Sher Khan withdrawing his forces before the battle; he also demanded the surrender of Chunar, but Sher Khan managed to hold on to it, convincing Humayun, who was eager to get back to Agra (to deal with Bahadur Shah, the king of Gujarat), to give up the siege.

Power, at Last

With Humayun safely occupied in faraway Gujarat, Sher Khan now prepared himself for the final leap to absolute power.

His most urgent task was to consolidate his own position in Bihar and deal with the many actual and potential opponents he still had among the Afghans themselves. He was a rich and powerful man now, and wealth and power always attract jealousy. First of all, he needed to neutralize Jalal Khan, his erstwhile suzerain and king of Bihar – old enough now to try and win his dominions back – and Jalal's many supporters: the local Afghan amirs in Bihar, mainly from the Lohani clan, traditional rivals of the Suri tribe to which Sher Khan belonged; and Jalal's powerful ally, Sultan Mahmud Shah of Bengal, whose powerful army was looming near the border.

***

Instead of bottling himself up in his strongholds, as many others would have done, Sher Khan resolutely took the initiative and invaded Bengal himself, annexing a large tract of land to his own dominions. The Lohani chiefs now conspired to have him assassinated, but he was, of course, much too cautious to be thrown off guard. The conspirators' position in Bihar now became untenable; they all fled in panic to Bengal to escape Sher Khan's wrath.

Interestingly and typically, Sher Khan did not assume his royal title at this point, as he could easily have done, with Jalal on the run. Legally and nominally, he remained Humayun's vassal – for now.

Sultan Mahmud Lodi, burning to take revenge for his earlier defeat, quickly rebuilt his army; accompanied by Jalal and his Lohani allies, he again marched westwards to regain the lost territory. Undaunted, Sher Khan met his adversaries on the plain west of Mungir (or Munger; now in Bihar) situated on banks of the Ganga. The encounter ended in complete victory for Sher Khan, with the enemy commander Ibrahim Khan killed on the battlefield. Not resting on his laurels, Sher Khan pushed on and went on the offensive, annexing Bengal territory as far as Bhagalpur (now in Bihar) before the rainy season of 1535. The following year, he resumed his campaign, this time capturing the capital Gaur and amassing a huge fortune in the process.

The sultan's humiliation had important strategic and political consequences. In the eyes of the old Afghan aristocracy, Sher Khan had always been a low-ranking upstart, a vulgar nouveau riche who just happened to get lucky; but now, he had become the one and only epicentre of Afghan power. His personal magnetism and well-earned reputation as a generous and equitable paymaster did the rest: Afghan leaders from far and wide now came flocking to him. He was ready to confront the Mughals.

By the time Humayun realized what was happening, it was way too late, and his strategy to deal with it, all wrong. The ensuing war over Bengal was nothing but a cat-and-mouse game, with Humayun jumping on the wrong targets hither and thither, and Sher Khan – now Sher *Shah* – patiently waiting for the moment to strike. Twenty-two months later, that moment had come. With two devastating blows – one at Chausa and the next at Kannauj – he crushed Humayun and drove him out of Hindustan, as already mentioned.

The Art of Government, Sher Shah Style

With Humayun on the run in Sindh, Sher Shah did not waste his time in chasing him – he had other and more important things on his mind than hunting down a hapless has-been. He consolidated his hold on the recently conquered territories in the Punjab and central Hindustan, then hastily travelled back to Bengal, where his local governor and erstwhile trusted general, Khizr Khan, had married the former sultan's daughter, occupied the *toki* (upper palace) and – while not formally assuming the royal title – was behaving like a king.

Seething with anger when he heard the news, Sher Shah dashed back, rapidly covering the approximately 2000 km by forced marches, and suddenly reappeared in Gaur at the head of his army, to Khizr Khan's understandable bewilderment. The latter still tried to appease his master by throwing a lavish welcome party, but Sher Shah was not impressed. '*Where did you get the idea that you could marry Mahmud Lodi's daughter and seat yourself on the* toki *without my orders?*' he thundered. Without further ado, the disconcerted governor was clapped in irons and unceremoniously thrown into jail. '*Let it be known,*' warned Sher Shah, '*that the nobles of this realm are not to do a single thing without their King's permission.*'

He was not kidding. To use the words of his biographer, Abbas Khan Sarwani, in his *Tarikh-i-Sher Shahi* (history of Sher Shah), he made sure that '*no man dared to draw a breath in contravention of his orders*'.

Divide and Conquer

Sher Shah understood full well that, unless adequate measures were taken, Khizr Khan would not remain an isolated case. History books abounded with examples – Sher Shah's own career being a case in point – of ambitious regional officials overthrowing their own kings. The answer, Sher Shah understood instinctively, lay in judicious *administrative* reforms: since the concentration of power in the hands of one individual was the problem, *division* of power had to be the answer.

Bengal was therefore immediately split up into a number of *sarkars* (districts), headed by district chiefs, directly appointed by, and responsible to, the king himself; and the provincial governor of yore was replaced by a regional coordinator, with no military power or disciplinary authority over the *sarkar* chiefs, who acted as the king's eyes and ears, and as arbitrators in disputes between regional officials.

Inside the *sarkars* themselves, power was further divided among:

1. a chief *shiqdar* or land tax collector (*shiqdar-i-shiqdaran*), responsible for law and order (except in big towns, which were treated as special districts and headed by a *kotwal* or town prefect);
2. a chief *munsif* or (*munsif-i-munsifan*) or judge, responsible for civil law and revenue matters; and
3. a *qazi* or judge (whose decisions were based on Islamic law).

In order to prevent the development of any vested interests, all provincial officials were given new assignments every two years. To make things complete, the border regions were held by military outposts or *thanas* of imperial troops personally appointed and changed by Sher Shah on a yearly basis.

In short: nearly two hundred years before Montesquieu,* Sher Shah instinctively understood that separation of powers was the best guarantee against any abuse of it.

'Political Power Grows Out of the Barrel of a Gun'

Sher Shah would have wholeheartedly subscribed to Chairman Mao Zedong's famous maxim:[30] in his world, much more than in ours, might was right, and no man understood this better than he did. Little wonder, that he placed paramount importance on the quality and discipline of his armed forces.

Fully aware of the defects of conscript armies, dependent on the often shifting loyalties of feudal tributaries, he maintained – supplemented by feudal levies when necessary – an immensely powerful and highly disciplined standing army under his personal leadership and control, consisting of 150,000 cavalry, 25,000 infantry, 5000 war elephants and a park of artillery. Like in the heydays of the Romans, powerful army divisions (called *fauj*, under the command of a *faujdar*) were stationed at several strategic places in his empire.

Sher Shah took a personal interest in the recruitment and training of his men and made every effort to maintain a close and individual a

*Charles-Louis de Secondat, Baron de La Brède et de Montesquieu, 1689–1755, was a French political philosopher known for his theory of separation of powers.

relationship with each one of them, personally fixing their salaries and making himself available to hear whatever complaint they may have had. A stern disciplinarian, but fair and dependable: that is how his men knew him and that is how he wanted to be known.

Pax Afghana

But force was not the only – and not the most important – thing Sher Shah understood about the art of government. There is no denying that he was a highly successful army leader and conqueror, but his accomplishments as an administrator have earned him an undying place in Indian history. Very few monarchs before him – and alas, very few leaders after him – have paid such close and constant attention to what is actually the core duty of any government: to further the legitimate interests of the governed.

While a staunch Sunni Muslim in his private life, his general policy in religious matters was one of pragmatism and toleration. Hindu religious practices were not interfered with and talented Hindus were readily employed in government service, both in the civil administration and the army. The vast majority of his infantry was Hindu, as was Barmazid Gaur, one of his most trusted generals. It should be remembered, incidentally, that a majority of his many wars were waged against fellow Muslims. And while he did use religious rhetoric and excuses to justify his misdeeds against Rajput adversaries, his motives were clearly imperialist, not religious. In summary: he was an imperialist who happened to be Muslim, not a '*Muslim conqueror*'.

An innovator in the true sense of the word, he was not: there was nothing entirely *new* in the measures he took. His remarkable strength lay in the consistent, pragmatic and efficient application of a few simple principles.

What exactly were those principles? Sher Shah never wrote any 'ruler's manual', but he would probably have agreed with the following summary:

- no power without prosperity;
- no prosperity without security;
- no security without justice; and
- no justice without enforcement.

No Power without Prosperity; No Prosperity without Security

Throughout his life, Sher Shah remained deeply convinced of the strategic importance of ordinary farmers as the very basis of all prosperity. Protecting them from any harm was high on his priority list. It is reported that he once personally cut off a soldier's ears for stealing from a field and had him paraded through the camp with the stolen corn around his neck. When invading an enemy's country, he never allowed the local peasantry to be plundered or harassed, but took every measure to protect them and their property. '*Those farmers are blameless,*' he said. '*If we oppress them, they will abandon their villages, the country will be ruined and deserted, and it will be a long time before it again becomes prosperous.*'[31]

Among his most acclaimed measures was his ingenious land revenue system, designed to settle revenues and taxes on the objective basis of the fertility of the soil and past average revenues. The purpose was clear: taxing the farmers fairly and leaving them enough surplus to encourage them to sustain and expand their activities, while, at the same time, ensuring a steady stream of revenue to the king's coffers.

The same principles guided Sher Shah's regulations on trade: local governors and tax collectors were summoned to watch over the safety and fair treatment of merchants and travellers. All taxes and imposts on merchandise were abolished and replaced by a uniform system of tax collection, one at the border where goods were imported, and one at the point of sale. Punishment for any contravention was swift and severe, so no one dared to impose any illegal levy. Prices were regulated to prevent usury and speculation; monetary stability was guaranteed through the issuance of new gold, silver and copper coins of fixed standard weight and purity.

Trade was also furthered by an impressive investment in infrastructure: new roads were built and existing ones repaired and improved. The backbone of the highway network was the east–west connection, all the way from Bengal to the Indus, branching out in north–south connecting roads like Lahore–Multan–Sindh and Agra–Rajasthan–Malwa–Gujarat. Wherever possible, the roads were lined on both sides with fruit-bearing and densely canopied, broad-leaved trees for sustenance and shade. Every seven kilometres or so, staging posts were set up to provide lodging and security to travellers (with separate arrangements for Muslims and Hindus) and stables for government mail horses.

No Security without Justice; No Justice without Enforcement

If his biographer is to be believed, India under Sher Shah was the safest place in the world: travellers felt free to encamp at night at every place, desert or inhabited, without fear; a decrepit old woman could place a basket full of gold ornaments on her head and go on a journey, for no thief or robber would dare to come near her, affirms Abbas Khan Sarwani, in his *Tarikh-i-Sher Shahi*.[32]

While this may be a gross overstatement, it is, nevertheless, an established fact that the crime rate under Sher Shah's reign was remarkably low. This has to do with his strict and oftentimes brutal, but always even-handed administration of justice, without any personal favour or partiality. '*Justice alone is the mainstay of government and the source of prosperity to the governed,*' he is reported to have said; and also '*injustice is the most pernicious of things; it saps the foundation of government and brings ruin to the realm*'.

He was imbued with the well-established – if often forgotten – principle that crime prevention is a function of two factors: the risk of getting caught times the severity of punishment. If the chances of getting caught are close to nil, even the death penalty will have no deterrent effect; if getting caught fails to entail any dire consequences to the perpetrators, there will be little respect for the law. Not only was law enforcement taken extremely seriously in Sher Shah's days, but also every local official and village headman was held personally responsible for any crimes committed in his precinct. While terribly unfair, the system ensured that no crime went unpunished, and more importantly, that every effort was made to *prevent* any kind of disturbance.

Sher Shah had no illusions about the honesty of ordinary mortals; he knew full well – and readily admitted – that he himself had acquired his own empire through corruption.[33] Little wonder that he was intensely preoccupied with all kinds of measures to prevent fraud, corruption and bribery, reinforced by an elaborate, efficient and much-feared network of secret informants.

Anti-fraud measures included a compulsory system of branding, which made sure that horses could not be lent out to other contingents at the time of muster calls. Similarly, individual descriptive records were kept about each and every soldier.

Decisive in Sher Shah's success was his hard work and tireless personal involvement in every detail. He made himself available to every complainant and worked – almost literally – day and night, rising before dawn every day and only interrupting his work for obligatory prayers, hasty meals and a short nap in the afternoon. '*It behooves the great to be always active,*' he is reported to have said.

The Time for the Evening Prayer Has Arrived

As stated above, Sher Shah was about fifty-four years old when he ousted Humayun in 1540. But he was not the kind of man to rest on his laurels. In the mere five years he still had to live, he managed to add vast territories to his already impressive empire. At the time of his untimely accidental death, he was ruling supreme over the vast arc of land formed by the basins of the Indus and Ganges and their tributaries, and pushing relentlessly to expand his borders southwards.

As in his earlier career, he preferred bloodless conquest wherever possible: Gwalior, Malwa and the powerful Rajput fortress of Ranthambor surrendered to him without a single shot being fired, thanks to the efforts of '*smooth-tongued ambassadors*'. If forced to fight, however, he did not shrink from any trick or treachery, however low, however despicable.

***

Leaving the conquest of Multan and Sindh (completed by 1543) to his generals, Sher Shah himself occupied Malwa and Ranthambor in 1542; then, in January 1543, he set out to conquer Chanderi and the great fortress of Raisen, approximately 45 km east of Bhopal (now the capital of Madhya Pradesh). After six months under constant heavy bombardment, Raja Puran Mal, the king of the fortress, offered to surrender, asking the Afghans to 'bind themselves by promise and oaths' and guarantee that he would 'suffer no injury in property or person'. This, Sher Shah solemnly swore, upon which the raja trustingly left the fortress along with his women and retinue. He was allotted a campsite surrounded by Sher Shah's army, with the promise that he would be allowed to travel unhindered on to Benares. But, late in the evening a few days later, Sher Shah brazenly broke his oath, ordering his troops to slaughter the Rajput men and enslave the women and children. As per their own gruesome custom, the Rajputs killed as many of their own women and children as possible, before being butchered themselves to the very last man; only a few women and children survived. A daughter of the raja was sold off to a band of itinerant musicians to be brought up as a dancing girl and three of his young nephews were castrated, so '*that the race of the oppressor might not increase*'.

Sher Shah's biographer has attempted to justify this scandalous act of treason, alleging that Muslim families from Chanderi had bitterly complained against Puran Mal, saying: '*We have suffered from this inhuman and malignant infidel all kinds of tyranny and oppression. He has slain our husbands, and our daughters he has enslaved, and has made dancing-girls of them, and has seized our lands, and all our worldly goods, for a long time past .... If you do not give us justice, hereafter, in the day of resurrection, when the first and the last of all men shall be collected together, we will accuse you.*'

Sher Shah then consulted his *ulama* (Muslim religious scholars), who conveniently delivered a legal opinion that the raja had to be put to death.

It was, most probably, a blatant lie: the raja does not appear to have had any Muslim slaves. But be that as it may, this mass murder was a heinous, inexcusable act of vile treachery, which has forever sullied Sher Shah's memory, and makes him, in spite of his many qualities, unworthy of his self-selected title, Sultan-ul Adil (the just ruler).

***

On the fall of Raisen (June 1543), Sher Shah briefly returned to Agra, where he decided to attack Marwar (Jodhpur), the then most powerful kingdom in Rajputana, ruled by its capable and energetic king, Rao Maldeo Rathore, who had been aggressively expanding his dominions at the expense of his neighbours. It is interesting to note here that several disgruntled Rajput chiefs had been asking Sher Shah to attack Rathore, out of revenge for the loss of their erstwhile territories. As has been stated above, it would be wrong to portray Rathore's struggle against Sher Shah as one of the last Hindu leaders desperately trying to fend off a Muslim invader. This was not a matter of one religious community fighting the other: India's feudal age was an utterly chaotic time, where rivalling principalities, ruled by Muslim or Hindu kings, fought against their Muslim or Hindu neighbours and rivals, and in the process, had no moral objections against betraying their own co-religionists if that suited their own selfish purposes.

Fully aware of the strength of his opponent, Sher Shah set out against Marwar at the head of a huge force of eighty thousand horse, until his further advance was blocked by Rathore's forces at the village of Sammel, about 100 km east of Jodhpur. For a full month, in late 1543, the armies merely kept facing each other. But time was running out for Sher Shah: he could not afford to stay entrenched for too long, as the supply problems for his huge army were becoming insurmountable; on the other hand, cautious as he was, he did not want to risk a frontal attack on so strong and experienced an adversary as Rathore.

Once again, he decided to take recourse to a ruse. Several forged letters – supposedly written by the Rajput king's generals and addressed to Sher Shah – were dropped in Rathore's camp. And the stratagem worked: suspicious about the loyalty of his generals, Rathore withdrew from the battlefield in early 1544 with the greater part of his army; and his duped generals, moved by misguided pangs of conscience and hurt pride, decided to redeem their lost honour with their own blood. At dawn the next day, they fell on the Afghan army with twelve thousand fanatical followers, bent on embracing death. Such was their fervour that they broke through Sher Shah's entrenchments and well-nigh succeeded in killing Sher Shah himself, before being cut down themselves. '*I had nearly given the kingdom of Delhi for a millet seed,*' Sher Shah later commented.[34]

Sher Shah's general, Khavass Khan, took possession of the city of Jodhpur and the surrounding territory from Ajmer to Mount Abu (250 km further south; now in Rajasthan), but Rathore himself succeeded in evading capture and would, about seven months later, reoccupy most of his lost territories.

Leaving Khavass Khan in charge of Marwar, Sher Shah himself marched further south, to Mewar, where the huge fortress of Chittor surrendered to him, without any resistance.

***

Sher Shah's next – and, quite unexpectedly, last – campaign was against the fortress of Kalinjar in Bundelkhand, about 230 km south of Lucknow and 195 km west of Allahabad. His forces surrounded the fort in November 1544, but in the face of staunch resistance, the siege dragged on for several months. The assailants built trenches running to the ramparts, and a tower overtopping the walls, from where they continually harassed the defenders. On the morning of Friday, 22 May

1545, Sher Shah went to supervise the launch of rocket grenades into the fort. As fate would have it, one of the grenades recoiled against the fortress wall and fell into a heap of ammunition near the spot where he was standing, leading to a huge blaze. Horribly burnt all over, he was carried posthaste to his quarters, but there was little the physicians could do – apart from sprinkling rosewater on his wounds. Mercifully slipping out of consciousness now and then, he kept shouting at his men, ordering them to continue the assault. That same day, he would, one last time, taste the sweet taste of victory: around the time of the afternoon prayer, his soldiers brought him the good tidings that the fort had fallen. '*Praise be to God!*' he sighed. '*This was my very desire.*' A few moments later, he breathed his last.

His body was temporarily interred at Kalinjar, but later transferred to the wonderful mausoleum he had himself ordered to be built at Sasaram, his childhood home. It is a harmonious, domed octagonal building on a square plinth with elegant *chhatris* (domed kiosks), serenely standing in the centre of a square artificial lake, connected to the mainland by a wide stone walkway. An inscription dates its completion to 16 August 1545, about three months after Sher Shah's passing.

***

Sher Shah is reported to have said, looking at a mirror one morning, shortly after his victory against Humayun: '*Alas! I have attained the empire only when I have reached old age, and when the time for the evening prayer has arrived. Had it been otherwise, the world would have seen what I would have accomplished.*'[35]

Pretentious as his claim sounds, he may very well have been right. In any case, it can hardly be denied that his achievements after a short reign of merely five years are absolutely outstanding. For all his faults, he has earned himself an enduring and well-deserved reputation as one of the most successful and efficient rulers India has ever seen. Very few monarchs in Indian history – Akbar being the obvious, if perhaps debatable exception – measure up to him.

His Father's Son: Islam Shah (1545–1554)

Sher Shah's untimely death left the Afghans with a problem: who was to succeed him? His youngest son, Qutub Khan, had fallen in the struggle against Humayun; but Sher Shah had failed to indicate who of his two surviving sons, Adil Khan and Jalal Khan, would be his successor. In an emergency conclave, the army leaders chose Jalal Khan, the younger one. It was a wise decision, for Jalal Khan had given more than sufficient proof of his competence, courage and military ability, whereas Adil Khan, despite his bodily strength, was little more than an indolent sluggard.

Nevertheless, choosing the younger of two brothers was an uneasy decision. There was tension in the air, and rightfully so, for the lack of a generally accepted order of succession would be the downfall of the mighty Suri dynasty.

Jalal Khan arrived at Kalinjar on 26 May, four days after his father's untimely death. He was enthroned the same day, assuming the royal title of Islam Shah.[36]

Enthroned he was, but not at ease: could he rest assured about his brother's intentions? Islam Shah, who clearly had inherited Sher Shah's cunning, now engaged in the kind of wily charade his father would have admired. He sent his brother a letter, assuring him that he had no other desire but to serve and obey him: he had only occupied the throne as a precautionary measure, he maintained, as his brother had been too far away at the time of their father's passing. But now, he would vacate the throne and leave it to Adil Khan.

Adil Khan, suspecting foul play, refused to leave Ranthambor, until four of the leading amirs, including Sher Shah's best general Khavass Khan, personally guaranteed his safety. When that guarantee was duly given, he reluctantly agreed to accompany his brother to Agra.

There, the painful comedy was staged to perfection, with Islam Shah urging his brother to ascend the throne and paying obeisance to him as a faithful subject; but Adil Khan, much less ambitious than his brother, rose from the throne and made Islam Shah sit on it again, paid his respects and withdrew to his chosen *jagir*.

Everything seemed to be under control, but Islam Shah, who also had inherited his father's suspicious nature, was still not at ease. How could he be sure Adil Khan was not lying? How could he be sure he would not become a figurehead for overly ambitious generals?

Consequently, he ordered his brother's imprisonment, but Adil Khan managed to evade capture, and the four nobles who had earlier guaranteed his safety, now sided with him. Sher Shah would have turned in his grave. Barely a year after his death, civil war had broken out among the Suris.

In the ensuing battle near Agra, Adil Khan's forces were routed; he fled towards Bundelkhand, never to be heard of again.

As a result of the civil war and a failed attempt on his life, Islam Shah's innate suspicious and vindictive character now degenerated into full-blown paranoia. With ruthless, murderous cruelty reminiscent of the Roman emperors, Tiberius, Nero or Caligula, he now embarked on a systematic purge of the great Afghan nobles, spreading such terror that, soon, no one dared to even lift a finger against him.

Islam Shah may have lacked his father's charisma and moral authority, but not his organizational talent. He spent the remaining years of his reign continuing in his father's footsteps, taking every measure necessary to centralize all the powers of state in his own hands. This even included the complete abolition of the *jagir* system, whereby the local governors were reduced to the status of civil servants, receiving their salaries from the royal treasury – precisely the kind of measures Akbar the Great would later take.

The Suri dynasty might have remained in power for many more decades or even centuries had Islam Shah been granted a few more years to prepare his eldest son and successor, but it was not to be. In the month of November 1554, while residing in his beloved city of Gwalior, he was suddenly taken violently ill with what appears to have been an acute and extremely painful disease of the urinary tract, with urine retention and a large and painful abscess on the penis, which he attempted to open himself, with fatal consequences: he died on 22 November 1554.

Abu'l Fazl, Akbar's biographer, later commented that it was a great pity that such competent men like Sher Shah and Islam Shah had not been in the Mughal service; coming from him, it is the ultimate tribute to their achievements.

The Bitter End

Islam Shah's needless murder of so many of his father's trusted veterans had made him strong, but at the expense of his own empire. His crimes now took their grim toll.

The first victim was Islam Shah's own twelve-year-old son, Firuz Khan, who was raised to the throne shortly after his father's death, only to be brutally murdered a few days later by his own maternal uncle (and paternal great-uncle) Mubariz Khan, son of Sher Shah's younger brother Nizam Khan and brother of the boy's mother. On the pretext of paying his respects to his nephew and new king, Mubariz Khan barged into the royal residence at Gwalior. The boy's mother, sensing what was about to happen, threw herself at her brother's feet, begging him to spare her son. But Mubariz Khan, unrelenting, tore the boy away from her and cut off his head before her very eyes. He then ascended the Suri throne with the title of Muhammad Adil Shah in late 1554.

Adil Shah now tried to conciliate the nobles and the army by a lavish distribution of money and titles, but it was to no avail. Soon, every corner of the empire was in open rebellion. Ibrahim Khan Suri, the governor of Agra and Adil Shah's brother-in-law, revolted and took possession of the central heartlands around Delhi and Agra. Ahmad Khan Suri, another brother-in-law and governor of Lahore, took the title of Sikandar Shah and set himself up as independent king in the Punjab. And over in Bengal, the local governor, Muhammad Khan Suri, also declared his independence, taking the title of Shams-ud Din Muhammad Shah.

Predictably, this was the beginning of the end, for the three Suri kings now started fighting among themselves. Sikandar, the strongest and most ambitious of the three, first marched against Ibrahim, defeated him, and took possession of Delhi and Agra. Defeated a second time by Hemu (aka Hemchandra), Adil Shah's capable Hindu *vakil* (prime minister), Ibrahim now fled to what is now Orissa (Odisha), where he died in obscurity.

Adil Shah, although caught between hammer and anvil, left all the fighting and the affairs of state to his trusted general, and wallowed in luxury in his capital Chunar, the only remaining territory under his control. There, as Eraly aptly put it,[37] he fiddled away – quite literally, for he appears to have been an excellent musician – in indolence and depravity. Three years later, he would be defeated and killed by the sultan of Bengal, his kinsman Khizr Khan Suri, son and successor of Shams-ud Din Muhammad Shah.

Meanwhile, as will be recounted later, Sikandar Shah had been soundly defeated by the returning Mughals. Just twelve years after Sher Shah's passing, by 1557, the proud Suris had wiped themselves off from the tables of history.

ACT FOUR: PARADISE REGAINED – AND LOST AGAIN

Humayun's Return to Hindustan

The civil war that broke out among the Suris after Islam Shah's death was the opportunity Humayun had been awaiting for so many years. At last, it was time for him to go back to Hindustan.

Typically, the decision to invade was taken on soothsaying. Thinking about Hindustan while on a hunting trip, Humayun decided to ask the names of the three first people he met. As luck – or Providence – would have it, the names of three people he met were Daulat Khwaja, Sa'adat Khwaja and Murad Khwaja – exactly the names of his erstwhile 'departments' of empire, auspiciousness and joy; clearly, a better omen was hardly imaginable.

Leaving behind his younger son Muhammad Hakim as the nominal governor of Kabul, under the care of the veteran general Munim Khan, Humayun crossed the Khyber Pass and reached Peshawar on 25 December 1554. Under his command was an army of five thousand men, all told – three thousand from Kabul and another two thousand from Qandahar – but it proved to be enough, given the utter chaos of the Suri civil war. Local garrisons simply fled on Humayun's approach, so that he was able to occupy the entire Punjab, including the major city of Lahore, without any effective opposition.

Alarmed at the Mughals' rapid advance, Sikandar Shah now sent a strong army of thirty thousand horse towards Sirhind. Undaunted by the enemy's superiority, Humayun's trusted general Bairam Khan crossed the river Sutlej before the arrival of the enemy. The two armies collided near the village of Machihwara (now in the Indian part of Punjab) in mid-May 1555. As it grew dark, it became impossible for any of the armies to fight, but then, as luck would have it, fire broke out in the area where the Afghan army was encamped. Under the cover of darkness, Bairam Khan's men started taking potshots at the Afghans, clearly visible now in the glow of the flames. After a brief engagement, the Afghans took to flight. A few weeks later, on 22 June 1555, the main Afghan force, led by Sikandar Shah himself, fared little better, in spite of its vast superiority in numbers. Under Bairam Khan's able leadership, the Mughals split their small but mobile fighting force in three; the central group under Bairam Khan stood its ground against a frontal Afghan attack; then, the left and right wings came out from behind and wheeled round the enemy, who, in a short time became a mass of confusion and fled in disarray, pursued by the victorious Mughals who slaughtered them by the hundreds. Sikandar Shah now fled hastily to the Siwalik hills in the north, leaving Delhi undefended. On 23 July 1555, Humayun triumphantly reoccupied the city, unopposed. Agra and the rest of Hindustan soon followed suit. There was a brief disturbance in the Punjab, when Sikandar Shah and his troops came out from the hills, but Bairam Khan, accompanied by young Prince Akbar, quickly drove them back.

Back in Delhi, Humayun spent the rest of the year '*in ease and enjoyment*', arranging his library, pursuing his abstruse astronomical studies, and thinking about how he would enlarge and administer his newly recovered dominions, perhaps along more sensible lines than his previous astrological follies.

But astrology remained critically – and as it would soon appear, fatally – important to him. In the afternoon of Friday, 24 January 1556, he went to the rooftop observatory of the Sher Mandal building, inside the so-called Purana Qila (Old Fort) in Delhi, along with several of his astrologers, to observe the first visible movements of the celestial bodies. In the west, *Esfand* (Pisces) was vaguely discernible on the horizon. From the observer's perspective, the sun was setting three fingers' breadth away from it, towards the south. A half hour later, Venus would be setting, close to exactly the same spot. Saturn, high up in the sky, and Mars, in the Bahman constellation (Aquarius), would then form a straight line above it. He must have been deeply convinced that it was all of profound significance, but whatever the stars' hidden message may have been, he sadly misread it. As he was about to retire to his quarters for a moment, and stood on top of the steep staircase, the muezzins' call to the late afternoon prayers suddenly resounded from the city's minarets. Humayun hastened down the steep and narrow flight of steps, in order to properly face the *qiblah*[38] and start his prayers, when his foot got caught in his robe, and he fell headlong down the stairs, receiving a violent blow on his right temple. The base of his skull must have been fractured, as blood was seeping out of his ear. He lingered on for a couple of days, regaining consciousness now and then, but on the evening of 27 January, he passed away. His last words, if we are to believe his pious chroniclers, were: '*I accept the Divine summons.*'

Thus ended, quite unexpectedly, but not entirely surprisingly, Humayun's eventful but tragic life. In the wry, often-quoted words of the British orientalist and historian Stanley Edward Lane-Poole (1854–

1931),[39] his end '*was of a piece with his character. If there was a possibility of falling, Humayun was not the man to miss it. He tumbled through life, and he tumbled out of it.*'

CHRONOLOGY

1533: Foundation of Din Panah.
1535: Humayun's campaign in Gujarat.
1537: Humayun's campaign in Bengal.
26 June 1539: Humayun's defeat at Chausa.
17 May 1540: Humayun's defeat at Kannauj; Sher Shah Suri's reign commences.
1541–42: Humayun in Sindh; marriage to Hamida Banu Begam.
15 October 1542: Birth of Akbar.
1544: Humayun in Persia.
22 May 1545: Death of Sher Shah; accession of Islam Shah.
November 1545: Recovery of Kabul and Qandahar by Humayun with Persian help.
1552: Kamran blinded and exiled.
22 November 1554: Death of Islam Shah; war of succession among the Suris; Humayun returns to Hindustan.
22 February 1555: Humayun again in power.
27 January 1556: Humayun dies in an accident on the stairs of his library.

Notes and References

1. S. Roy, 'Humayun', in R. C. Majumdar (ed.), *The Mughul Empire*, Bharatiya Vidya Bhavan's History and Culture of the Indian People, Vol. VII, Bombay, 1974.
2. Ferishta (aka Muhammad Qasim Shah) in J. Briggs (trans.), *History of the Rise of Mohammedan Power in India*, London, 1829, quoted by John Keay, *India: A History*, Grove Press, New York, 2000, p. 297.
3. Bamber Gascoigne, *A Brief History of the Great Moguls*, Carroll & Graf *Publishers*, New York, 2002, p. 34.
4. This carpet is reported to have seated 1400 people (see Abu'l Fazl Allamī, *The Akbar Nāmā*, in three volumes, translated from the Persian by H. Beveridge, 1902–39, Low Price Publishers, Delhi, reprinted 1989, p. 650, footnote 1).

5. Abu'l Fazl Allamī, op. cit., Vol. I, pp. 642–651.
6. 'Tiger Khan' (more accurately, 'Lion Khan'), an honorary title he had earned for himself by killing a tiger (or a lion?) single-handedly.
7. Abu'l Fazl Allamī, op. cit., Vol. I, pp. 313–316.
8. Gascoigne, op. cit., p. 39.
9. Haidar Mirza Doghlat was one of Babur's first cousins: his father, Muhammad Husain Mirza, had married the younger sister of Babur's mother.
10. Abu'l Fazl Allamī, op. cit., Vol. I, p. 354.
11. *Tazkirat-ul Waki'at* (relation of occurrences), written in 1587. The passage given here is quoted by Abraham Eraly, *The Mughal Throne: The Saga of India's Great Emperors*, Viking (an imprint of Penguin Books India and Penguin Books UK), New Delhi and London, 1997 and 2000, p. 63.
12. Abu'l Fazl Allamī, op. cit., Vol. I, p. 356.
13. Gascoigne, op. cit., p. 42; Abu'l Fazl Allamī, op. cit., Vol. I, p. 358.
14. Abu'l Fazl Allamī, op. cit., Vol. I, p. 367.
15. Eraly, op. cit., p. 66.
16. Sunday, the 5th of Rajab (the seventh month of the Islamic calendar) of the Islamic year 949. Beveridge, in his translation of Abu'l Fazl Allamī's *Akbar Nāmā*, comments that the date, in the current common reckoning, is actually late Saturday night of the previous day.
17. *Akbar* is the comparative/superlative of the adjective *kabir* (great). *Akbar* thus means '*greater/the greatest*'.
18. The printed version of Abu'l Fazl Allamī's *Akbar Nāmā* contains close to one hundred pages in small print (Chapters I–VIII, pp. 34–128) of detailed discussions of Akbar's horoscopes, calculated according to various traditions and methods (including Greek, Indian and Central Asian astrological methods), plus analyses of 'sundry secret annunciations and holy manifestations' and numerological studies of the hidden meaning and significance of the letters composing Akbar's name(s).
19. Originally from the area consisting of present-day north-west Iran, Azerbaijan, Armenia, eastern Turkey and northern Iraq. Bairam Khan himself was born in Badakhshan.
20. Abu'l Fazl Allamī, op. cit., Vol. I, p. 412.
21. Ibid., p. 414, footnote 1.
22. Ibid., pp. 418–431.
23. There appears to be some confusion as to the exact number; according to Beveridge (Abu'l Fazl's translator), three is probably correct.
24. A province in central Iran.
25. Near the Caspian Sea in north-west Iran – about 150 km northwest from Tehran and 160 km south of the Caspian shore.
26. Abu'l Fazl Allamī, op. cit., Vol. I, p. 489.
27. Gascoigne, op. cit., p. 52.
28. Abu'l Fazl Allamī, op. cit., Vol. I, p. 608.
29. Rather than to Lorenzo de' Medici (1449–1492, the de facto ruler of the Florentine Republic in Italy).

30. Mao Zedong's statement on 6 November 1938, given in *Problems of War and Strategy*, Foreign Languages Press, University of Michigan, USA. 1954.
31. Eraly, op. cit., p. 86.
32. Quoted in ibid., pp. 85–86.
33. Ibid., p. 84.
34. Ibid., p. 93.
35. Ibid., p. 73.
36. Although he was, in popular speech, often referred to as Salim Shah.
37. Eraly, op. cit., p. 98.
38. *Qiblah*: The direction of Mecca.
39. Stanley Edward Lane-Poole, *History of India* (in nine volumes), Vol. III, *Medieval India from the Mohammedan Conquest to the Reign of Akbar*, Doubleday, Page and Company, New York, 1906, p. 242.

Chapter 3
Akbar the Great

Larger Than Life

More than four centuries after his death, Akbar the Great (1542–1605) still looms larger than life over Indian history. In spite of the thousands of pages that have been written about him, he remains a somewhat enigmatic and often controversial figure. A brief search on the Internet will show that while the majority of commentators readily admit that he was a great man, he has his trenchant critics too, from both sides of the politico-religious spectrum: many Muslims consider him as a traitor to Islam, while right-wing Hindus often revile him as just another Muslim oppressor, responsible for the death of many tens of thousands of their co-religionists. The truth, as always, is somewhere in the middle, and much more complex than the simplistic stereotypes suggest; it is also elusive and will, regrettably, remain so, as it has become impossible to verify and reconcile the often conflicting accounts of his life.

Be all of that as it may, even his detractors will have to admit that he was one of the most spectacularly successful monarchs the world has even witnessed; and his eventful, often dramatic life story will remain a source of inspiration to many generations to come.

Sahar, Zohr, Shām

In my earlier book, *Akbar's Farewell** (an epic historical novel about Akbar's life and reign, written in the form of a fictional autobiography), I have him divide his own reign in three parts: Dawn (*sahar*); noon (*zohr*); and dusk (*shām*).

'Dawn' is the story of his adolescence, from his enthronement as

*Amaryllis, New Delhi, 2011/2024.

an immature thirteen-year-old, to the time when, against all odds, he managed to take the reins of the kingdom into his own hands. This part describes his evolution from an unruly, spoilt brat to a remarkably balanced, mature individual.

'Noon' spans the next four decades, a period when, in spite of fierce opposition from numerous enemies, everything seemed to be going his way, and when he revealed himself as a remarkably enlightened ruler, well ahead of his time, who attempted to build what one could call one of the world's first 'secular' societies, where people from all walks of life were truly free to worship God or the divine in the way they deemed appropriate.

'Dusk' describes Akbar's final years, troubled by the misconduct of his three adult sons: the two younger ones, Murad and Daniyal, dying at an early age from the effects of alcoholism, and Salim, the eldest and strongest of the three, in open rebellion against him. As will be related in due course, it is to no small extent thanks to the efforts of Salima – his cousin, preferred wife and soul mate – that Akbar succeeded in surmounting these difficulties and securing an orderly succession.

DAWN

The Unruly Boy King

At the time of his father's fatal accident, young Akbar was on his first official assignment: as Humayun's eldest son and crown prince of the empire, he had been appointed as governor of the Punjab. Together with Bairam Khan, his *ataliq* (guardian) and *sipahsalaar* (commander-in-chief) of Humayun's army, the young prince was leading the military operations against Sikandar Suri. Things were going quite well: Sikandar Suri was really no match for someone as deadly as Bairam Khan; it was only a matter of time before the entire Punjab would be pacified.

Late in the afternoon on 27 January 1556, Akbar and Bairam Khan were resting in the imperial army camp on the banks of the Ravi River near the village of Kalanaur (now in northern Punjab, India), when a messenger from Delhi came galloping into the camp, bringing them the message of Humayun's tragic accident.

Bairam Khan, who had been the driving force behind Humayun's restoration to power, now revealed himself as the most capable and faithful servant of the empire. Indeed, as stated earlier, young Akbar and the entire Mughal Empire owed their very survival to the loyalty and competence of this exceptionally talented and principled man.

Bairam Khan acted swiftly. Humayun's death was kept a secret for as long as possible; reassuring messages about his recovery were sent to Lahore; and back in Delhi, a loyal cleric by the name of Mullah Bekasi, who happened to have Humayun's build and the same shape of beard, was dressed up in the imperial robes, and made the usual daily appearance in front of the public from the balcony on the riverside of the fort.

Meanwhile, Bairam Khan moved on all fronts. First of all, he secured the loyalty of his personal rival, Tardi Beg, an influential Turkoman officer, appointing him as governor of Delhi. Next, he wisely resisted the temptation of riding into Delhi right away.

Indeed, at that stage, the Mughal hold on Hindustan was precarious at best. Faraway Kabul was ruled in practical independence by Akbar's half-brother Muhammad Hakim and his guardian, Munim Khan. In Hindustan proper, Humayun's forces did hold Delhi, Lahore and the other main cities, but the fight was far from over, as Sikandar Suri and other would-be heirs of Sher Shah's empire were waiting for an opportunity to strike back.

***

The weeks following Humayun's death were spent in preparation of Akbar's formal accession to the throne. A brick platform was built in a garden at Kalanaur, while astrologers engaged themselves in calculating the most auspicious moment for the enthronement ceremony. It was determined to be exactly at noon, on Friday, 14 February 1556. Three days before, the *khutba* had been read in Akbar's name for the first time in the mosques of Delhi, Agra, Lahore and the other cities of the empire.

The young prince ascended the coronation platform. His first official deed of government was to appoint Bairam Khan, his *ataliq*, as *vakil* (prime minister) of the empire, and to bestow on him the lofty titles of Khan Khanan (lord of lords) and Sipahsalaar I'tizad-i-Daulat Qahira (commander-in-chief of the army, mainstay of victorious dominion).

It all was very impressive, but in spite of all the pompous grandiloquence, the mood remained tense. In the days following Akbar's accession to the throne, Bairam Khan had to intervene more than once to restore discipline. The nobles' loyalty was conditional, at best. Any mistake from the young king's side or any setback in the fight against his enemies, and Akbar's host of followers would quickly evaporate before his very eyes.

Jalandhar

In the course of the following months, Bairam Khan and Akbar continued their military operations in the Siwalik hills, until the monsoon transformed the entire country into a swamp, making swift cavalry actions nearly impossible. Sikandar Suri withdrew further north, deeper into the hills, and the Mughal army moved south towards Jalandhar (now in Punjab, India), where it remained encamped for some five months.

Young Akbar, as usual, spent his time horse riding, hunting, bow and musket shooting, wrestling and practising his fighting skills. Throughout his life, he always would be a very physical man, fond of sports and the outdoors, a crack shot with bow and musket alike, strong like a bull and brave to the point of recklessness. From a very early age, he also showed a truly extraordinary aptitude with animals, elephants, in particular. He was particularly fond of them and handled them with amazing confidence and skill, as if he was one of their regular caretakers.

Bairam Khan also saw to it that his pupil's theoretical education continued. By that time, his teachers had given up all attempts to teach Akbar to read and write, but he very eagerly listened to all kinds of books being read to him by his new teacher, Mir Abdul-Latif of Qazvin, a Persian Sunni who had migrated to Hindustan to join Humayun's service.

Akbar was, as historian Abraham Eraly phrased it, an illiterate savant. Other than signing his own name, he is not known to have written anything, and Jahangir in his memoirs confirms that his 'illustrious father' was indeed illiterate.

This drawback, however, did not prevent him from being a great lover of learning and literature: throughout his life, whenever he had a moment's leisure, he had books of all kinds read out to him, and in his conversations with learned men from all religions, he amazed everyone with the breadth of his knowledge and the quickness of his wit. People who did not know him could hardly believe that a man of such vast knowledge was unable to read.

Panipat

A few more raids against Sikandar Suri and his weakening followers, and Akbar would be making his triumphant entry into Delhi. That was Bairam Khan's plan, and it seemed to make perfect sense. Little did he realize that it would take them nine more months, and a devastating battle against a formidable new adversary, before they would finally enter Humayun's capital.

As has been recounted earlier, Sikandar Suri was not the only one coveting the throne of Hindustan after Islam Shah's death. He was indeed the strongest of the three warring Suris, but the most powerful army leader to emerge from the fracas was not a Suri, but a remarkably talented Hindu general: Hemu.

A dwarfish little man of frail stature and very humble origins, but clever, tenacious and dangerous like a cobra, Hemu or Hemchandra had built himself a truly remarkable career. Born in 1501 (according to some sources) in a lower-caste, poor family, he originally had been eking out a meagre living as a greengrocer in the small township of Alwar (now in Rajasthan) when he started working for the local authorities. From there, he somehow managed to catch Islam Shah's attention, who appointed him as superintendent of the Delhi market. Such was his talent and dedication, that he quickly obtained a series of important additional assignments, including a number of highly confidential police and intelligence tasks.

After Islam Shah's death (on 22 November 1554) and the murder of his twelve-year-old son and heir by Mubariz Khan (Adil Shah), Hemu quickly filled the power vacuum. Adil Shah, an indolent good-for-nothing with no other interests than his own private pleasure, was more than glad to leave all the tedious affairs of government to this grovelling, but discreet and utterly dependable courtier, and appointed him to the position of *vakil*, the highest office in the state.

Applying himself diligently, Hemu grew more powerful by the day. A puny little man, who had never worn a sword and could not even ride a horse, amazingly, he revealed himself to be a talented general and a brilliant strategist, winning no less than twenty-two battles for his master. Outwardly, however, he maintained obsequious politeness to all. He accumulated immense wealth, only to spend it with cunning generosity, gradually buying himself the loyalty of the Afghan amirs. Patiently, he bided his time, determined to take full advantage of whatever opportunity would arise.

And that opportunity did arise when Humayun died, leaving a boy king on the shaky throne of Delhi. Hemu now persuaded his master to allow him to take the army westwards and chase the Mughals out of Hindustan for good.

***

Akbar and Bairam Khan were still encamped at Jalandhar, preparing themselves to resume the operations against Sikandar Suri, when they received the alarming news that Hemu was advancing against them from the south.

After taking Gwalior, Hemu had rapidly marched on to Agra and captured it without a fight, as the commander of the Mughal garrison in that city, Iskandar Khan Uzbeg, had withdrawn towards Delhi to join forces with Tardi Beg, the newly appointed local governor.

One would have expected those two commanders to hold the city and keep Hemu's army occupied until Akbar and Bairam Khan joined them with the main body of the Mughal army. Instead, Tardi Beg panicked. He allowed his vanguard to be slaughtered before his very eyes without intervening, and fled to the northwest, abandoning many fine horses, war elephants and other valuable booty to the enemy. So precipitous was his flight that Hemu, suspecting a ruse, did not dare to follow him.

Hemu entered Delhi in triumph. This was the opportunity he had been waiting for all his life. He distributed the captured treasures and horses among his Afghan nobles, keeping only the elephants for himself. He had coins struck in his own name and held his court under the imperial canopy, calling himself Raja Vikramaditya and donning the dress and adopting the style of the great Hindu kings of old. His Afghan commanders started calling him Hemu Shah, and one can only suspect that his Hindu followers must have been dreaming of a whole new era. The long years of hard work seemed to be coming to an end. He was ready to claim the throne of Hindustan for himself.

***

Bairam Khan was livid when he heard the news of Tardi Beg's shameful retreat. Leaving behind a small force in the Punjab to make sure Sikandar Suri would not be able to come down from the hills in the north and attack from the rear, Bairam Khan and Akbar rode south-east with the rest of the army as fast as they could. A courier was sent to Tardi Beg, carrying orders to meet the imperial army at Sirhind.

One can only speculate as to what might have happened, if Tardi Beg had been wise enough to apologize or at least keep his mouth shut. It is a historical fact that Bairam Khan greeted him courteously, affectionately calling him his *tüqān*,[1] and invited him to participate in the war council, but things went thoroughly wrong in the discussions that followed: Bairam Khan wanted to discuss the battle plan against Hemu, while Tardi Beg kept insisting that the enemy forces were far too strong, that Hindustan was lost, and that the Mughal army had to fall back to Kabul immediately. Bairam Khan then invited him for a private conversation to his tent, went out to wash before the afternoon prayer, and sent in two of his men, who, without further ado, plunged their swords into Tardi Beg's chest.

It has been hotly debated and will always remain a contentious issue, whether or not Bairam Khan had any ulterior motives for this summary execution – he and Tardi Beg had always disliked each other – and whether or not Akbar, who had conveniently gone hunting while it happened, had actually given his permission. The fact remains, that an open conflict inside the Mughal army would have been disastrous. One has to agree with British historian and Indologist Vincent Smith's statement:[2] '*... failure to punish ... Tardi Beg ... would have cost Akbar both his throne and his life.*'

For some time at least, Tardi Beg's execution had the desired effect: There was no more talk of fleeing to Kabul. Nevertheless, the morale of the Mughal troops left much to be desired. Hemu's generalship and the strength of his army formed the subject of many a whispered conversation. As Abu'l Fazl described it in his *Akbar Nāmā*, '*perturbation found its way into the hearts of imperial servants, through the instrumentality of empty-headed babblers, from whom no army is ever free, or rather, there are armies of such* [babblers] ...'

Bairam Khan and the senior officers did their best to counter the growing sense of defeatism. Through a judicial mixture of encouragement, promises, veiled and open threats and emotional appeals to the men's sense of honour and religion, they at least managed to keep an outer semblance of order and discipline.

***

Hemu, who must have been informed about the Mughal troubles through his spies, eagerly seized the opportunity and marched north as fast as he could. In the process, however, he became a little overconfident, which was a mistake against a strategist like Bairam Khan: he sent his heavy guns ahead towards Panipat, escorted by a relatively weak vanguard of ordinary troops. Undoubtedly, his plan was to prepare a defensive artillery position for his army, similar to the one Babur had used some thirty years ago. At Panipat, he would block the Mughal passage, forcing them to turn back and flee, or risk a suicidal frontal attack.

Had he succeeded in this plan, the Mughals would indeed have had no alternative, but to refuse battle and flee further north. Theirs was the smaller army – they would most certainly have been annihilated if they had dared to attack a strong defensive position.

Bairam Khan immediately sensed the danger when his scouts informed him about the arrival of Hemu's artillery at Panipat; he therefore formed a vanguard to ride ahead and seize the cannons before the main body of Hemu's army arrived.

Thus it was done. On 3 November 1556, the vanguard rode towards Panipat, still about 40 km further south, while Akbar and Bairam Khan followed with the remainder of the imperial army. According to Abu'l Fazl – writing many years later about things he never witnessed and which happened when he was only six years old – Akbar led the troops '*with a tranquil mind, an open brow, a prayerful heart, a just intent, a right principle, a wide capacity, a strong hand, a firm foot, a high spirit, a lofty soul, a right plan, a shining countenance, and a smiling lip* [sic!]'.

The next day, scouts came with reassuring news: Hemu's artillery had been taken. The enemy had fled in disarray without offering much resistance.

This was of course excellent news, but it only meant that Hemu could no longer use his artillery against the Mughals, but neither could the Mughal forces use it against him, unless they somehow managed to arrive there ahead of him.

Hemu, who was closer to Panipat than the Mughals, had made the same analysis, and drove his army as fast as he could. It was clear what he was up to: get his artillery back and bring it into position, or at the very least, prevent the Mughals from using those guns against him.

***

On the morning of 5 November 1556, when Akbar's army was still about 12 km removed from the town, scouts came in with the news he feared: Hemu's army had arrived and he was launching a massive attack to get his artillery back. The Mughal vanguard troops were fighting back as hard as they could, but were vastly outnumbered and in dire need of help.

Leaving their slower-moving artillery carts and supply train behind them, Akbar and Bairam Khan hurried towards Panipat.

By the time they arrived on the battlefield, the brave men of their vanguard were on the verge of defeat.

Bairam Khan left Akbar in the rear, with a group of cavalry on the fastest horses – they would be able to keep the young king safe if things were to turn out badly. He himself galloped to the front of the ranks and gave the order to attack.

For some time, the Mughal cavalry onslaught halted Hemu's advance on the flanks.

Yet, despite the initial successes, the battle did not go well. There seemed to be an unlimited supply of fresh enemy troops, and the enemy elephants were remarkably well disciplined, obedient to their mahouts and pushing forward despite many wounds. Slowly but surely, the Mughal flanks were driven back to the centre and their losses began exceeding the enemy's.

Suddenly, the ground started shaking, as the Mughals saw a grey wall of elephants rushing straight towards them: Hemu was moving in for the final kill.

In a last attempt to turn things around or at least slow down the enemy advance and organize an orderly retreat, Bairam Khan ordered as many archers as possible to the front line; thousands upon thousands of arrows were shot slant-wise in the air towards the enemy ranks behind the front line in an attempt to bring disarray to the enemy onslaught.

Initially, it all seemed of little avail: the enemy advance continued, and defeat was now becoming inevitable. Bairam Khan and the amirs began organizing their retreat, creating openings in the rear formations for the front line cavalry to fall back through. Maybe they could still escape with a sizeable combat force and come back to fight another day.

Then, suddenly, for no apparent reason, the enemy onslaught began faltering. Groups of two, four and then ten elephants broke the ranks and abruptly turned around; only moments later, the entire enemy was fleeing in utter panic.

It soon became clear what had caused the sudden turnaround, when a Mughal soldier came back with, strapped to a horseback, what seemed to be the corpse of a bony little man: the great Hemu himself. He had been turned over to the Mughals by his own mahout.

He was still alive, but barely so: an arrow was sticking out the bleeding socket of his left eye. It had been a stray arrow, one of the many hundreds shot randomly in the air to harass the enemy troops in the back. A lucky shot, or, as Abu'l Fazl preferred to put it, '*an arrow from the bended bow of Divine Wrath ...*'

Were history an adventure book, it would be considered bad writing, but this is how it actually happened: the entire Mughal Empire has been founded on one lucky stray arrow. God only knows what Hindustan would have looked like today, if Hemu had stayed a few more paces to the rear.

Bairam Khan drew his sword and handed it to Akbar. It was time for the young king to earn the title of Ghāzī.[3] Abu'l Fazl – who, as stated before, was but a child at the time of the battle and never witnessed it – wrote that Akbar magnanimously refused to kill Hemu, saying that '*there was no honour in slaying a defenceless wounded enemy*'. Like many other such stories, he probably heard this one from the mouths of flattering courtiers and repeated it, in a commendable attempt to demonstrate and exemplify the nobility of his master's character.

It is a great story, but it is, most probably, not true. What would have been the point of Akbar arguing with his guardian, who had just saved his throne, if not his life? And in the state Hemu was in, killing him quickly seemed to be the most merciful thing Akbar could do for him.

Irrespective of whoever struck the fatal blow, Hemu was beheaded without further ado, his head sent to Kabul and his trunk to Delhi, to be hung from a gibbet.

An advance party occupied Delhi, while the main body of the army rested on the battlefield, building, as per their gruesome Mughal custom, towers of enemy heads to commemorate their victory. Two days later, Akbar made his triumphant entry into Delhi, at the head of his troops and the immense booty they had captured, including many hundreds of heavy cannons and war elephants. Humayun's small invasion army had become the largest fighting force on the subcontinent; the Mughals were here to stay.

Mankot

Akbar and Bairam Khan stayed in Delhi for a month; then, they returned to the Punjab to deal with Sikandar Suri, who had come down from the hills in an attempt to seize Lahore. He was soon forced to flee and withdrew to the hill fortress of Mankot (in present-day Jammu and

Kashmir), where he resisted for another six months, hoping in vain for Afghan support to arrive from other parts of the country. On 25 July 1557, exhausted and deeply disillusioned, he surrendered. To his relieved surprise, he was treated courteously and given a fief in Bihar.

The next morning, Sikandar Suri, with a handful of followers and a strong Mughal army escort, left the Punjab forever. He never again caused Akbar any trouble – or, as Abu'l Fazl would have phrased it, he '*never again removed the neck of submission from the collar of obedience*'. He administered his province with commendable diligence and loyalty, until his death, barely two years later.

With him died the last of the remaining Suri kings.

***

The other Suri, Adil Shah (Mubariz), had already met his well-deserved fate further east. Hemu's death had left him utterly helpless; without his iron right arm, his downfall was only a matter of time. Sure enough, around the time Mankot fell into Mughal hands, the sultan of Bengal attacked and crushed Adil Shah's remaining army. Barely three years after butchering his defenceless young nephew, he himself was killed in April 1557.

Thus ended the glorious Suri dynasty: with the execution of an indolent, worthless murderer and the quiet passing of an obedient provincial administrator. It had taken a lifetime of hard work for one strong man to build a powerful kingdom; it took his successors less than twelve years to run it to utter ruin.

Family Matters

On the march to Mankot, Bairam Khan was gladdened by tidings of another nature, from his household back in Lahore:[4] he had become the father of a healthy son, Abdurrahim, who, as will be related in due course, would come to play a major role in the Mughal Empire.

The child's mother came from the family of the influential Khans of Mewat (now in Haryana), and his marriage to her had been one of important political convenience: after the (re)conquest of Delhi, Humayun and Bairam Khan had thought it opportune to marry the two daughters of Jamal Khan, the cousin of Hasan Khan of Mewat, one of the most powerful landowners in the region. In accordance with the generally accepted rules of hierarchy, Humayun had married the elder sister and Bairam Khan the younger one.

The Mankot campaign also saw the arrival of the noble ladies of the imperial household, who had stayed behind in Kabul until Hindustan was safe enough for them to travel. The party included Maryam-Makani Qadasi-Arkani Hamida Banu Begam,[5] Akbar's mother, and several other high-born ladies, including Haji Begam, one of Humayun's other spouses, as well as Humayun's half-sisters, Gulbadan Begam and Gulchihra Begam, and, last but not least, Akbar's charming cousin, Salima Sultan Begam. She was the daughter of Humayun's sister Gulrang,[6] and consequently, a granddaughter of Babur and one of the highest-born Mughal ladies.

From Mankot the imperial court travelled back to the palace at Lahore.

It was not an easy time. Not that there were that many problems – on the contrary, everything was for the best: each day, the Mughal hold on the recently acquired territories was growing stronger. Law and order were re-established, local chiefs and leaders made haste to pledge their allegiance, '*requesting the favour to kiss the threshold of the Sublime Court and* [pay] *homage*', as Abu'l Fazl liked to put it.

Yet, tensions were building at court. On the one hand, young Akbar took disappointingly little interest in the affairs of government; or, as Abu'l Fazl politely phrased it: '*in repose and pleasure, outwardly he wore the guise of one who did not attend to affairs*'. Most of the time, he went hunting, enjoyed himself listening to music in the company of dancing girls and left the day-to-day affairs to Bairam Khan.

And indeed, Bairam Khan, diligent and hardworking as always, readily filled the vacuum, taking charge of everything. Whenever Akbar was around, he would be courteous and obedient enough, but in the young king's absence, he acted as the true head of the empire.

Not surprisingly, this state of affairs did not fail to arouse the bitter jealousy of other courtiers – above all, Maham Anaga, Akbar's ambitious foster mother, and Adham Khan, her rowdy son. The imperial court was quickly turning into a hornets' nest of rumours, insinuations, accusations and complaints; and slowly but surely, this toxic atmosphere would not fail to do its poisonous work on the impressionable young emperor's mind.

***

After a stay of four months and a half in Lahore, the imperial court travelled to Delhi and then to Agra in 1559, halting on the way at

Jalandhar, where two important – if rather controversial – marriages were celebrated. Akbar, not yet fifteen, took his first wife, his cousin Ruqayyah, the only daughter of Humayun's brother Hindal. And Bairam Khan, then in his fifties, married the eighteen-year-old princess Salima[7] – an arrangement that had been agreed to by Humayun himself, in gratitude for the invaluable services rendered; and Akbar kept his father's promise.

Salima was the jewel in Bairam Khan's crown: after a lifetime of faithful service, he was now, quite officially, a member of the imperial family.

Needless to say, this state of affairs did not help to put his many rivals' mind at ease.

Bairam Khan's Downfall and Death

In January 1556, at the time when thirteen-year-old Akbar ascended his shaky throne, he had no safe territory to call his own – only a claim to a stretch of land along the Yamuna and Ganga Rivers, supported by a few garrisons. Five years later, all his father's enemies had been defeated, and law and order had been restored. He ruled over the heartland of Hindustan, including the western basin of the Ganga and Yamuna, as far east as Allahabad, and down to Gwalior in Central India. He also firmly held the entire Punjab, including the city of Multan (now in Pakistan) and the territory between the Indus and the Sutlej Rivers, and a vitally important part of what is now eastern Rajasthan, from the left bank of the Chambal river, up to and including the sacred city of Ajmer, where – then and now – the shrine of the venerable Sufi saint Khwaja Muin-ud Din Chisti (1142–1236) was (and is) honoured by thousands of Muslims and Hindus every year.

All of this had been Bairam Khan's work, and Akbar was honest enough to be grateful to him for it. Yet, slowly but inexorably, the two were drifting apart.

Much has been written about their gradual estrangement, but the reason for it is a combination of two factors: young Akbar's growing ambition on the one hand and Bairam Khan's suspicious nature and strong character, on the other.

Money was involved, as usual. Akbar deeply resented being kept on a leash as far as his own private expenses were concerned. He had no privy purse, and his household was poorly paid, while Bairam Khan's servants grew rich.

Power and status were involved, too. And as Akbar struggled for more autonomy, Bairam Khan grew more and more suspicious about his master's true intentions. In Abraham Eraly's words: '*As the scene changed and Akbar began to slip out of his control, Bairam Khan naturally grew anxious about his position, and that affected his judgement. Once a cool, suave, prudent leader, he now became irritable, brusque and overweening. He saw conspiracies where none existed, insults where none were intended.*'

The first – and worst – incident of this kind occurred rather early in Akbar's reign, during the campaign against Sikandar Suri: two fighting elephants had run into the tent where Bairam Khan, who was ill at the time, was resting. He immediately concluded that it had been a deliberate attempt on his life and could only with great difficulty be persuaded that it had been an accident. Both wisely decided to put the incident behind them, but the tension lingered.

What eventually brought about Bairam Khan's downfall, however, was his dictatorial style. In R. C. Majumdar's *The Mughul Empire*, S. Roy puts it rather strongly:[8] '*Bairam Khan was harsh in temper, overbearing in manner, arbitrary, dictatorial in method, highly ambitious and jealous of power, and would brook no rival. His administration, though efficient, was marked by high-handedness and nepotism.*'

Roy's verdict does seem harsh, but not entirely unfounded. In hindsight, Bairam Khan could and should have avoided the incidents that eventually caused him to fall into disfavour with his young king. At the very least, he should have involved Akbar more in his decisions: time and again, the young king would find himself confronted with decisions that had been taken unilaterally, things that had been done and situations that had been created, which had been forced down his throat and he could do nothing about.

Probably the worst and politically most significant instance of this kind of decision was when Bairam Khan unilaterally appointed a fellow Shia to the position of Sadr-i-Sudur, the highest legal office in the realm. However, despite the outrage this caused among the Sunni courtiers, Akbar chose not to intervene.

It was probably at the time when Bairam Khan unilaterally dismissed Pir Muhammad Khan, a former favourite of his, ordering him to go to Mecca that Akbar realized that things had really gotten out of hand. Bairam Khan may have had ample reason to be displeased with Pir Muhammad Khan – it was certainly true that he was an evil, arrogant and dangerous man – but the dismissal of a senior official without the emperor's prior approval was a blatant lack of respect, if not an outright insult.

A few weeks later, Bairam Khan made what would be his final mistake, when two of Akbar's favourite personal mahouts, both of them low-caste Hindus, were executed on his direct orders. One of them had not been able to restrain an imperial elephant, when it suddenly attacked and killed one of Bairam Khan's animals; the other mahout was executed when the elephant he was guiding along the banks of the Yamuna suddenly dashed into the water and almost overturned the small boat on which Bairam Khan was resting. This time, Akbar had enough of it all. Bairam Khan had to go.

The die had been cast. He had taken one of the most painful decisions of his life: he was about to dispose of the man whom he affectionately called Khan Baba (Daddy Khan), the man who had indeed been like a father to him, and to whom he owed everything, including his life.

It took him several more weeks, though, to work out a plan of action. Indeed, he needed to tread carefully, for Bairam Khan was not an opponent to be underestimated. In devising his plans, he could, of course, count on the support of Khan's many enemies, including his (Akbar's) own mother, his foster mothers Maham and Jiji Anaga, Maham's son Adham Khan, and Jiji's husband Shams-ud Din. Secret messages were sent to Pir Muhammad Khan – who had made his way back to Rajputana after having travelled as far as Gujarat on his way to Mecca, to keep himself ready to return as soon as possible – as well as to Munim Khan back in Kabul.

It was of course suggested that Bairam Khan be executed or assassinated, but Akbar would have none of it. Finally, it was decided that he would be banished, i.e., ordered to go on the Hajj to Mecca.

In the morning of Tuesday, 19 March 1560, Akbar left Agra on the pretext of another hunting trip, with only a small escort, in order not to arouse any suspicion. As prudence dictated, he did take along young Abu'l Qasim, Kamran's son: if Bairam Khan would choose to rebel he would at least not be able to rely on a grandson of Babur to legitimize the uprising. Once outside the city, Akbar headed to Delhi, on the pretext of visiting his mother, who either was or pretended to be ill. A message was sent to the governor of the city to strengthen the defences of the fort and prepare it to receive the emperor.

As soon as he reached the fort, Akbar ordered messages to be sent to all the amirs of the empire, informing them that now he had reached adulthood and he had decided to relieve Bairam Khan of his command and take the matters of government into his own hands.

It is said that Bairam Khan at first refused to believe the rumours about his impending dismissal. When, after a few days, he realized that they were true, his first reaction was to ask for a private audience with his emperor, but Akbar refused to see him. Instead, he sent him an imperial *firman* (edict), thanking him for his many accomplishments and giving him the permission '*to turn his attention to the bliss of pilgrimage*'. He did take care to add some friendly words, assuring Bairam Khan that he was like a father to him and remained dear to his heart, and that he would hand over to him '*whatever extent of land he wished in Hindustan, so that his servants might remit him the proceeds, harvest by harvest and year by year.*'

Rejecting the advice of his close friends and supporters, Bairam Khan refused to disgrace his career by taking up arms against his emperor. Early in April 1560, he left Agra, announcing that he was indeed going on pilgrimage to Mecca. At Nagaur (Rajasthan), he divested himself of his standard and insignia and sent them back to Akbar's court. Dismissing most of his followers except his close relatives and a small army, he proceeded on his journey to the Gujarat sea coast, where he would take a ship to Mecca.

The story would have ended then and there, had the so-called 'harem party' around Maham Anaga and Adham Khan not insisted on what soon proved to be a capital blunder: sending Pir Muhammad Khan with an armed force to trail Bairam Khan and '*pack him off to Mecca*'.

They should have known better. A man like Bairam Khan might accept injustice, but never an insult. Sure enough, when he became aware of Pir Muhammad Khan's approach, he promptly turned around to fight. At the first sight of Bairam Khan's Turkoman horse archers, Pir Muhammad Khan ran like a rabbit.

Much more worried than he cared to admit, Akbar tried to repair the mistake, sending Bairam Khan another *firman*, ordering him to continue on his pilgrimage, but it was too late. The matter would now have to be settled on the battlefield.

Bairam Khan and his small army quickly turned north, advancing into the Punjab. He left his family in the fort of Tabar-e-Hind (in present-day Bathinda), then headed south towards Jalandhar, clearly intent on later taking the important city of Lahore.

Hasty preparations were made, and Akbar left Delhi, sending Shams-ud Din ahead with a strong vanguard, to halt or at least slow down Bairam Khan's advance; Akbar followed with the main body of the army. The unthinkable had happened: the imperial army was marching against Bairam Khan.

Shams-ud Din did not waste any time. Driving his troops forward, he managed to block Bairam Khan's advance near the village of Gunecur near Jalandhar. He sent emissaries, in a last-ditch attempt to convince Bairam Khan to submit, but it was too late: his adversary had decided to stand and fight.

Morale among the imperial army was low. Bairam Khan's fighting force, though vastly outnumbered, was not to be underestimated: its men were excellent soldiers, devoted to their leader and commanded by the best general of their age.

Bairam Khan attacked immediately, preventing Shams-ud Din from deploying any artillery and taking advantage of the understandable fatigue of the imperial soldiers and their animals after the hasty advance. He had divided his small fighting force into two wings: a cavalry vanguard, led by his main lieutenant Wali Beg, and the main group, which he commanded himself and consisted of about fifty excellent fighting elephants, supported by another cavalry force.

Shams-ud Din's vanguard cavalry, though clearly superior in numbers, was quickly routed by the fierce onslaught of Bairam Khan's horsemen. Many imperial cavalrymen turned around and fled without a fight, more out of fear than due to enemy action.

Bairam Khan did not hesitate to seize the opportunity. He instantly attacked the main body of Shams-ud Din's force, which was standing on a small ridge behind a wide paddy field. In an unorthodox but bold move, he sent his elephants up front, in a direct attack through the field, while he and his cavalry came out from behind on the left flank, leaving the field on his right.

If things would have worked out as he had planned them, he just might have pulled it off: Shams-ud Din's army would have been caught in a deadly pincer, its flank would have been cut off and unable to move, while the centre would have been swept away by the elephants.

But luck would have it otherwise. The paddy field happened to be quite deep and its bottom soil unusually soft; Bairam Khan's elephants, advancing only very slowly and sinking almost up to their bellies into the mud, got bogged down. Harassed by clouds of arrows, a number of his leading mahouts died, and the attack faltered.

Shams-ud Din, an excellent soldier himself, was now free to launch a massive counterattack on his right flank.

Bairam Khan had gambled and lost – the battle was over for him. Unless he retreated immediately, his forces, much smaller in number than Shams-ud Din's, would soon be encircled and annihilated. Thanks only to his generalship and the discipline of his men did he manage to get away with the majority of his fighting force, but he paid a heavy price for it. His right-hand man Wali Beg, badly wounded in the battle, and several other trusted officers were taken prisoner, and a number of courageous men died while covering his retreat.

Shams-ud Din chased the fleeing enemy for about 8 km. Then, he prudently abandoned the pursuit and turned back with his army, joining the rest of the imperial forces, which, by that time, were encamped at Sirhind.

The news of Shams-ud Din's victory was greeted with elation. A major battle had been won against the great Bairam Khan! And the euphoria reached a new climax, when Munim Khan (guardian of Akbar's younger half-brother) joined the imperial army with reinforcements from Kabul.

Sumptuous celebrations were held. Shams-ud Din was, of course, hailed as a conquering hero and received lavish gifts, including the robes of honour, standards and kettledrums that once had belonged to Bairam Khan. The office of *vakil* and the title of Khan Khanan, however, were given to Munim Khan – most probably because Akbar did not want to concentrate too much power in the hands of a single courtier.

The prisoners taken on the battlefield were dragged before Akbar, who, contrary to what most attendants expected, did not have them executed, but, instead, had them incarcerated. With the exception of Wali Beg, who died of his wounds in prison, all of them were later pardoned, and, in time, reinstated as officers of the imperial army.

***

Meanwhile, Bairam Khan had withdrawn to the stronghold of Talwara (in northern Punjab, India) in the Siwalik hills. It is there that he finally decided to give himself up.

To Akbar's credit, he treated his old *ataliq* with every possible respect, using his own shawl to wipe away his tears and his own, and inviting him to sit down with him. He then offered Bairam Khan a choice among three alternatives: to remain at court as Akbar's personal adviser, to pick a *jagir* of his own choice, or to continue on the pilgrimage to Mecca. Declining to serve where he had ruled, as Roy aptly put it,[9] Bairam Khan chose the last option.

At peace with the world and himself, Bairam Khan leisurely continued his journey towards the coast of Gujarat, where he would board a ship to Jeddah. Upon arrival in the pleasant city of Pattan, he decided to stay for a couple of days and enjoy the beautiful sights.

On the day of his death, Friday, 31 January 1561, he had been enjoying a boat trip on the scenic Sahansa lake; back on the shore, he was ambushed and assassinated by a gang of Afghans led by one Mubarak Khan Lohani, whose father had been killed in the battle of Machhiwara (May 1555; referred to in Chapter 2).

Abu'l Fazl describes the incident as follows:

> *It appeared as if they had come to pay their respects to him, and so he called them to him. When that villain went up to him, he ... drew his dagger and struck Bairam Khan on the back with such force that the point came out at his breast. Another wretch struck him on the head with a sword and finished him. In such a condition did he, fortunate in his end, depart from this world with the words 'Allahu Akbar' on his lips.*

His body '*lay in the dust and in his blood*' until some local people charitably carried it to the precincts of the tomb of a Sufi saint nearby, where it was given a humble but decent burial.

Thus ended, sadly and unexpectedly, the life of the man without whom the Mughal Empire would never have existed.

Salima Sultan Begam and Abdurrahim at Court

Bairam Khan's camp was ransacked by the Afghan assassins, but his family and their retinue managed to escape to safety to Ahmedabad, where they stayed for several months.

When Akbar heard about their plight, he had them escorted back to Agra, where he married Bairam Khan's widow – and his own cousin – Salima Sultan Begam, and formally took charge of Bairam Khan's four-year-old son Abdurrahim. The young boy would grow up to become the great Abdurrahim Khan Khanan, the highest noble in the empire and one of the most successful and influential officials the Mughal era ever witnessed.

It seems that Akbar, unlike his son Jahangir or his grandson Shah Jahan, was not a very romantic man. While he is known to have had a voracious sexual appetite, particularly when he was still young, it seems he never had a real 'love of his life'. It is, however, well documented that his beloved cousin Salima, in spite of the fact that she did not bear him any children, was clearly his favourite. She was highly influential and would, as will be related in due course, play a crucial role in managing the conflict between Akbar and his successor. Her writings have been lost to posterity, but she appears to have been highly intelligent and exceptionally well-read, as well as an accomplished poetess.

'The Petticoat Government'

Akbar's marriage to Salima marked a turning point in his life: the transition from an unruly, pleasure-seeking youth to the great emperor he would soon turn out to be.

An easy transition, it was not: the period following Bairam Khan's downfall was marked by the desperate attempts of the so-called 'harem party' (Maham Anaga, her son Adham Khan, Munim Khan and Pir Muhammad Khan) to keep the young emperor under their control. They were soon to find out, however, that the era of the indolent and docile boy-king was over for good. In the course of the following eighteen months, a number of increasingly serious incidents and conflicts occurred, which would ultimately lead to their downfall.

The Conquest of Malwa

Akbar's first major confrontation with his supporters occurred at the occasion of the conquest of Malwa* in early 1561. True to his avowed and lifelong principle that '*a king should always seek conquest and war, lest his army become lazy and ineffective*', he had ordered Adham Khan and Pir Muhammad Khan to lead an army southwards and annex the region to his dominions.

At that time, Malwa was ruled by the self-declared 'Shah' Baz Bahadur, the son of a local Pashtun officer who had served under the Suri dynasty, and had come to govern his fief in practical independence

*Malwa now encompasses parts of western Madhya Pradesh and parts of south-eastern Rajasthan.

– if the word 'govern' can be used to describe an indolent life, dedicated solely to sensual pleasure, drinking and music.

The imperial troops advanced, virtually unopposed, to the capital Sarangpur (now in western Madhya Pradesh), where Baz Bahadur attempted to resist them. Deserted by his best officers, he was easily defeated by the imperial forces and put to flight.

Adham Khan and Pir Muhammad Khan celebrated their victory, spilling rivers of innocent blood. Dozens upon dozens of captives were brought before them and slaughtered like cattle, while the two imperial army leaders were cracking jokes. No one was spared – not even women and children, or venerable old Sayyids and Shaykhs with copies of the Holy Quran in their trembling hands.

It is highly unlikely that Akbar approved of all this. Throughout his career, he would only rarely be guilty of cruelty against defeated enemies, much less against innocent civilians. What truly infuriated him, however, was not the bloodshed, but the news that Adham Khan had kept all the captive women and choice spoils for himself, sending only a few elephants back to court at Agra.

Akbar did not hesitate one moment. He drummed up an escort of a few dozen reliable men, and set off to Malwa. Despite the blazing heat of early summer, he moved so fast, that he arrived at Sarangpur ahead of the fast courier a worried Maham Anaga had sent to forewarn her son. Completely taken aback by Akbar's sudden arrival, Adham Khan hastened to make obeisance, but the emperor coldly ignored him, refusing even a drink of water or a change of clothes.

Soon after, Maham Anaga herself arrived in Malwa, spending the next few days doing her utmost to patch things up between the angry young emperor and her impetuous son. Finally, after the booty was returned, Adham Khan was officially forgiven, but, even now, he was arrogant and foolish enough to secretly keep two especially beautiful girls for himself. When Akbar, already on his way back to Agra, heard about this, he halted the march and ordered a search of the Sarangpur palace. Maham Anaga, seized by panic at what would happen to her son if he would be caught stealing from the emperor a second time, then bribed one of the female harem guards to kill the two girls and bury them somewhere. '*Severed heads make no sound*,' she is reported to have said.

Akbar chose to ignore the incident for the time being and continued his journey back to the capital, but his mind was now made up. Relieved of whatever remaining debt of gratitude he still owed his foster mother, he would quietly use the following months to put her and her so-called 'harem party' out of action.

Upon his return, he made his first move: turning a deaf ear to Maham Anaga's pleas, he relieved Adham Khan of his command and called him back to Agra, leaving the Malwa campaign in the hands of Pir Muhammad Khan.

From a military point of view, it was a wrong move, for the impetuous Pir Muhammad Khan soon bit off more than he could chew. He headed further south, taking Bijargarh (now in Madhya Pradesh) – again, with general massacre – and invading the kingdom of Khandesh (now in northern Maharashtra), where Baz Bahadur had taken refuge. He even captured the fort of Asirgarh (now in southern Madhya Pradesh) and pushed forward all the way to Burhanpur (also in southern Madhya Pradesh), destroying and killing everything and everybody on his way, but that was where his luck ran out. His advance was checked by a coalition of three local rulers: Baz Bahadur himself, aided by Mubarak Khan of Khandesh and Tufal Khan of Berar (now in Maharashtra).

Outnumbered, Pir Muhammad Khan now hastily retreated towards Malwa. Having reached the Narmada River after dark, he insisted, against the good advice and repeated pleas of his officers, on crossing it during the night. It proved to be a fatal mistake. In the middle of the river, he was thrown off his horse and drowned – '*the just retribution,*' as the historian Abdul Qadir Badauni later phrased it, '*for the sighs of the orphans, the weak and the captives*'. The imperial army, now devoid of its leader, left Malwa, and Baz Bahadur even managed to temporarily recover his kingdom.

A minor defeat this was for the imperial army, but a major step forward for Akbar, because a potentially dangerous ally of Adham Khan, was now out of the way. The next year, 1562, Akbar would send another army to Malwa under Abdullah Khan Uzbeg, who quickly restored Mughal authority, this time for good.

Baz Bahadur remained a wandering, landless fugitive until November 1570, when he meekly surrendered to Akbar, who, typically, pardoned him and made him a musician at his court.

***

The removal of Adham Khan from active military duty had been Akbar's first move to clip the wings of the 'harem party'; a few months later, he made his second and decisive move, dismissing Munim Khan as *vakil*, and appointing Shams-ud Din in his stead. It was a masterstroke, for Shams-ud Din would prove to be a competent and loyal administrator, while Adham Khan, Munim Khan and Maham Anaga were now reduced to the position of powerless, second-rate courtiers.

With Shams-ud Din's competent assistance, Akbar now devoted himself in earnest to his duties as emperor. Following the example set by Bairam Khan, he made sure nothing escaped his attention, controlling, at random, even the smallest things.

Even more importantly, it was around this time that he started reflecting, quite open-mindedly, about his duties towards his subjects. Following the example of the great caliph, Harun-ar Rashid (763–809), he even started wandering in disguise around the streets and alleys of Agra after dark, informing himself first-hand about the actual living conditions, hopes and aspirations of his subjects. He also had many in-depth conversations with Mir Abdul Latif, his wise and broad-minded teacher, who impressed upon him the concept of *sulh-i-kul*, peace for all: the task of a monarch is to guarantee peace and prosperity for all his subjects, regardless of their religion. The significance of this concept – which would be further developed under Abu'l Fazl's influence – cannot be overestimated: it is thanks to this concept that Akbar would go down in history as one of the modern world's first and strongest proponents of universal tolerance and freedom of worship.

First Pilgrimage to Ajmer and Marriage to the Princess of Amber

It was in this enlightened and pious mood that Akbar – who was and would remain a deeply religious man all his life – decided to travel to Ajmer to pray and meditate at the blessed dargah[10] of the famous Sufi saint, Khwaja Muin-ud Din Muhammad Chishti.[11]

It was the first of eighteen annual pilgrimages that he would undertake to that place of worship, where he would find wisdom, peace and inner balance.

Crossing into Rajputana on his journey, he was greeted by Raja Bhar Mal of Amber (Jaipur), who offered him his eldest daughter in marriage. Akbar gladly accepted, and the wedding was celebrated at Sambhar in January 1562 on his way back from Ajmer. After the ceremony, Man Singh, nephew and adopted son of Raja Bhagwan Das, the heir of Raja Bhar Mal, accompanied the bridal cortège to Akbar's court. Little did Akbar realize at the time that this young Rajkumar (prince) Man Singh, would, together with Abdurrahim Khan Khanan, become his greatest general, who would fight and win dozens of battles for him.

***

It was indeed, in more than one way, a marriage made in heaven. Not only was the princess of Amber to become the highly respected Qadasī Arkānī Maryam-uz-Zamānī (pillar of purity, Mary of the age), the queen-mother of Akbar's first-born son and later successor: this marriage also sealed the mighty Rajput–Mughal alliance that would become the backbone of Akbar's military power and the very foundation of the Mughal Empire.

In itself, there was nothing unusual about Hindu kings offering their daughters in marriage to Muslim rulers as a token of their submission, but Akbar's attitude towards his wife and her family was significantly different. Contrary to the usual practice, he did not ask her to convert to Islam, but allowed her to maintain a Hindu shrine in the imperial residence; he himself would occasionally participate in Hindu religious festivities. Her relatives were not treated as mere vassals, but as true allies, friends and family members, in every respect equal or superior to the leading Muslim amirs. In short, Akbar's alliance to the Rajput house of Amber was the very cornerstone upon which his military might and the internal cohesion of his empire was founded. For the first time in Indo–Muslim history, Hindus could entertain, without any internal contradiction, truly patriotic feelings towards a state ruled by a Muslim king.

Maryam-uz-Zamānī's maiden name was Rajkumari (princess) Hira Kunwari alias Harkha Bai. Surprising though it may be, she is known to most Indians by the nickname Jodhā Bai or Jodh Bai, which means 'lady of Jodh(pur)'. This, however, is clearly a misnomer: the name Jodhā Bai should be reserved for one of Jahangir's wives, namely, the daughter of the so-called '*mota* (fat) *raja*': Udai Singh of Jodhpur.

The Downfall of the 'Harem Party'

As has been related earlier, it seemed an excellent idea to dismiss Adham Khan as an army leader and replace Munim Khan by Shams-ud Din: in two shrewd moves, Akbar had replaced a mediocre *vakil* by a competent and loyal one and reduced an overly ambitious and dishonest foster brother to the position of a powerless, second-rate courtier. Adham Khan and his mother felt deeply frustrated and humiliated by the demotion, and this was exactly how Akbar wanted them to feel.

Yet, he had underestimated the danger posed by them. All this spite and hatred was like a festering abscess, waiting to burst – and so it did.

In the hot afternoon of Saturday, 16 May 1562, at Agra, Akbar was resting in the *zanana*,[12] while Shams-ud Din and other officials were having a meeting in the neighbouring courtyard. Suddenly, Adham Khan walked into the courtyard of the imperial palace with a couple of his personal guards. They went straight to Shams-ud Din, who, unaware of any harm, courteously rose to greet them. Without any warning, one of Adham Khan's henchmen drew out a dagger and stabbed him in the chest. He tried to escape, staggering towards the gate, but the murderers easily caught up with him and struck him dead before he had taken five steps.

To this day, it is not clear why the guards did not interfere. Had they been bribed? Were they at a loss as to what to do, as this was apparently some kind of reckoning between prominent members of the imperial court? The fact remains that they did not intervene, and Adham Khan ran up the steps to the terrace outside the harem unhindered.

It is not clear what exactly he was up to. Most probably, he wanted to kill Akbar as well, or maybe he just wanted to present him with a fait accompli to extort a new appointment for himself; we will never know. In any case, the eunuch on guard had the presence of mind to shut and bolt the terrace door, preventing him from barging into the emperor's private quarters.

Meanwhile, Akbar had been woken up by the noise, and came out of his quarters to see what was going on. An old family servant, in panic, pointed through one of the windows at Shams-ud Din's body in the courtyard.

Without another moment's thought, wearing nothing more than a loin cloth, Akbar grabbed a sword from one of the eunuch guards and went out onto the terrace.

'You son of a *****,[13] what have you done?' he shouted, stepping in Adham Khan's direction.

'Wait a moment, Your Majesty,' he answered, taking hold of Akbar's right arm.

Maybe it was an attempt to overpower Akbar, or maybe he merely tried to prevent him from using his sword, but whatever Adham Khan's intentions, he had clearly picked the wrong tactic and the wrong opponent.

Akbar was only nineteen years old at the time, but strong as a bull, and well trained – very few men could hope to defeat him in hand-to-hand combat. And the insolent attempt to restrain him greatly enraged him. It did not take him much effort to pull his arm out of Adham Khan's grip, but he did not even bother to use his sword. In one swift move, he hit him straight in the face with his fist.

Adham Khan fell to the floor like a sack of flour, bleeding heavily – his nose was broken, and the chroniclers tell us that his face looked as if it had been hit with a mace. Regaining his composure, Akbar then coldly ordered the attendants to bind the assailant's arms and legs with their girdles and to throw him off the terrace.

'He has barged in here, head first,' he hissed, 'so throw him out, head first!'

They obeyed, but in a rather clumsy way: the victim landed on his legs, and although he probably did suffer a number of fractures, the fall did not kill him. Quite deaf to Adham Khan's desperate pleas for mercy, the emperor ordered the servants to drag him up on the terrace again, and throw him off, as many times as needed to kill him. They did not have to do it a third time: he fell on his head; his neck snapped and the brains dashed out of his fractured skull – a ghastly sight, no doubt, but all in all, a swift and rather merciful death for a would-be king slayer in sixteenth-century India.

Akbar ordered the bodies of both the victim and the murderer to be taken to Delhi for burial. Shams-ud Din's sons would later build a tomb for their father near the *dargahs* of Khwaja Nizam-ud Din Auliya and of the divine Amir Khusrau[14] – not too far from the spot where Humayun would later get his final resting place. Adham Khan's body was to be committed to earth approximately 10 km south of there, in a quiet area near the village of Mehrauli, about 300 metres west of the lofty Qutub Minar.[15]

Maham Anaga, who had been lying ill in her chambers for a couple of days, had heard some rumours that her son Adham Khan had landed himself in trouble again; apparently, however, nobody had found the courage to tell her what had happened. Brave and decisive as always, she asked for an audience, and despite her illness, came to beg Akbar's indulgence for whatever her son had done wrong this time.

Upon her arrival, Akbar reluctantly gave orders to admit her in his presence. He did not have the heart to tell her in so many words that her son was dead. Evading her glance, he said, softly, almost apologetically: 'Adham Khan killed our *atga* [foster-father] – we had to punish him.'

The brave old lady found the strength to reply: 'Your Majesty did well,' and retired to her quarters, never to leave them again. She ate and drank very little, and her illness, whatever it was, worsened quickly. Clearly, the will to live had left her. Forty days later, she expired.

Akbar, who had an essentially forgiving nature, paid homage to her body, and ordered it to be taken to Delhi, to be interred near her son. He even accompanied the bier for a short distance on its way, and had a beautiful tomb erected above their graves, at his own personal expense. Whatever one may think of him – he was indeed, as he would have readily admitted himself, by no means a saint – examples of people paying for the mausoleum of their would-be assassins, 'for old times' sake', must be few and far between indeed. The tomb is quite a graceful building, with a classical, Afghan-style dome and an octagonal gallery of twenty-four elegant arches, where the people from the neighbourhood come to enjoy the shade and a quiet stroll in the evening.

A Whole New Kind of Government

With Adham Khan's summary execution, the atmosphere at court changed markedly: everybody tried to keep as low a profile as possible, and anxiously awaited the young emperor's next initiative.

It was of course widely expected and feared that he, in furious and justified anger at Shams-ud Din's murder and the attempt on his own life, would wipe out the entire Maham Anaga clique, guilty or innocent. In any case, it seemed to be beyond any doubt that at least the main conspirators would be duly executed, as a stern, but just, warning to any other would-be rebels. The only question was: how far would the emperor go?

Following the same line of reasoning, everybody was expecting the *atga khail*, or 'foster-father horde', as Shams-ud Din's family was commonly called, to become all-powerful at the imperial court. It will be remembered that Shams-ud Din was the emperor's foster father on account of his marriage to Jiji Anaga, and that his sons therefore enjoyed a position of high prestige and influence at court as the emperor's *kokas* or foster brothers – united with him, as the expression went, '*by a river of milk*'.

But all these speculations proved to be sorely mistaken. All of Shams-ud Din's relatives, after having been judiciously placated with the sight of Adham Khan's bloodied corpse, were given lucrative and important, but far-away fiefs and military assignments in remote border regions.

Rather than rising to absolute power as generally expected, the *atga khail* had thus, tactfully, but effectively, been removed from court.

As far as Munim Khan was concerned, as he had been Maham Anaga's main supporter and trusted friend for many years, and was widely regarded as the real ringleader behind Shams-ud Din's murder, nobody believed there was even the remotest chance for him to escape death.

Similar thoughts must have crossed his own mind, for he attempted a hasty and desperate, if futile, escape westwards, to Kabul probably or Persia perhaps. A detachment of the imperial guard tracked him down without too many difficulties and arrested him in a small village not far from Agra. The soldiers dragged him from a shabby peasant hut and brought him to the imperial residence, trembling with fear.

To his great relief and utter astonishment, however, the emperor did not order his execution, but reinstated him as *vakil* of the empire.

Rather than a mistake or a sign of weakness, this, too, proved to be a true masterstroke. The highest office in the empire was now in the hands of a mediocre yes-man, competent and experienced enough to be an emperor's assistant and messenger, but much too weak and much too scared to harbour any dangerous ambitions of his own. It must be said that he learned his lesson well: for the rest of his life, he served his king with unwavering, exemplary loyalty, in grateful obedience and to the best of his abilities.

***

Akbar's message to the imperial court had been crystal clear: from now on, his word, and his word only, would be law. As the world would soon find out, a great empire was in the making.

NOON

The Enlightened Imperialist

By mid-1562, after Adham Khan's execution, Akbar could have retired, had he wanted to. His grandfather's dominions were his again; he had at his disposal the strongest army in all of northern India; not one of his courtiers or neighbours was in a position to challenge him. He could have looked forward to a life of leisure and luxury.

But that was neither his hope nor his ambition. Akbar, for all his personal charm and enlightened views on government, was an avowed and ruthless imperialist.

He made his first and relatively modest move in February 1564, against the small neighbouring kingdom of Garha-Katanga or Gondwana,[16] which was then administrated by Rani (queen) Durgavati, a descendant of a famous Hindu dynasty, acting as governor on behalf of her young son Bir Narayan. As she had repeatedly refused to submit to Akbar's authority, he sent one of his generals, Asaf Khan, with an army to subdue the kingdom.

Against the Mughals' overwhelming numbers, many of the rani's twenty thousand soldiers deserted her before the first shot was fired. But despite the hopelessness of her situation, she refused to yield and made a gallant stand with the remainder of her forces, near the town of Narhi (near Ballia in eastern Uttar Pradesh). She led her men with remarkable bravery, seated on a mighty war elephant, until she was herself disabled by two arrow wounds. Choosing death rather than disgrace, she stabbed herself in the heart on the battlefield. Two months later, Asaf Khan marched on to her capital Chauragarh (in Madhya Pradesh), where, pointlessly gallant like his mother, Bir Narayan chose to offer battle, and was slain as well.

Towards the end of his authoritative biography, Vincent Smith wrote that '*his* [Akbar's] *ruling passion was ambition. His whole reign was dedicated to conquest. His aggressions, made without the slightest regard to moral considerations, were not determined in any instance by a desire to better the condition of the people in the kingdom attacked*'.[17] Smith's judgement is quite harsh, but not entirely unjustified: Akbar was an absolutist if there ever was one. Neighbouring states were attacked without provocation, and scores of people, whose only crime it had been that they had wanted to stay independent, were ruined, imprisoned, or killed. The undeserved and bitter fate that befell Rani Durgavati and her son is a perfect example of this harsh reality.

Yet, despite the reservations one may – and should – have vis-à-vis Akbar's brutal, unapologetic imperialism, it is impossible to deny that he was a much better human being and a much more impressive king than many conquerors before or after him. Unlike Genghis Khan, Timur, Alexander the Great and so many others, Akbar was a true statesman, moved by an unfeigned and profound desire to further the interests of his subjects, and to rule over them with justice and impartiality. At a time when Europe found itself plagued by fanaticism, persecution and bloody religious wars, he made one of the very first conscious attempts in human history to create a truly 'secular' state, where the sovereign obligates himself to remain neutral and impartial and to treat all his subjects equally. His tolerance in religious matters, which he pushed through in spite of stiff opposition and at great personal risk, was truly exceptional, and that alone merits him a place among the greatest rulers in history.

First Measures vis-à-vis Religious Tolerance

As far back as the days of Adham Khan, during the conquest of Malwa – possibly under the influence of his Hindu wife or her Rajput relatives – Akbar had already issued an explicit ban against the enslavement of the inhabitants of conquered territories, even of prisoners of war. '*We do not wish to lay waste to the lands that are added to our dominions*,' the *firman* stated, '*we do not merely want to conquer them; we wish to rule over them in justice and in accordance with the will of Allah, so that they may prosper. From now on, it is therefore forbidden to deprive the dwellers of those lands of their freedom.*'

Undoubtedly, this was no religious, but merely a pragmatic, measure, much like the ones introduced by Sher Shah Suri, intended to temper the army commanders' lust for plunder and to protect the country's main source of wealth: the people who labour on its soil.

***

It was in 1563, while on a hunting trip near a Hindu place of pilgrimage, that Akbar took his first truly religious measure – at the expense of his own treasury. Discovering that taxes were being levied on every pilgrim, in keeping with the custom of earlier Muslim kings, he immediately forbade the practice throughout his kingdom, on the grounds that no one should be taxed for worshiping the Creator in the way he or she knew best.

The next year, in 1564 – around the time he attacked Rani Durgavati of Gondwana – he went even further, abolishing the infamous *jizya* or poll tax on non-Muslims. Technically, the tax is based on a stipulation in the Holy Quran that the so-called *ahl al-kitāb*, or people of the book – that is to say, people who worship God, without adhering to the Muslim creed – are entitled to protection and remain free to worship according to their own ways, provided they pay the *jizya*. It caused quite a bit of consternation among the orthodox Muslim scholars that the young emperor dared to abolish a tax expressly mentioned in the Quran, but Akbar stuck to his decision: since the *jizya* was a tax imposed on non-Muslims exempt from military duty, and since he did not intend to exempt any Hindus from military duty, he was under no obligation to impose the tax. Clearly, Mir Abdul Latif's influence on the young emperor was making itself felt. It would be his first, but definitely not his last, confrontation with the Muslim *ulama*.

Uzbek and Mirza Rebellions

Akbar's empire in 1564 was vast and wealthy, but landlocked and therefore inherently vulnerable. To secure its borders, and even more importantly, to keep control over the profitable trade with the outside world, it needed – ideally – to annex Bengal in the east and Gujarat in the south-west. And the road to Gujarat could not safely be held without capturing the great fortresses of southern Rajputana: Chittor and Ranthambor. But once those goals were achieved, and Hindustan, Bengal, Gujarat and Rajputana were firmly united under a single government, it would only be a matter of time before the smaller sultanates of the Deccan, and, ultimately, the entire southern tip of the subcontinent would eventually fall into Akbar's hands.

Those must have been Akbar's considerations after the successful conquest of Gondwana in 1564. To his surprise and utter dismay, however, his grandiose plans were to be seriously upset: before long, he found himself fighting in every part of his empire, trying to suppress, among others, the dangerous revolt of his own Uzbek army leaders.

To understand the deeper causes of this rebellion, it is important to remember that the Uzbek war chiefs who had helped Humayun to recover the throne of Hindustan were not really interested in a place to settle down. They were adventurers on the lookout for a war to join, thirsting for excitement and easy spoils. Their alliance with, and personal loyalty to, Akbar's family were essentially temporary and lukewarm at best.

As long as Akbar had kept them in sight, he had them under control; but in sending them off to remote regions, far away from the imperial court, he made the mistake so many other Indian kings before and after him made and would be making, i.e., to underestimate the inherent dangers of physical *distance*: in an environment where communications were slow, distance inevitably bred estrangement, estrangement bred ambition and ambition bred rebellion.

That was how and why a trusted officer and excellent soldier like Abdullah Khan Uzbeg eventually turned into a rebel: back in the days of Adham Khan, Akbar had sent him to recapture Malwa; but instead of calling him back to court, he had allowed him to stay on as the local governor. And sure enough, once the victory was won, distance and greed started exerting their poisonous influence: the soldier became a governor, the governor set up a sumptuous court of his own, and, suddenly, the emperor seemed far away. Abdullah Khan Uzbeg started keeping part of the imperial revenues for himself, and when the first embezzlements appeared to go undiscovered, went on stealing more and more.

Unfortunately for him, he grossly underestimated both the resolve of his young emperor and the perceptiveness and competence of his emperor's minister of finance, Raja Todar Mal, erstwhile an unknown, humble Hindu scribe from Laharpur (now in Uttar Pradesh), but now the most trusted and powerful of the emperor's ministers. The story of Todar Mal's rise to power is as simple as it is telling about Akbar's way of recruiting. Immediately after Adham Khan's execution, Akbar decided to hire a financial expert to rectify the steadily declining revenue stream. His eye fell on old Khwajah Phul Malik, a learned eunuch who had been working for several years at the court of Sher Shah Suri's son Islam Khan, earning himself the lofty title of I'timad Khan[18] on account of his well-deserved reputation as an outstanding and incorruptible administrator.

As usual, Akbar's choice proved to be excellent. The old eunuch and his helpers worked day and night to put the imperial court's affairs in order: counting all the stocks, verifying every revenue account and sending inspectors to the farthest corners of Akbar's dominions. Their efforts soon met with remarkable success: after only a few months, the stream of revenues to the imperial treasure more than doubled. And as it was so aptly phrased in the chronicles: '*A stone fell on the glass of great men's reputations*.' Quite a few local officials were found guilty of embezzlement. All of them were summarily dismissed and heavily fined; a few of them, guilty of the most flagrant outrages, '*had their arms duly shortened*', as Abu'l Fazl put it so eloquently.

Like all wise and capable men, old I'timad Khan had the good foresight to avail himself of the assistance of skilled helpers, regardless of their background. Among them was Todar Mal, the taciturn Hindu scribe who, on account of his outstanding competence and sense of duty, soon managed to attract the king's attention. Exceptionally quick-witted, he showed himself so amazingly proficient with numbers and gifted with such limitless capacity for hard work that very soon, the most delicate and difficult assignments were entrusted to him. After a few years, to the surprise and envy of many, he was appointed as I'timad Khan's replacement when the latter retired from office. Unbelievable as it sounded, it was but the first example of many.

As usual, Todar Mal had been quick to draw Akbar's attention to the growing irregularities in the revenues coming from Malwa and the evasiveness of its governor's letters. And, as usual, Akbar had been equally quick to react: on Monday, 17 July 1564, he left Agra at the head of a powerful expeditionary force and swiftly headed south to Malwa.

He who hastens grips the world: the rebels were taken by complete surprise by Akbar's rapid advance, and he overtook their main force near Mandu (now in south-western Madhya Pradesh) before they had the time to organize their defence.

A number of them were killed; the rest fled in disarray into Gujarat, from where, after a short while, they were thrown out by the local king – to whom Akbar had sent a letter, demanding their immediate expulsion. Their small remaining fighting force disintegrated completely, while Abdullah Khan Uzbeg himself seemingly vanished from the face of the earth. It later appeared that he had made his way to Jaunpur up north, where he placed himself in the service of the local Uzbek officers, who, as will be related in due course, had ventured onto the ruinous path of rebellion themselves as well. But God spared Akbar the grief of having to punish his old comrade himself. He died of natural causes before the Uzbek rebellion was finally – and quite literally – crushed.

***

Having thus defeated Abdullah Khan Uzbeg, Akbar headed back to Agra in early October 1564, looking forward to a period of repose and leisure.

He thoroughly enjoyed the taming of a large herd of wild elephants, which he had managed to capture along the march, and ordered the building of a beautiful hunting palace – aptly called Nagarchain, or Amanabad (i.e., abode of peace) – about 10 km south of Agra. The reconstruction of the fort at Agra was making excellent progress as well.

It seemed to be an auspicious time for him. One of the slave girls in the *zanana* was pregnant and expected to give birth a few months later.

Akbar was overjoyed: until then, not one of his many wives and concubines had ever borne him a child, and he was getting worried, that maybe, for some reason, God had decided that he was to remain childless .... But now, three months before the beginning of the tenth year of his reign,[19] twin sons were born unto him.

He of course ordered grandiose festivities to be held, and publicly announced that the children would be called Hasan and Husain. By choosing two names that are more popular with the Shia than with the Sunni, he again made it clear to everyone that he did not want any strife among the various denominations of Islam.

His joy, however, soon proved to be premature. The two children were underweight, weak and in bad health, and in spite of the physicians' and astrologers' best efforts, died in less than one month. What Akbar had thought to be an auspicious period in his life, now suddenly was full of pain, darkness and menace.

Unfortunately, his misgivings proved to be correct: soon after his two infant sons' death, he found himself confronted with a second and far more dangerous rebellion of his Uzbek officers.

This time, the main instigator was Ali Quli Khan, the competent army leader who had earned himself the title of Khan Zaman at the Battle of Panipat in 1556. With him were his brother, Bahadur Khan; their uncle Ibrahim Khan, governor of Surhurpur (now in Uttar Pradesh); and Iskandar Khan, governor of Awadh (also in Uttar Pradesh).

Having grown suspicious about the Uzbeks after Abdullah Khan's earlier misconduct in Malwa, Akbar had ordered Iskandar Khan to come to Agra – he wanted to probe their intentions and assure himself of their continued loyalty and support.

His suspicions, unfortunately, proved to be justified. Iskandar Khan blatantly disobeyed his orders and fled to Jaunpur, taking Ibrahim Khan with him. Under the leadership of Khan Zaman, the three now broke out in open rebellion, defeated Akbar's local garrison at Nimkhar (in Uttar Pradesh) and besieged the fortress of Manikpur in Awadh.

Akbar immediately sent out Munim Khan to block any further rebel advance to the west, and crossed the Yamuna himself at the head of a large army about three months later, on 24 May 1565.

The situation was grave and Akbar found, not entirely without reason, that he could not afford to take any political risk: he saw no alternative but to order the private execution of his young cousin Abu'l Qasim Khan, the son of Kamran, Humayun's treacherous brother and bitter rival. It was an act of cruel, Machiavellian *Realpolitik*: even though Abu'l Qasim was innocent of any wrongdoing, his death made sure that the rebels could not use him as a figurehead.

The preparations for the campaign being completed, Akbar headed east, joined up with Munim Khan's troops at Kannauj, and immediately marched on to Lucknow, causing Iskandar Khan to hastily flee that city, whereupon Khan Zaman, alarmed at the rapid advance of the imperial forces, abandoned the siege of Manikpur and fled eastwards.

After a few further skirmishes of little importance, Akbar managed to corner Khan Zaman near Allahabad, and prepared himself for battle.

Having seen the might of the imperial army and clearly fearing that he was no match for it, Khan Zaman sent a messenger to Munim Khan, asking for clemency and offering submission.

For old times' sake, Akbar decided to forgive and forget, and extended a general amnesty to the Uzbeks, leaving it to Munim Khan to work out the terms and conditions of the truce. Among others, it was agreed that all Uzbek forces would remain north of the Ghaghara or Gogra River (flowing through present-day Nepal, Uttar Pradesh and Bihar), until Akbar had returned to Agra.

***

While still in the east, he took the opportunity of visiting the Hindu holy city of Benares (aka Varanasi, in Uttar Pradesh) on the Ganga, spending a few leisurely days, fascinated by the sight of the colourful crowds of pilgrims, priests and sadhus, and captivated and horrified at the same time, like so many visitors before and after him, at the sight of the many funeral pyres and the omnipresent smell of scorching human flesh.

His rest and tranquillity were short-lived, however. No sooner had he reached Varanasi, when Khan Zaman's Uzbeks violated the terms of the truce, again crossing the Gogra and menacing the cities of Ghazipur and Jaunpur.

Akbar immediately turned back and attacked them on several fronts, easily routing them wherever he found them.

Again impressed by the speed and the overwhelming force Akbar was capable of, Khan Zaman reopened negotiations for peace, promising complete submission and unwavering loyalty.

It clearly was a mistake, but Akbar allowed himself to be persuaded yet again. His troops were weary of the long and exhausting campaign and the many forced marches, and he himself longed for the tranquillity of Agra. Once again, he forgave the rebels and reinstated them in their positions. On 6 March 1566, he headed back to the capital.

***

Things appeared to go well at first, but it proved to be the lull before the storm. Eight months later, Akbar received the perplexing news that his half-brother Muhammad Hakim had left Kabul and was crossing the Khyber Pass at the head of a large invasion army. And in Jaunpur, the *khutba* was now being read in Muhammad Hakim's name: the Uzbeks had actually invited him to invade Hindustan. It was, so they said, every good Muslim's duty to fight the emperor: he had turned Shia, or maybe even Hindu.

Beside himself with rage, Akbar immediately marched north into the Punjab to repel Muhammad Hakim's invasion. It did not take long before he had his incompetent half-brother on the run: after a few minor skirmishes, all of them disastrous for his forces, he meekly headed back across the Khyber Pass, without offering battle.

Akbar would have pursued him, all the way to Kabul if necessary, but that was quite impossible as long as the Uzbeks had not been dealt with.

To make things even worse: while still in the Punjab, he received an alarming message from Munim Khan, that back in Agra, the Mirzas had broken out in open rebellion.

The Mirzas were, in fact, distant cousins of Akbar's: they descended from Timur's second son Umar Shaykh Mirza, whereas Akbar's line descended from Timur through his third son Miran Shah. Their ancestors had joined Babur's service, but that did not prevent them from harbouring ambitions of their own.

The whole family had joined the uprising: Muhammad Sultan Mirza, Ibrahim Husain Mirza, Muhammad Husain Mirza, Mas'ud Husain Mirza, Aqil Husain Mirza, Ulugh Mirza and Shah Mirza. They roamed here and there, plundering the countryside and, at one moment, even threatened Delhi.

Akbar immediately headed back from the Punjab towards Agra. Upon his arrival, he was relieved to find that Munim Khan had already done excellent work: he had attacked the rebels head on, managing to capture Muhammad Sultan Mirza, and had chased the others into Malwa.

This victory allowed Akbar to focus his attention on the Uzbeks. On 6 May 1567, he left Agra at the head of his troops and marched east.

Finding upon his arrival that the enemy had crossed over to the south bank of the Ganga, with a view to proceeding west towards Kalpi (in southern Uttar Pradesh), Akbar, as Vincent Smith put it, '*displayed his customary zeal and contempt of personal danger*': he made the elephant he was riding swim right across the swollen Ganga. About fifteen hundred brave men crossed the river with him, while the main body of the army, under Raja Bhagwan Das, proceeded further west.

For the last time, the Uzbeks made the mistake of underestimating Akbar. Nearly all of them had been spending the better part of the night carousing and getting dead-drunk, and they had posted far too few sentries. At dawn on 9 June 1567, despite the weakness of his forces, Akbar carried out a surprise attack on their camp.

He had placed musketeers and rockets at three carefully chosen locations, and ordered them to fire no less than half of all their ammunition in the first attack. It all went as he expected: the Uzbeks, bewildered by the devastating fire from all sides, and seeing the imperial standards, assumed that the entire army had fallen upon them, and fled without offering battle. A few kilometres further west, as planned, they ran into the main body of Akbar's troops. There was nowhere to run; all they could do was to surrender or fight.

As Akbar expected them to do, they attempted to break out of the encirclement, concentrating their entire fighting force on the point where they thought Akbar's formation was the weakest: away from the imperial standards, towards the Rajput foot soldiers. It was their last and fatal mistake. The Rajputs' discipline was impeccable; they held their ground, and well-aimed rocket and mortar fire caused deadly carnage in the enemy ranks. A final cavalry and elephant charge finished off the enemy, with very few losses on the imperial side.

***

Khan Zaman had fallen in battle, while Bahadur Khan, who had been captured alive, had been beheaded immediately after the fight.

This time, Akbar was no longer in any mood for clemency. A few of the surviving younger officers, who could still be of use for his army, had their lives spared; the rest were herded together in a circle and trampled to death by his war elephants – killed, as Abu'l Fazl aptly put it, '*under the feet of the elephants, or rather, under the weight of their sins and ingratitude*'. The great Uzbek rebellion, the gravest menace Akbar had to face since Panipat, had been – quite literally – crushed.

In triumph, he headed back to Agra, where he dispatched one of his generals to Malwa to deal with the Mirzas. Upon his arrival, they fled in disarray into southern Gujarat, where, for some time at least, they would find refuge. There were no more rebels left to fight.

Chittor

Other people in Akbar's situation would have been more than glad to take a few months rest, after so long a campaign and so many hundreds of kilometres of marching and fighting in the blazing sun. Not Akbar. He had work to do: he wanted to conquer Gujarat, the rich coastal province that once belonged to Humayun, the province that would give him access to the sea and control over the lucrative coastal trade.

But in order to get to Gujarat from Hindustan, he had to at least control the roads leading to it, and the mighty Rajput fortresses guarding those roads: Chittor and Ranthambor. This, however, was where Akbar's ambitions clashed with Rajput pride.

Through his marriage to the princess of Amber, he had already shown himself to be a respectful and dependable ally; thanks to his tolerance and fairness in matters of religion, he had earned himself the unwavering loyalty and friendship of the powerful rajas of Amber, who had become his closest friends and most trusted allies. Their brave fighting forces had become the backbone of his army. But not all of the Rajputs agreed to follow suit.

The Ranas of Mewar prided themselves as the greatest among all the kings of Rajputana. They were said to have taken a solemn vow: never to 'sully their blood' by giving a princess of their family in marriage to a Muslim.

That in itself did not bother Akbar all that much – he had more than enough wives and could easily do without a Mewari bride. The one thing he did want to secure was loyalty – an unconditional recognition of his sovereignty. And here, their attitude had been half-hearted at best.

Rana Udai Singh, the son of Maharana Sangram Singh (aka Rana Sanga, whom we have come across in Chapter 1), did send his son Sakat to Akbar's court as a conciliatory gesture, but refused to attend on Akbar in person, and even refused to accept an invitation for a friendly visit. There were also consistent rumours that he had been helping the Mirzas in their uprising.

Akbar wasted no time on further negotiations: the treachery of the Uzbeks had made him weary of parleys and treaties. He stayed in Agra no longer than strictly necessary to prepare for the new and major campaign. Allowing himself but little leisure, he did meet a few new artists recently admitted to court. Among them was a talented young poet, named Abu'l Faizi, son of one Shaykh Mubarak; little did Akbar realize that he had just made the acquaintance of the elder brother of the man who, some years later, would become his most influential courtier: Abu'l Fazl.

***

The preparations for the campaign made good progress, and on 9 September 1567, barely two months after the final suppression of the Uzbek rebellion, he marched south into Mewar, heading straight for its capital, Chittor.

His advance through the countryside was unopposed. Rana Udai Singh, a spineless weakling, '*the unworthy son of a noble sire*', as Vincent Smith aptly described him, left his capital under the command of his army leader, Jai Mal, and ran to hide himself deep in the Aravalli hills, where he would found the beautiful lake city of Udaipur (in Rajasthan).

On 23 October 1567, the Mughals pitched their camp – 12 km long – in sight of the western cliffs of Chittor and started preparing themselves for a lengthy siege. The heavy mortars (needed to hammer breaches in the fortress' massive walls) were cast on the spot: it would have been much too cumbersome and time consuming to lug them along.

It was not going to be easy. Chittor is really a heavily fortified, steep cliff, rising abruptly from the surrounding plain, about 400 metres high. Its length from north to south is over 5 km; at its broadest point, it is about 1200 metres wide; at its base, it is no less than 13 km in circumference.

Upon arrival, Akbar ordered a frontal assault from the north-east and north-west, but the defenders were well prepared. Two Mughal attack waves were repulsed with heavy losses, and Akbar had no alternative but to withdraw his troops beyond the range of the enemy guns and to start the encirclement of the hill.

It took him more than a month of hard work before he finally succeeded and had Chittor completely sealed off. As of then, no one could approach, enter or leave it without Akbar's permission. The noose was around Chittor's neck; now came the long struggle to pull it tight.

Direct assaults having proven costly as well as pointless, Akbar's men began the long, cumbersome travail of digging so-called *sabats* – large ditches, protected against enemy projectiles by heavy logs of wood covered with rawhide. The excavation works were executed under the competent direction of Raja Todar Mal and Qasim Khan, the master builder of the Agra Fort. Akbar ordered the *sabats* to be built wide enough for horses to advance through them in rows of ten and deep enough to be ridden through by a man, spear in hand, seated on the back of the largest elephant bull. While this process was, of course, quite time consuming, it would make the final assault much easier and less dangerous.

***

Again, it was painfully apparent that the defenders were determined, well-led, and amply stocked with gunpowder and projectiles. As soon as the *sabats* came within reach of their fire, they did whatever they could to hinder them, pounding them with nearly incessant musket and cannon fire. Despite the movable ramparts used to protect the workers, heavy casualties were inflicted upon their ranks – sometimes over one hundred died in a single day.

In spite of this stiff resistance, the works continued to make steady progress. Every day, the *sabats* wormed themselves a bit closer towards the foot of the hill, like fat, giant snakes, slowly crawling towards their victims, waiting for an opportunity to strike.

As the assailants edged closer to the foot of the cliff, they managed to inflict increasing losses on the defenders. Through loopholes in the *sabat* roof and the movable bulwarks, Mughal musketeers fired incessantly at the defenders on the ramparts, forcing them to take cover. Akbar personally spent several hours every day in the *sabats* himself, firing one musket after the other – he had over one hundred and fifty of them – while his attendants busied themselves reloading. He reportedly did more than his fair share of the killing, which was hardly a surprise: he had been shooting muskets since age five, and countless hunting parties had made him an excellent marksman.

Despite the cover provided by the bulwarks, standing in the *sabats* was quite a dangerous activity. On one occasion, Akbar was nearly hit by a cannon ball that smashed through the *sabat* roof and killed several of his men. But he determinedly refused to move to safety, despite the pleas of his officers to do so.

At long last, one of the *sabats* reached the foot of the hill. Under Qasim Khan's direction, workers began digging a deep shaft, in which gunpowder charges would be set off to bring down Chittor's wall.

Everything seemed to go as planned. The charges were placed, the fuse was lit – there was a massive explosion, causing a landslide, which brought down a part of the wall with it. Only ten paces wide, the breach was not as wide as Akbar had hoped, but sufficient for the storm troops to force their way through. On Todar Mal's orders, they launched a massive assault.

It was a costly mistake. The assailants failed to realize that *two* charges of gunpowder had been placed, both of which, unfortunately, had not gone off simultaneously: as the assault troops were rushing towards the breach, the second charge exploded. A few dozen defenders standing on top off the crumbling ramparts were killed as well, but, by far, the majority of the victims were from the Mughal camp. Over two hundred of Akbar's men, including some of the best and the bravest, perished in the blast. He was forced to call off the attack and had to witness how the defenders quickly repaired the breach and erected new defences. Hearing their mocking laughter and insults, he swore to himself that he would make them pay dearly.

***

The next few weeks were spent in building new *sabats* and in further weakening the defences. However, despite all the hard work and the daily losses inflicted on the defenders, they still showed no sign of weakness.

The days passed by without any real progress being made, and losses on both sides continued to be heavy. Then, in the afternoon of 23 February 1568, the tide finally turned. As usual, Akbar was standing in the *sabat*, when he suddenly saw on the ramparts a tall man in heavy *hazar mikhi*[20] armour, directing the enemy troops, and asked for Sangram, his favourite gun. Akbar squeezed the trigger and saw the man being knocked backwards. The chaos on the ramparts and the frantic yelling and screaming confirmed his suspicion: this had been a very important man.

Less than an hour later, most defences had been deserted and large fires were burning in several places inside the fortress: it appeared that Akbar had killed the enemy commander, Jai Mal. In accordance with the gruesome Rajput code of honour, the leaders were preparing themselves to die – burning their own women and children, lest they should fall into enemy hands.

Akbar now ordered coordinated attacks on several points throughout the night. Musket fire kept the ramparts clear, while heavy mortars hammered the walls and new gunpowder charges were brought forward. Just before the break of dawn, his men had again breached the wall and the assault troops stormed in, thirsting for booty and revenge. Akbar himself followed right after the first attack wave, amidst a large group of battle elephants.

A few thousand enemy soldiers still staged a few valorous, if utterly futile, attacks – more eager, so it seemed, to fall in battle than to win it; and the Mughals, of course, obliged them. After about an hour, the last resistance broke down. A few dozen survivors made their last stand around Patta Sisodiya, Chittor's second-in-command; after a brief struggle, they were all trampled to death under Akbar's elephants.

Most of Chittor's regular soldiers had perished in the battle, but much of the fighting had been done by farmers who had taken refuge in the fortress. Contrary to his usual practice, Akbar ordered the general massacre of all adult male prisoners. Not only had the stubborn resistance and the loss of so many of his best men angered him, but also he wanted to break Mewar's remaining fighting capability. Only a few hundred mercenary musketeers managed to escape, passing themselves off as Mughal troops and driving their women and children bound in front of them, as if they were their prisoners.

***

Akbar ordered Chittor to be vacated, its massive gates to be unhinged and transported to Agra as war trophies and strictly forbade any repairs to its ramparts and defences. It was to remain like it was: dauntingly impressive, but powerless and emasculated, a tribute to the might of its conqueror.

Aftermath: Further Conquest of Rajputana

Udai Singh never again left his refuge in the Aravalli hills, and Akbar let him be: the isolated hill range was of no strategic importance to him and he had much more ambitious plans. After Udai Singh's death in 1572, his son and successor, Pratap (he later came to be called Maharana Pratap), seemed inclined initially to keep the peace, sending his son

Amar Singh to Akbar's court. Like his own father, however, Maharana Pratap refused to come to the Mughal court in person. Further incidents led to new hostilities and to the advent of the Mughal expeditionary force into Mewar, which repeatedly defeated Maharana Pratap's forces and even occupied Udaipur. Maharana Pratap, however, refused to give up. He retreated into the jungle, from where he waged what would now be called a low-intensity guerilla war, retaking lost territories as soon as the Mughal expeditionary force had left them. The situation would drag on until Amar Singh, Maharana Pratap's successor, submitted to Jahangir in 1615.

Maharana Pratap's struggle against Akbar has often been portrayed as a desperate and noble struggle for Hindu independence against the overwhelmingly superior forces of a Muslim invader, but, as most historians agree, it was hardly that. Akbar's expansionism was purely imperialist, not at all anti-Hindu; the backbone of his armies consisted of Rajput and other Hindu fighting forces, led by prominent generals like Raja Bhagwan Das and Raja Man Singh; the Hindu kings of Amber, Bikaner and Bundi were with him, and even Maharana Pratap's own brother Sagaraj Singh. Maharana Pratap's army, on the other hand, included large Afghan contingents. Only thirty years before the fall of Chittor, an earlier Rana of Mewar had marched against the neighbouring king of Malwa in alliance with the Muslim sultan of Gujarat. In other words, the Mewar conflict was essentially one of local rivalries. As Bamber Gascoigne described it: '*Among so many long-established principalities, some Hindu and some Muslim, but all jostling for space, most alliances were made along lines of political self-interest. And the local rivalries helped the Mughal power to expand just as they would later help the British.*'

***

Within months of taking Chittor in February 1568, Akbar laid siege to the equally daunting fort of Ranthambor, held by the Hara clan, vassals of the Rana of Mewar. Luckily, this campaign was a brief and virtually bloodless one: after a token resistance, the occupants surrendered the fort, and Akbar, in turn, offered them exceptionally honourable terms in accordance with his usual carrot-and-stick policy: respect, high rewards and true friendship to those who submitted, but brutal, relentless pressure on those who attempted to resist.

Around the time Ranthambor submitted, the fortress of Kalinjar (now in Uttar Pradesh) – where the great Sher Shah Suri had met his doom – surrendered as well; within three months, the Rajput kingdoms of Marwar (Jodhpur), Bikaner and Jaisalmer peacefully associated themselves with Akbar.

Apart from the remote and insignificant Aravalli hills, all of Rajputana was now firmly under Akbar's control, with his troops able to move about unhindered from Amber to the Thar Desert and from the Punjab to the borders of Gujarat. At barely twenty-six years of age, he ruled supreme.

Ajmer and Fatehpur Sikri

Right after the conquest of Chittor, Akbar headed straight to Ajmer. Eager to show his gratitude and humility before almighty God, he covered most of the distance on foot, and spent several hours in prayer on his knees before the sacred tomb of Khwaja Muin-ud Din Chishti. There was a lot he had to be grateful for, but one thing was bothering him: in spite of his many wives, he still had no living heir. He decided to seek the advice and blessings of a living member of the Chishti order, one Shaykh Salim Chishti, who lived in Sikri, a village on a rocky hill, about 35 km west of Agra. The good Shaykh assured Akbar that his prayers would be answered, and that not one, but three healthy sons would be born unto him.

Barely three months after Akbar had returned from this memorable visit, the imperial court was buzzing with rumours that the princess of Amber was with child. After much deliberation and consultation of every teacher, physician and astrologer he could find, Akbar decided that his pregnant spouse was to go to Sikri, where she and her servants and midwives were to reside until after the delivery. This, so he reasoned, would avail her of the utmost benefit of the saint's orisons.

With great dispatch, a nice house was built for her, spacious and comfortable, on the flank of the hill overlooking the riverbank. As soon as the construction work had progressed sufficiently, she and her retinue moved to Sikri, where, under the protection of the Shaykh's prayers, everything went well. At noon on Tuesday, 30 August 1569, in the middle of the season when the monsoon rains bring life in abundance to the countryside, she gave birth to a remarkably strong and healthy boy, of whom the astrologers immediately predicted that he would grow up to be a just, mighty king of kings, who would walk in his illustrious father's footsteps.

The fortunate mother received the lofty title of Maryam-uz-Zamānī,[21] whereas the newborn prince himself was given the name Salim – Shahzada[22] Sultan Muhammad Salim, to be complete – in grateful recognition of the holy man's prayers and in an effort to ensure his lifelong protection and blessings.

Akbar, however, rarely if ever called his son by his official name: even when he had grown taller than his own father; he would always affectionately call him Shaykhu Baba (little Sheikh).

***

A healthy son and a successor! Akbar was overwhelmed with joy. The successor he had prayed for so ardently was born, at last; the future of the empire was assured.

In accordance with a solemn vow he had taken, Akbar again set out to Ajmer. While escorted, as usual, by an impressive cortège with hundreds of soldiers and richly adorned, mighty war elephants, he covered the entire distance – 365 km – on foot.

He arrived in Ajmer on 2 March 1570, and stayed there until shortly before the celebration of the fifteenth anniversary of his enthronement, spending his time in prayer and administering justice and charity. Then, he decided not to return directly to Agra, but to travel to Delhi instead and pay his respects at Humayun's tomb, a sublime monument, commissioned and financed by one of Humayun's widows.[23]

From Delhi, the imperial cortège unhurriedly made its way back to Agra; Akbar, as usual, amused himself with grandiose hunting parties. Back in Agra, he celebrated the birth of the second of the three healthy sons the good Shaykh had promised would be born unto him: Shahzada Murad had beheld the first light of day at Sikri, on Wednesday, 7 June 1570.

At Sikri, once again. It could, so Akbar thought, hardly be a coincidence. His mind was made up: he would take up residence in that most blessed place, so that its auspiciousness might continue to protect him and his family. The piteous village of Sikri was to become the glorious Fathabad (city of victory) Sikri. Before long, the sleepy little town of yore would change beyond recognition: on the rocky ridge, where there had been nothing but wilderness, structures such as palaces, mosques, courtyards, towers and gates would be rising up, like young greens in the monsoon season. The Khari Nadi, the local seasonal river, was dammed, and the ensuing lake formed a wonderful water reservoir for the growing city.

Two more carefree, leisurely years slipped by, nearly unnoticed. But new conquests were around the corner.

Gujarat: The First Campaign

Gujarat .... Its unfettered independence had been a thorn in Akbar's flesh for quite a long time, but now, he finally saw his way clear to add it to his dominions. Indeed, the kingdom had fallen prey to utter chaos and anarchy. The rebellious Mirzas, driven out of Hindustan, had made themselves masters of the southern part of the territory, whereas in the north, Muzaffar Shah III, the nominal king – himself a prince of doubtful legitimacy, as Vincent Smith aptly put it – had become a mere puppet in the hands of adversarial nobles who had partitioned the country among themselves.

One of them, I'timad Khan, cornered by an alliance between Muzaffar Shah and a nobleman named Sher Khan Fuladi, sent Akbar a urgent message, begging him to intervene and reclaim the throne of Gujarat, which once, however briefly, had belonged to Humayun.

This was all the encouragement Akbar needed. To conquer Gujarat was his right; it was, as the Americans would later phrase it, his manifest destiny. Thus, on Wednesday, 2 July 1572, the imperial army left Sikri and headed west.

En route, in the sacred city of Ajmer, it gave Akbar great pleasure to supervise the arrangements for yet another imperial birth: one of the ladies in the *zanana* was with child.

She and her retinue were installed in the house of the venerable old Shaykh Danyal, himself one of Khwaja Muin-ud Din Chisti's successors and the most prominent attendant of the sacred shrine. If the child was a boy, he would be called Danyal, in honour of his esteemed protector.

***

For the attack on Gujarat itself, a powerful force of ten thousand horse was to ride ahead, while Akbar would follow about two weeks later with the rest of the army. The strength and mobility of this advance guard and the distance between his two fighting forces would allow him to keep fully abreast of the strength and whereabouts of the enemy forces, and adapt his battle plans accordingly.

On 12 August 1572, the vanguard rode out of Ajmer; on 1 September, Akbar himself marched forth at the head of the remaining troops.

***

Apart from an altogether insignificant incident in southern Rajputana, where he had to crush and exterminate a band of rebels – loyalists of the Rana of Mewar, no doubt – who had made the fatal mistake of trying to hinder his vanguard, his advance into enemy territory was quite uneventful. In fact, the whole journey seemed more a leisurely excursion than an arduous army campaign.

One day, while the army was hunting to replenish the supply of meat for the troops, Citr Najan, Akbar's favourite cheetah, was chasing a deer, when, suddenly, a ravine appeared in front of them. The deer leapt into the air and jumped across. To the troops' delight, the cheetah, in its eagerness to catch its prey, did not even slow down before the forbidding obstacle, but cleared the ravine with a lightning jump and, going on at the same breathtaking speed, caught and killed the deer. It was, so everyone acknowledged, a very good omen.

A good omen it was, indeed: only a few days later, Akbar received the news that, on 9 September 1572, Danyal, his third son, had been born back in Ajmer. The child was in excellent health; Shaykh Salim Chishti's prophecy had been fulfilled.

Akbar did not return to Ajmer to pray at Khwaja Muin-ud Din's shrine – there was a war to be fought and the advance guard counted on his support – but did decide to strike camp for a few days, spending many hours in prayer at the local mosques and organizing splendid feasts in celebration of the birth of the new prince. Generous gifts were distributed to all the people in the area; as Abu'l Fazl phrased it: '*... the coin of liberality was poured into the lap of the world.*'

Akbar further ordered that as soon as Danyal would be one month old, he was to be sent to Amber, and entrusted to the care of Raja Bhagwan Das' spouse – yet another sign of the bonds of friendship and loyalty that united him to his Rajput allies.

As the imperial army neared the Gujarat border, the reports were highly encouraging indeed. Muzaffar Shah, the ruler in Gujarat, struck by panic on hearing about the approach of the mighty imperial army, had, head over heels, deserted his capital Ahmedabad, leaving his former ally Sher Khan Fuladi in charge of its defence. The latter, however, deserted the city immediately thereafter. He was now heading south, to the region of Surat, where, no doubt, he was hoping to find new allies.

***

Akbar ordered the army to proceed straight on to Ahmedabad, but first sent Raja Man Singh with a body of troops in pursuit of Sher Khan Fuladi's two sons: according to his informants, their father had sent them to the area of Pattan to bring their family and goods to places of safety; they were now heading south to rejoin their father. As expected, Man Singh routed their force without too much trouble. The two brothers managed to escape in the wilderness, but their valuable baggage fell into Man Singh's hands.

On 7 November 1572, Akbar himself crossed the Gujarat border and marched triumphantly into the city of Pattan, hailed and cheered by the local people as their liberator.

For a few days, he struck camp before the gates of Pattan, and went, together with young Abdurrahim, to pay his respects at Bairam Khan's tomb nearby; the imperial army headed further to Ahmedabad.

On the march, Akbar tasted the satisfaction of accepting the submission of the fugitive king, Muzaffar Shah – his scouts had found him, hiding in a field, scared to death. A few days later, I'timād Khan and his allies came to make their submission as well. It seemed that, at least for the moment, there were no opponents left in northern Gujarat. On 20 November 1572, Akbar marched in triumph through the gates of Ahmedabad, without a single shot being fired.

Provisional arrangements were made for setting up the government of the new province: Akbar appointed his foster brother Aziz Koka as governor of the territory north-west of the Mahi River,* whereas I'timād Khan, whom he wished to give the benefit of the doubt, was made responsible for the southern part.

After a few days, on 8 December to be precise, Akbar left Ahmedabad and headed south towards the coast, to the port of Khambhat (Cambay), where, for the first time in his life, he saw the sea. Deciding to stay on

*The Mahi has its source in present-day Madhya Pradesh. After flowing a bit through Rajasthan, the river enters Gujarat and flows into the Arabian Sea.

and relax for a few weeks, he even went on a boat trip, when alarming reports compelled him to resume his campaign.

Ahmedabad and the north seemed to be under control well enough, but further down south, the Mirzas – Ibrahim Husain in particular – persisted in their rebellious ways, determined, so it seemed, to defy Akbar. Ibrahim Husain was marauding around Baroda (Vadodara), barely two days on foot from Ahmedabad, practically under Akbar's nose. Muhammad Husain still held the important port of Surat in the south, and Champaner, east of Baroda (about 50 km away), was occupied by Shah Mirza.

***

Akbar had always been a daredevil: his courage bordered on the verge of recklessness at times. In the days of Adham Khan, for instance, on the return journey from Malwa, he had killed an attacking tigress, on foot and singlehandedly, reportedly with just one blow of his sword. On another occasion, on a hunting trip, he had personally led the charge against a gang of armed robbers, driving his elephant right through the wall of the house where they had taken cover – taking no less than seven arrows in his shield. Many times, and with remarkable prowess, he had tackled enraged elephants and calmed them down.

Now, however, in his indignation and youthful impetuousness, he almost made a fatal mistake. Rather than taking his time and crushing the Mirzas one by one, as he could have done quite easily, he insisted on dealing with the three of them at once.

On reaching the outskirts of Baroda, he dispatched one of his generals with about half of his army towards Surat, near the mouth of the Tapti River. Another force was to head east and take Champaner.

Akbar himself stayed near Baroda, with little more than a personal guard –two hundred horse, all in all – to protect him and his staff.

But when he learned that Ibrahim Husain and his gang had been spotted nearby, moving north, no doubt in an attempt to escape the clutches of the imperial army, he did not hesitate for one moment, and headed as fast as he could to the Mahi River, to cut off their escape.

His forces were, of course, much too small to give battle to any opponent worthy of that title, but he stubbornly refused to hear his officers' desperate pleas to wait for reinforcements.

Upon reaching the banks of the Mahi, they found that the enemy, over one thousand strong, had already crossed the river, and was camping in the small town of Sarnal. Against his better judgement, Akbar attacked immediately. Without any further scouting or preparation, and without even giving any command, he drove his mount through the ford in the river and scrambled up the steep bank on the other side, forcing Man Singh, Bhagwan Das, Todar Mal and the others accompanying him to do the same.

Ibrahim Husain, upon seeing this wild bunch crossing the river and approaching the town, hurried out of it from the other side, looking for space to deploy his superior force. Like many other Gujarati towns, however, Sarnal was surrounded by a maze of narrow roads and tiny fields, all fenced with thorn bushes and prickly pear cactus – more unsuitable terrain for a cavalry battle was hardly imaginable.

This state of affairs led to two consequences. The most important and advantageous one was that the enemy was unable to exploit his numerical superiority and move around to encircle Akbar's force. On the other hand, the fight amidst this maze of bushes and thorns bore no resemblance to an orderly battle; it was little more than a vulgar, man-to-man street fight between two rival gangs.

Man-to-man scuffles, indeed. Behind the front – or so he thought – Akbar was looking for higher ground from where to better direct the battle, when suddenly, he found himself face to face with three enemy troopers.

It is not clear whether they realized who was in front of them, but from his shining armour and the magnificent caparison of his horse, they must have guessed that he was quite an important man. Keen on plunder and booty, they fell on him. He managed to fend off the first attack when, suddenly, one of his assailants was hit in the stomach by a Rajput spear: Raja Bhagwan Das had come to his aid.

The two remaining enemies realized that they now stood two against two. They quickly turned around and made haste to save their skin; Akbar and Baghwan Das, on their part, were prudent enough not to take any further unnecessary risk and returned to their troops.

The battle, meanwhile, had been taking a favourable turn for Akbar. In the fighting inside the maze, the opposing bunch of marauders, man for man, proved to be much inferior to Akbar's elite troops. After their front men had been cut down like grass, the next row of men was seized with such panic that they turned around and fled, hindering the others in their advance. That, in turn, led to further chaos and confusion, which Akbar's men did not fail to exploit, chasing the gangsters wherever they went and cutting them down by the dozen. Ibrahim Husain himself, however, managed to escape under the cloak of darkness.

The next morning, Akbar's group returned to camp and reunited with the reinforcements arriving from Champaner. The two hundred men who had fought so valiantly were showered with rewards, and Raja Bhagwan Das was decorated with an amir's banner and accorded his personal kettledrums, an honour never before bestowed on a Hindu.

***

The Battle of Sarnal (21 December 1572) has been hailed as one of Akbar's most glorious victories; and it indeed witnessed remarkable feats of bravery. Objectively speaking, though, it was maybe the worst military blunder of Akbar's reign, a wholly unnecessary act of recklessness, which could easily have cost him his life. His whole empire could have ended then and there, in that insignificant skirmish, because of his stubbornness and daredevilry; and several good men, including Raja Bhagwan Das' own brother Bhupat, paid for this vainglory with their lives.

Chroniclers and poets may love pitched battles and great deeds of valour, but a wise king knows that what counts is not battle, but victory.

***

With most of the Mirzas gone from the area – or so Akbar thought – only Surat remained to be conquered. At dawn on the last day of the solar year (1572) – a uniquely auspicious moment, according to the astrologers' calculations – Akbar left Baroda and leisurely travelled south, hunting and administering justice on the way.

Eleven days later, he reached the outskirts of Surat, where he joined the men of his vanguard, who, he was pleased to find, had not been idling away their time: the area had been successfully pacified, the city surrounded and its supplies cut off. The only thing left to do was to smoke the enemies out.

Sure enough, after six weeks, the defenders were forced to capitulate. Much to their surprise and relief, Akbar spared their lives. Only the garrison commander – a former officer in Humayun's army – had his tongue cut off.

The taking of Surat would not be worthy of further mention were it not for Akbar's first encounter with the Portuguese. Akbar had just started the siege operations against Surat, when he was informed of the arrival of a strong war fleet in the port of Daman, a Portuguese trading post and stronghold on the southern border of Gujarat. Emissaries were sent, and it soon appeared that the intentions of the Portuguese were friendly. The Mirzas had sent them a request for help under the pretence that Akbar was marching upon Daman. Upon their arrival, however, they quickly realized that the Mirzas were a spent force, and clearly did not want to get caught up in a war that was not theirs. Recognizing Akbar's suzerainty over Cambay – the name they had given to Gujarat – they expressed the hope that they could live in peace with the king of Hindustan.

Akbar, for his part, had no problem with a few trading posts on the coast, and was, in fact, quite taken with and intrigued by the Firanghis ('Franks', i.e., Europeans). The peace treaty was quickly agreed to and signed: the Mughals would not attack the Portuguese coastal settlements and the Firanghis would neither interfere in the ongoing hostilities nor try to expand any of their settlements inland; their warships would continue to protect the Muslim pilgrims on their way to Mecca. It is, incidentally, quite remarkable that, for over a century, Portuguese warships dominated the entire Arabian Sea between the Strait of Hormuz and the Indian west coast; Muslim pilgrims on their way to Mecca could not travel overseas unless they procured themselves a Portuguese passport – duly stamped with crucifixes and images of Jesus Christ and the Holy Virgin.

The further conquest of Gujarat posed no problems. Surat capitulated in a matter of weeks, and up north, Aziz Koka, Akbar's foster brother, inflicted a crushing defeat on the last remaining enemy army in the area. Muhammad Husain Mirza, Shah Mirza and a few survivors fled to the Deccan. Peace and calm had returned to the region – or so it seemed to Akbar.

The Second Campaign in Gujarat

On Thursday, 2 April 1573, Akbar started out on the long journey back to Sikri, which, so he decreed, would henceforth be named Fathabad (city of victory). Soon, however, it would be called Fatehpur or Fathpur Sikri in popular parlance, and Akbar, apparently, was quite taken by the new name. Places in India with names ending in '*bad*' (say, Ahmedabad or Moradabad) have been founded or conquered by Muslim rulers, and names ending in '*pur*' refer to Hindu origins. Akbar's capital, however, would be special: it would be a truly Hindustani city, uniting Hindu and

Muslim building styles and combining, in its name, a Muslim concept with a Hindu ending.

After all those hectic and strenuous months of war, Akbar was very much looking forward to the leisurely life at court, but his return to Sikri was rather significant for another reason: on the very day of his triumphant return, amidst the interminable series of congratulatory speeches by enthusiast courtiers and flattering sycophants of all sorts, he made the acquaintance of a humble Shaykh, who had been allowed to present himself at court, through a letter of recommendation from Akbar's foster brother Aziz Koka.

Mubarak of Nagaur was his name, and he was accompanied by his two eldest sons: Abu'l Faizi, whom the emperor already knew as a talented poet and employed at the imperial court since the days of Chittor, and another, rather chubby young man, not much older than twenty. Little did Akbar realize that this young man was to become his most important minister and adviser: Abu'l Fazl.

But the late-night conversations about God, truth, goodness and politics would have to wait, for alarming reports began coming in from Gujarat: the region was again aflame with an unexpectedly violent and dangerous new insurrection. Muhammad Husain Mirza had come back from the Deccan with a large army; his hordes had invaded the area of Surat and occupied Cambay, chasing out the local imperial garrisons. Together with Sher Khan Fuladi's sons and a local Gujarati warlord named Ikhtyar-ul Mulk, he was now threatening Ahmedabad itself.

What was Akbar to do? The Gujarati invasion army had been disbanded; most troops had returned to their *jagirs*. To call them back, to reconstitute the forces and equip an entirely new invasion army would take several weeks; and the march back down to Gujarat, at the very least, another month or so. Ahmedabad was more than 800 km away – trading caravans needed two full months to cover that distance.

There clearly was no time to be lost. The empire stood to lose the entire Ahmedabad garrison, and Aziz Koka's life was in danger. In a matter of two days, Akbar hastily assembled a striking force: barely three thousand cavalry; not nearly enough, but all hand-picked, battle-hardened, excellent men and generously equipped at the imperial treasury's expense.

Well-meaning friends and advisers implored him to wait, but he wanted nothing of it. '*The hooves of my own horse will be the first to cross the Gujarat border*,' he swore, making sure to repeat this oath several times in front of the troops.

Thus it was done. Akbar along with his troops left Fatehpur Sikri on Sunday, 23 August 1573, speeding through the countryside despite the infernal heat and humidity, covering over 80 km per day. Barely nine days later, he was standing on Gujarat's soil.

He sent scouts down to Ahmedabad, to inform Aziz Koka: the imperial expeditionary force would press on as fast as possible and attack the enemy's rear; this would allow Aziz to break through the encirclement and crush the rebels between hammer and anvil.

Unfortunately, however, it did not quite work out that way. Aziz, suspecting an enemy ruse to lure him into the open, stayed safely behind Ahmedabad's ramparts. The enemy, on the other hand, did not take any chances. Hearing the rumours about the advent of an imperial army, Muhammad Husain Mirza left his ally Ikhtyar-ul Mulk behind to block the gates of Ahmedabad with five thousand men, while he rode out, at the head of fifteen thousand, determined to check Akbar's advance at the Sabarmati River.

It must have been quite an unpleasant surprise for Akbar to descry in the distance, on the other side of the river, not the imperial standards, but the detested red banners of the Mirzas, and a strong enemy host, complete with dozens of war elephants.

Impetuous and stubborn as he was, however, he refused to listen to prudence or reason; he drove his horse through the river and ordered the attack, even though there was no sign yet of Aziz and his men and even though the enemy clearly outnumbered his forces, five to one at least.

The rest is history: it was quite a pitched battle, but against all odds, the much better-trained imperial troops won – collecting over two thousand enemy heads on the battlefield against a loss of barely one hundred of their own.

***

But unlike at the Battle of Sarnal, Akbar's decision to attack was not merely a matter of impetuousness or daredevilry. He simply *had* to attack before the enemy had the chance to fully draw out his own troops. Even more importantly, he had to lure him into a fight on the narrow stretch of flat land near the bank of the river: when a large army is forced to fight on a narrow, restricted battlefield, its numbers are an impediment rather than an advantage, because they will slow it down and hinder it in its movements.

And perhaps even more decisive in this case was the difference in the fighting spirit and ability of the men on either side. Akbar commanded a small but effective fighting force of hand-picked, battle-hardened soldiers, each and every one of them devoted to their emperor. The Mirza army, by contrast, impressive though it looked, was nothing but a bunch of hoodlums out for plunder: adventurers, robbers and mercenaries – nothing more.

Akbar divided his troops into four fighting forces: Turkoman horse archers on both flanks; heavily armed, unflinching Rajput shock troops in the centre. Behind the front line on both flanks, he positioned his best marksmen, ordering them not to fire at random into the enemy host, but to carefully target the enemy leaders and their bravest soldiers. Around his own person, he kept a bodyguard of two hundred of the best men on the fastest horses, enough to escape unharmed if things would turn against him.

As mentioned earlier, it was a pitched battle. Akbar's men, though far better and braver than the enemy, were initially pushed back and nearly overwhelmed by the enemy's larger numbers. To make things worse, Akbar's horse got hit by a musket bullet and collapsed under him. This setback very nearly cost him the battle: for a moment, his men thought he had been killed, and the Mughal battle lines started to falter. Fortunately, he was soon back in the saddle of another horse, just in time to prevent a complete rout. Seeing him alive and well, his men attacked with renewed courage and, after some time, Akbar's strategy finally started bearing fruit: most enemy leaders had been killed, and the Rajputs were now making deep, bloody inroads into their ranks.

Muhammad Husain Mirza, realizing that his army was on the verge of collapse, pushed forward to encourage his men, when, suddenly, one of his elephants, seized with panic as a result of an exploding rocket, wreaked havoc in its own rearguard. The ensuing pandemonium marked the end for him: his battle lines collapsed completely. Everywhere, his men were fleeing in disarray; they were being slaughtered by the hundreds by the victorious Mughals. Muhammad Husain himself, wounded in the melee, was captured alive.

The battle was over. Most of Akbar's men were resting by the river bank, apart from a few who had been assigned the task of collecting enemy heads, digging graves and building funeral pyres for the fallen Mughal heroes.

Suddenly, a few of Akbar's scouts signalled that another army was approaching.

Akbar first thought it was Aziz Koka and his garrison, but for the second time that day, he was in for a most unpleasant surprise: this was the other enemy army under Ikhtyar-ul Mulk, who, probably alerted by an emissary, had come to his ally's aid. Akbar quickly had Muhammad Husain beheaded, and ordered the battle lines to be formed.

His men, fortunately, remained calm; taking their positions, they advanced towards the enemy.

The enemy soldiers, from their side, were seized with panic, horrified at the sight of Muhammad Husain's bleeding head on a Rajput lance, and the tower of heads in the making in the background.

They did not even try to put up a decent fight: even before Akbar's men had reached their front lines, the entire enemy host had been transformed into a panic-stricken herd of sheep. Akbar's men butchered them with virtual impunity – he probably did not lose a single soldier in the entire engagement.

***

Ikhtyar-ul Mulk desperately tried to save himself, but Sohrab Turkman, one of Akbar's best scouts, spotted him, hunted him down, and, as Abu'l Fazl phrased it so elegantly, '*relieved his shoulders of the burden of his head*'.

Thus, after barely a few hours of fighting, the rebellion was totally crushed. There was a brief moment of panic when, to the men's bewilderment, a third army arrived at the scene, but this time, it was Akbar's own Ahmedabad garrison under Aziz Koka.

Akbar and his men had themselves a great feast on the river bank. As for the enemy, this time, the Mirzas had tried Akbar's patience once too often. He personally ran his spear through the man who had slain Raja Bhagwan Das' brother in the battle of Sarnal and ordered the summary execution of all the others.

***

Akbar stayed in Gujarat no longer than strictly necessary. Leaving the governorship of the province in the hands of Aziz Koka, he gave Todar Mal the special assignment to busy himself with the organization of revenue and tax collection – a task in which, as usual, he would acquit himself admirably. Only a few weeks later, the incoming revenue from Gujarat would swell, from the disappointing trickle it had been before, into an impressive and incessant stream of wealth, with which Akbar could amply fund his further plans and ambitions. The province was finally his.

Barely three weeks later, on 5 October 1573, spear in hand, Akbar rode through the gates of Fatehpur Sikri, amidst the cheering crowds. He had been absent from his capital for forty-three days, all told.

It was the fastest and one of the most impressive military campaigns in Indian history. Never had so complete and decisive a victory been won in so little time against so distant and powerful an opponent.

Campaign in Bengal and Bihar

Gujarat was not yet fully under Akbar's control, when the situation in the east, in Bengal and Bihar in particular, suddenly demanded his urgent attention.

Up to that moment, those territories had never been a primary concern of his. Traditionally, they had always been more or less dependent on the sultans of Delhi; that situation did not change when Akbar came to power and defeated Sikandar Suri: the Suris who ruled over Bengal made haste to swear allegiance to him.

In the ninth year of Akbar's reign, power in Bengal was seized by the Afghan general Taj Khan Karanani, a former army leader of Sher Shah Suri; however, both he and his successor and younger brother, Suleiman, were sensible and prudent enough never to provoke Akbar and fully recognized his authority. All over Bengal, the *khutba* was read and coin was struck in Akbar's name and sumptuous gifts were sent to the imperial court on a regular basis.

When Suleiman died (in early October 1572) – much regretted by his subjects, the chroniclers say – the problems started. Suleiman's elder son, Bayazid, who had succeeded him, was murdered a few months later by Afghan army leaders, who raised his treacherous younger brother Da'ud to the throne.

Da'ud, '*a dissolute scamp who knew nothing of kingship*', as Vincent Smith described him, thus inherited his father's vast treasure and powerful army, but not his prudence. Taking advantage of Akbar's absence, he assumed all the dignities of independent royalty, ordering coin to be stamped and the *khutba* to be read in his own name. Soon, he pushed the insolence further, attacking and destroying the imperial frontier fort of Zamaniya in the Ghazipur district (now in Uttar Pradesh).

When Akbar heard about these disturbances, he ordered Munim Khan, who had stayed behind in Agra during Akbar's absence, to chastise the rebels forthwith.

Munim Khan hastily assembled a striking force and marched east, towards Patna. After the first skirmishes, he was approached by Da'ud's chief minister Lodi Khan, who, with lavish gifts, flowery compliments and solemn oaths of friendship and submission, sought to placate him. Munim Khan, well into his seventies and weary of the hardships of travelling, was more than happy to end hostilities, and granted peace on exceedingly lenient terms.

When Akbar was informed about this development, he immediately sent the more level-headed Todar Mal to the region, with additional reinforcements. The events that followed soon proved him right: Da'ud, demonstrating the viciousness of his nature, rewarded his faithful minister by confiscating his goods and having him executed, and entrenched himself in the fortress of Patna. Akbar's men had to start all over again.

Munim Khan, ashamed and angered, laid siege to the city. Soon thereafter, however, realizing that his force was not quite up to the task and, fearing that he would provoke Akbar's anger if the siege dragged on too long, he sent the emperor a message, imploring him to take personal charge of the campaign.

So Akbar did. On Tuesday, 15 June 1574, he left Agra at the head of a powerful army, accompanied by his two main Hindu generals, Raja Bhagwan Das and Raja Man Singh. The monsoon season being at its height, all the rivers were dangerously swollen. Nevertheless, not wanting to waste any time, he insisted on travelling by boat: this allowed him to speedily transport the cannons and other heavy material, which otherwise would have gotten stuck in the soggy mud of the rain-soaked roads.

A couple of weeks later, he reached Varanasi on the banks of the Ganga River, where he stayed for three days, deeply fascinated, once again, by the ancient city's frantic hustle and bustle.

He proceeded from there to anchor near Saidpur, about 50 km away, where the Gomti flows into the Ganga. On the same day, he was joined by the rest of the army, which had travelled overland. The ladies and children were escorted to safety in Jaunpur, while Akbar himself advanced at the head of his army to the infamous ferry at Chausa, where, thirty-five years ago, his father had been defeated by Sher Shah Suri. This time, however, the omens were much better, for, upon arrival, he received the happy tiding that the fortress of Bhakkar in Sindh had just been added to his dominions.

Apart from the loss of one of his prize elephants, he managed to bring the army safely across to the southern bank of the river and proceeded to Patna, where he arrived on Saturday, 3 July 1574.

***

It must have been quite a painful surprise for Da'ud to suddenly see the imperial army, complete with heavy cannons and war elephants, setting up camp near his gates. Never before in the history of Hindustan had a major battle been fought in the middle of the monsoon season: it was thought impossible for a large army to cover any large distances before the end of October. And yet, here was the emperor …

After careful scouting of the surroundings, Akbar decided to first take the small fortress of Hajipur on the other side of the river, as this appeared to be of vital importance to the supply of the enemy garrison. The detachment he sent to accomplish this task did excellent work: despite the difficulties caused by the wild and dangerous river – over 4 km wide in that season! – and the tough resistance of the defending Afghan garrison, Akbar's men successfully stormed the fort. The heads of the enemy leaders were thrown into a boat and brought back to Akbar, who, of course, did not fail to forward them to Da'ud, '*as a hint of the fate that awaited and in due course befell him*', as Vincent Smith aptly put it. Along with the heads, Akbar sent Da'ud a personal message, challenging him to meet him in a man-to-man combat.

As was to be expected, Da'ud declined. That same night, he and his garrison sneaked out of the city and fled, as fast as they could, back to Bengal. Akbar personally chased the fugitives all the way up to Daryapur (in southern Bihar). They managed to escape, but he did return with a fabulous amount of booty, including two hundred and sixty-five prize elephants.

***

With Bihar (including Patna) now firmly under his control, Akbar decided to return to Delhi, leaving an army of twenty thousand men under Munim Khan and Todar Mal to complete the annexation of

Bengal. The border towns fell in quick succession, and, after the Mughal scouts had taken out the enemy defences, Munim Khan marched triumphantly through the fortified Teliyagarhi Pass, right into the Bengali capital Tanda, which he took, with little enemy resistance, on 25 September 1574. Da'ud now fled into Odisha, while the Mughal forces continued their advance, easily establishing imperial authority in Satgaon, Burdwan (both in present-day West Bengal) and Ghoraghat (in present-day Bangladesh).

After some months, however, tensions began growing within the Mughal camp. The soldiers, exhausted after the long and strenuous campaign in the heat and humidity of Bengal's marshes, were desperate to get back home, and morale among the army leaders was not much better. Todar Mal faced immense difficulties in convincing the aged and weary Munim Khan to leave the relative comfort of the Bengal capital and pursue the campaign into Odisha.

***

Through his informants, Da'ud must have heard about the growing battle weariness and discord in his opponent's army: he saw his chance and marched against the slowly advancing Mughal troops, his army clashing with theirs near the village of Tukaroi (now in Odisha).

Munim Khan found himself compelled to engage the enemy before he was fully ready for the battle. The result was that his fighting force, consisting almost entirely of cavalry, did not have enough artillery to support it. Da'ud's general, Gujar Khan, cleverly exploited this drawback and opened the battle with a massive elephant charge. His strategy very nearly worked: the Mughal vanguard and centre were completely scattered by the irresistible mass of charging elephants; and Munim Khan himself, severely wounded, barely escaped with his life.

Defeat would have been inevitable had it not been for Todar Mal's tenacity and skill. Leading the Mughal left wing, he wheeled around the flanks of the attacking elephants, killing several enemy mahouts and wounding many of the huge and bulky animals. He then fell on the enemy with such vehemence that the right wing was routed and driven off. The rest of the Mughal troops now took heart, regrouped and launched an all-out counterattack.

It was the death of Gujar Khan that decided the fate of the battle. The Afghans fled in disarray, and the Mughals, eager to avenge the losses they had sustained at the outset, pursued and slaughtered them by the hundreds. To paraphrase Abul Fazl's words: '*Munim Khan's wounds and lacerations were healed by the balm of conquest.*' He ordered all the prisoners to be brought before him, and '*had their bodies separated from their souls*'; the collected heads, so it is reported, served to build *eight sky-high minarets* on the battlefield.

Da'ud and the surviving Afghans fled to the fort of Cuttack (also in Odisha) where, on 12 April 1575, he submitted to Munim Khan, handing over his nephew as a hostage.

Mun'im Khan, eager to put an end to the strenuous campaign, allowed himself to be talked around, and Da'ud again got away with a treaty offering overly generous peace terms, including the governorship over much of Odisha.

Todar Mal, smelling deceit and foul play, openly opposed the treaty and refused to sign it. He would soon be proven right.

***

A few weeks later, Munim Khan headed north to quell some disturbances in the Ghoraghat region. Ignoring the advice of his officers, he insisted on moving his capital from Tanda to the ancient capital Gaur, which, so he had heard, abounded with the finest buildings. Unfortunately, the persistent rumours about pestilence in that region proved to be true. So many hundreds perished that the living no longer bothered to bury the dead; they just threw their comrades' corpses into the nearby Ganga River.

Mun'im Khan, gravely ill himself, retreated to Tanda, only to die upon arrival there on 23 October 1575.

***

Pending the arrival of new instructions, the soldiers appointed a new leader among themselves. The new commander, however, was not strong enough to maintain discipline. In utter disorder, the imperial army retreated to Bhagalpur in Bihar.

Da'ud, who, owing to Munim Khan's ill-considered leniency, had been left in command of substantial forces, did not hesitate to again take advantage of the situation; he reoccupied all of Bengal, including Tanda and the Teliyagarhi Pass. It was his last and fatal mistake.

When Akbar got word of the vexing news, he sent Khan Jahan, governor of the Punjab, to deal with the situation. At Bhagalpur, Khan Jahan intercepted the retreating imperial army; with the able help of

Raja Todar Mal, who had arrived from Fatehpur Sikri carrying Akbar's personal instructions, he managed to bring the soldiers back to do their duty.

Khan Jahan reinvaded Bengal and, to Da'ud's surprise and dismay, quickly recovered the important Teliyagarhi Pass. Joining forces with Muzaffar Khan, governor of Bihar, he engaged the enemy near Rajmahal, and after a pitched battle, defeated and captured Da'ud.

This time, Da'ud's promises and pleadings were of no avail. When Akbar was barely one day's march outside of Fatehpur – he had decided to travel to Bengal and take personal charge of the campaign – he had the great pleasure of receiving his enemy's severed head. He had it put on a stake, and returned in triumph to the capital, where great feasts were organized, and, to put it in Abul Fazl's words, '*waves of largesse quenched the thirst of the needy*'.

Bengal was finally Akbar's – although imperial authority remained mainly confined to the cities. On the countryside, local Hindu and Afghan landlords would, to a large extent, continue to lay down the law for many more years. And it would be in Bengal's marshes that, only a few years later, the most dangerous rebellion against Akbar's authority would break out.

Maharana Pratap

Before Da'ud finally met his doom at Rajmahal, Akbar also found himself compelled to deal once more with his old enemy, the Rana of Mewar.

As has been related earlier, Udai Singh had fled to the Aravalli hills, where he set up a new capital, and Akbar had let him be – at the time, the conquest of wealthy Gujarat was of much greater importance and urgency to him – and Udai Singh had meekly stayed in Udaipur until his death in 1572, without giving Akbar any further trouble.

Udai Singh's son and successor, Pratap Singh, however, had inherited more of the pride and the fighting spirit of his forefathers than his father. As S. Roy put it, '*race feeling taught him to hate the foreigners, ancestral pride to despise them, and high martial spirit, his grandfather's legacy, to resist them*'.[24] Slowly but surely, he started to recover large stretches of the land that once belonged to his ancestors.

In April 1576, Akbar sent Raja Man Singh with an army to deal with Pratap Singh. About three months later, on 21 June 1576, his advance was opposed by Pratap Singh's forces at the entry of the Haldighati Pass.

Pratap Singh and his men fought with remarkable valour. Wave upon wave charged the imperial lines with utter contempt for death. But despite their bravery and the few hundred casualties they managed to inflict on Raja Man Singh's expeditionary force, they were no match for the firepower of the imperial army, with its many field cannons and gun swivels mounted on the backs of camels and elephants. Pratap Singh, though seriously wounded, managed to escape to the nearby hills, saved by his swift and faithful steed Chetak: the exhausted imperial cavalry horses were unable to catch him.

Despite the victory, Akbar was greatly vexed when he learnt that his enemy had managed to escape. And as has been related, Pratap Singh never gave up. Although he was forced to retire deep into the wilderness, and one by one, his strongholds fell into Mughal hands, later in his life, during the thirteen years that Akbar transferred his capital up north to complete the conquest of Kashmir (in 1586), he again managed to recover much of his lost territory. His war with the Mughals would end only when thirty-nine years later, in 1615, his son and successor, Amar Singh, would submit to Akbar's son and successor, Jahangir.

Ibadatkhana and Debates on Religion: The Infallibility Decree

Supreme lord and master of a vast and mighty empire, Akbar enjoyed a period of relative calm. Outside of the many hours he still kept devoting scrupulously each day to the affairs of state, he finally found the leisure to occupy himself with his favourite pastimes: religion and philosophy.

Akbar had always been a deeply religious man. It is well documented that, throughout his life, he spent several hours every day in prayer and meditation, usually around or before dawn, sitting on a large flat stone in a lonely spot. But he was also a rationalist, deeply interested in – not to say obsessed by – religious truth. '*Discourses on philosophy have such a charm for me, that they distract me from all else,*' he once confessed in public. '*I sometimes have to forcibly restrain myself from listening to them, lest I should neglect the necessary duties of the hour!*'

In January 1575, he ordered the construction of the Ibadatkhana (house of worship), which was to be a sacred meeting place dedicated solely to the study of God, where the most learned scholars of Hindustan and beyond would be invited to join him in studious reflection on the divine mysteries.

***

At the outset, only Muslims were invited for discussions. There were four groups:

- the amirs or leading nobles;
- the ulama, learned specialists of Sharia law;
- the Sayyids, descendants of the Prophet Muhammad through his daughter Fatimah and Ali; and
- finally, to phrase it in the words of Abu'l Fazl, '*Sufis of clear heart, absorbed in beatific visions*': a diverse group of shaykhs, faqirs and other holy men, who by virtue of their pious life and studies, were reputed to have attained a special communion with God.

But if Akbar hoped that the meetings would bring the participants to more profound insights and consensus, he was to be sadly disappointed.

At first, everybody was allowed to go and sit wherever he pleased in the building. This led to such acrimonious quarrels over who should take precedence over whom that the emperor found himself obliged to assign separate quarters to each group. A semblance of peace had returned, but the bickering about precedence at the meetings was only a foretaste of the squabbling and the strife that were to come.

As was to be expected, the verbal duels soon started in real earnest, with bitter arguments and accusations flying back and forth between Sunni and Shia. The atmosphere became so heated that the emperor ordered them to speak in turns, without interrupting each other, but this move hardly helped in soothing the frayed tempers.

After some time, the emperor grew tired of it all. He asked the participants to refrain, for the time being, from further debates on the Sunni–Shia divide and invited them to instruct him in what he hoped would be a less controversial subject: Sharia law and jurisprudence. That was of no help either, for he soon grew bored of the legalistic trivia, which, in his opinion, had little to do with true religion and the will of God.

It has been postulated that it was then and there, in the course of those heated debates, that Akbar lost his faith and ceased to be a true Muslim. That, however, is not entirely accurate. Akbar never formally renounced Islam, neither publicly nor privately, and whether or not he was still a Muslim when he died, depends, as shall be argued later, on one's definition of Islam. In late 1575, he allowed several of his female relatives – including his cousin and favourite spouse, Salima Sultan Begam – to leave the safety of the imperial court for several years and undertake the hazardous voyage to Mecca; upon their return in 1582, he revered with conspicuous respect and devotion the Prophet Muhammad's petrified footprint, which the ladies had brought back to court. It is also a well-documented fact that he donated large sums of money from the imperial treasury to pay for the pilgrimage (Hajj) of poor Muslims and that he deeply yearned to become a Hajji himself; his courtiers could only persuade him with great difficulty that God required him to stay with his subjects.

***

It is true, though, that the debates in the Ibadatkhana did change him profoundly, in more than one way. It was there that his personal outlook on religion took its final shape: tolerant, free-thinking and eclectic, bordering on the heretical. Those personal views and insights, in turn, ended up estranging him completely from religious authority in general and from the court ulama in particular. Akbar, an absolutist par excellence, found it increasingly difficult to accept any source of legal authority next to his own. On 2 September 1579, he made his final move against the ulama, obtaining from them a famous official declaration (Mahzar), which has been referred to by historians as the so-called *infallibility decree*. The name is perhaps a bit misleading, but the text – skilfully drafted by the erudite old Shaykh Mubarak, probably aided by his brilliant son, Abu'l Fazl – did determine that Akbar, as the just ruler (Sultan-i-Adil) was higher than the highest *mujtahid* (authority on law), and therefore could make final and binding decisions in case of any conflicting views. The decree also empowered him to issue new and binding rules, provided they were in conformity with the Quran. It was a masterstroke: from now on, he was, by and large, free to act as he pleased.

***

The inability of the various Muslim sects and jurists to reach an agreement on any issue had made Akbar even more interested in the insights, beliefs and practices of other religions. By the end of 1578, the Ibadatkhana had become a true religious parliament, where not only Muslims, but also Hindus, Jains and Parsis (Zoroastrians) were invited. In this respect, he appears to have taken a distinctly rationalist stance.

'*I do not wish to take a single step on the path of faith, unless it be lit by the torch of reason,*' he is reported to have stated. It is also quite telling that he refused to be convinced by any story of a miracle as 'proof' of the truth of one or another denomination: '*Wondrous occurrences are seen in every religion,*' he claimed, and added: '*People everywhere tend to confuse the unexpected and the unusual with the miraculous.*'

While, as stated earlier, he never renounced Islam, Akbar became more and more of an eclectic free-thinker, who was interested in, and influenced by, the insights, beliefs and practices of all religions. For hours on end, he would listen to the teachings of Parsi *mubids* (fire priests), Jain monks and Hindu teachers.

Akbar also became increasingly intrigued by what he had heard about Christianity. Near the end of December 1578, he sent an emissary to Goa (where the Portuguese had set up a base), carrying an official request to send '*a delegation of learned men with books*' to Fatehpur Sikri, as, so he stated, he wished to be instructed in their faith.

The imperial emissary arrived in Goa few months later, and the letter he was carrying was received with understandable elation. Hasty preparations were made and three Jesuit priests set sail for the port of Daman on the southern border of Gujarat, from where they travelled overland to Fatehpur Sikri.

As the eldest of them was taken quite ill with a persistent and rather severe indisposition of the bowels, the padres made but slow progress. Then, at long last, early in the evening of 28 February 1580, two of them finally arrived at the imperial court, to be followed a few days later by their ailing colleague.

The emperor, who had been impatiently awaiting their arrival, received them with every possible honour. So eager was he to see them that he had them brought to his presence immediately.

He was much taken with the presents his visitors had brought with them. Of particular value to him was a beautiful painting representing the Blessed Virgin Mary; he took it in both hands with great respect, bowed and placed it above his head, and ordered it to be fixed high on the wall in his private quarters. High, the painting had to be placed, as it would, so he explained, be quite unbecoming for him to look down upon the Blessed Virgin.

The padres then presented him with the precious and world-famous Polyglot Bible, a work of exceptional scholarship, printed by Christopher Plantin of Antwerp (in present-day Belgium), containing the Christian holy scriptures in five languages: Hebrew, Aramaic, Syriac, Greek and Latin. Akbar took each of the eight volumes in his hands, respectfully kissing them and placing them on his head. He then asked which volume contained the *Injil* (i.e., the Gospel). They pointed it out to him, upon which he again took that particular book in his hands, kissed it again, and placed it over his head.

***

As was customary with important visitors, Akbar ordered lavish amounts of gold to be handed to the padres as a welcome gift. To his surprise, however, they politely but firmly declined to accept anything other than food, shelter and simple sustenance, explaining that accepting anything else would be contrary to the solemn vow of poverty they had taken. Greatly fascinated by his visitors, Akbar ordered that they be provided with ample and comfortable living quarters, worthy of the highest-ranking ambassadors, and, without them even asking for it, assigned to them a spacious room, which they were free to furnish as a chapel.

The weeks came and went, and as was to be expected, the presence of the Firanghi padres and the growing influence they seemed to have on the emperor became the subject of almost every conversation at the imperial court.

But the emperor did not seem to care. On the contrary, he would seize every occasion to visit the padres or to invite them to his presence, paying them great respect on every occasion, even though he clearly did not always agree with what they said or believed. Each time he entered the chapel, he would remove his head gear, kneel down and make the sign of the cross as the Jesuits had taught him, showing great reverence for the crucifixes, pictures, relics and all the other religious objects and ornaments and praying in front of the crucifix or the sanctuary lamp.

Not unexpectedly, rumours and speculations about his imminent conversion to the *Isawi* faith (i.e., Christianity) started spreading like wildfire. Understandably impressed and pleased with these signs of deep and sincere reverence, the padres, too, must have thought that it was only a matter of time before the emperor would convert to their faith. They were, however, to be sadly disappointed. The first Jesuit missionaries left in 1582, after a stay of almost three years, without having accomplished anything. They were to be followed by a brief second mission (1591–1592) and a third, more permanent one (from

May 1595 onwards). By that time, however, it had become clear that the missions were much more important from a diplomatic than from a religious perspective: while Akbar allowed the Jesuits every freedom to build their churches and to try and win converts, their successes remained disappointingly limited – which, of course, had everything to do with their failure to convince the emperor himself.

What neither the Jesuits nor their Muslim adversaries seemed to realize was that the harder they tried to win the emperor's favour, i.e., the more radical and fanatic their arguments, the less convinced he was. He was looking for the truth; they wanted to teach him their doctrine. He wanted to unite, conciliate and bring people together; they only wanted to accuse, condemn and exclude others. He wanted to free people's minds; they only wanted to subjugate them.

***

Akbar no longer believed that any particular religion could lay claim to the truth. Under the influence of kindred, free-thinking spirits, above all, that of the erudite old Shaykh Mubarak and his brilliant son Abu'l Fazl, he began dreaming aloud about a cult that would surmount all differences and peacefully unite all religions, and about a role for himself, not only as a political, but also as a *spiritual* leader of the entire population.

His religious practices soon became more and more openly eclectic and unorthodox. Under Hindu and Jain influence, he became increasingly averse to the killing of animals, to the point of breaking off hunting parties, adopting a vegetarian diet and strictly regulating the slaughter of animals. He was also very much taken by the fire symbolism of the Parsi *mubids*: a sacred fire was established in the palace, and at least by early 1580, he openly prostrated himself before it and the sun.

Predictably, Akbar's unorthodoxy provoked much fear and resentment among the more conservative Muslims. It is hard to imagine that he did not sense the impending danger, but if he did, he chose to ignore it – probably assuming that no one was strong enough to challenge him. It very nearly cost him his throne.

The Great Uprising

When in February 1580, towards the end of the twenty-fifth year of his reign, Akbar was informed that a number of local zamindars in Bengal were refusing to pay their taxes, he was not overly alarmed.

Little did he realize, that only a few months later, he would be facing the most dangerous rebellion of his reign, with powerful enemies rising up in arms against him in the three corners of his vast empire: Bengal and Bihar in the east, the Punjab in the north-west and Gujarat in the south-west.

It all began with what looked like a simple tax collection issue. Suspecting that the governor of Bihar, Muzaffar Khan Turbati, was possibly a bit overzealous or heavy-handed, Akbar sent Raja Todar Mal to appease the parties involved and remove the causes of discontent. But a few weeks later, truly alarming reports started reaching Fatehpur Sikri. All conciliation attempts were unsuccessful, and, every day, new zamindars were joining the ranks of those who opposed Akbar.

To make matters worse, the newly appointed *qadi* (Muslim judge) of Jaunpur, Mullah Muhammad Yazdi, had the audacity to issue a fatwah, condemning the emperor's *bidah* or 'religious innovations'.

The rebellion against Akbar, thus legitimized, spread like wildfire, into Bihar, Odisha, Ghazipur, Varanasi and Allahabad, and the outnumbered local imperial garrisons suddenly found themselves confronted with an all-out war.

The beginning of its campaign against the rebels was an outright disaster for the imperial army. The Bengali rebels crossed the Ganga at Rajmahal, where they joined forces with their comrades from Bihar. They defeated the local government forces led by the brave Muzaffar Khan Turbati, who was captured and put to death, after what reportedly was the worst imaginable torture.

Raja Todar Mal, now in peril, with forces much too small to take on the enemy, was, of course, unable to avenge the unfortunate governor's death. But despite the grave danger, he staunchly refused to flee back to the safety of Fatehpur Sikri and retreated to the fortress of Munger (in Bihar), where he and his men were besieged by the rebels.

***

Akbar was getting ready to head east himself, when he received an even more disturbing dispatch: the rebels had started reading the weekly *khutba* in the name of the ruler of Kabul, his half-brother Muhammad Hakim – a worthless drunk, to be sure; but, conveniently, an orthodox Muslim …

Gone were Akbar's lofty musings and his grandiose plans: what had started as a rather trivial dispute over taxes and local autonomy had now assumed the pretence and legitimacy of jihad against his throne. He hastily conferred with his leading generals. Where should he attack first? On the one hand, the greatest military threat clearly lay in the east: vast and rich territories had fallen into rebel hands, and many of them were experienced army commanders. On the other hand, the greatest danger to the throne actually loomed across the Khyber Pass: if Muhammad Hakim managed to get his hands on the treasures of Lahore, Delhi or Agra, Akbar's position would have become untenable.

Clearly, Akbar needed to deal with both threats at the same time. He ordered one of his generals, Amir Shahbaz Khan, to march east with all his troops, and sent an urgent dispatch to his foster brother Aziz Koka to join Shahbaz Khan as soon as possible with another strong contingent, relieve Todar Mal and occupy the strategic Teliyagarhi Pass to contain the enemy.

Man Singh was sent westwards to secure the Punjab.

The events that followed soon proved the soundness of Akbar's strategy. Encouraged by the support of the Bengali rebels, Muhammad Hakim indeed prepared for war. Two scouting expeditions in December 1580 were repulsed with relative ease by the imperial border garrisons; a few weeks later, however, Muhammad Hakim himself attacked in force, with his entire army.

He crossed the Indus and headed straight towards Lahore, where his advance was brought to an abrupt halt, thanks to Raja Man Singh's staunch resistance. Muhammad Hakim, who clearly had counted on a general uprising in his favour, was sadly disappointed to find that nobody in the Punjab was prepared to join him: not the Rajputs, not the Sikhs, not the local Muslims. When he then learnt that Emperor Akbar himself was not safely occupied in faraway Bengal as he had hoped, but was actually advancing against him, he beat a hasty retreat. Indeed, such was his panic that four hundred of his men perished in crossing the Chenab River.

***

Meanwhile, Akbar had left nothing to chance – absolutely nothing. Personally busying himself with the campaign preparations, day and night, in every possible detail, he had, in no time, managed to assemble a force of truly overwhelming strength: no less than fifty thousand horse, over five hundred prime war elephants and a host of foot soldiers and cannon! Each soldier received eight months' pay in advance: army loyalty, in the first instance, was based on a sound treasury.

On 8 February 1581, this huge, magnificent army headed north-west, with amazing speed and precision. The Jesuits, travelling with the army, were astounded at the perfect organization of the supplies for such an immense host of people and animals.

Near the town of Sirhind, scouts brought Akbar the happy tidings that Muhammad Hakim had taken to flight, head over heels. But that did not change his decision: this time, he decided to personally chase the rebel all the way to Kabul, and make him eat dust.

Advancing via Kalanaur (in northern Punjab, India) and Rohtas (in Punjab, Pakistan), the imperial army reached the Indus, which was crossed with understandable, but no less irritating, difficulty and loss of time. To make things worse, the Hindu commanders faced immense trouble in persuading their men to cross over to the 'unclean' lands on the other side. Akbar did his best not to lose his temper, but was almost literally bursting with impatience. He had no time to lose; he needed a quick and decisive victory and he could not afford to have his forces tied down in a protracted siege of a big city like Kabul. Much to his relief, Raja Man Singh managed to restore order and discipline among the Rajputs, and volunteered to ride ahead with a fast and powerful vanguard of 20,000 horse to catch up with the rebels before they reached the city. Akbar's son Murad, barely eleven years old, insisted on riding with them. So full of fighting spirit was the lad that he kept on pestering Akbar until he finally let him have his way.

***

On to the Khyber Pass! Akbar hardly allowed himself the time to enjoy the sight of the majestic landscape, spending his time conferring with the army commanders, devising battle plans and preparing for every conceivable eventuality, good or bad.

He did not need to wait much longer. Ably guided by the scouts, Man Singh and his men caught up with Muhammad Hakim's army and attacked it, showing neither hesitation nor mercy. They inflicted on it a defeat so crushing and bloody that Muhammad Hakim did not have a glimmer of hope left of making a stand at Kabul. Scared to death, he fled to the mountains further west. Akbar's strategy had worked perfectly.

And thus, on 10 August 1581, the great imperial army of Hindustan proudly marched through the wide-open iron gates of Kabul: Akbar the Great made his triumphant entry into his grandfather's ancient capital. Awestruck at the sight of his magnificence and power, the inhabitants received him with humble reverence and every possible honour, but with visible dread: what kind of punishment would be meted out to the city? How terrible would be the inevitable mass executions, rapes and plunder?

Fear, fortunately, quickly turned to relief and then enthusiasm, when, for the first time, the people saw for themselves the kindness and clemency Akbar was capable of. Leaving everything and everybody in peace, he had alms distributed to the destitute and needy, and with conspicuous piousness, rendered himself immediately to the great Ali Masjid, where he humbly removed his armour, turban and boots. Barefoot and in plain white clothes like the humblest of worshippers, he prostrated himself in silent prayer, thanking God for his victory.

***

Anxious to get back to Fatehpur Sikri, and to quell the dangerous rebellion in Bengal, Akbar stayed in Kabul for only seven days, just the time required to settle the affairs of the local government. He officially appointed Bakht un-Nissah, Muhammad Hakim's sister and his own half-sister, wife of Khwaja Hasan of Badakhshan, as governor over the province, giving her clear and written instructions: that the government of Kabul and Badakhshan was entrusted to her *personally*; that Akbar would take it back, if and when he pleased; that he did not care if Muhammad Hakim, whose name he never wanted to hear again, returned to Kabul or not; and that she should warn him, that in the event of any new misbehaviour or misadventure, he should no longer expect the kindness and clemency shown to him now.

Muhammad Hakim would indeed never bother Akbar again. During his few remaining years, he confined himself to the only thing he was good at: drinking himself to death. When in July 1585, he did indeed die, barely thirty-one years old, Akbar did not have a single rival left alive. For the rest of his life, he would think, say and do as he pleased.

After crossing the Khyber Pass, the Indus and the great rivers of the Punjab once again, Akbar triumphantly made his way back to the capital. On the first day of December 1581, he arrived at the gates of Fatehpur Sikri, where grandiose feasts were held to celebrate the victory.

***

Meanwhile, in the east, the tide had turned in Akbar's favour. The rebels besieging Todar Mal had fled upon Aziz Koka's arrival; Bihar, Allahabad, Jaunpur had all been recovered by the victorious imperial armies. The back of the insurrection was broken: slowly but surely and thoroughly, Bengal and the eastern provinces would be pacified and brought under control.

But Akbar's worries were not over yet. The victorious imperial armies were still busy mopping up the last pockets of resistance in the rebellious east, when, in late 1583, a new and equally dangerous revolt broke out in the opposite corner of the empire: Gujarat. It had nothing to do with religion this time, but with taxes. Disgruntled local zamindars suddenly found themselves a ringleader when the former Gujarati king Muzaffar Shah, who had been captured during the conquest of Gujarat, but had managed to escape, reappeared from his hiding place. Soon, he succeeded in bringing together a sizeable force and cleverly took advantage of the temporary weakness of the imperial garrisons, due to the retirement of the former governor, Shihab-ud Din, and his replacement by his successor I'timād Khan. Against vastly superior numbers, Ahmedabad fell to the enemy, and a few weeks later, Qutub-ud Din, the loyal governor of Baroda, was also defeated and treacherously killed when he surrendered after having been promised a safe conduct out of the country. All of Gujarat, except the city of Pattan, had fallen to the enemy.

***

Akbar reluctantly started preparations for another major campaign, when young Abdurrahim, Bairam Khan's son, asked permission to ride out against the rebels.

He proved to be as resourceful as his illustrious father. Advancing rapidly through Rajputana, he allied himself with the '*mota* (fat) *raja*' (namely, Udai Singh of Jodhpur, who would become Jahangir's father-in-law and Shah Jahan's grandfather) and other local leaders.

Abdurrahim's force – small in numbers, but of excellent quality – crossed the Gujarat border, and came upon the rebel army at Sarkhej, south-west of Ahmedabad, on 14 January 1584. The enemy fielded an overwhelming force of forty thousand horse and about one hundred thousand foot soldiers against Abdurrahim's mere ten thousand horse and five hundred elephants. Many imperial officers implored him to retreat, but Abdurrahim refused to yield and attacked without hesitation.

Protecting his right flank by using the town walls, he employed the same bold and daring tactics his father had once used against Shams-ud Din: a massive elephant charge in the centre, combined with a furious cavalry attack on the left, in a deadly pincer movement. Only here, there were no paddy fields to slow down the elephants; the enemy was literally crushed between hammer and anvil.

In less than a quarter of an hour, Muzaffar Shah's huge army was on the run, leaving behind several thousand dead. Abdurrahim pursued him to Cambay (on the sea coast) and from there, north to Baroda and Nandod, where he inflicted on him a second and final defeat, again resulting in several thousand casualties. Muzaffar Shah managed to flee the carnage and went into hiding – until his capture, a few years later. Seeing no escape, he would slit his own throat, sparing Akbar the trouble of ordering his execution.

When the good tiding of this new great victory was brought to Akbar, he did not hesitate one instant: Abdurrahim ibn Bairam Khan, the brave young officer who once had come to Akbar's court as a shy four-year-old orphan, was appointed Khan Khanan (lord of lords) and head of the imperial armies – just like his father was before him. He was about to become one of the most influential courtiers in Mughal history.

Din-e-Ilahi

Things quickly returned to normal.

Mullah Muhammad Yazdi, the *qadi* of Jaunpur, the jurist who had supported the rebels with his ill-considered fatwa, was invited to present himself '*at the sublime threshold*' along with his colleague, the *qadi* of Bengal. No official reason was mentioned in the *firman*, but there could be little doubt: the emperor wanted them in court to account for their treacherous attitude during the rebellion. But those expecting to witness a sensational trial, were bitterly disappointed: the two learned mullahs perished on their way to Fatehpur Sikri, when the boat carrying them suddenly and inexplicably foundered in the middle of the river.

Whether it had been planned like this or not, the result was strikingly effective: order and discipline were restored. Never again would a mullah dare to pass judgement on the emperor's policies, not even in private. Emperor Akbar reigned and he reigned alone.

With no one left to criticize let alone challenge him, Akbar once again indulged in his favourite intellectual pastime: religion. He seemed to have lost interest in formal public debates, of which he convened but few; private audiences, however, were granted almost on a daily basis, sometimes throughout the night. He appeared truly insatiable in this quest for knowledge and wisdom; and the more unworldly and mysterious his interlocutors and their teachings, the more they seemed to evoke his interest and respect.

***

To the dismay of some, but with the consent of many, the Hijri lunar calendar fell into disuse at court: events were henceforth recorded using the Persian solar calendar, with the chronology starting in the year of Akbar's accession to the throne.

Every day, at dawn, noon, dusk and even midnight, he now publicly worshipped the sun – either directly, outside, in the open air, or through the symbols of fire and light. He issued orders that, henceforth, each evening when the lamps were lit, all courtiers were to rise to their feet and bow their heads, for to light a candle was to commemorate the rising of the sun and the sun was the sacred symbol of God's eternal majesty.

One would be inclined to conclude from all this that he had become a confirmed Parsi fire worshipper, but that would not be entirely accurate, for the Parsi *mubids* were clearly not the only people to enjoy his favour and attention.

Sitting on the balcony of his private quarters, he listened, night after night, for weeks on end, to the teachings of a feeble old Brahmin priest named Debi. The priest, as per his own express request, was hoisted up the wall of the imperial residence in a cot made of thick hemp ropes, as it would be impossible for him to set foot in a *mlechcha*[25] home, albeit the palace of a highly respected and admired king.

And the Brahmin priest was just one of many teachers introducing him to the many branches of the Hindu tradition. Particular mention should be made of three venerable Jain monks residing on the palace grounds, who seemed to exert a remarkable influence on the emperor. Heeding the imperial summons to come to court to instruct him in their faith, the three old sages had walked all the way from Gujarat to Fatehpur, politely declining the comfortable transportation provided for them.

***

Thenceforth, Akbar refrained from hunting; he abstained from consuming meat, onions, leeks and garlic and rarely took more than one meal a day. On more than one hundred days per year, the killing of animals was prohibited throughout the empire and the slaughter of cows was banned altogether, as it would be in a Hindu state.

So that the wisdom of the Hindu Mahabharata may become accessible to all, he ordered it to be translated from Sanskrit into Persian, under the reluctant supervision of Maulana Abdul Qadir Badaoni, an orthodox Muslim scholar.[26] Hindu symbols, customs and rituals became commonplace at court: Holi, Diwali, Navaratri, Durga Puja and all the other Hindu festivals were celebrated as they would be at the palace of a Hindu king. Sometimes, he actually dressed like one, complete with a *bindi* (a red vermilion dot) on his forehead and a *rakhi*[27] around his wrist. Deeply convinced that all creeds were equally respectable and that wisdom was to be found everywhere, he seemed to belong to all religions, and to none. As Abu'l Fazl expressed it with his usual discernment and wit: '*... the emperor is Parsi in his rites, Hindu in his food and Sufi in his heart*.'

***

And then, in early 1582, during the month of Bahman towards the beginning of the twenty-seventh year of his reign, it all became official: the emperor solemnly promulgated Din-e-Ilahi, the Religion of the One God, the one religion peacefully uniting all others. '*Thus*,' the *firman* stated, '*honour will be rendered to God, peace will be given to the people and security to the empire.*'

Or, as Abu'l Fazl observed in the *A'in-i-Akbari*, with the usual flattery:

> *Whenever, from lucky circumstances, the time arrives that a nation learns to understand how to worship truth, the people will naturally look to their king, on account of the high position he occupies, and expect him to be their spiritual leader as well; for a king possesses, independent of men, the ray of divine wisdom, which banishes from the heart everything that is conflicting.*

Genius, a Folly, or Both?

In more than one way, the promulgation of Din-e-Ilahi was truly the high point of Akbar's life and reign. It is all the more ironic that it was also his greatest failure.

It remains unclear what his motives were at the time he promulgated his Din-e-Ilahi. Was he actually hoping that the masses of Hindus and Muslims would convert, by the hundreds of thousands, to his mysterious new religion? He must have realized that any such initiative was doomed to failure. More likely, he merely intended to establish a religious order of his own, a fellowship similar to the Sufi orders, but open to like-minded people of all backgrounds, Muslims and non-Muslims alike. And most certainly, Din-e-Ilahi was a symbolic, *political* gesture to drive home the point that Akbar was the one and only worldly *and* spiritual highest authority in the land, standing above any religious and communal divide.

As a new cult, however, it was hardly a success. On the contrary, it nearly estranged Akbar from some of his closest friends.

It angered Aziz Koka, his faithful but rather bigoted foster brother, to the point that he left and sailed for Mecca, without seeking Akbar's permission. Upon his return two years later, however, he was eager to make amends, and even became one of the most fervent Din-e-Ilahi disciples: the merchants of Mecca had fleeced him so thoroughly that his Islamic ardour had cooled off.

Raja Man Singh was not happy either with the new cult, and even had the courage to tell it straight to Akbar's face, when the latter brought up the subject of the raja becoming a Din-e-Ilahi disciple. Man Singh retorted: 'Forgive me, Your Majesty, but I do not know what you mean by me becoming your disciple. If it is my willingness to lay down my life for you, have I not given you more than sufficient proof of that? But if it refers to religious faith, I do not know what it is you want to achieve. I am a Hindu, to be sure. If you command me to become a Mussalman, I am prepared do so. But I know of no other religion than these two!'

In any case, Akbar was wise enough not to try and force the issue. There never was any pressure on anyone to join the new religion; no attempts were made to win any converts; no doctrines were issued to disprove or supersede any others; and membership remained limited to a rather small number of devoted courtiers and sycophants, who were eager to please the emperor and proud to belong to his inner circle.

***

Din-e-Ilahi was an utter failure, destined to die with its founder. But, in one way, it was the also high point of Akbar's life, the symbol of everything his reign stood for. It was the living proof that he truly answered to no one but to the one God; and it was – and remains – a powerful message to all people of goodwill: God, if He exists, is less interested in the formal creed we belong to, than in our deeds. A God who truly is all-good, compassionate and merciful, really does not care too much whether we believe in the divinity of Christ, the virginity of Mary, the Holy Quran or any other religion or dogma. If God exists, He wants us to live our lives in the service of truth and goodness; He wants us to leave the world a better place than we found it; and He wants us to be a source of happiness to other people, and through that, also to ourselves.

Campaigns in the North

In late 1585, Akbar was informed of the death of his half-brother Muhammad Hakim back in Kabul. Less than one month later, he abandoned Fatehpur Sikri to set up court further north.

Akbar's decision to move may seem rash, but was actually quite rational. Reports had come in that the Uzbeks had taken possession of Balkh and Badakhshan (northern Afghanistan), the country across the Hindu Kush mountains north of Kabul and south of the Amu Darya. With the dangerous void Muhammad Hakim's death had left in Kabul, Akbar wanted to bring his army closer to the northern border to keep the Uzbeks at bay; and his presence up north had the added advantage that it allowed him to finally conquer the exquisite gem he had been longing to add to his crown for many years: Kashmir. The local king, one Yusuf Khan, had been refusing to submit to Akbar for many years, while trying to placate him with vague promises and half-hearted signs of friendship. It was time to put an end to this situation.

It was a final farewell to Fatehpur Sikri: it would never again serve as Akbar's capital. The affairs of state would keep him in the north of the country for no less than thirteen years, and, by the time he finally returned to the area for a hasty visit, he would find that the erstwhile bustling city had become a ghost town, as good as deserted: the imperial residence untouched, beautiful and imposing as ever, but most of the surrounding shops and houses in pitiful decay. With the emperor gone, most people had left; besides, since the bursting of a part of the dam and the ensuing water supply problems, Fatehpur Sikri was hardly the place anymore to sustain a large population. It had become a monument, a testimonial to its maker, a symbol of the Hindustan he created, with its Muslim-style arches and domes, combined, blended and unified with Hindu pillars, terraces and *chhatris*[28] – *sulh-i-kul* (universal peace) in stone.

***

Barely three months after leaving Fatehpur, Akbar set up camp near the town of Attock (now in northern Pakistan), where the Kabul River runs into the mighty Indus. Not a very comfortable place, but an ideal base for military operations. From here, Akbar oversaw the entire north; from here, his troops could reach Kabul and/or Kashmir in a matter of days.

Together with his army leaders, Akbar took stock of the situation. The roads around the Khyber Pass and the Sulaiman Hills were infested by unruly Afghan tribesmen, but Kabul itself was perfectly safe. The new governor appeared to have everything under control: no unrest, no sign of any Uzbek incursions.

Kashmir under Yusuf Khan, on the other hand, prepared for war, but its resistance was futile: a mere eight months after Akbar's arrival at Attock, the victorious imperial army under Raja Bhagwan Das marched into Srinagar. Yusuf Khan and his son had but one alternative: unconditional surrender. Akbar, however, did not show them his usual leniency. No public reconciliation, no appointments to high office and no fat stipends: they were carted off to Bihar, where they remained imprisoned like common criminals for over a year, after which Akbar assigned them to humble positions well below their rank, a warning to all other would-be rebels. Their proud kingdom was history; without too much ceremony, it was annexed to the empire, not as a separate *sarkar* as everyone expected, but as a mere *suba*, joined to the *sarkar*[29] of Kabul.

***

If the campaign against Kashmir, at first sight a major war, passed off rather smoothly, in any event easier than expected, the operation against the Yusufzai and Mandar Afghan tribes, supposedly a routine job, turned into an outright disaster.

The start of the operations was successful enough. Simultaneously with the attack on Kashmir, Akbar ordered a punitive expedition into the Afghan mountains under a commander named Zain Khan. In accordance with his orders, he invaded the tribal territories with a two-pronged attack: one via the Bajaur territory to the west and the second one due north into the Samah Plateau between the Kabul and the Swat Rivers. After duly chastising any opposing brigands, he crossed the Swat and occupied the town of Chakdara, where, in an entirely strategic manner, he built a stronghold from where he could further harass the tribesmen and pacify the country. So far, so good. As his forces were exhausted from the strenuous marches in difficult country, he sent a messenger back to Attock to ask for reinforcements.

Here, Akbar made a tactical blunder – one of the very few in his career. A number of his courtiers – bored by the tranquil life in the camp, probably – started quarrelling among themselves for the honour of leading the reinforcement troops. In fact, there were so many candidates that the dispute was resolved by drawing lots. Fate appointed Raja Birbal (born as Mahesh Das Bhatt) – one of Akbar's favourite courtiers and one of the famous *navratnas* (nine gems) of his court – together with one Hakim Abul Fath.

It was clearly a mistake to allow two inexperienced courtiers, an administrator and a physician, to lead an army into an insurgent-infested wilderness without clear instructions. Ignoble disputes broke out between Birbal and Zain Khan – the former, believing himself to be the latter's superior and too proud to acknowledge the better judgement of an experienced soldier. On the one hand, Zain Khan maintained – quite correctly – that the fortress needed to be held in strength, while the number of insurgents could be further reduced in a series of punitive raids. Birbal, on the other hand, insisted on returning to the base camp in Attock. To make things worse, Birbal refused to withdraw through the rather broad and much more easily surveyable Malakhand Pass as Zain Khan recommended, but instead insisted on going back through the Karakar and Malandarai defiles. It was a terrible mistake – one that would cost Birbal his life. The retiring imperial army, though grievously harassed by the Afghan tribesmen, still held its own in the narrow Karakar defiles, but when it reached the Malandarai Pass further south and again found itself under attack, the withdrawal degenerated into a humiliating and disastrous rout, a headlong flight where every man tried to save his own skin, without putting up even a semblance of resistance. Zain Khan and Hakim Abul Fath survived with a little over half of the army, but eight thousand men, including Birbal himself, were slaughtered like sheep.

Akbar was devastated, unable to eat or drink or sleep for days on end: not only because he was mourning the loss of a dear old friend but also because his mighty army had been humiliated by a bunch of tribesmen.

He made them pay dearly. They had shed the blood of a Hindu courtier; Hindu warriors would shed theirs. Todar Mal, after taking a number of well-placed fortresses, harried the eastern mountain tribes so brutally that they were soon begging for peace; and near the Khyber Pass, Man Singh inflicted on the western tribes a defeat so crushing that it took them years to recover from it. The roads were safe again, with the mountain passages cleared and order restored.

Thirteen Years in Lahore

After the successful campaign in Kashmir and after meting out punishment to the inimical Afghan tribes, the northern borderlands were safe again. Safe enough, anyway, for Akbar to retire to the more cultured comfort of Lahore, which was to remain his capital city for the next thirteen years.

From thence, he further built up and consolidated his mighty empire: through war and conquest, of course, but equally and, at times more importantly, through carefully worded correspondence and elegant conversation, artfully blending courtesy with thinly veiled threats.

If strategy is like playing chess, the entire decade was really a gigantic game between Akbar and the Uzbek king, Abdullah Khan Uzbek. A game with very high stakes indeed: the entire balance of power in the north-west – among the Persians, the Uzbeks and the Mughal Empire – depended on it. A game that Akbar would win brilliantly, using the Uzbeks to wear down the Persians, and then the Persians to chastise the Uzbeks; and while those two were at each other's throats, he quietly helped himself to the spoils.

Persia was in dire straits at the time. Its wealthy western provinces – including the eternal city of Baghdad itself – had been lost to the Ottoman Empire of Turkey; its north-western borders were under constant threat of invasion by the increasingly arrogant Uzbeks.

For the entire thirty-first year of his reign (1586), Akbar found himself involved in lively correspondence with his two quarrelling neighbours: the old, tremulous and half-blind Persian king, Muhammad Shah Khudabanda, and his ruthless, land-hungry Uzbek adversary.

It was not difficult to discern what was behind all the lavish gifts and pledges of everlasting friendship they both kept sending Akbar: they both wanted his support, or at least his neutrality, in the longstanding feud that divided them.

If he were to have followed his heart, he would have combined forces with the mild-mannered old Shah and crushed the Uzbeks, once and for all. After careful consideration, however, he chose not to. What good would it have done to strengthen a potential adversary? He stayed put, and from behind the safety of his borders, watched his foes weakening each other.

Before long, the Uzbeks did invade the Persian north-east and quickly seized Herat, Sistan and Mashhad from the ill-prepared Persians. Humiliated, the powerless Shah had no alternative but to abdicate in favour of his sixteen-year-old son Abbas, whose first worry was to stay alive, amidst a wasp's nest of strife and court intrigues – which the boy successfully managed to overcome, as will be related in due course.

***

While the Persians and the Uzbeks kept each other occupied, Akbar had his hands free for his own plans.

His first target was the province of Sindh. After all, it was unthinkable that he would leave the Punjab's natural access to the sea, the fertile plains around the lower reaches of the Indus, and his own birthplace, Umarkot, in foreign hands. When amicable overtures were of no avail, in 1591, he sent down Abdurrahim with an army to make Jani Beg, the local ruler, see reason. The enemy attempted to resist, but, of course, was no match for Abdurrahim, who made quick work of Jani Beg's army and fleet of warships. Meekly surrendering all his cities and fortresses to Abdurrahim, Jani Beg travelled to Lahore to prostrate himself at Akbar's feet.

Akbar decided to give him another chance and allowed him to return to his native region as its governor. As usual, Akbar's instinct did not fail him. For the remainder of his life – which, unfortunately, ended prematurely in a drinking bout a few years later – Jani Beg served his emperor faithfully, fighting at his side in the Deccan and becoming a confirmed Din-e-Ilahi adept.

Now that Sindh was under control, Akbar was able to consolidate the other south-western regions. In the beginning of the fortieth year of his reign (1595), his forces invaded Baluchistan (now part of Pakistan) and quickly captured the fortress of Siwi in the Kirthar Mountains, south-east of Quetta. Barely two months later, the jewel in the crown fell into Akbar's lap when the Persian governor of Qandahar, fearing an imminent invasion by the Uzbeks, delivered the city to him. No sooner had Akbar's troops taken over the city and manned the territory's borders that the Uzbeks withdrew.

With Sindh, Baluchistan and Qandahar now firmly in his hands, Akbar could finally rest assured that the north of his empire was safe behind well-nigh impregnable natural borders, with its two entrance gates (Kabul and Qandahar) well guarded.

***

Meanwhile, in the Persian–Uzbek feud, the tables had been turned completely by the energetic young Persian emperor, Shah Abbas. Swiftly dealing with any would-be rivals – that is to say, having them blinded, poisoned or strangled – he quickly patched up a peace deal with his powerful adversaries in the west, ceding them some additional territories; and while the Ottomans were revelling in their easy victory, he quietly availed himself of a number of European military advisers. With unremitting zeal, he strengthened and reorganized his armed forces, similar to the model of his Ottoman opponents. Cannon foundries were built virtually everywhere, hundreds of thousands of muskets fabricated and ample supplies of gunpowder stockpiled all over the land. With spectacular success: barely ten years after his father's humiliating defeat, Shah Abbas' victorious armies washed over the Uzbek occupants like a tidal wave; only a handful of maimed and blinded survivors were allowed to stumble back to Bukhara and give Abdullah Khan Uzbek the tiding that his grandiose plans had failed. A few years later, in 1598, the old Uzbek king died, in the certain knowledge that there was no one of value to succeed him. Gone were the dreams of a great Uzbek empire.

With Abdullah Khan Uzbek out of the way, his forces decimated by Shah Abbas and his successor an impotent weakling, Akbar was tempted to march north, to Samarqand: Samarqand, where the bones of his great ancestor Timur were resting; Samarqand, the priceless jewel that was stolen from his grandfather by the Uzbek usurpers. But unlike his father and grandfather, Akbar was not a Central Asian anymore; his future did not lie in faraway northern regions where he never had set foot, but in his own Hindustan.

Akbar realized he was growing old – fifty-six already – and much remained to be done. He decided to move back to Agra, from where it would be easier to direct the operations against the recalcitrant sultanates of the Deccan.

Little did he imagine that his last adversary was not to be some Deccan ruler, but his own firstborn son.

DUSK

A Great King, but a Failed Father

Akbar's thirteen years at Lahore – the period roughly between the thirtieth and the forty-third year of his reign, i.e., between the annexation of Kashmir and his return to Agra – constituted what one could call the afternoon of his reign. To be sure, vast, rich and crucially important territories had been and were being added to his empire: Sindh, Baluchistan, Qandahar, Odisha, Berar (once a part of Hyderabad in the Deccan), Asirgarh (in southern Madhya Pradesh) and Ahmednagar (now in Maharashtra), all fell into his hands. He had never been more powerful, had no one to fear, but for the first time, he began to feel the curse of advancing age. He lost many of his most trusted, lifelong friends, and with growing despair, he had to witness how his three promising, wonderful sons – Salim (who would later take on the title Jahangir), Murad and Danyal – rather than making him proud like before, were becoming a cause of grave concern and disappointment.

In 1586, his dear old friend Birbal had been killed in battle; three years later, Todar Mal and Raja Bhagwan Das had died, barely one week from each other; and four years after that, the wise old Shaykh Mubarak had passed away as well. Of the famous *navratnas*, only three were left: Raja Man Singh and Abdurrahim Khan Khanan, his two strong army leaders, and Abu'l Fazl, his closest friend and adviser.

The pain of these losses, however, had been more than alleviated by the birth of three healthy grandsons: Khusrau on 5 August 1587, Parvez on 31 October 1589 and Khurram on 5 January 1592.[30] Khurram, in January 1628, would succeed Jahangir as Shah Jahan and would achieve everlasting worldwide fame as the builder of the Taj Mahal.

Khusrau's birth in particular had been a cause of great rejoicing. Not only was he Salim's (Jahangir's) firstborn but also he did ensure the continuity of the dynasty: the fact that he was born to Salim's first-wedded wife, the princess of Jodhpur, again reinforced the bonds of kinship and friendship that united the Mughals with the Rajputs. (Parvez was born to a Muslim mother.) In terms of 'blood', Khusrau and Khurram both were three-fourth Rajput, one-eighth Persian and one-eighth Central Asian Turkish. The 'Mughal' dynasty had become truly Indian.

***

From a personal perspective, Akbar's life had changed a great deal, and not for the better. At the time he left Fatehpur Sikri in 1585, he was forty-three and at the peak of his power (both physical and political), and everything and everybody revolved around him. His three sons were then mere boys of sixteen, fifteen and thirteen, respectively; promising lads – spoilt, no doubt, but strong and talented.

By the time he decided to return to Agra in 1598, he was a white-haired, aging man, and those three wonderful sons of his had changed beyond recognition into conceited, quarrelsome and indolent drinkers, well on their way to become total failures. And even more worrisome was that the brotherly love and friendship that once had united them had given way to barely hidden mistrust and resentment. Abu'l Fazl and the other courtiers did their best to spare Akbar's feelings, but they could not hide from him the reality that the imperial court was rife with rumours – rumours that the princes were looking for allies in the war of succession that would surely break out from the moment Akbar would have laid down his weary head and that all three of them were living in constant fear of being assassinated.

All this was a cause for great concern for Akbar, but there was little he could do about it. Somewhere along the line, he had failed as a father, and perhaps, even more importantly, as a succession planner. This shortcoming would be the Achilles' heel of the Mughal Empire in the centuries that followed, generation after generation.

Failed Campaign in the Deccan

If everything would have gone the way Akbar planned, his borders would have extended considerably further south than they actually did at the time of his death in 1605. It was not to be, because of his sons' misbehaviour and disobedience.

Akbar wanted the Deccan. The continuing independence of the sultanates there had been a thorn in his flesh for many years.

As early as during the wars in Gujarat (beginning in 1572), he had been sending envoys to Khandesh (spread over parts of present-day Maharashtra and Madhya Pradesh) and other places to invite the rulers to join the Mughal Empire. But their submission had only been temporary and half-hearted at best. On the contrary: Burhan Shah of Ahmednagar had been insolent enough to seek Akbar's help when he needed it to defeat his local enemies and then ignored him as soon as he got what he wanted. In August 1591, Akbar gave it one last try: he dispatched four missions, to Khandesh, Bijapur (now in Karnataka), Ahmednagar and Golkonda/Golconda (now in Telangana, near Hyderabad), under the leadership of Shaykh Abul Faizi. Patiently, he waited, but the vague reports he kept receiving were far from promising. Two years later, his worst misgivings were confirmed: the envoy returned with a meagre fourteen elephants and a handful of jewels as a so-called *token of friendship*; but none of the Deccan kings had submitted or pledged allegiance.

Akbar sent Abdurrahim Khan Khanan at the head of an army and instructed Murad – who was at the time governor of Gujarat – to join up with him. The two imperial armies met at Chandur (now in Telangana) and crossed the border virtually unopposed, laying siege to the fortress of Ahmednagar on 26 December 1595. However, things did not go well at all between the two commanders: Murad was too drunk and arrogant to take advice from a seasoned warrior and the latter too proud and stubborn to keep his mouth shut. More preoccupied with their own private feuds than with the war they were supposed to fight, they quickly patched up a peace deal with the enemy, whereby the siege was lifted in exchange for the territory of Berar.

Akbar was beside himself with rage when he was informed about this failure, but there was little he could do. Given the distance between Agra and the Deccan (more than 1000 km), dispatches back and forth took over a week to reach their destinations; all he got was a few polite letters with vague reassurances, while the disturbing rumours about the drinking bouts and violent rows continued unabated.

The dispatch he received late 1598 was the drop that made the cup run over. The enemy had broken the peace deal, and Abdurrahim – not a word about Murad – had fought them at Ashti near Supa (now in Maharashtra) on the banks of the Godavari River. The enemy army had been much stronger than expected, and an indecisive victory had been the result: Abdurrahim had managed to rout them, but his own losses had been so heavy that he had been unable to pursue and annihilate the fleeing enemy.

This time, Akbar had had enough. He sent Abu'l Fazl to assess the situation in the Deccan and summoned Murad back to the Agra court. But it was too late: weeks later, Abu'l Fazl's messenger presented himself, a blue handkerchief around his wrist, which could only mean one thing: someone very close to the emperor had died, someone so close, that the messenger did not dare to speak his or her name. It appeared that Murad had drunk himself to death – he had passed away on 1 January 1599. Towards the end, things had become so bad that his friends had to spoon-feed him two cups of arak every morning before he was able to do anything, because he was shaking so badly.

After six months of mourning, Akbar decided to take matters in his own hands. On 10 July 1599, he headed south, to Khandesh and the fortress of Asirgarh, to pick up where his son had left off; but what should have been the start of his last and most glorious conquest, was to become an embarrassing spectacle.

***

Akbar left Salim in charge of Agra, and ordered him to lead a campaign into southern Rajputana to bring the Rana of Mewar to heel. He unsuspectingly headed south, and reached the border of Khandesh near the end of the year. Upon his arrival, he found that the local ruler, Mirhan Bahadur, and most of his forces had taken refuge in the fortress of Asirgarh, and quickly seized the opportunity. Bypassing the fortress, he marched further south to the capital Burhanpur, which he took, virtually unopposed, on 31 March 1600. Abdurrahim and Akbar's other remaining son, Danyal, were sent ahead further into Ahmednagar, where they surrounded the town, and took it by storm on 19 August, imprisoning the local king and his family and putting the defending garrison of about fifteen hundred to the sword. Meanwhile, Akbar had laid siege to the fortress of Asirgarh. It was there that things started to go seriously wrong.

Asirgarh was at least as strong a fortress as Chittor, its ramparts high up on well-nigh inaccessible cliffs with the added difficulty that all the ground around it was solid rock, preventing the construction of *sabats*. It had its own potable water from numerous wells and reservoirs inside its walls and supplies sufficient to feed the entire defending garrison for over ten years, affirms Vincent Smith. As the ramparts could not be stormed and as Akbar did not have enough heavy cannons at his disposal to breach the walls, he found himself stuck. He sent an emissary to Goa, with a message requesting the Portuguese to come to his assistance with a good number of their heavy guns.

As he waited in vain for the Portuguese to arrive – they were apparently not so eager to help Akbar conquer the Deccan and thus become his neighbours – and was devising alternative plans to either bring in additional artillery from up north or to found extra cannons and mortars on site from locally available bronze and iron, highly disturbing dispatches came in from Agra: Salim was in open rebellion against his father. He had attempted to seize the treasuries in Lahore, Delhi and Agra, raised a large army and taken Allahabad, where he had set up court as an independent king.

What was Akbar to do? He clearly could not afford to stay away from his capital, with a major rebellion going on, and thus hastily proceeded to secure the last and most inglorious victory of his life. Through the intermediary of a few local nobles, secret negotiations were opened with the leading defenders; as he hoped and expected, gold and silver bribes quickly proved to be far more effective than steel and gunpowder. After a few weeks, Asirgarh opened its gates, and without a single drop of blood having been shed, the imperial standard flew over the ramparts.

He paid a hasty visit to the newly conquered fortress, and headed back to Agra, to secure his capital from his own son. His firstborn, the successor he had so ardently prayed for, was threatening his treasure, his throne, and possibly even his life.

Salim's Rebellion

As soon as his father had left for the Deccan, Salim had headed west towards Mewar, as he had been ordered to do. Before even reaching Ajmer, however, he went back to Agra. Refusing to talk to Man Singh and refusing even to go and see his grandmother, despite her desperate pleas, he seized as much treasure as he could lay his hands on –

thirty million rupees, reportedly – and headed east, taking the city of Allahabad, where he set up court as an independent king, dismissing his father's officers and appointing confidants of his own, everywhere from Kalpi to Bijapur. In 1601, to add insult to injury, he had coins minted in his own name – nothing short of a declaration of independence.

***

An all-out rebellion, however, it was not. Salim did not attempt to conquer any adjacent territories, and Akbar, on his part, did not attack his son's army. On the contrary, he made every attempt to settle the issue amicably. When this failed, he sent Abu'l Fazl as an emissary, hoping that his chief minister would be able to convince Salim to see reason.

That move, however, worked like a red rag to a bull. Salim, who deeply resented Abu'l Fazl for the strong influence he had on his father, instructed a local warlord, Raja Bir Singh Deo of Orchha (about 120 km south-east of Gwalior), to kill him.

Abu'l Fazl had been forewarned by informants, but clearly underestimated the danger. Early in the morning of Thursday, 12 August 1602, a large group of heavily armed horsemen scattered his escort and, before he could even lift a finger, the enemy speared him like a boar. The assassins cut off his head and took it to Allahabad, to collect their blood money; Salim, accepting the gruesome gift with glee, casually had it tossed into the latrines.

Akbar seethed with impotent rage when he heard about his best friend's assassination. But the troops he sent to Orchha came back empty-handed: though wounded, Bir Singh Deo had managed to escape.

***

What exactly made Salim revolt against his father remains a matter of conjecture, notwithstanding lavishly mounted romantic films. He was thirty-three years old at the time, obviously tired of waiting and eager to shake off the yoke of a loud, overbearing and domineering father. For some reason, he became convinced that Abu'l Fazl was intriguing against him and that he was about to convince his father to appoint someone else – his eldest grandson, probably – as his successor. That was, most probably, the reason why he set up his own court in Allahabad; and that was, most certainly, why he had Abu'l Fazl assassinated.

In his memoirs,[31] Salim/Jahangir testifies, with his usual candour:

> *Toward the end of my exalted father's reign, Shaykh Abu'l Fazl, one of the Shaykhzadas of Hindustan who was outstanding in his learning and wisdom, had ostensibly adorned himself with loyalty and sold it to my father at an exorbitant price. He was summoned from the Deccan, and since his feelings towards me were not honest, he both publicly and privately spoke against me.*[32] *At that time, because of the corruption of mischief-makers, my exalted father's mind was quite turned against me, and it was certain that if* [Abu'l Fazl] *succeeded in reaching him he would create more discord and prevent* [me] *from rejoining* [my father]. *It was therefore absolutely necessary that he be prevented from reaching him. Since Bir Singh Deo's territory lay in his path, and at that time* [Bir Singh] *was in the circle of insurgents, I sent him a message that he should waylay the miscreant and dispatch him to nonexistence, in return for which he could expect great rewards from me. Success smiled on the endeavour, and as* [Abu'l Fazl] *was passing through* [Bir Singh's] *territory,* [Bir Singh] *blocked his path, scattered his men in a skirmish, and killed him, sending his head to me in Allahabad. Although this caused distress to [my father], in the end it resulted in my being able to proceed to kiss the threshold of my exalted father's court without fear, and little by little the bad blood between us subsided.*

Uneasy Reconciliation

The last sentence of the above quote more or less summarizes the sequel. Akbar, in spite of his grief and anger, could not bring himself to start a ruinous civil war against his own son. Late in 1602 or early in 1603, he allowed his favourite consort, Salima Sultan Begam, to travel to Allahabad. Thanks to her adroit diplomacy, Salima succeeded in bringing about an official reconciliation: in March 1603, the rebel prince presented himself at court, with lavish gifts, including twelve thousand gold pieces and no less than seven hundred and seventy elephants – three hundred and fifty-four of which were accepted and placed in the imperial stables, the rest – plus Akbar's best elephant – being given to the prince. Akbar even took off his own turban and placed it on Salim's head, publicly recognizing him as heir to the throne. As Vincent Smith remarks, Salima must have felt justifiably proud at her diplomatic success.

It was, however, but a half-hearted reconciliation. Between father and son stood a past that neither of them could forget and a future that was equally worrisome to both. Apart from a few official court sessions, they saw very little of each other. Salim stayed as much as possible on his own in Fatehpur Sikri and spent much time with the Jesuit priests at court, ostensibly out of interest in religion and Western art, but in reality, to secure the help of the redoubtable Portuguese guns in the civil war that was bound to take place after Akbar's death, for it was increasingly clear that Khusrau was still harbouring dangerous ambitions of his own.

***

In the fall of 1603, Akbar again asked Salim to lead an army into southern Rajputana and force the defiant Rana of Mewar into submission. Salim, however, had little appetite for a war in a faraway hill region, where little plunder was to be gained, and more importantly, where he would be unable to keep things under control at court, should anything happen to his father. After weeks of procrastination, delays and extravagant demands for unnecessary reinforcements, Salim asked for permission to return to Allahabad.

Akbar gave up. He gave the desired permission, adding that Salim was free to return to court at any time he pleased. On 10 November 1603, Salim left Fatehpur Sikri, crossed the Yamuna River near Mathura and went back to Allahabad. Upon his arrival there, he organized extravagant festivities, celebrating the reconciliation with his father.

Shortly after his arrival, however, Salim suffered the painful loss of his first wife, Man Singh's adopted sister and Khusrau's mother (who took on the name Shah Begam). A passionate woman, prone to depression, she had been deeply distressed by the continuing rivalry of her son against her husband, and in a fit of despair, had taken an overdose of opium.

'*In consequence of her death,*' writes Salim/Jahangir, '*from the attachment I had for her, I passed some days without any kind of pleasure in life or existence, and for four days ... I took nothing in the shape of food or drink.*'[33]

The quote is a typical illustration of the complex character of this man, who, throughout his life, remained a strange mixture of opposites: a cold cynic who could be moved to tears by romantic love, works of art or the beauty of nature; a lover of justice, but capable of unspeakable cruelty; a hopeless drunk and a drug addict, and yet, an effective ruler.

Akbar sent his son a touching letter of condolence, accompanied by a precious robe of honour and the turban from his own head, again a confirmation of Salim's position as heir to the throne.

The rapprochement was, however, disappointingly short-lived. Akbar was much vexed with increasingly unsettling reports about drunken depravity, vicious cruelty and excesses of all kinds on Salim's part. The most fearful penalties were inflicted for trivial offences, writes Smith;[34] pardon was never thought of, and even his adherents were dumbstruck with terror. A courtier convicted of a plot against the prince's life was flayed alive while Salim calmly watched. Akbar must have attended the celebrations for the beginning of the forty-ninth year of his reign in the most sombre of moods: was this the kind of man to succeed him?

Danyal

Any hopes Akbar may have entertained vis-à-vis his other surviving son were rudely shattered, when early in May 1604, he got the sad tiding that Danyal, his youngest, had died in the Deccan. Danyal, in spite of his gentle character and many talents, was a hopeless drunkard like his two brothers, and the problem had been growing increasingly worse. The Khan Khanan (Abdurrahim), to whose daughter Danyal was married, had done his best to talk some sense into him, and when that had failed, to cut off his supply of liquor, but his efforts had been in vain. The prince had bribed his friends and servants to get him his daily ration – the liquor was smuggled in, in phials hidden in turbans and clothes, and even in musket barrels. At last he was beyond help, and passed away in early April 1604, after six weeks of acute illness.

The Death of the Queen Mother

Akbar was facing a terrible dilemma, perhaps best summarized in the following quote from my historical novel, *Akbar's Farewell*:

> *You see my problem, Salima? If I appoint Khusrau, or one of my other grandsons, there will be civil war – maybe I will be able to prevent it during my lifetime, but it will certainly break out when I'm gone, and that would be an absolute disaster! Not only will kindred blood be spilt – which in itself is terrible enough – but no matter who wins this civil war, he will inherit a weakened and deeply divided land. How*

long do you think it will take, before the Uzbek Khan, or the Persian Shah, or some or other ambitious zamindar tries to take advantage of this weakness?

*So you see, my dear, there are hardly any options I have left! If I do not appoint an official heir, if I just leave things to run their course as they are today, I'm effectively condoning the partition of the empire I fought for all my life, undermining my own authority, and sowing the seeds of lawlessness and war. If I die while Salim is still in Allahabad, Khusrau and his supporters will almost certainly disavow him, saying that he forfeited his right to the throne because of his rebellion. On the other hand, if I do appoint Khusrau, it is almost certain that Salim will either go to war to claim his birthright, or declare independence and split up the empire.**

***

The reports were extremely worrying: Salim was well on his way to end up like his two younger brothers. Angry and desperate, Akbar resolved to go to Allahabad in person, and drag him back to Agra – by military force, if necessary. On 24 August 1604, amidst the heavy monsoon rains, he prepared his army for war. Not to conquer the Deccan, as had been his plan; not to invade Persia or Central Asia, as he may have considered at some point in time; but to fight his own flesh and blood.

The preparations were plagued by all kinds of mishaps: his camp on the bank of the Yamuna was inundated and partly destroyed under a deluge of rain and the barge he wanted to travel in got stuck on a sandbank in the middle of the river, but these setbacks did not change his resolve. He marched on, at the head of his invincible army.

He had not gone far, when the news reached him that his mother was critically ill. At first, he ignored the message, but when it was reconfirmed, he felt bound to abort the campaign.

By the time he arrived at his mother's bedside, he found her barely conscious and unable to speak. Five days later, on 29 August, at the age of seventy-seven, the old empress passed away.

Akbar was profoundly saddened by her demise. As a sign of mourning and filial piety, he took off his turban, shaved all the hair on his head – even his whiskers and eyebrows – and fasted for several days.

*Dirk Collier, *Akbar's Farewell*, Amaryllis, New Delhi, 2011/2024; 41st Letter.

Hamida Banu Begam's body was conveyed to Delhi by a relay of noblemen, to be laid to rest at the side of Humayun, her husband, whom she had outlived by more than four decades.

Akbar's Farewell

Something seemed to have broken inside Akbar after his mother's death; he did not pursue his planned march on Allahabad. After a few listless days, during which he hardly appeared in public, he unexpectedly accorded a private audience to Mir Sadr Jahan, an orthodox mullah and one of Salim's confidants. The audience lasted for a full two hours; when it was over, the mullah, carrying secret instructions with him, hastily packed a few belongings and left for Allahabad. Nobody knows what was written in the instructions, but it is not hard to guess: one of them, most certainly, was an official letter written by the court scribe, informing Salim of the passing of his grandmother, and inviting him to court to share in his father's mourning. The second one, most probably, must have been a personal message to Salim, warning him that if he did not immediately present himself at court, Akbar would officially disavow him and appoint Khusrau as his successor.

Whatever was in the letters, it certainly had its intended effect. Soon after Mir Sadr Jahan's arrival in Allahabad, Salim started his journey to Agra, ostensibly with the intention of offering his condolences on the death of his grandmother. On Friday, 9 November 1604, he arrived at court, accompanied only by a small retinue of four attendants, having left his troops at a considerable distance from the city limits, as Akbar had ordered him to do.

The reunion between father and son was again reassuringly warm and friendly. Salim was welcomed with full honours, in the presence of the entire court, and after a brief but friendly exchange of civilities, he was invited to join his father in the *zanana*. Inside the *zanana*, however, Akbar dragged him into a room, violently slapped him in the face and showered him with a torrent of abuse.

He then stated that his son was ill, in need of medical treatment, and ordered him to be locked in a bathroom under the charge of a physician, without any alcohol or opium. At the same time, Salim's army was disbanded, his horses and elephants accommodated in the imperial stables and his main supporters thrown in jail.

A few days passed, and the *cold turkey* treatment seemed to have had some beneficial effect. Akbar personally brought his son a small supply of opium to alleviate his distress, and a bit later, officially pardoned him and assigned to him a residence worthy of his royal rank.

The rebellion was over. Until Akbar's death in late October 1605, Salim continued to live in the imperial residence, in ostensible amity and harmony with his father; in official ceremonies, he occupied the place closest to the throne. And while he still drank a lot and used opium every day – he would continue to do so throughout his life – he seemed to keep things more or less under control.

***

The court intrigues, however, continued unabated, with a powerful faction, led by Aziz Koka (Khusrau's father-in-law) and Raja Man Singh (his adopted maternal uncle), strongly advocating Khusrau's cause.

It was in this uneasy atmosphere that, in late September 1605, Akbar ordered an elephant fight between Salim's prize bull Giranbar and Khusrau's champion Abrup. The contest, in which Khusrau's elephant was defeated, ended in an unseemly squabble between the two camps, where Khusrau made a terrible scene, which greatly upset Akbar. He hardly slept that night; the next morning, he was taken ill with the intestinal disease that would eventually kill him.

As usual, under similar circumstances, there have been widespread speculations, all of them unproven, that Akbar had been the victim of poisoning, probably by Salim's or Khusrau's supporters. It even has been suggested that his death was accidental, and that he mistakenly took poison, which was, in fact, intended to kill someone else. There is, however, no evidence whatsoever to prove that his death was due to anything other than natural causes.

The illness followed a rather erratic course, with brief intervals of improvement, alternating with acute attacks. Despite the desperate efforts of Hakim Ali Gilani, Akbar's personal physician, the symptoms gradually worsened. Mild remedies seemed to have little effect; after one week, the physician administered stronger astringents, which indeed stopped the diarrhoea, but brought on a dangerously high fever, accompanied by severe belly cramps, stabbing flank pains, and – the most alarming symptom of all – the utter inability to pass water. Administration of the astringents was discontinued; herbal infusions relieved the kidneys and brought down the fever, but soon after that, the diarrhoea returned and worsened to acute dysentery, with alarming and increasing amounts of blood in the stools.

As Akbar's condition worsened, the intrigues around his succession continued unabated. Aziz Koka and Man Singh tried to convince the other nobles that Salim was unworthy and had to be set aside in favour of his son; a majority of the amirs, however, rejected the proposal as contrary to tradition and natural law. Anxious to prevent civil war, the amirs then exacted from him two solemn oaths: first, that he would neither punish or injure any of Khusrau's supporters nor hold any grudge against them, and secondly, that he would protect the religion of Islam. The prince accepted both conditions, took the oaths, and, it must be said, kept them honourably.

***

Meanwhile, the battle for the dying emperor's soul continued. On Saturday, 12 October 1605, the Jesuit padres presented themselves at Akbar's quarters in the morning and once again tried to persuade him to embrace the Christian faith.

The emperor, however, while courteous as always in spite of his ailments, made it clear that he was in no mood for religious debate. He seemed rather relaxed and cheerful, in slightly better health than in the days before, and spent the remainder of the afternoon and evening in the company of his courtiers. By the following Monday, however, his condition had become critical. The Jesuits once again attempted to talk to him, but this time, they were refused an audience. Instead, the emperor sent for his son. The prince, who had up to that moment not found the courage to visit his father, possibly out of fear that he might be rejected as heir to the throne, presented himself immediately. The dying emperor, unable to speak, made a sign that he should put on the imperial turban and gird himself with Humayun's sword; it was his last deed as emperor of Hindustan.

Outside the imperial apartments, the amirs and other members of the imperial court took turns kissing the ringed hands of their future new emperor.

As the days went by, Akbar's condition further worsened, and in the early hours of Thursday, 17 October 1605,* he passed away.

***

*Corresponding to 27 October on the Gregorian Calendar (introduced by Pope Gregory XIII in October 1582, adopted in Great Britain in 1752).

The next morning, in accordance with a time-honoured Sunni custom, his mortal remains were taken to their last resting place. A gap was broken in the sandstone wall of the fort; Salim and his sons took the bier upon their shoulders and carried it to the Diwan-i-Aam (hall of public audience). From there, all the eminent amirs and courtiers followed each other in quick succession, carrying the bier out of the fort. The entire court, heads and feet bare, followed the cortège to the tomb at Sikandra, about 13 km north-west of the Agra Fort, where the emperor's body was placed in the mausoleum, still under construction at that time, which he had designed himself.

***

The structure is like the great king whose mortal remains it houses: open to light and air from all directions, eclectic and, at times, incongruous, an unsuccessful attempt to unite different architectural styles and traditions.

On the southern entrance gate is an elegant inscription, sculpted by one of Akbar's best calligraphers: 'These are the Gardens of Eden. Enter them, to live forever.'

Akbar's mortal remains would, however, not be left in peace. Eighty-six years after his death, during the reign of his great-grandson Aurangzeb, the tomb was pillaged by a band of Jats, who dragged out Akbar's bones and threw them into a fire. It was, as Abraham Eraly remarked, *a Hindu end for Akbar, after all.*

Akbar's Persona

Like many other rulers, leaders and demagogues – both good and bad, from Julius Caesar to Mahatma Gandhi, Mao Zedong or Adolf Hitler – Akbar appears to have had a truly mesmerizing personality, a mixture of personal charm and awe-inspiring authority, as well as an extraordinary ability to adapt himself to his audience, '*to be great with the great, and lowly with the lowly*'.[35]

Father Pierre du Jarric S.J. (1566–1617, a French Jesuit missionary testifies that '*to his own family he was most dear; to the great he was terrible; to the lowly, kind and affable. With small and common people he was so sympathetic and indulgent, that he always found time to gladly hear their cases, and to respond graciously to their requests. Their little offerings, too, he used to accept with such a pleased look, handling them and putting them in his bosom, as he did not do with the most lavish gifts of the nobles, which, with discreet pretense, he often seemed not even to glance at.*'[36]

Akbar's conversation would, in general, be reassuringly pleasant, polite and kindly; yet, he radiated awesome power and majesty, and his innermost thoughts would usually remain hidden behind a faint, inscrutable smile. The way he moved, his demeanour, everything about him was '*in such perfect accord with royal dignity, that anybody would instantly recognize him as a great king*', the Jesuits noted.

He rarely lost his self-control. At times, however, he did display a quick, not to say violent, temper. Occasional outbursts of wrath could put him beside himself, at which point he proved to be extremely dangerous. Once, for instance, he found a guard asleep at his post, and in his anger, had him thrown off the fortress ramparts. On another occasion, he ordered the feet of one of his senior palace servants cut off for robbing the shoes of a poor man.

He later felt remorse at the severity of his verdict, and as he gained maturity with the passage of time, he ordained that whenever he would sentence an offender to death or to the mutilation of a limb, he should be reminded three times before the sentence could actually be carried out.

As far as his personal appearance was concerned, he was of medium height, probably around 1.7 m, and strongly built. He walked with a slight limp, and was markedly bow-legged, most probably the effect of many hours on horseback, hunting parties and violent sports in his early years. His head dropped a little towards the right shoulder. His nose is described as moderate sized, with a bony knobble in the middle, and rather wide nostrils; a small mole, the size of a small pea, connected the left nostril with the upper lip. His complexion was dark rather than fair, his eyes rather narrow, a vestige of his Central Asian ancestry. He was clean-shaven, apart from a small moustache, but unlike his Turkish ancestors and most Muslims, he allowed his hair to grow long in the Rajput fashion. His attire, too, was a mixture of Muslim and Hindu elements, with a tunic that reached a little below the knees, rather than the ankle-length robes worn by most Muslims. And on his head, he invariably wore a small, tightly rolled, bejewelled turban which combined Hindu and Mussalman modes as well.

He was extremely moderate in his diet, taking but one substantial meal in the day, which was served whenever he asked for it – not at any fixed hour. He appears to have been extremely fond of fruit, especially grapes, melons and pomegranates. Under Hindu and Jain influence, he hardly ever ate any meat in the later years of his life. '*It is not right that a man should make his stomach the grave of animals,*' he is reported to have said. He did drink hard liquor and used opium, and there is more than one example of shockingly drunk misbehaviour, but, in general, he did not allow his drinking habit to interfere with his other activities and he most certainly was not a hopeless addict like his sons were.

From early boyhood, he was fond of all kinds of sports, and absolutely fearless, to the point of recklessness. He was a crack shot, a perfect horseman, and better than anyone else in handling all kinds of animals: elephants, horses, dogs, camels, cheetahs and others. As far as the more peaceful amusements were concerned, he adored song and music – he is reputed to have been an excellent drummer himself – as well as storytelling and witty conversation, often well into the night.

As is often the case in hyperactive people, he also had a pensive, often melancholy temperament, and as has been related, a deeply religious, mystical disposition, combined with a level-headed, rationalist approach. Jahangir declares in his memoirs that his father '*never for one moment forgot God*'. Throughout his life, he was preoccupied with religion and the harmonious coexistence of various religions and denominations. It was this rather amiable and commendable trait that made him so very remarkable as a ruler.

Akbar's Religious Views and Their Historical Significance

Here is a quote from my historical novel, *Akbar's Farewell*, bringing out the views of Akbar's personal physician:[37]

> *Was our beloved emperor still a Muslim when he died? Had he turned Pārsī as people say, or Hindū? Was he guilty of* ilhād, *had he become a* murtadd?[38]
>
> *I have given this matter much thought, and have come to the conclusion, that he lived and died as a true believer – albeit admittedly a highly unorthodox one – and that whether or not one can still call him a Muslim, depends more on the outlook of the beholder, than on the piety of our emperor.*
>
> *What gives me the right to say that he remained a true believer? First of all, because he believed in God's unity and worshipped Him, all his life, with all his heart and soul. Second, because he never converted to another religion. He highly respected the Hindūs and the Jains, to*

the point of rejecting the slaughter of animals and believing that there might be some truth in the idea of transmigration of souls, but he had no use for any of their gods and statues and rituals; he liked the Pārsī fire symbols, but did not find much use in their concept of God; he revered the Prophet Īsā [Jesus Christ] *and his saintly mother – upon both of whom be peace! – but found it impossible to accept the obvious nonsense of a triune divinity, the virgin birth of a God-man, and all those other errors and superstitions.*

What made him unorthodox, to the point of incurring, not entirely undeservedly, the reproach of being a heretic and an unbeliever? I think his worst heresy from the point of view of Islām was the rather low esteem in which he held the Prophet Muhammad and the Holy Qurān: in his eyes, they were merely a prophet and a sacred scripture among others. The constant quarrels among the ulamā had convinced him that the Muslim law and religion were far from indubitable, since there were so many differences between the scholars themselves. In the Ibādat-Khāna, he had been looking for unity and insight, but had found nothing but confusion and disagreement.

In the end, his concept of religion was a rather simple one. There is but one God, and all must worship and honour Him, and allow other people to do so in the way they prefer. All must subdue evil passions and practice virtue. All must be led by reason and not merely bow to the authority of any one man or tradition. Differences in creed or ritual are of little importance: the people of the land should be united under their king, whom God has placed above them, and whose duty it is to serve God through bringing justice and prosperity to the people entrusted to his care.

Was Emperor Akbar a Muslim, or a kāfir? Bīrbal – or was it Ab'ūl Fazl? – once said: 'Our Emperor is a Hindū in his food habits, a Pārsī in his rites, and a Sūfī in his heart.' As far as I am concerned, he was like the Sikh Gurū Nanak, or the great poet Kabīr: both men denied they were either Muslims or Hindūs, for such names seemed useless to them. As Kabīr sang so eloquently:

> *Hindūs call Him Rām, Muslims Khudā*
> *Kabīr says: whoever lives should not bother about this:*
> *Ka'bah becomes Kashi, Rām becomes Rahīm*

Abdul Haqq [1551–1642], *the great scholar, [in] his book on the lives of great Muslim saints, wrote that his father, when still a child, had asked his own father whether Kabīr had been a Muslim or a Hindū. The grandfather replied that Kabīr had been a muwahhīd, a believer in the Unity of God. His father then asked whether a muwahhīd was a kāfir or a Muslim. Upon which the old man replied: 'To understand this is difficult: you will understand when you grow up.'*

Allāh willing, one day, when it grows up, the world will understand.

***

Hundreds, if not thousands, of pages have been written about Akbar's religious beliefs and practices.

From a dogmatic point of view, Akbar's beliefs appear to have been the result of two competing tendencies in his mind. On the one hand, he had an inquisitive, fundamentally rationalist mind: according to him, beliefs were to be based solely on evidence and reason – had he been a European monarch, he would have been called a typical Renaissance man. On the other hand, he was also a melancholy mystic, with a profound humility before the Creator, an almost obsessive interest in religious truth and an unfeigned respect for every religion.

'*Just as all groups and the practitioners of all religions have a place within the spacious circle of God's mercy,*' writes Jahangir, '*in my father's realm ... there was room for practitioners of various sects and beliefs, both true and imperfect, and strife and altercation were not allowed. Sunni and Shiite worshiped in one mosque and Frank* [Firanghi] *and Jew in one congregation. Utter peaceableness was his established way. He conversed with the good of every group, every religion and every sect, and gave his attentions to each in accordance with their station and ability to understand.*'[39]

***

Did he renounce Islam? As I have Hakim Ali Gilani state in Epilog 1 of *Akbar's Farewell*, the answer appears to be dependent on one's definition of Islam. If a Muslim is defined as a person who holds the profound belief that there is one God, lord of the universe, to Whom every human being should humbly submit, then Akbar was still a devout Muslim. However, when one considers the other central tenets of Islam – in particular, the unique position held by the Holy Quran and the Prophet Muhammad – Akbar was no longer a Muslim, or at best a highly unorthodox one, for in his mind, the Prophet Muhammad and the Holy Quran occupied a much less prominent place than they do in orthodox Islam.

It has frequently been pointed out that if Akbar was tolerant towards other religions, he was much less so towards Islam. More than one chronicler has claimed that he actually persecuted the religion of his ancestors, or, at least, was clearly prejudiced against it. While the evidence for that claim is much less convincing than some sources suggest, it is definitely true that Akbar was extremely critical of the Muslim clerics of his time – partly for religious, but mostly for political reasons. Akbar was an absolutist, with very little tolerance for anybody else having real power. Both the so-called 'infallibility decree' and the Din-e-Ilahi cult were deliberate attempts to neutralize the power of the Muslim jurists and strengthen his own position as padshah (emperor).

However, it is equally important to emphasize that Akbar never formally renounced Islam and never converted to any other religion, publicly or privately. He had an unfeigned and profound respect for Jesus of Nazareth, but clearly rejected the fundamental tenets of Christianity, i.e., the divinity of Christ and the concept of the Holy Trinity. It is equally clear that he never became a Hindu or a Jain or a Parsi, impressed and heavily influenced though he was by their philosophy, practices and symbols.

Akbar fundamentally was an eclectic, a rationalist as well as a mystic, who came to regard all religions as merely human attempts to honour and serve an ineffable, unattainable Reality. In his own words: '*Each person, according to his personal condition, gives the Supreme Being a Name, but in reality, to name the Unknowable is vain*.'

From a Muslim point of view, Akbar's eclecticism may seem vexingly unorthodox, but in a way, it was profoundly (Sufi) Islamic, too. Although it tends to be forgotten much too often these days in so-called 'Islamist' or 'fundamentalist' circles, Islamic theology teaches that all creeds have their own *shar'a*, i.e., their own rituals and prayers, which may be very different from one tradition to the other; but at their core and at the core of every ethic worthy of that name lies the same *din*, the true spirit of religion, the actual devotion to the Deity, or if one prefers to put it in non-confessional terms, the commitment to truth, justice and love. Arguably, only din truly matters; for, as Mahatma Gandhi once put it, with provocative simplicity: 'God has no religion.'[40]

Akbar's undying contribution to history is to have demonstrated just that.

CHRONOLOGY

14 February 1556: Akbar enthroned at Kalanaur.
5 November 1556: Second Battle of Panipat. Hemu defeated by Bairam Khan.
Early 1557: Annexation of Ajmer.
25 July 1557: Surrender of Sikandar Suri at Mankot.
February 1559: Annexation of Gwalior.
31 January 1561: Bairam Khan assassinated.
1561: 'Petticoat government'. Akbar's wanderings in disguise.
November 1561: Shams-ud Din appointed *vakil*.
14 January 1562: Akbar's first pilgrimage to Ajmer. Akbar's marriage with the princess of Amber. Raja Man Singh at court.
16 May 1562: Execution of Adham Khan.
1563: Abolition of the pilgrimage tax on non-Muslims.
Early 1564: Abolition of the *jizya* tax on non-Muslims.
July 1564: Uzbek rebellion.
Late 1564: Birth and death of Akbar's twin sons.
1566: Invasion by Muhammad Hakim.
1566–1567: Rebellion of the Mirzas.
October 1567: Siege of Chittor.
February 1568: Fall of Chittor. Pilgrimage to Ajmer on foot.
March 1569: Capitulation of Ranthambor.
30 August 1569: Birth of Prince Salim. Start of construction at Fatehpur Sikri.
7 June 1570: Birth of Prince Murad.
1570: Akbar's marriages to the princesses of Bikaner and Jaisalmer.
2 July 1572: Start of campaign in Gujarat.
9 September 1572: Birth of Prince Danyal.
21 December 1572: Battle at Sarnal.
26 February 1573: Capitulation of Surat.
23 August 1573: Rebellion in Gujarat; start of second campaign.
2 September 1573: Battle of Ahmedabad.
1574: Abu'l Fazl presented at court.
End 1574: Campaign in Bengal.
12 July 1576: Battle of Rajmahal; death of Da'ud.

December 1578: Invitation for Jesuit priests sent to Goa.
3 September 1579: The 'infallibility decree'. Last pilgrimage to Ajmer.
28 February 1580: Arrival of first Jesuit mission in Agra.
1580–1581: Rebellion in Bengal; invasion by Muhammad Hakim.
July–August 1581: Akbar crosses the Indus and takes Kabul.
Early 1582: Din-e-Ilahi proclaimed.
Early 1584: Din-e-Ilahi calendar adopted.
February 1584: Marriage of Prince Salim.
10 October 1585: Death of Muhammad Hakim.
5 February 1586: Defeat and death of Raja Birbal.
Later in 1586: Annexation of Kashmir.
5 August 1587: Birth of Prince Khusrau.
November 1589: Death of Raja Todar Mal and Raja Baghwan Das.
1591–1592: Second Jesuit mission in Agra.
1592: Conquest of Odisha.
April 1595: Annexation of Qandahar.
1 January 1599: Death of Prince Murad.
Early 1600: Campaign in the Deccan.
July 1600: Rebellion of Prince Salim.
12 August 1602: Murder of Abu'l Fazl.
March 1603: Reconciliation with Prince Salim, brought about by Salima Sultan Begam.
10 November 1603: Return of Salim to Allahabad.
8 April 1604: Death of Prince Danyal.
September 1605: Akbar's fatal illness.
27 October 1605: Akbar's death.

Notes and References

1. *Tūqān:* elder brother.
2. Vincent A. Smith, *Akbar the Great Mogul 1542–1605*, Clarendon Press, Oxford, UK, 1917; second (revised) edition and third Indian reprint, S. Chand & Co., Delhi, 1966, p. 27.
3. *Ghāzī*: victorious warrior, slayer of the infidel.

4. At the time of the campaign against Hemu, Bairam Khan had left his pregnant wife and the rest of his family in relative safety at Lahore.
5. Maryam-Makānī: occupying the place of (the Virgin) Mary; Qadasī-Arkānī: pillar of purity.
6. Gulchihra: flower-faced; Gulbadan: flower-bodied; and Gulrang: flower-coloured.
7. She was born on 23 February 1539; the marriage took place some weeks before her nineteenth birthday.
8. S. Roy, 'Akbar', in R. C. Majumdar (ed.), *The Mughul Empire*, Bharatiya Vidya Bhavan's History and Culture of the Indian People, Vol. VII, Bombay, 1974, p. 109.
9. Ibid., p. 111.
10. Dargah: Tomb, shrine.
11. See Note 16 under Prologue.
12. *Zanana*: Women's quarters.
13. According to some historians, Akbar called him *batchā-i-lada* in Persian, i.e., young of a dog, or *babesyā* (Hindi), i.e., a catamite, someone in the habit of getting sodomized.
14. Nizam-ud Din Auliya Chishti (1238–1325) was a revered Sufi sage, and Amir Khusrau (1253–1325), a famous musician, scholar and poet who wrote in Persian and Hindustani. The Nizamuddin area still is an important place of pilgrimage in Delhi.
15. 'Axis of Islam', a 73-metre-high minaret tower of victory, one of Delhi's main historical sights. Its construction started in 1193, under Qutub-ud Dīn Aybak, first of the Muslim sultans of Delhi.
16. Gondwana is now mainly in Madhya Pradesh.
17. Vincent A. Smith, *Akbar the Great Mogul - 1542-1605*, Delhi, 1917; second (revised) edition; third Indian reprint, 1966.
18. *I'timad*: (person in whom one has placed one's) reliance, dependence, confidence. Hence: support(er), help(er). I'timad-ud Daula: supporter of the realm.
19. Late 1564.
20. *Hazār mīkhī*: thousand nails.
21. Mary of the Age.
22. Son of a shah, i.e., prince.
23. It should be noted that a number of the Mughal Empire's monuments – tombs, mosques, madrasas and the like – have, in fact, been commissioned by women.
24. Quoted by S. Roy in R. C. Majumdar, op. cit., p. 131.
25. *Mlechcha*: foreign, barbarian, impure, unclean.
26. Maulana Abdul Qadir Badaoni would write a highly critical history of Akbar's reign.
27. Hindu protection charm. A *rakhi*, a thread with a small decorative ornament attached to it, is tied by a sister on her brother's wrist during the annual

Rakshabandhan festival. The brother promises to protect his sister throughout his life.

28. *Chhatris*: Umbrella-shaped cupolas, usually resting on four pillars, used as ornaments on walls, terraces, minarets and other structures.
29. *Sarkar*: province. *Suba*: district.
30. Khusrau: a Persian royal surname, means beautiful/handsome; Parvez: victorious, fortunate; and Khurram: cheerful, happy.
31. *The Jahangirnama: Memoirs of Jahangir, Emperor of India*, translated, edited and annotated by Wheeler M. Thackston, Oxford University Press, New York, 1999, pp. 32–33 and Smith, op. cit., pp. 221–222.
32. This sentence as quoted by Smith, op. cit., p. 221.
33. Ibid., p. 226.
34. Ibid., p. 227.
35. Father Jerome Xavier et al, quoted in ibid., pp. 242 ff.
36. Pierre du Jarric, *Akbar and the Jesuits*, Gorgias Press, Piscataway Township, New Jersey, USA, 2008 edition.
37. Dirk Collier, *Akbar's Farewell,* Amaryllis, New Delhi, 2011/2024, Epilog 1.
38. *Ilhād*: heresy; *murtadd*: apostate, person who has renounced Islam.
39. Thackston, op. cit., pp. xxiii and 40.
40. See, for example, Dirk Colllier, *Paths to Peace: Religion, Ethics and Tolerance in a Globalizing World*, Vakils, Feffer & Simons, Mumbai, 2013.

Chapter 4

Jahangir the Hedonist

Underrated Monarch, Intriguing Man

In India's collective memory, Jahangir is little more than an insignificant transitory figure between his father Akbar the Great, the military and political colossus, and his son Shah Jahan, the apogee of Mughal magnificence and builder of the incomparable Taj Mahal.

To some extent, this is inevitable: Jahangir's reign (1605–1627) was relatively uneventful, if we compare it to other episodes in Mughal history; as he readily admitted himself, he neither had his father's genius nor his stamina. More often than not, he was an indolent, debauched weakling, a slave of wine, women and opium; on several occasions, he revealed himself as a fickle-minded tyrant, capable of unspeakable cruelty.

But that is not the entire story. If we are to judge Jahangir by the security, justice and prosperity enjoyed by his subjects – arguably, the most important criteria for any ruler to be judged by – he stands head and shoulders above any other Mughal emperor, with the exception of his father. On the whole, in spite of his many vices and weaknesses, he was a successful and just monarch who honestly desired the welfare of his subjects and sincerely tried to treat all of them equitably, irrespective of their religion, rank or birth. A well-known anecdote in this respect is that upon his accession, he had a long chain with gold-plated bells suspended from the Agra fort battlements reaching down to a stone column on the bank of the Yamuna; whosoever rang the bells could be assured that the emperor himself would personally hear his case. That chain, by itself, may have been of rather limited practical use to people living outside Agra, but it was a telling symbol of the peace, law and order that reigned during the first two decades of his tenure and which made him deservedly popular with the common people. There was no hunger in Hindustan under Jahangir and no unjust taxation; people lived in relative safety and commerce and culture flourished.

***

Jahangir's relative success was, of course, built on the strong foundations laid by his father, and he was honest enough to frankly admit to this. Whatever had estranged him from his father ended as soon as Akbar passed away and was no longer a rival to him. Jahangir invariably spoke with great praise and reverence about him, and often visited his mausoleum in Sikandra (on the outskirts of Agra) to invoke, as he writes in his memoirs, the support of his *revered father's* spirit; each time, he would dismount at the gate, walk on foot to the tomb, kneel down and rub his forehead on the marble doorstep.

Generally speaking, Jahangir did try to follow in his father's footsteps. He was, for instance, wise enough to realize that Akbar's policy of religious tolerance and equality under the law constituted the very backbone of the empire; therefore, by and large, he followed exactly the same rules and practices – absence of discriminatory taxes, equal opportunities for appointments and promotions and so on. He permitted non-Muslims to build places of worship and celebrate their religious festivals without hindrance; he even gladly participated in them on several occasions.

Publicly, Jahangir conformed to the rituals and practices of Sunni Islam; privately, he was a free-thinker, much less mystically inclined than his father. Sir Thomas Roe (1581–1644), the first English ambassador to the Mughal court in January 1615, even claims he was an outright atheist. That may or may not be the case; he most certainly was no dogmatic fundamentalist of any creed. He respected other religions' philosophical insights and enjoyed open intellectual debate; he was fond of the company of saints and hermits of all religions, and came to view Sufi mysticism and Hindu Vedanta as 'almost identical'. Above all, he was an inquisitive, level-headed rationalist and a sceptic with precious little patience for stories of miracles and superstitious old wives' tales.

One of many examples in this context is Jahangir's own description of one Shaykh Ahmad Sirhindi, a charlatan who pretended to have ascended to several stages of sanctity and mystical union with God (stages designated by such arcane names as 'Dual Lights', 'Faruq',

'Siddiq' and the highest stage: 'Beyond the Caliphs') and was making good money on the backs of the naïve and the credulous.

'[He] *had spread a net of deceit and deception,*' writes Jahangir. '*He had also sent into every city and region those of his devotees, whom he called khalifas, who were best versed in setting up shops in which mysticism could be peddled and people hoodwinked. One of the pieces of nonsense he wrote for his disciples and believers was a book called Maktubat, a miscellany of drivel in which he had penned the basis of his claptrap.*'[1]

Summoned to court to explain himself, the charlatan '*couldn't give a reasonable answer to anything I asked him. He appeared, in addition to his lack of wisdom and knowledge, to be extremely conceited and self-satisfied. I saw that the only thing* [for] *him was to spend a few days in prison so that the frenzy in his mind would settle down,*' Jahangir notes in his wry, matter-of-fact style.

***

In non-religious matters, too, Jahangir adopted the same sceptical, empirical and almost modern scientific attitude. His memoirs are literally studded with examples of his lively interest in natural sciences. When told by local people in Kashmir that a nearby lake was extremely deep, he immediately had it fathomed – only to find out that it was, in fact, rather shallow. The claim that bitumen was supposed to be helpful in the treatment of broken bones was proven to be wrong when a chicken's leg – broken on purpose for the occasion – failed to heal any faster than through the usual means. He ordered the dissection of the liver of a lion in an attempt to find an anatomical explanation for the animal's ferocity. For no less than five years, he personally followed the vicissitudes of a pair of cranes, called Laila and Majnun (the Arabian equivalent of Romeo and Juliet). He had a meteorite dug up while still hot, and knives' blades were forged from its iron. A convict was fed an entire *seer* (about 500 grams) of saffron to find out whether or not it was true that this spice caused laughter and was poisonous in large doses, as the physicians claimed. Needless to say, they, too, were proven wrong by their sceptical emperor. In short, Jahangir was an enthusiastic amateur scientist *avant la lettre*.

***

While Jahangir was by no means a religious bigot, there have been, throughout his career, a number of outrageous – if coincidental – lapses, which would have been quite unthinkable under Akbar. Admittedly, most of these incidents appear to have been politically motivated. In Gujarat, for instance, he had Jain temples demolished and one of the statues thrown on the steps of a mosque, for the Muslims to step on, but this was a punishment of what he saw as an act of open rebellion: at the time of Khusrau's insurgence in 1606, a Jain leader had prophesized that Jahangir's reign would come to an end within two years. Similarly, as will be related in due course, the execution of Guru Arjan Singh Dev in May 1606, the fifth of the ten great Sikh Gurus, was not religiously, but politically, motivated. Probably the worst and most deliberate religious outrage Jahangir committed for 'political' reasons was in 1620, when, after taking the fort of Kangra (in present-day Himachal Pradesh) in the foothills of the Himalayas, he had a cow slaughtered while Muslim prayers were being said.

Apart from the foregoing cases, there have been other instances where, in a fit of – usually drunken – rage, Jahangir suddenly ordered the wanton destruction of religious sanctuaries and artifacts. At Pushkar (in Rajasthan), for instance, he found himself so disgusted by an image of Varaha (Lord Vishnu's third avatar, represented by a man with a wild boar's head), that he ordered it destroyed and thrown into a water tank. It is also reported that he forbade Muslim converts in Kashmir – on pain of death! – from offering their daughters in marriage to non-converted Hindu families, while the opposite – Hindu girls marrying into Muslim families – was permitted and even encouraged.

These incidents may have been isolated and the result of anger and drunken fickleness rather than policy, but they foreboded the resurgence, under Shah Jahan and Aurangzeb, of an ill-advised 'orthodoxy' wherein non-Muslims were again considered – and treated – as second-rate citizens; predictably, this would lead to the downfall of the empire and the ultimate disintegration of India.

***

When crossed, Jahangir was capable of furious anger and extreme cruelty, and it has been reported how he would watch, with sadistic glee, the most horrible forms of torture. Nevertheless, in the fourteenth year of his reign (1619), he found it necessary to take measures to in some way protect himself and his subjects from the consequences of his rage. Describing how he had once condemned a man to death and later ordered his life to be spared, only to find out that the execution had already been carried out, he admits that he regretted his rashness: '*Although that murderous villain deserved to be killed, I regretted the circumstances and decreed that henceforth whenever anyone was ordered to be executed, no matter how insistent I was, he should be held and not killed until sundown. If by that time a rescinding order had not come, they could proceed with the execution.*'[2]

Jahangir's capriciousness was obviously aggravated, if not caused, by his hopeless addiction to alcohol and opium. With his usual candour, he describes his lifelong struggle with the drink demon:

> *I myself did not drink until the age of eighteen .... After that, I started drinking wine, increasing it day by day until grape wine had no longer an effect on me, and I started drinking liquor. Little by little, over nine years, it increased to twenty phials of double-distilled spirits, fourteen during the day and the rest at night .... Things got so bad that in my hangovers my hands shook and trembled so badly I could not drink myself, but had to have others help me. Finally I summoned Hakim Humam, Hakim Abu'l Fath's brother and one of my exalted father's confidants, and informed him of my condition. In perfect sincerity and compassion he said, with no beating around the bush: 'Highness, the way you are drinking, in another six months – God forbid – things will be so bad it will be beyond remedy.' Since his words were spoken in benevolence, and life is precious, it made a great impression on me.*
>
> *From that date I began to decrease the amount .... Over a period of seven years, I got it down to six phials, the weight of a phial being seventeen and three-quarters mithcals. I have now been drinking like this for fifteen years without increase or decrease ...*[3]

Nevertheless, it is well documented that official audiences in the evening often ended with the emperor passing out in a drunken stupor – in fact, he rarely drew a sober breath after the sun had set. It is all the more strange that he was extremely particular about *other* people's drinking: courtiers attending official audiences had their breath sniffed by the guards and were denied access at the slightest hint of alcohol consumption, and he even attempted to outlaw the production and sale of wine and narcotics throughout his empire.

Despite all his weaknesses and shortcomings, Jahangir revealed himself as one of the most gifted and, at times, the most endearing of the Great Mughals. He was an intelligent, well-educated man, fluent in Persian, Turkish, Khariboli (from which Hindi evolved) and Arabic, apart from being a refined connoisseur of the arts, a deserving amateur scientist, a shrewd politician, a pragmatic and wise ruler, a respectful son, a passionate lover, a devoted husband, father and grandfather, and a talented writer. His remarkably candid autobiography, written in an exceptionally lively, straightforward and, at the same time, elegant and refined Persian, is, in fact, more deserving of accolades than the much better-known *Baburnama*.

Like in his father's days, artists and artisans from all over the world were invited to Jahangir's court; he was a passionate lover of beauty, who could be moved to tears by the daintiness of a single flower. His contributions to India's artistic heritage are manifold: the beautiful Shalimar Gardens in Srinagar (the capital of Jammu and Kashmir) and other deserving works of architecture – such as the tomb of I'timad-ud Daula (meaning 'pillar of the realm'; more about him later) in Agra and his own mausoleum in Lahore, to name but a few examples – were commissioned during his reign. Above all, however, he was an unequalled expert in (European, Persian and Indian) painting.

'*As regards myself,*' he boasts in his autobiography, '*in judging (paintings) I have arrived at such a point that when any work is brought before me, either of deceased artists or the present day, without the names being told to me, I say on the spur of the moment that it is the work of such and such a man. And if there be a picture containing many portraits, and each race be the work of a different master, I can discern which face is the work of each. If any other person has put in the eye and eyebrow of a face, I can perceive whose work the original face is and who has painted the eye and eyebrows.*'

While capable of terrible cruelty, Jahangir also appears to have had an emotional, tender heart. It has been related earlier that he was deeply saddened by the loss of Shah Begam, his first wife and Khusrau's mother: '*In consequence of her death,*' he writes, '*from the attachment I had for her, I passed some days without any kind of pleasure in life or existence, and for four days ... I took nothing in the shape of food or drink.*'[4]

Another example of such endearing sensitivity is when he relates the passing of an infant granddaughter (one of Khurram's children), on 5 June 1615. Jahangir was so saddened by the loss, that he found himself unable to continue his diary: '*On this date an event took place of which, no matter how much I wanted to, my hand and heart would not let me write. Every time I took the pen I felt so depressed that I had to tell I'timad-ud Daula to write it for me,'* notes Jahangir. I'timad-ud Daula then proceeded to describe how the emperor refused to leave his room for two days, and then went to his son's house to offer his condolences. '*Along the way,*' writes I'timad-ud Daula, '*no matter how much he desired to control himself, involuntary tears poured from his blessed eyes, and for a long time at the mere mention of a word that reminded him of her, he broke down.*' Even weeks later, '*... he could not control himself, and every time familiar words came to his ears, he burst into tears*'.

Accession to the Throne

One week after Akbar's death on 27 October 1605, Prince Salim ascended the throne in the Diwan-i-Aam (the hall of public audience) of Agra's Fort.

The imperial crown, which had been crafted in the days of Akbar in the pattern of the ornament worn by the great kings of Persia, was brought to him. He put it on his head, and, as an omen auspicious to the stability and happiness of his future reign, kept it there for a full hour. As a formal sign of his accession, he assumed the grandiose title of Nūr-ud Dīn (light of religion) Muhammad Jahāngīr (seizer of the world).

Upon accession, he issued a proclamation consisting of twelve regulations, including the abolition of certain unjust taxes, the prohibition of barbarous punishments (i.e., cutting off noses and ears), the protection of private property and inheritances, the establishment of hospitals for the treatment of poor people, and – remarkably enough – the prohibition of wine and narcotics.

As he had promised before his father's passing, he took no vindictive action against Khusrau's supporters or anyone else who had opposed him. Most of the government officials, high and low, were confirmed in the posts and responsibilities they had held under Akbar. Raja Bir Singh of Orchha, Abu'l Fazl's killer, was handsomely rewarded for his services; but in a conciliatory gesture, Abu'l Fazl's son Abdurrahman was appointed as a high-ranking officer in the imperial army as well.

Other important new appointments included the promotion of Ghiyas Beg (who would become known to posterity as the father of Nur Jahan and the paternal grandfather of Mumtaz Mahal, the lady of the Taj Mahal) to the position of diwan, with the lofty title of I'timad-ud Daula (pillar of the realm, as mentioned earlier).

Conciliatory, but not naïve, Jahangir did take the precautionary measure to separate his two most powerful potential adversaries, keeping his rebellious eighteen-year-old son Khusrau close by his side in the Agra Fort, while sending Man Singh, the boy's maternal uncle and most powerful potential supporter, back to his station as governor of Bengal. It proved to be a prudent move: merely five months later, young Khusrau would rise in open rebellion against his father.

Khusrau's Rebellion

According to contemporary sources, Khusrau appears to have been a handsome and amiable lad, quite pleasant company and 'exceedingly beloved [to] the common people'. That may or may not have been the case; but a faithful son, he clearly was not.

Unable to stomach the humiliation of a life in semi-confinement when the throne had been within his grasp only a few months before, he started plotting a coup. On 6 April 1606, he left the fort with his retinue on the pretence of visiting Akbar's mausoleum in Sikandra, but sped on towards Delhi. On the way, he was joined by Husain Beg Badakhshi, one of his most devoted sycophants, at the head of three hundred horse, a number that would soon swell to twelve thousand. En route, the rebels seized an imperial money convoy carrying one hundred thousand rupees, and, bypassing Delhi, made their way to Lahore. On the way, they were joined by Abdurrahman, the diwan of the Punjab province; Khusrau's revolt had surged to a dangerous tidal wave.

***

However, his luck turned abruptly. Arriving at Lahore, he found its gates closed by the garrison loyal to the emperor; he laid siege to the fort, but was unable to take it. Shortly thereafter, Jahangir himself arrived on the scene: in a highly unusual display of energy, the usually indolent emperor had assembled a striking force and personally set off in pursuit of his rebel son. Khusrau left a detachment to block the gates and keep the garrison bottled up in the fortress and himself turned around at the head of the main body of his army to give battle to the pursuing imperial army.

The two armies clashed on the plain of Bharowal (now in Punjab, India), and in spite of its superior numbers, Khusrau's army was badly defeated. He managed to escape with a handful of followers – including Abdurrahman and Husain Beg Badakhshi – leaving most of the stolen treasure behind. Following the advice of Husain Beg Badakhshi to head west to try and take

Kabul and raise a new invasion army, the fugitives attempted to cross the Chenab River near the Shahpur (in Punjab, India) ferry. Without the help of professional boatmen, however, they accidentally grounded their bark on a sandbank in the middle of the river and pathetically sat there until Jahangir's men arrived to take them prisoner.

In chains, with Abdurrahman and Husain Beg Badakhshi on either side, the prince was brought before his father at Lahore. He attempted to prostrate himself and formally surrender, but Jahangir was not in the mood for reconciliation and had him unceremoniously thrown in jail.

Khusrau's two principal followers were sewn into the wet skins of a freshly slaughtered ox and ass, seated on donkeys, facing the tails, and in this guise paraded through the streets of Lahore all day, in the sweltering heat. Husain Beg Badakhshi died within twelve hours, due to constriction and suffocation; Abdurrahman somehow survived the ordeal and was pardoned after twenty-four hours.

Khusrau's humbler followers were less fortunate. Jahangir had them impaled alive on a mile-long row of stakes, and a horrified Khusrau was forced to ride past them, seated on an elephant, '*to receive*', as Jahangir put it with cruel irony, '*the homage of his followers*'.

***

Another victim of Jahangir's wrath was Guru Arjan Singh Dev, the fifth of the ten great Sikh Gurus. On his way through the Punjab, Khusrau had asked him for help, which the holy man had at first refused, stating that whatever money he had was for the poor, not for princes; but in the end, when Khusrau pleaded he was destitute, the Guru had given him five thousand rupees. Jahangir now condemned him and asked him to pay a fine of two hundred thousand rupees. When the Guru refused to pay, the emperor had him executed – horribly tortured to death, according to some Sikh sources. Quite obviously, this ill-advised execution (on 30 May 1606 at Lahore) had nothing to do with religious bigotry per se; nevertheless, it deeply shocked and angered the Sikhs and forever estranged them from the Mughal authorities, leading to a dangerous revolt in the days of Aurangzeb. It was, as Charles-Maurice de Talleyrand (1769–1821)* would have said, worse than an injustice: it was a mistake.

***

*An astute French bishop, diplomat and politician in the days of Napoleon Bonaparte.

Khusrau's rebellion had been crushed within a month, and the prince himself now spent the next year in chains, being moved about with the imperial camp during Jahangir's travels to Kabul and the Qandahar area (which, as a result of the turmoil, had come under threat of a Persian invasion).

However, barely had Khusrau been released from his chains, when, in August 1607, he started hatching a new plot to have his father assassinated during a hunting trip. The secret, however, leaked out, and Khurram, who got scent of it, immediately informed his father. Some four hundred nobles were said to be involved, but Jahangir wisely avoided detailed inquiries and contented himself with the summary execution of the four known ringleaders. Significantly, he also ordered Khusrau to be blinded – by having his eyelids sewn shut, most probably, for his vision was partially restored in one eye when physicians were later allowed to treat him.

The hapless, half-blind rebel spent the rest of his life in confinement, moving around with the imperial army. On rare occasions, he was allowed in the emperor's presence, '*but he showed no signs of frankness of spirit and always seemed sad and downcast, so I forbade his coming to see me,*' Jahangir coldly notes.

In 1620, towards the end of his life, Khusrau would be put in Khurram's custody (at the latter's own request); shortly thereafter, in late January 1622, he died – officially of an 'attack of colic', but more than probably, murdered in cold blood on Khurram's orders.

Nur Jahan and Her Clan

As Bamber Gascoigne notes,[5] the most important development of the first half of Jahangir's reign was the twin rise to power of his newly wedded wife Mehr-un Nissa (sun among women) and of his third son Khurram, soon to be known as Shāh Jahān (king of the world).

Mehr-un Nissa was the daughter of Ghiyas Beg, a Persian who had entered Akbar's service after having fled his home country. His own father had been *wazir* to the governor of Khorasan in Persia, but after his death in 1582, the family had fallen into discredit, and Ghiyas Beg resolved to seek his fortune in India. Accompanied by Asmat Begam, his pregnant wife, his daughter Sahlia and two sons, Muhammad Sharif and Abdul Hasan (Asaf Khan), he joined a merchant caravan travelling eastwards. Unfortunately, while still on Persian territory, the caravan was attacked by robbers and Ghiyas Beg's family lost almost everything it owned. Left with only two mules, they made their way to Qandahar, where, on 31 May 1577, Asmat Begam gave birth to Mehr-un Nissa, her fourth child and second daughter.

There, on Mughal territory, Ghiyas Beg's good luck came back to him. He managed to enter Emperor Akbar's service, and, thanks to his refined education and astute skills, quickly rose through the ranks and made himself a fortune.

***

In 1594, when she was seventeen years old, Mehr-un Nissa was given in marriage to Ali Quli Istajlu, a Persian officer in the imperial service, who, as a member of Prince Salim's (Jahangir's) retinue, had earned himself the title of Sherafgan (lion thrower) for single-handedly killing a lion or a tiger on a hunting trip. Although he had sided with Akbar in the days of Salim's revolt, he was granted an important *jagir* in Bengal upon Jahangir's accession.

Something, though, must have been going wrong, for in 1607, Sherafgan was suspected of rebellious designs. Jahangir ordered the new governor of Bengal, Qutub-ud Din Khan (who had succeeded Raja Man Singh in August, 1606) to interrogate Sherafgan and bring him to court. Upon the governor's arrival in Agra in late May 1607, there was a skirmish in which an infuriated Sherafgan attacked and fatally wounded Qutub-ud Din Khan and one of his men, before being himself '*chopped to pieces,*' and '*dispatched to hell*', as Jahangir puts it in his memoirs. '*It is hoped,*' he vengefully adds, '*that the disgraced wretch's place will forever be in hell.*' As for the unlucky governor, Jahangir informs us that he '*passed away to God's mercy in his own quarters, four watches* [12 hours] *later*'.

Thus prematurely widowed, young Mehr-un Nissa was sent to the imperial *zanana* together with her little two-year-old daughter, Ladli Begam, to serve as lady-in-waiting to Salima Sultan Begam, the late Akbar's favourite wife and Jahangir's stepmother.[6] The year 1607 was decidedly a bad one for Mehr-un Nissa's family: her money-grubbing father found himself demoted upon charges of embezzlement, and both her elder brother Muhammad Sharif and a cousin of her mother were summarily executed on the emperor's orders for their involvement in Khusrau's assassination plot.

Four years later, however, in March 1611, her fortune took a spectacular turn for the better, when she managed to catch the emperor's attention at the annual palace Meena Bazaar[7] during the New Year spring festival. Forthwith smitten by her beauty, Jahangir married her two months later. Jahangir's infatuation with his new bride became evident from the lofty titles he chose to bestow on her: Nūr Mahal (light of the palace), soon upgraded to Nūr Jahān (light of the world); as of 1613, the entire court was officially referring to her as Pādshāh Begam (lady empress), the first woman in the realm, and, as soon became apparent, its true centre of power.

***

One of the countless fabricated stories with which Indian history abounds is the hypothesis that Jahangir had been in love with Mehr-un Nissa before her ill-fated first marriage and that he had a hand in Sherafgan's downfall and violent death. This version is, of course, entirely unsubstantiated, and quite evidently, blatant nonsense. For all we know, Jahangir never laid eyes on Mehr-un Nissa before the fateful Meena Bazaar meeting in 1611. If he had known and wanted to marry her before, he could easily have done so, and he most certainly would not have needed to wait for four long years after she became a widow.

Jahangir thought his beautiful new wife was a godsend, and as far as he was concerned, she certainly was – most of the time, anyway. At thirty-four years of age, she still was – and would remain for many more years – a radiant beauty; but much more than a physically attractive bedfellow, she was his confidante and true soul mate. Like her husband, she was quick-witted and highly intelligent, educated and cultured, fond of poetry, music, architecture and painting. She had excellent aesthetic taste and was herself a gifted artist, who devised new styles of dress, ornaments and decoration. The small, but wonderfully elegant mausoleum she built for her parents on the right bank of the Yamuna in Agra is, arguably, one of the absolute apogees of Mughal architecture, less overwhelming, but aesthetically on a par with the Taj Mahal.

She appears to have been endowed with great physical stamina and good health; she was an excellent hunter and a crack shot, reputed to have once felled four tigers with only six bullets. She was sociable, mild-mannered and even-tempered; towards the poor and the downtrodden, she was compassionate and charitable, donating vast amounts of money to charity on a daily basis.

Above all, however, she was an astute, hard-working and extremely ambitious politician. Her husband's indolent character, his – usually justified – blind trust in her and her many personal skills and dedication would soon make her the most powerful person in the empire. Jahangir even had coin struck in her name – a unique event in Mughal history – with the inscription: '*By order of Emperor Jahangir, gold has a hundred splendours added to it by receiving the impression of the name of Nur Jahan, the Queen Begam.*'

If Nur Jahan was a godsend to Jahangir, she was even more so to her relatives. Under her influence, her next of kin – the junta/clique around her, as many an unsympathetic commentator has preferred to call it – soon became all-powerful. The members of this 'gang of four', apart from Nur Jahan herself, were I'timad-ud Daula (Ghiyas Beg); her surviving brother Asaf Khan, an able and hard-working administrator just like his father; and, last but not least, Prince Khurram (later Shah Jahan), Jahangir's favourite son and heir-apparent. Khurram, on 10 May 1612, married Asaf Khan's beautiful nineteen-year-old daughter Arjumand Banu Begam, better known under her honorary title, Mumtaz Mahal, meaning 'the preferred/most excellent one of the palace'.

The erstwhile destitute Persian migrants had all but become full members of the imperial family – I'timad-ud Daula even enjoyed the exceptional privilege of being allowed to enter the *zanana* without the ladies having to veil themselves; literally nothing in the realm happened without the knowledge and permission of Nur Jahan and her family/clique.

It will come as no surprise that many a courtier deeply resented this state of affairs, but the few muffled protests that reached the emperor's ears were of no avail: Nur Jahan and her party would rule supreme for eleven years, until Khurram's revolt in 1622, which, as will be related in due course, would cause a dramatic rift in the family.

The Conquest of Mewar

The military strength of the empire allowed Jahangir to rest on his father's laurels throughout most of his career. Akbar had left out just one 'beauty spot': the Aravalli hills (i.e., the area around Udaipur), where Rana Udai Singh of Mewar had gone to hide himself after the loss of Chittor in 1568. The area had been of little strategic importance to Akbar at the time: after all, the road to Gujarat and the mighty fortresses of Chittor and Ranthambor were firmly in his hands, and as we have seen, he had many more pressing priorities. Thus, Udai Singh had been allowed to live undisturbed in his hills; an independent Mewar was to Akbar little more than a nuisance, a small stone inside his boot, annoying enough to make itself felt from time to time, but not enough to bother to stop and get rid of it.

Things took a turn for the worse when the meek Udai Singh was succeeded after his death in 1572 by his defiant and bellicose son Pratap Singh, who managed to recover a substantial part of his father's erstwhile dominions. A Mughal expeditionary force under Raja Man Singh soundly defeated him on 21 June 1576 (in the Battle of Haldighati), but he refused to give up: though seriously wounded, he managed to escape into the jungle. From there, in the following years, he mounted a successful guerilla operation, retaking lost territories as soon as the Mughal expeditionary forces had left them and managing to remain free and independent until his death from natural causes on 29 January 1597. His son and successor Amar Singh, though not as strong a leader as his father, continued with his father's policy of resistance.

This was the situation Jahangir inherited at the time of Akbar's death in on 27 October 1605. Immediately upon his accession to the throne, he ordered a new attack on Mewar, which, however, was aborted on account of Khusrau's rebellion. Hostilities resumed in 1608 and dragged on for six years with one Mughal commander succeeding the other, until, in 1614, supreme command of the Mewar operation was entrusted to Prince Khurram. Eager to prove himself, the prince launched an all-out campaign until Amar Singh's followers entreated their king to sue for peace. Clearly, the resources of tiny Mewar were no match for the Mughal Empire's infinite supply of men and resources.

***

Elated and also relieved at the conclusion of a costly war that had been dragging on for so many decades, Khurram and Jahangir were happy to offer honourable terms to their adversary. The treaty was signed in 1615: Amar Singh recognized Jahangir as his sovereign, but remained in charge of Mewar as its governor; even the region around Chittor was restored to him, although the fortress was not to be fortified and not even repaired. He was exempt from attending the Mughal court in person: his son would represent him and assist the emperor with a contingent of troops and the Rana's entire family was exempt from marrying any of its princesses into the Mughal ruling family.

Both parties honourably kept their word. From then on, the Ranas of Mewar would remain loyal allies to the Mughal throne, until, two generations down the line, Aurangzeb's ill-advised policies would drive Raj Singh to rebellion.

War in the Deccan: Malik Ambar

The other front where Jahangir intended to pick up where his father had left off was the Deccan – the independence of which had always been a thorn in Akbar's side. At the time of Akbar's death in 1605, the Mughals controlled the whole of Khandesh (in northern Maharashtra) and a sizeable part of Ahmednagar (in central Maharashtra), but the region remained defiant. It was now Jahangir's task to put an end to this defiance and conquer the rest of Ahmednagar. He would then try and take over Bijapur and Golconda, and if possible, the rest of the subcontinent.

***

In 1608, while still engaged in Mewar, Jahangir sent Abdurrahim Khan Khanan at the head of an army of twelve thousand well-equipped elite cavalry to complete the conquest of Ahmednagar. In spite of his considerable military experience and the strength of his forces, however, the Khan Khanan soon found himself on the defensive – which had everything to do with the military genius and skilful tactics of Malik Ambar (1549 to 13 May 1626), Ahmednagar's fearless and highly competent prime minister and army leader.

Malik Ambar's career had been remarkable, to say the least. Born in dire poverty near the city of Harar in the Adal Sultanate (eastern Ethiopia), he was sold into slavery by his own parents and travelled from country to country with his successive masters. Via Yemen, Mecca and Baghdad, he finally ended up in south-central India, where he rose to the position of prime minister of the Nizam Shahi dynasty of Ahmednagar in 1615.

A European witness, the Flemish/Dutch merchant Pieter van den Broecke (1585–1640), described him as '*a black kaffer*[8] *from Abyssinia with a stern Roman face*'. This '*kaffer*', for one, proved to be an exceptionally talented leader, both in times of peace and war. He is credited, among other achievements, with the establishment of a highly efficient fiscal administration and with the foundation of the city of Khadki (in Maharashtra; later called Aurangabad), with its ingenious canal water supply system. Also, and perhaps more importantly, however, his courageous and highly effective resistance against Mughal supremacy foreboded the rise of the Maratha nation under Shivaji Maharaj, two generations later (in the late seventeenth century). The erstwhile slave would have been proud to know that his political heirs would later become the nemesis of the mighty Mughals.

Confronted with the Mughal invasion, Malik Ambar engaged his adversaries with deadly hit-and-run guerilla tactics, avoiding open pitched battles, but constantly harassing the invaders with his Maratha militiamen. Its ranks decimated and demoralized and its officers hopelessly divided, the erstwhile seemingly invincible Mughal army proved to be unequal to the task: soon, Ahmednagar city itself was lost.

***

After two frustrating years of humiliating cat-and-mouse games, the unfortunate Khan Khanan was recalled in disgrace and replaced by Prince Parvez and his guardian, Asaf Khan. But neither these two, nor the other generals sent down to support them, fared any better than their predecessors: in the end, they did hardly anything but arguing and blaming each other for the army's constant failure to come to grips with the ever-elusive Maratha warriors.

In 1616, eight years after the triumphant start of a campaign, which hitherto had produced nothing but dishonour and painful losses of men, resources and territory, an utterly frustrated Jahangir decided to move the imperial court from Ajmer to Mandu[9] to be closer to the war, and put his favourite son Khurram in charge of the campaign. The prince was given the lofty title of Shah Sultan, plus ten million rupees for campaign expenses.

***

Khurram reached Burhanpur by March 1617, and, at once, opened peace negotiations with his adversaries. Awed by the overwhelming military force at Khurram's disposal, Malik Ambar and his ally, the sultan of Bijapur, were pragmatic and shrewd enough to bend with the wind rather than break in the storm, and quickly accepted the terms offered: the city of Ahmednagar and all the territories seized during the guerilla war would be returned to the Mughal throne, and tributes would be paid. As a result, 1.6 million rupees worth of presents were offered to Khurram and a peace treaty was signed.

The treaty – which, in fact, did little else than restoring the status quo under Akbar – was hailed and celebrated at the Mughal court with extravagant pomp and magnificence, as if it had been the result of the most decisive of victories. Jahangir invited Khurram to sit next to him on the imperial balcony in the Diwan-i-Aam, had trays of gems and gold coins poured over his head and bestowed on him the grossly overblown title of Shāh Jahān (king of the world).

But there really was not all that much to celebrate. Malik Ambar had not been beaten; his ambition and self-assurance remained unabated. No sooner had Jahangir returned to the north that Malik Ambar forged an alliance with Bijapur and Golconda, besieged Ahmednagar and threatened Burhanpur; his guerillas even carried out raids as far as Mandu, deep in Mughal territory.

In response to his Deccan garrison's desperate appeal for reinforcements, Jahangir resolved to once again send Shah Jahan to punish the rebellion, but as the prince was tied up in the siege of the Kangra hill fortress, the counteroffensive was delayed for some time. The prince also laid down an important condition for his renewed mission in the south: he demanded – and got – custody over his half-blind brother Khusrau.

***

Things were changing at the Mughal court, and with Jahangir's health becoming increasingly uncertain, Khurram had little appetite for a prolonged absence far away from the centre of power. True, he was his father's favourite and clearly more competent than his three brothers – Khusrau was half-blind and disgraced, Parvez a hopeless drunk, and Shahryar, born through a concubine, a good-for-nothing nincompoop – but as long as his father and brothers were alive, he could not let his guard down.

Besides, cracks were starting to appear in the erstwhile seemingly unbreakable Nur Jahan bloc. As Jahangir's health began to fail – the effects of years of alcoholism, opium addiction and chronic asthma were making themselves felt – she was growing increasingly worried about the future. Clearly, she was smart enough to realize that as soon as Shah Jahan would occupy the throne, her reign would be over: the prince was far too strong-willed to allow anyone, much less his stepmother, to rule in his stead; and over the years, he had become a staunch, conservative Sunni, increasingly weary of Nur Jahan's liberal, Shia persuasion – another reason for him to clip her wings.

It was no doubt with these thoughts in mind that, in early 1620, she decided to betroth Ladli Begam (her daughter by her first husband) to Prince Shahryar, Jahangir's youngest offspring.

In a way, the marriage was a kind of insurance policy: it made sure that, one way or the other, Nur Jahan's family would continue to hold sway over the Mughal Empire for at least another generation. However, this move also introduced a deeply divisive new element in the family relations. If, as expected, Shah Jahan would turn out to be Jahangir's successor, Mumtaz Mahal (his favourite spouse and Asaf Khan's daughter) would become the first lady; if, however, Shahryar could somehow manage to seize the throne, Nur Jahan would continue to call the shots like before.

Whether they liked it or not, Nur Jahan and her brother Asaf Khan had become potential rivals, rather than allies. And with the death of their parents – their mother passed away on 9 October 1621 and their father followed her to the grave on 27 January 1622 – they lost the two most important potential mediators between them. From then on, they were on their own – all of them.

***

With Khusrau in his custody as he had requested, Shah Jahan left Lahore and headed for the Deccan in late 1620. From Ujjain in Malwa, he dispatched two powerful cavalry forces to drive away the Maratha raiders from the Mandu area. This activity was done without too much difficulty, and with the same ruthless resolution he had shown himself to be capable of, some six years earlier in Mewar, he quickly took over Burhanpur and Ahmednagar. When his forces reached Patan (now known as Satara and located in Maharashtra, about 170 km south of Pune), the unthinkable happened: the seventy-two-year old Malik Ambar sued for peace. Shah Jahan, eager to get back up north, quickly agreed to the terms offered: Ahmednagar was to return all the territories it had taken from the Mughals, plus throw in an additional 50-km-wide strip of land along the border; in addition, the states of Ahmednagar, Bijapur and Golconda agreed to pay a tribute of 1.2, 1.8 and 2.0 million rupees, respectively. Mughal honour was thus saved. In mid-1621, after less than a year of military operations, Shah Jahan was back in Burhanpur to celebrate, rest and bask in his glory.

Malik Ambar's capitulation was the apogee of Jahangir's – and Shah Jahan's – military career, although it was, all things considered, a rather meagre result, compared to Akbar's spectacular triumphs. It had taken the mighty Mughal Empire more than twelve years of war to win a few extra square kilometres of territory and a bit of treasure – much less than what it had invested and lost in the wars. Moreover, the Deccan states had only been beaten back, but by no means crushed, and old Malik Ambar remained a force to be reckoned with until his death in 1626.

But that was not the way Jahangir chose to see the situation. Apart from Khusrau's rebellion, it had, on the whole, been smooth sailing for him so far. The heartlands of his empire enjoyed an unprecedented period of prosperity, tranquillity and rule of law; moreover, all the enemies of state had been brought to heel. With the conquest of Mewar and the capitulation of the recalcitrant Deccan states, he had succeeded where his illustrious father had failed, and he felt immensely proud about his achievements.

Alas, it proved to be the calm before the storm, the peak before the abyss. Soon, fate would have one setback after another in store for him.

Qandahar: A Bone of Contention

The Persian Shah Abbas must have sensed it, right from the start: with Akbar gone, the great Mughal Empire no longer was the invincible superpower it once had been; with a less forceful emperor on the throne, it was only a matter of time before it would start slipping. Early in Jahangir's reign, probably encouraged by Khusrau's rebellion, Shah Abbas had made a move to seize Qandahar, but withdrew when Jahangir moved closer to the area, and explained it away as the unauthorized action of a local commander. Nevertheless, Qandahar remained a symbolic bone of contention between him and the Mughal emperor – not important enough to go to war over, but too prestigious to forsake one's claims on it. And as far as legal claims were concerned, his were, without any doubt, more legitimate: after all, it was Humayun who had stolen it from the Shah and not the other way round.

Towards the end of 1620, the Shah's patience had come to an end. He sent an official ambassador to the Mughal court, carrying a friendly letter emphasizing the cordial relations between them, but openly – albeit verbally by the ambassador – demanding the return of the city to Persia. When this overture failed to produce the desired response for a full year, he sent an army to Qandahar, which took the fort there after a forty-five-day siege.

In an unbelievably flowery, convoluted letter, Shah Abbas tried to explain away the incident as a trivial matter, not worth the aggravation. A remarkable opening sentence set the stage: '*May breezes of prayers, whiffs of response to which cause the rosebud of desire to open and perfume the nostrils of unity and flashes that drive away the darkness of disagreeableness be perceived by that illuminated mind* [i.e., Jahangir's]'.[10]

The Shah goes on to explain that after he had inherited the throne from his father, he managed to chase away his enemies (i.e., the Uzbeks and the Ottomans) from all his ancestral territories. He noted that Qandahar had always been safe in the hands of '*that brother as dear to me as life itself* [i.e., Jahangir]' and that he had expected it to be handed back to him '*in a spirit of cooperativeness and brotherliness*'. He regretted that Jahangir had failed to react to his request, probably because '*that petty country was not worthy of his* [Jahangir's] *notice*'. He then declared that he had then decided to go on a hunting trip ('*without arms or armaments*') in the area and that he had expected to be received as a guest of honour in the fortress, but the local commander had stubbornly refused to let him in. It was then that the Shah had ordered the fortress to be taken, after which, he had granted amnesty to the defenders. He concluded that, on the whole, the entire incident was a trivial matter and that he hoped that unity, concord and brotherly affection would continue to rule their relationship. The letter ended with gushing best wishes: '*May your exalted banner be always and ever embraced by divine protection*.'

In a well-nigh equally flowery response, Jahangir confirmed his feelings of undying friendship, while – ever so subtly, politely, but unmistakably – calling the Shah a cheat and a liar and voicing his anger that the Shah had '*without provocation or cause caused to wither the garden of amity, friendship, brotherliness and unity, which should not have been clouded by the dust of contention until the end of time*'. Expressing hope for an amicable settlement, the letter ended with the pious wish that God would, at all times, preserve and protect the Shah.

The letter was sugarcoated with pledges of brotherly affection, but it was clear that Jahangir was seething with rage. He cared little about Qandahar, but all the more about his honour; this insult would not go unpunished. Grandiose plans were made, not only to retake Qandahar but also all of Khurasan, and maybe, with the help of the Uzbeks of Samarqand, even the Persian capital Isfahan itself. And, of course, Jahangir's iron right arm would have to do the job. An imperial *firman* was sent down to the Deccan: Shah Jahan was summoned back to court to assume command of the Qandahar campaign.

Shah Jahan's Rebellion

In mid-1622, upon receiving his father's orders, Khurram/Shah Jahan dutifully left Burhanpur and headed north. It soon became apparent, however, that he was not at all pleased with the prospect of a new, lengthy and even further remote campaign, when he had a throne to defend, a father whose health was declining and a powerful stepmother whom he no longer trusted. Already at Mandu – about 1250 km south of Lahore and a full 2400 km from Qandahar where he was supposed to go – he decided to halt, explaining in a message to his father that he would advance further when the monsoon was over. Also, he laid down several conditions for his continuing involvement: he wanted sole command of the army, the governorship of the Punjab and the great fortress of Ranthambor as a safe residence for his family.

Jahangir did not like it one bit. '*From the contents of the letter* [Khurram's] *and the requests he made the aroma of goodness did not come – indeed, signs of rebelliousness were apparent,*' he writes in his memoirs.[11] His misgivings were soon confirmed when reports came in that Khurram had been seizing some of Nur Jahan's and Shahryar's *jagirs* in the Dholpur area (in eastern Rajasthan). In no uncertain terms, Jahangir ordered Khurram to immediately desist: '*An order was issued with the following points: henceforth he would mind his own business, not step off the highway of propriety, and be content with the estates the supreme administration had assigned him.*' He was still welcome at court, added Jahangir, if he wanted to pay homage to his father, but he was to immediately send a large number of his followers (all veterans of the Deccan campaign) to join the Qandahar expedition. Jahangir then cautioned: '*... if he acted contrary to orders, he would regret it.*'[12] A few weeks later, on 12 August 1622, Shahryar was officially appointed as head of the Qandahar campaign, promoted to the rank of 12,000 *zat* and 8000 *suwar** and bestowed with a number of important *jagirs* that had previously been given to Khurram/Shah Jahan.

*Ever since the days of Akbar, each Mughal official was given a rank called *zat* (referring to a rate of pay, out of which the holder, in theory, was required to maintain a certain quota of horses, elephants, beasts of burden and carts), in addition to a *suwar* rank, which allowed the officer to add a supplementary body of *suwar* or horsemen.[13] The whole system became highly inflated under Akbar's successors, with ever increasing numbers of nobles being awarded higher and higher ranks – without any real military or other substance behind it.[14]

Deeply alarmed by these developments, Khurram sent his diwan (Afzal Khan) with a personal letter to his father. The diwan arrived at Agra on 5 October and was allowed to read out his message, but Jahangir was not in the least impressed. '*Cloaking his outrageous behaviour in apologies, he had sent Afzal Khan in* [the] *hope that he might be able to advance his interests with slick talk and smooth over his rough spots. Paying not the slightest attention, I didn't even turn my face to him* [Afzal Khan],' he notes.[15] The tables had been turned: the once good-for-nothing nobody had managed to become the heir-apparent or at least a privileged pretender to the throne; the erstwhile favourite had fallen into utter disgrace.

***

Shah Jahan saw no other way out of his predicament than to rise in open rebellion. At the head of the troops loyal to him, he sped to Agra, intent on seizing the treasury.

Jahangir was appalled. '*Of the patronage and favours I showered upon him I can say that until now no monarch has showered upon any son,*' he complains in his memoirs. '*Of which of my pains should I write? Is it really necessary for me, with my illness and weakness, to get on a horse and gallop around in such hot weather, which is extremely disagreeable to me, running off after such an undutiful son?*' Henceforth, he decreed, Khurram was to be referred to as '*bedaulat*' (the pauper). An additional cause of frustration to the ailing emperor was that many amirs, including the seventy-year-old Abdurrahim Khan Khanan himself, had joined the rebellion.

But the rebels underestimated the astuteness and the resolve of the emperor, and above all, of his queen. The Qandahar campaign was aborted, and Mahabat Khan, the best and most trusted general of the empire, summoned from Kabul. Similarly, Jahangir's second son Parvez was recalled from Bihar with all his men, and the raja of Amber (now in Rajasthan) and the other Rajput chiefs were ordered to send strong contingents in support of the imperial forces. '*By the time I reached Delhi,*' affirms Jahangir, with a touch of hyperbole, '*such an army was assembled, that the whole country was covered with men as far as the eye could reach.*'

Meanwhile, Khurram and Abdurrahim invaded and plundered the defenceless city of Agra in April 1623. Unable to take the fort and the treasure within it, they were compelled to turn north to meet the rapidly advancing imperial army. Near Mathura (about 50 km northwest of Agra), Shah Jahan stayed behind and sent his best general, a Hindu named Sundar Das aka Raja Vikramajit, to face Mahabat Khan's forces.

There was a moment of panic in the imperial army when Abdullah Khan, who commanded the vanguard, but, in reality, was one of Shah Jahan's spies, promptly went over to the rebels. History might have taken a completely different turn here had it not been for '*a bullet fired by Fate*' that hit and killed Sundar Das. The death of their commander completely demoralized the rebel army, which now took a terrible beating; decimated and in complete disarray, the survivors fled until they reached Shah Jahan's camp, some 80 km away.

Discouraged by this unexpected disaster and also by the loss of his most competent general – '*it was as though this Hindu dog was his* [Shah Jahan's] *fortune, ambition, and mind,*' observes Jahangir contemptuously in his memoirs – Shah Jahan hastily retreated to Mandu, and from there, across the Narmada River, into the Deccan. After lodging his family in the fortress of Asirgarh, he proceeded further south to Burhanpur, the capital of the Mughal Deccan, from where he piteously appealed to his erstwhile adversaries, Malik Ambar and the sultan of Bijapur, for help against his father.

***

Success has many fathers, but failure is an orphan. Malik Ambar had precious little appetite for waging a new war against the Mughal Empire for the sake of a forlorn prince, and neither had Bijapur. Shah Jahan's men now began deserting him in droves. Even the old Khan Khanan, whom Shah Jahan had sent out to negotiate a peace deal with Mahabat Khan, switched over to the imperialists as soon as he had crossed the Narmada, in spite of a solemn oath on the Holy Quran that he would never betray him. Shah Jahan had no alternative but to flee posthaste eastwards, across the Tapti River into Golconda. The sultan there refused to help him, but allowed him to flee through his territory into neighbouring Odisha.

The imperialists now briefly rested on their laurels. The victorious army under Mahabat Khan returned to Burhanpur to pass the remainder of the rainy season, and Jahangir himself felt safe enough again to leave Ajmer and travel to his beloved Kashmir.

***

It provided a most welcome breathing space for Shah Jahan. The province of Odisha surrendered to him without a fight, and he now quickly retook the initiative, invading and soon thereafter occupying Bengal and Bihar, where the remaining imperial garrisons were too weak to resist. Patna and Jaunpur fell to his forces, ably led by his valiant new commander, Prince Bhim Singh of Mewar. Even Allahabad and Awadh would have been captured by Shah Jahan, had not Parvez and Mahabat Khan hastened from Burhanpur to relieve both cities.

Once again, the tables turned quickly. Astute manoeuvring by Mahabat Khan cut off Shah Jahan's supplies and compelled him to fight unprepared, with devastating results, his army severely defeated and its valiant commander killed in battle. He found himself forced to flee posthaste to Rohtas (in southern Bihar), where he left Mumtaz Mahal, too weak to travel after childbirth, in the security of the fortress. From there, he withdrew back to the Deccan via Odisha and Golconda, where he even entered into a short-lived alliance with the old ironside Malik Ambar, who at that time was battling it out with the sultan of Bijapur.

Whatever plans Shah Jahan and his new ally had were rudely interrupted by the advent of the main body of the Mughal army under Parvez and Mahabat Khan. To add to his misery, Shah Jahan fell seriously ill, and Abdullah Khan, his only remaining supporter of any stature, abandoned, out of sheer frustration, all worldly pursuits to become a fakir.

This was the end of the road for Shah Jahan. In sheer despair, in late 1625, he wrote his father a grovelling letter, begging his forgiveness and promising unconditional loyalty and obedience.

Jahangir's reply was prompt and surprisingly lenient. Khurram would be fully pardoned if he surrendered the fortresses of Asirgarh and Rohtas and sent his sons Dara Shikoh and Aurangzeb[16] – then aged ten and eight, respectively – to the imperial court. Much relieved, Shah Jahan complied immediately. He was appointed governor of Balaghat (now in south-eastern Madhya Pradesh) – an insignificant *jagir* in comparison the lofty position he once had held, but much better than he had dared to expect. He later withdrew to Junnar (in Maharashtra, about 150 km east of Mumbai) to rest after three exhausting years full of anguish and frustration and bide his time. Three years of ruinous civil war had come to an end in April 1626.

***

In the days of Khusrau's rebellion, Jahangir had retaliated with mass executions, imprisonment and, ultimately, the blinding of his own son. Why was he so lenient this time? Did he, in spite of everything, still have a soft spot for the most talented of his sons? Was he anxious to assuage Asaf Khan's feelings? Or was it, as many authors have speculated, Nur Jahan who convinced him to be sympathetic towards Khurram? Indeed, the empress was anxious to thwart Mahabat Khan's fast-rising power and influence and, therefore, wanted to put an end to the civil war as quickly as possible. We do not and cannot know for sure. One thing was certain: the worst humiliation for the imperial couple was yet to come.

Mahabat Khan's Coup d'état

Nur Jahan was far too astute a politician not to realize how dramatically Shah Jahan's rebellion had changed the political landscape. Shah Jahan himself was licking his wounds, in virtual exile; Khusrau was dead; and Shahryar, now that the Qandahar campaign had been aborted, was again what he always had been: an absolute nobody. The only prince left with any real power was Parvez, the victorious leader of the imperial campaign against Shah Jahan's rebellion. True, he was a self-indulgent weakling and a notorious drunkard, but he was Jahangir's eldest surviving son, perfectly loyal and obedient to his father, and, therefore, a likely successor to the throne. And he and Mahabat Khan – by far the best general in the army and the real mastermind of the campaign against Shah Jahan – got along quite well. Mahabat Khan, on the other hand, made no secret of his disapproval of a woman running the empire; he hated Asaf Khan, whom he suspected – not without reason – to be jealous of him and bent on ruining him.

What would happen to Nur Jahan and Asaf Khan if Parvez were to become the next emperor? There was little doubt that Mahabat Khan would become the real power behind the throne and they would be completely sidetracked. Brother and sister, allies again, began manoeuvring against their common enemy, with cunning and consummate skill.

The first masterstroke was to physically separate their rivals: Parvez was sent to Gujarat and Mahabat Khan to Bengal, i.e., to the opposite corners of the empire. Next, the siblings skilfully started casting doubts on Mahabat Khan's honesty and loyalty: he was ordered to account for all the booty he had taken during the campaign and surrender all the elephants to the imperial stables. A final blow was the extraordinarily brutal treatment of his newly wed son-in-law, an imperial officer named Khwaja Barkhurdar, who had accepted Mahabat Khan's daughter in marriage without first obtaining Jahangir's formal permission. The young man was dragged in front of the emperor and thrown in jail, with his hands bound to his neck. And to add insult to injury, the lavish wedding presents Mahabat Khan had given him were all confiscated.

This time, Mahabat Khan had had more than enough. Rather than waiting for Nur Jahan's next move, he decided to travel to the Punjab (where the imperial family happened to be at the time, on their way to Kabul) and personally plead his case with the emperor.

***

Things, however, would quickly take a dramatically different course.

Upon arrival near the imperial camp on the banks of the Jhelum in mid-1626, he was ordered to remain where he was and wait for an order to present himself in front of the emperor – again, a clear sign that he had fallen into disfavour. He obediently set up camp for himself and his retinue of about five thousand Rajput soldiers. Then, after what must have been a sleepless night, he decided to take matters into his own hands. Most of the imperial army had crossed over to the right bank of the river, while the emperor, Nur Jahan and their personal retinue were still encamped on the left bank. On an impulse, Mahabat Khan ordered some two thousand of his horsemen to block the boat bridge across the Jhelum and prevent the army from crossing back, while he dashed to the imperial enclosure at the head of the rest of his forces.

Alerted by his servants, Jahangir came out of his tent and took a seat in the palanquin that had been readied to take him across the river. Mahabat Khan stepped forward, saluted him respectfully, and pleaded that since Asaf Khan was bent on his destruction, he had come to throw himself at the mercy of his emperor. Jahangir several times laid his hand on the hilt of his sword, but one of his attendants cautioned him – in Chagatai Turkish, a language Mahabat Khan did not understand – to remain calm and bide his time.

***

It was one of the oddest coups d'état in world history – entirely unplanned, perpetrated in an impulse, and from then on, improvised and clumsily executed. Mahabat Khan first pleaded with the emperor to ride out with him as if on a hunting trip; he offered him his own horse, but Jahangir refused and mounted a steed from his own stables. After riding for a few hundred metres, Mahabat Khan thought it wiser to have Jahangir seated on an elephant rather than a horse, for everyone to see that everything was all right; however, the two soldiers who brought him the elephant were killed, when Mahabat Khan's men mistakenly took their action for a rescue attempt. The bizarre cortège then proceeded to Mahabat Khan's camp, where the emperor was placed in the custody of the general's sons.

Back in his camp, Mahabat Khan realized that in the hurry, he had forgotten all about Nur Jahan, the real power behind the throne. He dashed back to the imperial tents, only to find that the queen had already crossed the river.

It seems that she had been completely unaware about the incident at first: she had just used the bridge as planned the day before; Mahabat Khan's Rajputs had allowed her to do so, as their orders were only to prevent the army from crossing back.

But once she realized what had happened, she went, seething with anger, to her brother's tent, where she summoned the main army leaders. After showering them with all kinds of abuse, she ordered an all-out attack to rescue the emperor. Preparations were made for improvised crossings at dawn the next day via fords in the river – the bridge had meanwhile been destroyed by Mahabat Khan's Rajputs.

The attack was a complete disaster. The fords proved to be narrow and hazardous, and there was an utter lack of leadership and coordination. Consequently, the attackers got divided, and very few men managed to get across the river. In the fracas, many of them were cut down by the Rajputs or drowned in the river; others deserted their companions and ran for their lives, or simply went over to Mahabat Khan's side. Nur Jahan herself, seated on an elephant with Shahryar's infant daughter on her lap, had to turn around in mid-river when her elephant and the baby's nurse were badly wounded by arrows.

One of the fugitives was Asaf Khan – never much of a general – who abandoned his sister and his emperor to their fate and fled posthaste to take refuge in the fort of Attock, where he was later forced to surrender to Mahabat Khan's troops. Seeing no way out, Nur Jahan now capitulated and joined her husband in semi-captivity.

***

For a few months more, the strange charade would continue, with the imperial couple seemingly reconciled to their figurehead role and Mahabat Khan calling the shots, though, at all times, he was outwardly courteous and deferential towards his emperor.

But the general had bitten off more than he could chew. He was a great soldier, but neither an administrator nor a politician. Apart from his faithful Rajput soldiers, there was no one he could trust – neither the imperial couple nor the amirs, all of whom were envious of his success. Slowly but surely, the reins of power were slipping from his hands.

His biggest mistake was to allow the emperor to proceed to Kabul as had been his original plan. Mahabat Khan should have ensured that Jahangir remained in Hindustan, where his faithful Rajputs felt at home: in faraway Kabul, where the general's troops were resented by the local population, he was entirely on his own. A trivial incident (involving the grazing of Rajput horses in a hunting ground reserved for the emperor) escalated into a full-scale riot, in which several hundred Rajputs were killed and Mahabat Khan had to resort to brutal and bloody reprisals to restore a semblance of order. Meanwhile, Nur Jahan and her husband were quietly hatching plans to regain full power.

On the way back home from Kabul, they struck. Jahangir ordered Mahabat Khan to ride one stage ahead as he wished to review his own troops and wanted to avoid any possibility of friction between them and Mahabat Khan's Rajputs. The general, who must have been fed up with the whole situation and come to the conclusion that it was a dead end, complied and marched ahead, but instead of halting after one day's march, sped on towards Lahore, taking the sons of Danyal and Asaf Khan and his own son with him. On Nur Jahan's orders, he released his hostages a few days later, and continued on his journey.

***

In the meantime, Shah Jahan, upon hearing of the coup d'état, had proceeded – with a small force of barely a few hundred men – from the Deccan to Sindh, ostensibly in an attempt to come to his father's rescue. By then, however, Nur Jahan was back in the saddle, and curtly ordered him to go back where he came from. Deeply frustrated, the prince had no alternative but to comply. The only bright spot was that his brother Parvez had managed to drink himself to death in Burhanpur (in late October 1626). It would be him against Shahryar.

Parvez's death resulted in another strategic advantage: Mahabat Khan would now be on Shah Jahan's side. After a failed attempt to seize a treasure convoy coming from Bengal, the disgraced general and some two thousand of his troops joined up with Shah Jahan at Junnar.

***

The whole bizarre charade had lasted eight months. Started in an impulse, ill-considered and clumsily executed, the coup had collapsed under its own weight, like a house of cards. But now, in the service of the very prince he had campaigned against for three years, Mahabat Khan's troubles were over. Soon, Jahangir would be dead, and upon Shah Jahan's rise to the throne, he would first be appointed as governor of Ajmer and later transferred back to the Deccan, where he would die in 1634 as what he had always aspired to be: a competent and well-respected officer, loyal to his emperor.

The Struggle for Succession

In late 1627, with Shah Jahan back in the Deccan and Mahabat Khan safely out of the way, Nur Jahan found herself back in control, at last. Her brother Asaf Khan, now *vakil* to the emperor, was the effective head of the entire administration, and she, as empress, called all the shots. But the fairy tale would soon be over.

Jahangir was by now a complete physical wreck – plagued, not only by the devastating effects of forty years of alcohol and opium addiction but also by his ever-worsening asthma. After the travails of the past months, he had hoped to find some much-needed rest and relief in his beloved Kashmir, but his condition failed to improve even there. Soon, he became so ill that he lost all appetite for food. He even had to stop taking opium and drinking hard liquor, consuming nothing but a few cups of wine per day.

Another misfortune befell the imperial family when Prince Shahryar suddenly developed what appears to be a case of *Alopecia universalis*, a condition whereby he lost all the hair on his body and head, even his eyebrows and eyelashes. It was, of course, a very bad omen: how was a man, cursed with as 'dishonourable' an ailment as this one, ever to become a credible emperor? The luckless prince was advised to forthwith return to Lahore and the rest of the family decided to follow him.

On the way, the imperial retinue halted at Bairamkala (at the foothills of the Himalayas), one of Jahangir's favourite hunting grounds, where the ailing emperor decided to once more try his hand. Reclining on a comfortable pillow, the barrel of his musket resting on a tripod, he waited for the drivers to chase a herd of deer toward him. In spite of his ailments, he apparently still had the knack: one of the deer bounded in the air and fell, mortally wounded; then, with a final effort, it managed to struggle to its feet and tried to rejoin its herd. Jahangir's elation at his perfect shot turned to horror, when one of his soldiers, who had gone after the dying deer, slipped and fell to his death in a ravine. The emperor was disconsolate. This clearly was no coincidence: the poor man's misfortune foreboded his own demise; soon, the angel of death would come for him. In a deeply depressed mood, he continued his journey until a few days later, on Saturday, 6 November 1627, near the town of Bhimber on the edge of the foothills of the Himalayas, his condition turned critical. The next morning, soon after sunrise, he breathed his last.

***

As had been widely feared and expected, the emperor's demise triggered a high-stakes, no-holds-barred power play among the pretenders to the throne and their respective supporters.

In the melee, Asaf Khan immediately revealed himself as the most accomplished Machiavellian of all. As the head of the Mughal administration, he first bypassed his sister, effectively holding her incommunicado: when she summoned a meeting of the leading amirs to discuss the succession, her call was coldly ignored. The emperor was dead; the days of the empress were over.

Asaf Khan's next move was to win time for his son-in-law, Shah Jahan, who had the support of the majority of the amirs, but was still far away in the Deccan: it would be weeks before he could reach Lahore to ascend the throne. Shahryar, in contrast, was in Lahore and ready to proclaim himself emperor – supported, no doubt, if not pushed, by his wife Ladli Begam and his formidable mother-in-law, Nur Jahan. Asaf Khan needed a counterweight, someone to challenge Shahryar's legitimacy in expectation of Shah Jahan's arrival. His eye fell on Dawar Bakhsh, a son of Khusrau. The youngster (then in his early twenties) must have sensed what fate had in store for him and desperately attempted to decline the honour, until Asaf Khan and the amirs had bound themselves with stringent oaths to protect him. Then, he accepted – and, by that act, signed his own death sentence: his reign would last exactly seventy-two days.

***

On Monday, 8 November 1627, the day after Jahangir's passing, the imperial retinue moved into Bhimber, from where, after the funeral rites, his mortal remains were conveyed to the Shahdara Gardens on the banks of the Ravi River in Lahore. For the first time, the *khutba* was read in Dawar Bakhsh's name. In the Lahore court, however, Shahryar proclaimed himself emperor, seized the local treasury, and, in an effort to secure his position, distributed some seven million rupees amongst the noblemen. Mirza Baisinghar, son of the late Prince Danyal, deserted the other camp to join him and was appointed head of Shahryar's army. But neither Shahryar nor his novice general was up to the task. Their army was easily dispersed by Asaf Khan's forces and Lahore was taken. Soon, Shahryar, who had tried to hide himself in the harem, was dragged before Dawar Bakhsh, forced to pay homage to him, thrown in jail, and, for good measure, blinded.

***

Meanwhile, while on his way back to the north, Shah Jahan sent his father-in-law an imperial *firman* – his first – written in his own hand. It stated that '*it would be well at this time … if Dawar Bakhsh and the other son, and the useless brother of Khusrau* [i.e., Shahryar], *and the two sons of Danyal, were all made wanderers in the plains of non-existence*'.[17]

Asaf Khan complied promptly. Early in the morning of 2 February 1628, Shahryar, Dawar Bakhsh, his brother Garshasp, and Danyal's sons Tahmuras and Hoshang were seized and executed without further ado, after which the *khutba* was read in Shah Jahan's name. Asaf Khan's mission had been accomplished.

Shah Jahan proceeded to Agra, where he made a triumphant entry, mounted on a beautifully caparisoned elephant. A few days later, Asaf Khan arrived from Lahore with the rest of the imperial court to pay homage to his son-in-law; as a reward for faithful services rendered, he was confirmed as *vakil* of the empire. At last, Shah Jahan's worries were over; all that was left for him to do was to bask in his glory as the world's most exuberantly wealthy monarch.

***

Nur Jahan had prudently stayed behind in Lahore, together with her daughter Ladli Begam. A level-headed pragmatist above anything else, she stoically accepted her retirement and went on with her life, without ever looking back. With a generous state allowance of two hundred thousand rupees per year – over and above her private fortune, which must have been more than immense to begin with – she henceforth busied herself with the construction of her husband's mausoleum and all kinds of charitable work, never attempting to get involved in politics again. She died on 18 November 1645, sixty-eight years of age, and was buried in the graceful tomb she had designed and built for herself, 400 metres westwards from her husband's final resting place.

Around four and a half years earlier, in June 1641, her brother Asaf Khan, too, had passed away. Symbolically and significantly, his tomb is adjacent to Jahangir's and stands in between the tombs of the emperor and his beloved empress.

CHRONOLOGY

27 October 1605: Akbar dies.
3 November 1605: Jahangir ascends the throne.
6 April 1606: Khusrau rebels.
1607–1609: Emissary sent to Goa.
May 1611: Marriage of Jahangir to Mehr-un Nissa/Nur Jahan.
1612: Consolidation of Mughal rule in Bengal. British East India Company sets up a trading post at Surat defeats Portuguese navy.
10 May 1612: Khurram marries Arjumand Banu Begam, the daughter of Nur Jahan's brother Asaf Khan.
1613: War with the Portuguese.
1614: Khurram defeats Rana Amar Singh of Mewar.
1615: Sir Thomas Roe at Jahangir's court.
1615–1618: Embassy of England set up; additional rights granted for English traders.
1616: Khurram officially given the title Shah Jahan (king of the world).

1620: Ladli Begam (Nur Jahan's daughter by her first husband) betrothed to Prince Shahryar, Jahangir's youngest son. Conquest of Kangra in the foothills of the Himalayas. Khurram gets custody of Khusrau.
January 1622: Death of Khusrau.
June 1622: Qandahar lost to the Persians, but Khurram refuses to march against them.
1622–1625: Khurram rebels but is defeated and retreats to the Deccan, then to Bengal and then back to the Deccan. His reconciliation with Jahangir takes place when he sends his minor sons Dara Shikoh and Aurangzeb to the Mughal court as hostages.
March–November 1626: Coup by Mahabat Khan.
October 1626: Parvez dies.
8 November 1627: Jahangir dies; war of succession begins.
18 November 1645: Nur Jahan dies.

Notes and References

1. *The Jahangirnama: Memoirs of Jahangir, Emperor of India*, translated, edited and annotated by Wheeler M. Thackston, Oxford University Press, New York, 1999, p. 304.
2. Ibid., p. 272.
3. Ibid., pp. 21 and 185.
4. Quoted by Vincent Smith, *Akbar the Great Mogul 1542–1605*, Clarendon Press, Oxford, UK, 1917; second (revised) edition and third Indian reprint, S. Chand & Co., Delhi, 1966, p. 226.
5. Bamber Gascoigne, *A Brief History of the Great Moguls, Publishers*, Carroll & Graf *Publishers*, New York, 2002, pp. 127 ff.
6. A few sources state that she was assigned to serve Akbar's first wife, Ruqayyah Begam.
7. Meena Bazaar, also known as Kuhs Ruz or Khush Roz (days of joy), was a fancy fair set up on the palace grounds during the Noruz (New Year) spring festival ever since the days of Humayun. The ladies of the imperial *zanana* and the wives and daughters of the most important noblemen set up their own market stalls to sell items such as cloth, jewellery and handicrafts, while the emperor, the princes and a few privileged nobles came to purchase the goods, usually at exorbitant prices.

8. '*Kaffer*' is a Dutch/Afrikaans word, derived from the Arabic *kafir* (infidel), used by the Arabs when referring to people in subSaharan Africa. Originally a neutral term referring to black people, the word has over the years become a highly offensive racist term, equivalent to the word nigger in English. Pieter van den Broecke was born in Antwerp in present-day Belgium, but his Calvinist family migrated to Amsterdam. He joined the Dutch East India Company (Vereenigde Oostindische Compagnie, VOC) and spent many years in Africa and Asia.
9. Mandu was then in Malwa (it is now in western Madhya Pradesh), approximately 435 km north of Ahmednagar and 525 km north-east of Mumbai.
10. Thackston, op. cit., pp. 383 ff.
11. Ibid., p. 379.
12. Smith, op. cit., pp. 263-264.
13. Gascoigne, op. cit., p. 188.
14. Thackston, op. cit., p. 380.
15. Ibid., p. 381.
16. Dara Shikoh meaning 'the glory of Darius', a renowned Persian king's name (circa 550–486 B.C.) and Aurangzeb meaning 'the jewel of the throne'.
17. Fergus Nicoll, *Shah Jahan: The Rise and Fall of the Mughal Empire*, Haus Publishing, London, 2009, p. 155.

Chapter 5

Shah Jahan the Magnificent

On Monday, 24 January 1628, laden with jewels and proud as a peacock, Abul Muzaffar Shihab-ud Din Muhammad Shah Jahan, Sahib-i-Qirani ath-Thani, Padshah Ghazi[1] mounted the long-coveted imperial throne.

That the throne was stained with the blood of two brothers, two nephews and two cousins did not bother him in the least. Those who covet the throne have no next of kin, and no one understood this better than the ice-cold and ruthless Shah Jahan, who turned emotional only when his next of kin was involved.

But a sin tends to bring its own punishment. Not only would his own murderous example mark a ruinous tradition in Mughal family history for generations to come: it would soon come to haunt him personally. His own flesh and blood would invoke it against him, and he would live to see his favourite grandson and two of his sons brutally executed and a third one perishing in exile, while he himself was to spend the last eight years of his life as a hapless prisoner. A cruel fate, no doubt, but hardly an undeserved one.

The Bejewelled Decline

If Jahangir is usually underestimated in Indian historiography, Shah Jahan tends to be much overrated, both as a monarch and as a human being.

Who was he? As the epitome of Mughal grandeur, he sits, larger than life, gilded and glittering, in the dead centre of Mughal history – literally and figuratively. The grandiose vestiges of his reign are still there to be admired; the imprint he has left on Indian history, art and architecture is indelible; he is, quite literally, impossible to overlook or ignore. Yet, for all his conspicuousness, he very much remains an enigma.

'*There are three meticulous chronicles of the reign of Shah Jahan, official histories by courtiers, every chapter of which was approved by the emperor personally or by his authorized representative,*' observes Abraham Eraly,[2] '*but they tell us little about the man. Probably no one ever knew Shah Jahan as a person, for there was a cold hauteur about him that did not permit intimacy*'.

'*I never saw any man keep so constant a gravity*,' affirms Sir Thomas Roe, the first English ambassador to the Mughal court. He never smiled or deigned to show any kind of respect or sympathy to anyone in public; the only emotions apparent on his stone-cold face were extreme pride and utter contempt for others. So, if he remains an enigma, it is because he quite consciously chose to be one. He wanted to be regarded and treated as a superhuman demigod, the epicentre of the empire, if not of the world; that his people could have had any other goal or purpose than the glorification of their king never seems to have entered his mind.

***

Shah Jahan appears to have been obsessed with wealth and ostentation. It is reported[3] that it would have taken an expert fourteen years (*sic*!) to go through and evaluate all the emperor's personal jewels; he himself, for that matter, appears to have outclassed the finest professional jewellers when it came to assessing the quality and value of precious stones. Friar Sebastião Manrique (*c.* 1585–1669), a Portuguese Augustinian monk who travelled through the whole of northern India and visited Shah Jahan's imperial court, was taken aback to witness how the emperor hardly deigned to look at twelve scantily clad, beautiful dancing girls sent to entertain him at the end of a banquet one evening, busying himself instead with the examination of a set of jewels presented to him by his father-in-law, Asaf Khan.

It is also quite telling that one of Shah Jahan's very first acts of government was the commissioning of the famous Peacock Throne (Takht-e-Taus), the richest and most extravagant throne the world has ever seen, made of pure gold and precious stones and surmounted by a lavish, jewel-studded enamel canopy supported by twelve emerald pillars. On top of each pillar, there were two peacocks on either side of a tree, set with diamonds, emeralds, rubies and pearls. Contemporary estimates of its value vary from thirty to over one hundred million rupees – an incredible amount of money in a day and age where entire families subsisted on a few dozen rupees per year.

But ostentation has a price, and in this case, it was paid by the common people.

Long before Adam Smith's classic *Inquiry into the Nature and Causes of the Wealth of Nations* (1776), level-headed administrators like Sher Shah Suri (see Chapter 2) and Todar Mal, Akbar's brilliant minister of finance, intuitively understood that the common working people – farmers, artisans, labourers and traders – were (and are) the backbone of any country's power and prosperity, and that it was therefore a king's duty to protect their interests to the best of his ability. A certain amount of 'luxury spending' (for example, investment in gardens, beautiful buildings, works of art, and so on) no doubt contributes to the people's quality of life, but only if it is based on, and remains proportional to, wealth creation. In other words: a paradise of luxury and ostentation cannot be maintained on an economic graveyard.

But that was exactly what Shah Jahan did. Rai Bhara Mai, a historian (the former diwan to Prince Dara Shikoh) writing during Aurangzeb's reign (1658–1707), proudly stated that imperial revenue under Shah Jahan had trebled since the days of Akbar, but simultaneously admitted, apparently without realizing the dramatic implication, that expenditure had grown fourfold.[4] This kind of conspicuous consumption at the top was the result not of economic progress, but of increasingly oppressive tax collection, itself much worsened by corruption and illegal extortions by an increasingly unscrupulous and bloated bureaucratic apparatus. In spite of charitable initiatives here and there, there was an appalling and widening gap between the ostentatious glamour of the ruling classes and the wretched squalor and poverty in which the masses were forced to live. The result was a ruinous vicious circle, a downward spiral of economic decline, with a steady exodus of peasants and merchants from the land, followed by increasing extortion and oppression of those left behind.

***

In the days of Akbar and Sher Shah Suri, the state revenue had been increasing steadily, not only as the result of more just and judicious tax collection policies and much leaner and less corrupt administrations, but also because of territorial expansion: new conquests had invariably brought new sources of income. That process, however, had been completely reversed during the reign of Shah Jahan. Mughal military might by then had become, as Eraly aptly phrases it, '*more flab than muscle*', and constant but largely failed attempts to expand the empire's borders constituted an additional drain on the national treasury, rather than being a source of revenue.

Justice and the rule of law, too, were on the wane. Judging by the sharply declining number of court cases and appeals to imperial justice, public trust in the equitable administration of justice had all but disappeared; the gap between the oppressed people and their distant emperor had grown all but unbridgeable.

Another victim of Shah Jahan's mismanagement was the budding political union between the various sections of the population, Hindus and Muslims in particular. Akbar had consciously strived for a society where differences in creed or ritual would no longer matter, where people of all religions would be united under one God and one king; and Jahangir, while conformant to Sunni ritual, had followed in his father's footsteps.

Shah Jahan, humourless and self-centred as he was, utterly lacked his forefathers' political astuteness. Like many a misguided fundamentalist before and after him, he conveniently confused ethics with orthodoxy, goodness with outward observance. In particular after the death of his Shia wife, Mumtaz Mahal, on 17 June 1631, he appears to have come quite strongly under the influence of bigoted Sunni ulama.[5] Court practices were reIslamized: he wore a beard (with a pointed tip at the chin), abjured wine, modified the manner of obeisance to Muslim custom, forbade amirs from wearing miniature portraits of the emperor in their turbans and abolished Akbar's solar Din-e-Ilahi calendar, replacing it with the conventional – if much less practical – lunar (Hijri) calendar.

***

In late 1632, he took the extremely aggressive step of ordering the demolition of all newly built Hindu temples throughout the empire: although this kind of drastic intolerance has no foundation in the Holy Quran itself, conservative Muslim jurists are of the opinion that *dhimmis* – non-Muslims living in Muslim countries – are allowed to retain their own places of worship, but not to repair them, nor build any new ones. It is reported that in the district of Benares alone, seventy-six Hindu temples were thus razed to the ground; similarly, several Christian churches in Agra and other parts of the empire were demolished. In the same vein, Shah Jahan reintroduced the taxes on Hindu pilgrimages and ordered Hindus to keep to a specific style of dress, with their tunics tied on the left, as opposed to Muslims, who tied them on the right. While actively encouraging conversions to

Islam, he strictly prohibited Muslims from changing their religion; Hindu men were forced to convert to Islam if they wanted to marry a Muslim woman; adult male enemies – such as the Rajputs of Bundelkhand (the name given to parts of Uttar Pradesh and Madhya Pradesh) and the Portuguese at Hugli or Hooghly (about 40 km north of Kolkata in West Bengal) – were offered a choice between Islam and the sword.

It appears that towards the end of his reign, he became somewhat more moderate – under the influence, most probably, of his son Dara Shikoh and his daughter Jahanara – but the damage had already been done: Shah Jahan's grandiose empire was an apartheid-ridden society, where the vast majority of people were considered – and treated – as second-rate citizens.

Needless to say, this sorry state of affairs was hardly conducive to the development of any patriotic feelings towards the state or its ruling dynasty; predictably, it would lead to the downfall of the empire and the ultimate disintegration of India.

***

Shah Jahan was an egocentric, rather mediocre, often misguided ruler; his track record in matters both civil and military was deeply disappointing vis-à-vis his predecessors'. Using the analogy of a family business, he was the proverbial 'prodigal son', frivolously squandering the better part of the fortune his grandfather and father spent a lifetime to build and maintain, nearly bringing the business to its knees in the process. Yet, in India's – and the world's – collective memory, his fame remains remarkably unscathed. This has to do with two undeniable feats: first, few monarchs in history have managed to leave behind a legacy of such exquisite beauty, and, second, the love he felt for his wife has appealed to the imagination of all generations since.

AN EVENTFUL REIGN

An Easy Start

With all his potential rivals duly eliminated, a huge army at his disposal and treasure chests full to the brim, Shah Jahan began his reign in an atmosphere of profound optimism. After a joyful reunion with Dara Shikoh and Aurangzeb, their two sons who had been residing at

Jahangir's court, he and Mumtaz Mahal now enjoyed a life of carefree luxury and security, which had not been theirs for the last six years.

***

The first – rather minor – disturbance was the rebellion (in late 1628) of Jujhar Singh, son of Bir Singh Deo, the killer of Abu'l Fazl and the ruler of Orchha. The rebel was quickly defeated, but continued creating trouble; in 1635, Shah Jahan had to send another army against him, commanded this time by seventeen-year-old Prince Aurangzeb, who revealed himself a capable, resolute and brutal adversary. Jujhar Singh, decisively defeated, escaped into the nearby jungle, where he was soon killed by Gond tribesmen.

Shah Jahan personally joined in towards the end of the campaign; he and his even more bigoted son soon made it clear that the days of religious tolerance were over. The great temple built by Bir Singh Deo was destroyed and a mosque built in its place. Jujhar Singh's family was brought to Agra, where the women and girls were consigned to the harem and the young boys separated from their families and raised as Muslims. The adult males, who had been given the choice between Islam and the sword, died with honour.

Trouble in the Deccan

A much more serious military threat was posed, in 1629, by the rebellion of Khan Jahan Lodi, an Afghan officer who was a descendant of the old Delhi sultanate and governor of Malwa. He had always been one of Jahangir's favourites, but Shah Jahan deeply mistrusted him, and as would soon become apparent, not without reason. After having been recalled to Agra, Khan Jahan Lodi escaped at the head of two thousand men to the Deccan, where he allied himself with Nizam-ul Mulk, the last of the Nizam Shahi rulers of Ahmednagar. Soon, the entire region would be aflame.

Shah Jahan needed no further pretext or encouragement: he launched a massive invasion, with the avowed design of annexing the entire Deccan. In December 1629, he personally moved to Malwa to be closer to the theatre of operations.

It took the mighty Mughal army more than a full year of hard campaigning before it achieved its first objective: Ahmednagar, exhausted by famine and ruined by the brutal war, sued for peace. Khan Jahan Lodi, now finding himself alone, fled the region, but was hunted down and killed in February 1631. That, however, did not put an end to the ruinous conflict, which would, as will be related in due course, drag on till May 1636.

Tragedy Strikes

Shah Jahan's personal involvement in the military operations came to an abrupt end, when on 17 June 1631, five weeks after his nineteenth wedding anniversary, his beloved queen Mumtaz Mahal unexpectedly died at Burhanpur, reportedly after thirty hours of excruciating labour, while giving birth to her fourteenth child, Gauharara Begam. The unfortunate queen's mortal remains were committed to earth within the day, as Islamic law prescribes, in a provisional grave in a walled pleasure garden nearby (called Zainabad, meaning abode of grace/beauty) on a bank of the Tapti River. A pillared cenotaph was erected over the tomb, awaiting the queen's reburial in Agra.

The emperor was absolutely devastated by her death. He had lost the one and only true love of his life, his closest friend and confidante, his soul mate. They had been nearly inseparable for over two decades – betrothed in 1607, when they were fifteen and fourteen years old, and officially married five years later, in 1612.

Shah Jahan did marry other women, both before and after his marriage to Mumtaz: Qandahari Begam, a Persian princess, was his first spouse, and Izz-un Nissa, Abdurrahim Khan Khanan's granddaughter, his third. But these marriages had been political alliances before anything else. It was Mumtaz who became, for all practical purposes, his only consort. '*His* [Shah Jahan's] *whole delight was centred on this illustrious lady*' confirms the contemporary historian Inayat Khan (as quoted by historian and architect Giles Tillotson in *Taj Mahal*),[6] '*to such an extent that he did not feel towards the others one-thousandth part of the affection that he did for her.*' Significantly, Mumtaz was the mother of all his surviving children, with the one exception of his first child, Princess Purhunar, daughter of his first wife.

With the queen's passing, a dark period of intense sorrow and mourning began for him. The first week, he stayed in his private quarters, refusing to participate in any official activity or to see anyone. Then, on 26 June, nine days after her death, he finally found the strength to drag himself to her provisional grave for a tearful first visit. It is reported how, for two years, he forswore any kind of pleasure, including rich foods, fancy clothes, perfumes, music and dance. Whenever he set foot into Mumtaz's former palace apartments, he would burst into tears. And as contemporary portraits show, his hair and beard went white in a matter of months – white, the colour of mourning, the colour he would wear every year thereafter during the fateful month of Dhu al-Qi'dah, the month in the Islamic calendar in which his beloved queen had passed away.

Something inside him had snapped. Henceforth, he would become less and less directly involved in the affairs of state, leaving, for instance, the command of the armed forces to his sons, whilst he stayed behind in the capital.

He lingered on in Burhanpur for another few months, visiting Mumtaz's temporary grave every Friday to recite the Fatiha.[7] Then, disgusted with the Deccan – where severe famine was plaguing the war-torn countryside – he decided to go back to Agra and leave the military operations to his generals. Mumtaz Mahal's mortal remains were to be escorted back by Prince Shah Shuja, their second son. The funeral cortège left Burhanpur on 11 December 1631, and, on 8 January the next year, Mumtaz Mahal's body was reburied in Agra at another temporary location, near the site where her final mausoleum was to be built. Shah Jahan himself returned to Agra six months later, on 11 June, in time for the ceremonies commemorating his wife's first death anniversary[8] or *urs*.[9]

THE TAJ MAHAL

An Ambitious Project

The emperor had carefully selected the spot where the final mausoleum was to be built: a plot of land on the west bank of the Yamuna, just around the meander where the river flows eastwards. This spot would allow an unobstructed view from the Agra Fort palace residences as well as an absolutely perfect north–south orientation. Perfect, from an aesthetic perspective, for the building would never have to be approached against the sun and would get optimal light, whatever the season, from dawn to dusk – not to mention the enchanting moonlit nights. Perfect, also from a symbolical and religious perspective, as it allowed the burial of the deceased along the monument's main axis of symmetry, exactly in the centre of the mausoleum, with her head at the north and her face turned to the left, westwards, facing Mecca.

There was one small administrative detail to be taken care of: the land – as well as the lavish, domed mansion built on it – belonged to Mirza Raja Jai Singh, ruler of Amber, a great-grandson of the noble Raja Man Singh, Akbar's trusted Rajput general. Reportedly and understandably, the raja was not at all pleased with the unceremonious expropriation of a valuable river-front estate that had belonged to his family for four generations. Somewhat belatedly, Shah Jahan decided to compensate the disgruntled raja, offering him four villa properties in exchange for the river-front plot. The official transaction, however, was not finalized until 28 December 1633, by which time the work on the mausoleum was well underway.[10]

***

At every stage of the construction, detailed designs and scale models were presented to the emperor for his comments and approval. The Taj Mahal (as the structure came to be called later) is, in fact, the collective achievement of a *team* of people, whereby the decisive role of the emperor – an accomplished aesthete himself – is by no means to be underestimated. In this context, writes Abdul Hamid Lahori (the court historian during Shah Jahan's reign): '*The royal mind, which is illustrious like the sun, pays full attention to the planning and construction of these lofty and substantial buildings, which … for ages to come will serve as memorials of his abiding love of … ornament and beauty. The majority of the buildings he designs himself and on the plans prepared by skilful architects after long consideration he makes appropriate alterations and amendments.*'[11]

Speculations, Stories and Outright Lies

It is, alas, rather typical of Indian historiography in general, and of the Taj in particular, that the facts often get clouded by a mist of claptrap, urban legends, outlandish confabulations and outright falsifications.

The Name

Even the origin of the name remains somewhat of a mystery. The historians and poets of Shah Jahan's era constantly referred to it as: the Rauza-i-Munnawara (the illumined tomb); the Rauza-i-Muqqadas (the holy tomb); or the Rauza-i-Mutahhara (the pure tomb – the word *rauza* refers to a tomb in a garden). As the renowned architectural historians Ebba Koch and Giles Tillotson remark,[12] these phrases have very strong religious connotations: the name Rauza-i-Mutahhara, for instance, is used to designate the tomb of the Prophet Muhammad at Medina.

Exactly when and who started calling it Taj Mahal (literally meaning crown palace), we do not know for sure. What we do know is that the Englishman Peter Mundy, an agent of the East India Company who was in Agra at the time of the construction, affirms that '*the King is now building a Sepulchre for his late deceased Queen Tage Moholl*',[13] and that local people refer to the adjacent bazaar as '*Tage Gunge*' (i.e., Taj Ganj or crown treasure).

Decades later, in a letter dated 1 July 1663 – still during Shah Jahan's lifetime – the French physician François Bernier enthusiastically sings the praises of the completed mausoleum, raised '*to the memory of* [Shah Jahan's] *wife Tage Mehale, of whom her husband was so impassioned that it is said that while she was alive, he never even saw the beauty of another, and that when she died, he thought it would kill him as well*'.[14]

It thus appears safe to assume that well before Shah Jahan's death (on 22 January 1666), the name 'Taj Mahal' was in use quite commonly. Communication between European travellers – expressing themselves, no doubt, in beginner's Persian and sign language – and the local people they interviewed must have been less than perfect, so we do not know for sure whether those local people actually used the expression as an abbreviation of 'Mumtaz Mahal', as the Europeans assumed (probably mistakenly), or just as the honorary title for her mausoleum (more likely). All we know is that Taj Mahal quickly and deservedly became the name under which the monument became known to posterity, inside and outside India.

The Builders and Designers

As far as the people behind the design and construction are concerned, we know the following to be true, beyond any reasonable doubt:

1. The chief *sarkar* – i.e., the administrative coordinator and overseer of the project – was a Persian from Shiraz called Mullah Murshid Makramat Khan (meaning the master of noble qualities).
2. The *sarkar*'s chief assistant and construction supervisor was Mir Abdul Karim Mamur Khan, the doyen of architects, who had won his spurs under Jahangir.

3. The Quranic calligraphy was written by Abdul Haqq Shirazi, known by his title Amanat Khan, who had also been responsible for the calligraphy on Akbar's tomb in Sikandra. The Taj actually bears his signature, an inscription near the text at the base of the interior dome that reads: '*Written by the insignificant being, Amanat Khan Shirazi*.'
4. Last but by no means the least, the leading architect *(mim'ar)* – i.e., the actual designer of the monument – appears to have been Ustad (meaning master) Ahmad Lahori. This is at least what it says in the *Diwan al-Muhandis*, written by Ahmad Lahori's second son Lutfallah Muhandis, himself a deserving architect as well. Although hardly impartial, the younger Muhandis' testimony does seem plausible, since Lahori is known to have worked on several other critically important projects, including the Red Fort in Delhi – one of Shah Jahan's personal pet projects[15] – and to have received the lofty honorary title of Nasir al-Asr (wonder of the age).[16]

Myths and Urban Legends

In contrast, we know the following stories to be mere confabulations.

The Black Taj[17]

One of the most persistent urban legends around is that the Taj is only half of a much grander scheme, which included a mirror image tomb in black marble across the Yamuna River, where Shah Jahan himself would find his final resting place. The origin of this story appears to be an innocent remark in the travelogues of Jean-Baptiste Tavernier (1605–1689), a wealthy French merchant trading in costly jewels and other precious wares, who visited India on several occasions between 1640 and 1667. Tavernier commented that Shah Jahan had begun the construction of his own mausoleum on the other side of the river, but had not been able to carry out his plan after Aurangzeb had dethroned him in 1658.

Tavernier's remark finds no confirmation whatsoever in any contemporary Indian source, but even if it did, it says nothing at all about the black replica, the planned bridge across the Yamuna, or any of the other fanciful embellishments that have been added later on. Moreover, the story of a second tomb – black or other – is entirely inconsistent with the findings of archaeological excavations in 1995–

1997, which revealed nothing more – nor less – than the remains of a garden, perfectly aligned with, and of the same proportions as, the garden on the other side of the river (and, needless to say, not a trace of any black marble). These archaeological findings, incidentally, happen to be entirely consistent with contemporary Mughal sources, which refer to a Mahtab Bagh (moonlight garden) across the river. The Taj therefore found itself not merely at the end of a mirror-pool garden, but in the middle of an even more impressive, symmetrical complex of carefully landscaped gardens and water streams, which included the river itself.

Does this mean that Tavernier knowingly lied about the supposed construction works on Shah Jahan's tomb? Not necessarily: it is perfectly possible that he and the people living in the neighbourhood honestly mistook the ongoing construction of the garden walls, reflecting pools, and so on, for the beginning of a much larger project.

In fact, one may well ask: what kind of burial did Shah Jahan want for himself? Did he actually plan to be buried alongside his wife? As Tillotson aptly states, '*the honest truth is that we have no way of knowing what Shah Jahan's private intentions were, or even if they remained consistent between his commissioning of the Taj in 1631 and his loss of freedom to act in 1658. There is no record of him expressing a preference either for a separate tomb or to share his wife's. His burial …* [in 1666] *was managed by his most trusted daughter* [Jahanara], *but whether its manner coincided with what he would have most wished for, we cannot know*'.

What we do know is that Shah Jahan's cenotaph is the only asymmetric, incongruent element in the entire Taj Mahal. It was added alongside Mumtaz's grave, appreciably larger than hers, to the west and therefore slightly closer to Mecca – but not quite in the middle. That in itself does not need to prove anything, as the arrangement is exactly the same as in I'timad-ud Daula's (Jahangir's father-in-law) tomb; but it is undeniable that to admirers of perfect symmetry, its position is slightly disturbing.

Again, we will never know what Shah Jahan had in mind for himself. But, judging from the historical evidence available, it was definitely not a black Taj.

The European-designed Taj

The prize for the most preposterous story about the Taj should probably go to Friar Sebastião Manrique, who, in his *Itinerario de las Missiones de la India Oriental*,[18] blandly stated that '*the architect of these works* [Taj Mahal et al] *was a Venetian, by name Geronimo Veroneo, who had come to this part in a Portuguese ship and died* [in 1640] *in the city of Laor* [Lahore] *just before I reached it*'. The good friar does not offer a single shred of evidence for this bold assertion, which, by his own admission, is only hearsay, as he never met Veroneo, who died before Friar Manrique's arrival.

The Englishman Peter Mundy, who did know Veroneo quite well, does not make the slightest mention of his friend as the alleged architect. And not only that: we know that Mundy left Agra for Surat on 4 March 1632, and that, among the people accompanying him, was Veroneo, whose absence from Agra at such a crucial time clearly shows that he could not have been employed on the tomb in any significant capacity.[19] So, if he was of any help at all, it must have been as a supplier of gemstones.

Howsoever preposterous, the Veroneo legend was later revived by a number of European writers – including, alas, the otherwise outstanding historian, Vincent Smith. It was done, most probably, out of a misplaced sense of Western superiority: the incomparable Taj simply *had* to be, as Smith put it, '*a combination of European and Asiatic genius*'.

The discussion probably had to do with intra-European rivalries. Indeed, as Giles Tillotson aptly points out, many controversies around the Taj find their origin in European commentators' eagerness to *dis*prove someone else's theory. A telling example was the influential English arts administrator and historian E. B. Havell's (1861–1934) enthusiastic support for 'Ustad Isa' (supposedly a Turkish architect, who turned out to be, in all probability, fictitious) as the main designer of the Taj. Such support seemed to be motivated primarily by Havell's concern to prove that it was not created by an Italian.[20]

***

There are a few areas where European art may actually – if indirectly – have influenced the builders of the Taj: for instance, the extensive use of the so-called *pietra dura* or *parchin kari* stone inlay technique (whereby highly polished coloured stones are inlaid in the walls to create images and glued together so precisely and meticulously that the contact between the component parts is practically invisible and impalpable): it is very well possible and even probable that Mughal craftsmen imitated – or were inspired by – this technique from the many pieces of inlaid European furniture that had been assembled over the years at the Mughal court.

As Koch points out, the Mughals were not worried at all about borrowing from non-Muslim sources, both Hindu and European. They happily combined all these influences into a harmonious and quite distinct new style, which was entirely their own. For instance, the vases with flowers in marble relief decorating the central tomb chamber – both the shape of the vases as their flower arrangements – are clearly influenced by European herbals and other imagery available at the Mughal court, but that hardly makes them any less Indian.[21]

Another example of this kind of intercultural influence in Mughal art is the use of halos or aureoles (the rings of light that surround the heads of saints in Christian iconography): Jahangir, who was an aficionado of European painting, fondly introduced the practice in Mughal state portraits – whereupon it readily evolved into an established tradition; but that does not make Mughal painting – which artfully combines the pre-existing Hindu traditions and techniques with Persian and (to a much lesser extent) foreign influences – any less Indian.

The Hindu Taj

Another rather bizarre theory was the claim that the Taj is, in fact, a pre-existing Shiva temple named 'Tejo Mai Mahal', built by Raja Jai Singh or his ancestors. While forcefully argued by a few[22] and willingly believed by many, this theory seems extremely unlikely, if not impossible. We know for a fact that the land on which the Taj was built was allocated, shortly after Akbar's marriage to the princess of Amber in January 1562, to Jai Singh's great-grandfather Raja Man Singh. Just like all the other leading nobles at the imperial court in Agra, Man Singh used his riverside property to build himself a lavish mansion, which remained in the Singh family until it was razed to the ground after the expropriation by Shah Jahan.

Apart from the fact that the Taj's architectural concept bears precious little – if any – resemblance to any Hindu temple worldwide, it does not, to say the least, seem plausible to assume that a pious Rajput like the great Raja Man Singh would have disfigured a pre-existing temple to turn it into a private residence.

The Blood-stained Taj

'*When the Taj was finished, Shah Jahan is said to have had the architect's eyes gouged out and the hands of the craftsmen chopped off, so that nothing as beautiful could ever be built again.*' This story and similar other horror stories are still being told today by self-appointed 'experts'. Needless to say, such stories are utter claptrap. Not only is there not a shred of evidence for such old wives' tales, but also it is well documented how Shah Jahan rewarded his people quite handsomely and also continued to employ them in many other projects, Shahjahanabad (Old Delhi) being the most obvious example.

The Pinnacle of Mughal Building Art

In summary, the Taj was conceived in the minds of a few truly brilliant men – including the widowed emperor himself – who managed to combine their skills, expertise and refined taste into a common, perfectly harmonious vision. Assisted by what must have been a well-oiled machine made up of several hundred extremely skilled craftsmen and thousands of workers, Hindus as well as Muslims, they managed to design and create one of the – if not *the* – most beautiful buildings ever built.

Says François Bernier: '*This monument deserves much more to be numbered among the wonders of the world than the pyramids of Egypt*.' Leaving aside the question whether or not this kind of comparison is entirely fair or even relevant, it is undeniable that few buildings in the history of humankind are as flawlessly beautiful and impressive.

Literally thousands of pages of architectural studies and comments have been devoted to the Taj; it seems hardly relevant to add a few more in this framework. Suffice it to make a few general observations.

First of all, the great merit of the Taj is not its originality, not some kind of striking innovation: it is a uniquely masterful, perfectly harmonious blending of pre-existing Central Asian, Persian, Ottoman and Indian influences and traditions. What makes it so remarkable, is that it manages to combine these well-known, pre-existing techniques and architectural insights to create something surprisingly new and absolutely unique. Literally every aspect of it – the orientation, landscaping, proportions, volumes, building materials, calligraphy and ornamentation – has been thought through with such thoroughness, virtuosity and originality that the result is beyond comparison. It is magnificent, imposing, grandiose, and regal; yet, at the same time, strikingly elegant, feminine, intimate, gentle and deeply moving. Every detail of it has been crafted with meticulous precision; yet the whole seems effortless and totally spontaneous.

The entire concept works towards the end result; take away a single detail, and there would be diminishment. For instance:

- The approach and the general view would be much less imposing without the portal in the screening wall and the ingenious positioning of the monument at the end of the garden, rather than in the middle of it.
- The uniqueness of the celestial, white mausoleum is highlighted by the contrast with the earthly, red sandstone of the two flanking buildings (i.e., the mosque on the west and the *mihman khana* or guest house on the east).
- The main building would have looked substantially less elegant without the chamfering of the corners and the addition of recessed pishtaq arches. What we now have is a dynamic yet harmonious interaction of the five interlocking irregular octagons, surmounted by five cupolas: the perfect 'onion' or 'guava' (*amrud*) dome and its surrounding four smaller *chhatris* (dome-shaped pavilions).
- For all its delicate elegance, the tomb would have looked much heavier without the plinth on which it stands or without the elegant slenderness of the four flanking ornamental minarets.
- These four minarets are leaning outwards, correcting the parallax (i.e., the optical illusion that parallel lines appear to converge in the distance) and creating an impression of complete openness towards – and indeed, intimate communication with – heaven above. As many commentators have remarked, an added practical benefit of this arrangement is that in case of an earthquake, the minarets would fall outward, away from the tomb.
- In reality, the tomb is a top-heavy structure of bricks, stone and rubble, sheathed in marble. Yet, thanks to that marble, the building suddenly appears ethereal, almost translucent. On a misty morning, it appears to be floating in the air, merging with the clouds that surround it; with its ever-changing colours, it actively partakes in the eternal spectacle of day and night.

In short, the Taj is the absolute zenith of Mughal building art. It is, arguably, the dynasty's greatest achievement and its most permanent legacy to humankind.

And that is why, despite all his faults as a monarch and a human being, Shah Jahan fully deserves his place in the pantheon of the most magnificent rulers this planet has ever witnessed.

The Shift from Agra to Delhi

Time is the great healer .... It appears that soon after the Taj was completed (the building itself was quite finished by 1648, seventeen years after Mumtaz' passing, although work on the subsidiary buildings continued until 1653[23]), Shah Jahan altogether lost interest in it. He returned for two more anniversary visits, but once he had proclaimed his new capital city of Shahjahanabad (Old Delhi) as the 'seat of the caliphate', his visits to Agra became few and far between. From then on, virtually all his aesthetic energy went into Delhi, with the Friday mosque (Jami or Jama Masjid) and the Red Fort (Lal Qila) within which was the white marble Moti Mahal (Pearl Mosque) and a magnificent palace complex, where the emperor lived a life of pomp and circumstance.

Inside the Lal Qila, on the north and south walls of the Diwan-i-Khas, the hall of private audience, is repeatedly inscribed a rather pretentious-sounding couplet, attributed to the multitalented Amir Khusrau (1253–1325):

> *Agar firdaus bar ru-yi zamin ast,*
> *Hamin ast, o hamin ast, o hamin ast!*
> (If there be a paradise on earth,
> It's here, it's here, it's here!)

***

Meanwhile, back in Agra, maintenance at the Taj was neglected, which becomes evident from a letter written by Aurangzeb on 9 December 1652: four days earlier, on his way to the Deccan, the thirty-four-year-old prince had stopped at Agra to pay his respects at his mother's mausoleum and had found it in a pitiful state of disrepair: the roof was leaking and the beautiful Mahtab Bagh had been inundated by the waters of the Yamuna. The emperor's last visit to the Taj was on 27 December 1654 – together with Dara Shikoh, his eldest son and heir-apparent. It was his first visit in more than ten years; seemingly, obviously, the great Queen Mumtaz Mahal was a thing of the past.[24]

In fact, it is widely rumoured that when Shah Jahan finally came out of mourning, approximately two years after Mumtaz Mahal's death, he began to lead an active and quite licentious sex life, involving several concubines, dancing girls and married women; and if we are to believe the contemporary gossip, he even had an incestuous relationship with his favourite daughter, Jahanara.

Are we really to believe these rumours?[25] We do know that Jahanara was clearly his favourite child, and quickly became his closest confidante, just like her mother had been during her lifetime. Shah Jahan bestowed on her half of Mumtaz Mahal's movable property (worth ten million rupees at that time), while the remainder had to be shared among her six other children; Jahanara's annual allowance was also raised from 600,000 rupees to a staggering one million. We do know that Shah Jahan was inconsolable when, on 4 April 1644, Jahanara (then thirty) nearly lost her life in a fire accident: he summoned the best physicians in the empire and beyond to treat her; for months in a row, he stayed with her, personally dressing her wounds.

But that in itself does not prove anything, and in the absence of more conclusive evidence, we should give Shah Jahan the benefit of the doubt: he and his daughter obviously loved each other very much, but for all we know, they both went elsewhere to satisfy their sexual urges. Bernier does affirm that father and daughter were lovers, adding that several courtiers justified it, stating that the emperor had 'the privilege of gathering fruit from the tree he had himself planted'; Niccolò Manucci (1639–1717; an Italian writer and traveller), however, who claims to have been deep in the confidence of the principal ladies and eunuchs in Jahanara's service, dismisses these affirmations as scandalous slander. He does state, as does Bernier, that Jahanara did lead quite a licentious love life herself: she is supposed to have indulged in Bacchanalia with lots of drinking and dancing, and had lovers smuggled into her residence on a regular basis. Once again, we will never know what really happened.

Fading Glory

As an aesthete, Shah Jahan is virtually unrivalled. His artistic legacy surpasses that of most, if not all, other monarchs who earned themselves the title of *magnificent*, such as Sultan Sulaiman I (1494–1566) in Istanbul, Lorenzo de' Medici (1449–1492) in Florence, or João V (1689–1750) in Portugal.

The same, however, can by no means be said about Shah Jahan's track record as a ruler and an army leader. His ill-advised economic and communal policies have been discussed earlier; we should now have a brief look at his military career, which is little more than a concatenation of Pyrrhic victories (as Eraly aptly called them), strategic blunders and humiliating setbacks. Akbar's unstoppable bulldozer, the invincible Mughal army, seemed to have run out of steam.

The Capture of Hugli

The early years of Shah Jahan's reign saw the first major clash with a European colonial power: in 1631, he ordered Qasim Khan, the Mughal governor of Bengal, to chase the Portuguese from their settlement at Port Hugli (now known as Hooghly). With the Portuguese levying exorbitant tolls on trading ships sailing past their settlement, forcibly converting local people to Christianity and conniving with local pirates and slave traders, the colony had become a major irritant.

Besides, as Eraly remarks,[26] Shah Jahan bore a personal grudge against the Portuguese: they had sided with the imperial forces at the time of his rebellion against Jahangir and had seized some of his boats and abducted two of his slave girls. To add insult to injury, at the time of his coronation, they had neglected to send him the customary presents and make amends.

The siege operations began in the summer of 1632 and went on for three months, after which the Mughals succeeded in blowing up a part of the battlements; the city was then captured, regrettably, with tremendous bloodshed. A group of colonists succeeded in escaping by the river route, but several hundred – mainly women and children – were taken captive and forced to walk to Agra, an arduous march of eleven months, during which many more perished. The survivors were paraded before the emperor, who invited them to convert to Islam; the majority, however, refused and suffered imprisonment and maltreatment of all kinds. Many of them, notes Shah Jahan's court historian Abdul Hamid Lahori, 'passed from prison to hell'.

Things cooled down a few years later, thanks to the continuing efforts of Portuguese Jesuit missionaries: by the end of the 1630s, the situation of the small Christian community in Agra was almost back to normal.

Peace in the Deccan

By June 1633, two years after Mumtaz Mahal's passing, Shah Jahan's forces in the Deccan, under the able leadership of Mahabat Khan, had stormed Daulatabad, Ahmednagar's main stronghold, and seized Husain Shah, the country's boy king. The poor lad's capture and lifelong imprisonment in Gwalior effectively put an end to the Nizam Shahi dynasty, which had ruled the territory since 1490, but it did not end the war. The powerful Maratha chieftain and guerilla expert Shahji Bhonsle – father of the great Chhatrapati Shivaji, founder of the Maratha empire – who had been siding with the Mughals at first, suddenly switched sides and set up another descendant of the Nizam Shahi dynasty on the throne as a figurehead king to thwart the Mughal ambitions. The rest of the Deccan, including Bijapur and Golconda, remained equally defiant. It proved to be too much for the old ironside. Frustrated and exhausted by the travails of constant campaigning, his health undermined by a debilitating chronic fistula,[27] the old general died in October 1634.

After another frustrating year with little if any progress, Shah Jahan decided he would intervene personally. It proved to be an excellent move: on his arrival at Daulatabad, Golconda meekly capitulated, agreeing to pay an annual tribute of 600,000 rupees; and Bijapur, soundly beaten after barely four months of fighting, signed a peace treaty (in May 1636), in which it recognized Shah Jahan's overlordship and agreed to pay a tribute of two million rupees per year. In exchange, Bijapur was allowed to annex a large part of the now-extinct state of Ahmednagar. Shahji Bhonsle, now on his own, soon capitulated and entered the service of Bijapur. Peace finally reigned.

The treaty would endure for two decades, allowing Shah Jahan to concentrate on his northern frontier and other areas of the empire, while the tributary sultanates of the Deccan found themselves free to expand their southern frontiers without having to worry about the hostile Mughals in the north. Prince Aurangzeb, not even eighteen years old at the time, was appointed viceroy of the four Deccan provinces (Khandesh, Berar, Telangana and Daulatabad), a post he would fill with diligence and success for the next eight years. Meanwhile, Dara Shikoh – Shah Jahan's eldest and favourite son – remained at court with his father.

Qandahar and the Central Asian Adventure

Shah Jahan was well aware that he was personally responsible for the loss of Qandahar back in 1622, for it was his refusal to march against the Persian invaders and his subsequent rebellion against his father that had prevented Jahangir from recovering the city. But in 1638, the opportunity arose to redress the situation: Ali Mardan Khan, the local Persian governor, had fallen out of favour with his king, Shah Safi, and was quickly persuaded to surrender the city to the Mughals. In exchange, he was showered with money and presents and appointed the governor of Kashmir, to which the Punjab was added later on.

For a while, there was little the angry Shah Safi could do about it: he had rebels to deal with; moreover, the Ottomans on his western frontier were a constant headache. But ten years later, in the dead of the winter of 1648, led by the young Shah Abbas II, his energetic successor, the Persians would be back – to stay.

Before that, however, Shah Jahan freely indulged in grandiose dreams. With the Deccan pacified, was it not high time he expanded northeastwards – to Central Asia, and above all, to Samarqand, where the bones of Timur, his glorious ancestor, were resting? In 1646, when a civil war broke out among the Uzbeks, he finally saw his way clear. Led by the twenty-two-year-old Prince Murad Bakhsh (Shah Jahan's youngest son) and General Ali Mardan Khan, a Mughal invasion army swiftly occupied all of Balkh and Badakhshan, the region between the Hindu Kush mountains and the Oxus River (Amu Darya). Virtually unopposed, the army even crossed the river, occupying the town of Termiz (now in southern Uzbekistan).

Unfortunately, Shah Jahan had bitten off more than he could chew, and his own army now proved to be its own worst enemy. Samarqand was only 370 km – two weeks' march – away from Termiz, but Prince Murad Bakhsh was in no mood for a rough campaign in the frigid highlands of Central Asia. In vain, Shah Jahan tried to persuade him, dangling the prestigious governorship of Samarqand before his nose, but the prince remained adamant: he yearned to get back to the warmth and comfort of Hindustan. Abruptly and without permission, he relinquished his command and returned to Lahore, whereupon an angry Shah Jahan stripped him of his rank and forbade him to set foot in court again, but the damage had been done. The spineless attitude of the commanding prince had set an extremely bad example for the rest of the army; it hardly boded well for the campaign.

In the days of Babur, the Mughal soldiers could hardly wait to get out of Hindustan and its sweltering heat. Now, it was the other way around: they all loathed the frigid highlands of Central Asia. Following the bad example of its commanding prince, an entire Rajput contingent deserted its post and headed back to India; it was only stopped at the

Indus River on Shah Jahan's explicit orders, and convinced, with great difficulty, to return to its post. At his wits' end, Shah Jahan now decided to call back Aurangzeb and entrust the campaign to him.

It was during that fateful war that Aurangzeb earned himself his undying reputation for piety and personal courage: one day, when the hour for the evening *namaz* happened to fall in the middle of a major battle, he calmly spread out his prayer carpet and knelt down, unarmed, in the middle of the melee. But personal bravery is sometimes not enough: the tough new commander fared little better than his epicurean brother. In a harsh campaign reminiscent of the Vietnam war or the Soviet campaign in Afghanistan, his army won every major engagement; yet, in the end, the Uzbeks managed to drive it out of the country. His troops demoralized, suffering from the inclement weather and constantly harassed by the Uzbeks and wild Turkoman tribes, Aurangzeb failed to make any progress; in the end, he had no alternative but to retreat. He patched up some kind of more or less honourable peace, returning Balkh to its Uzbek ruler in exchange for the latter's formal submission and then made his way back to Kabul.

The campaign had been an outright disaster: twenty million rupees in expenses, against a revenue of barely 2.2 million rupees; five hundred men slain in battle; about ten times that many (including camp followers and servants), plus a large number of animals, perished in the cold of the snow-bound passes across the Hindu Kush; and not a square centimetre of territory to show for it.

It was only the first in a series of humiliations. Sometime later, in December 1648, the fortress of Qandahar found itself under siege by a Persian army.

It should not have been a surprise, for in his correspondence with Shah Jahan, the young Shah Abbas II had demanded, in no uncertain terms, the immediate and unconditional restitution of the province. Still, the Mughals were taken aback by the boldness and timing of the attack: in the middle of the winter, when the snows made it virtually impossible to send any serious reinforcements from the plains. The garrison, although 7000 strong and amply provisioned to withstand a long siege, soon panicked and meekly surrendered in mid-February 1649, after barely fifty-seven days.

***

Upon hearing the news that Qandahar was under siege, Shah Jahan summoned Aurangzeb from Multan (now in Pakistan), where he was now serving as governor, to lead an army northwards to relieve the city. It was a rash, ill-prepared operation, for Aurangzeb and his 50,000-strong army got bogged down in the mountains, and reached Qandahar only by mid-May 1649, a full three months after its surrender to the Persians. Ill-equipped for the siege, with far too few heavy guns and siege engines, the Mughals were unable to make any progress against the defenders. The Persian garrison stood firm, and after a frustrating one hundred and ten days of siege, fearing harsh winter conditions and the arrival Persian reinforcements, Aurangzeb was compelled to withdraw, disgraced and empty-handed.

Seething with anger, Shah Jahan prepared for revenge – sparing neither trouble nor expense. By now, Qandahar had become much more than a border dispute: it was a matter of personal prestige. Three years later, in 1652, his powerful new army of 50,000 men was ready: extra heavy guns had been cast, supplies readied and a strong reserve force of 40,000 men stationed in Kabul, from where the emperor would personally direct the operations. But again, the operation was a complete failure. The costly new guns proved to be of inferior quality, cracking and sometimes even exploding after repeated use; whereas the Persian defenders revealed themselves as true masters in artillery – a skill their western (Ottoman) neighbours had taught them the hard way. After a siege of barely two months, Aurangzeb was recalled in disgrace, much to the delight of Dara Shikoh's followers, and sent back to the Deccan. The estranged father and son would never see each other again.

One year later, Dara Shikoh – who had boasted that he could take the city in a week – appeared before the walls of Qandahar with an even larger army of 70,000 men, reinforced, this time, with European mercenary artillerymen. But in spite of this overwhelming force, he failed just as dismally as his brother: after five months of siege, fearing the advent of winter, he slunk off with his tail between his legs.

***

It has been estimated that the Mughals' triple failure to retake Qandahar cost them an incredible 120 million rupees – half the annual revenue of the entire empire.[28] But the loss in morale was much worse and their military prestige and aura of invincibility were gone forever. Gone forever also were the grandiose dreams of expansion into Central Asia and Persia. On the contrary, in May 1739, barely three decades after

Aurangzeb's death in 1707, the unthinkable would happen, with the Persians marching into Delhi, mass-slaughtering its inhabitants and carting off the entire Mughal treasure, including the celebrated Peacock Throne. Thus passes the glory of this world ...[29]

Throughout Aurangzeb's long reign (1658–1707), Mughal forces would be pushing their southern borders nearly to the tip of the subcontinent, but it was clear even then – to Aurangzeb himself and to everybody else – that his great empire was falling apart. His hold on the south was precarious at best, and never undisputed; perhaps even more importantly, his throne appeared to have lost much of its authority and legitimacy. Dangerous revolts by non-Muslim communities – Jats, Sikhs and Rajputs – were breaking out in what used to be the very heartlands of Mughal power, and could barely be kept in check; chaos and disintegration were looming everywhere.

It is time at this stage to take a closer look at the remarkable career of this grim, but highly talented and, all things considered, deeply tragic man, who, with a bit more political astuteness, could have grown into another Akbar the Great – but ruined his empire while trying to be one.

Aurangzeb's Bumpy Career

As mentioned earlier, after the 1636 peace treaty with Bijapur and Golconda, Aurangzeb was appointed as governor of the four Mughal Deccan provinces (Khandesh, Berar, Telangana and Daulatabad). It was an extremely important assignment to give to a seventeen-year-old, but, as related earlier, the young prince had more than won his spurs in the war against Jujhar Singh, the rebel chief of Orchha. And three years before that, on 28 May 1633, in spite of his rather frail stature, he had already shown his mettle against an enraged war elephant[30] stampeding through the army camp. Undaunted, the lad had valiantly stood his ground and struck the animal right on its forehead with his lance. Akbar would have been elated, and so was Shah Jahan: he gave him his weight in gold plus two hundred thousand rupees worth of presents and conferred upon him the well-deserved title of Bahadur (the brave).

Shortly after his appointment to the Deccan, in 1637, he married the Safavid Princess Dilras Banu Begam,[31] a direct descendant of the great Persian Shah Ismail I (reign: 1501–1524). The young bride – quite a hot-tempered woman, reportedly – was to become his first wife and chief consort. She would bear him five children, including Muhammad Azam Shah, who would later succeed his father; princess Zeb-un Nissa (jewel among women), an accomplished poetess and Aurangzeb's favourite daugher; Princess Zinat-un Nissa (ornament among women), titled Padshah Begam; and Sultan Muhammad Akbar, Aurangzeb's favourite son – until his rebellion in 1681.

In spite of his young age, Aurangzeb soon proved himself as a dedicated and talented administrator – to such an extent that his father promoted him to the rank of twelve thousand *zat* and seven thousand *sawar* in 1637 and to fifteen thousand and nine thousand two years later.[32] It is all the more surprising that, on the occasion of a visit to Agra in the summer of 1644, he was suddenly and dishonourably dismissed from his position and stripped of his rank and allowance.

What happened? We don't know exactly. He had come to the bedside of his sister Jahanara, who, in March that year, had been critically injured in a fire accident. For several months, she had been on the verge of death, and Shah Jahan was beside himself with grief and worry; it was in these dramatic circumstances that Aurangzeb was dismissed.

How did he incur his father's displeasure in the first place? Again, we don't know. But more than likely, it had everything to do with court intrigues. Dara Shikoh and Aurangzeb hated each other's guts – not only because they were both boundlessly ambitious and natural-born rivals but also because their respective characters and outlook on life could not have been further apart: Aurangzeb, utterly humourless, austere and bigoted; Dara Shikoh, in contrast, was suave, worldly, broad-minded, universalist, but vexingly self-important and overconfident.

***

Dara Shikoh had always been his father's favourite, although it is, at first sight, hard to see why: when it comes to character, or religious bigotry, Aurangzeb was very much his father's son, much more than Dara Shikoh – very much a free-thinker and a strong proponent of inter-religious dialogue and universal tolerance. Why, then, did Dara Shikoh become Shah Jahan's favourite? Dara Shikoh is supposed to have been much better company than dour Aurangzeb: his courtly manner must have been quite pleasing to his protocol-obsessed father; and, most probably, he was an excellent flatterer. In addition, Shah Jahan must have felt anxious to ensure an orderly transition; and, in theory at least, in the absence of compelling reasons to deviate from the rule, the firstborn son had to take precedence over the others.

Shah Jahan's own coronation had been preceded by a destructive civil war and a family bloodbath, even though he had been his father's favourite and the heir-apparent for many years. The reason for this, so he figured, was that he had been away from court for much too long: distance is bound to breed misunderstandings, distrust and estrangement. This was a mistake he would not make: he would keep Dara Shikoh close by his side in the centre of power, while the others, Aurangzeb in particular, could do the dirty work in the field. The unintended result of these measures was the exact opposite of what he had planned: when push came to shove, shrewd and battle-hardened Aurangzeb was perfectly prepared for the civil war that would soon prove to be inevitable.

Aurangzeb's disgrace in 1644 did not last very long. By the autumn of the same year, Princess Jahanara was out of danger, and in November, grandiose festivities were organized to celebrate her recovery. On this occasion, Shah Jahan reinstated Aurangzeb in his former rank, and later on, appointed him as governor of Gujarat – a task to which, once again, the prince would apply himself with skill and dedication.

***

As has been discussed earlier, Aurangzeb was moved from Gujarat to Balkh in 1647; then, after the Central Asian debacle, to Multan and Sindh. His failed efforts in 1649 and 1652 to dislodge the Persian occupants of Qandahar earned him his father's renewed displeasure, and in early 1653, he was back in the Deccan provinces, which, in the meantime, had been substantially impoverished under the yoke of several interim governors.

His requests for extra funds from the central treasury, however, were turned down by Shah Jahan. He therefore reintroduced a number of judicious measures – going back to the days of Sher Shah Suri and Akbar's minister Todar Mal – including loans for poor peasants to stimulate cultivation and a much leaner and tighter land administration. These, however, were longer-term measures, insufficient to cover his short-term cash needs. The fastest way out – and the best way to redeem his tarnished military reputation – was the conquest of new territories.

His first victim was the neighbouring, immensely rich state of Golconda – an easy prey ruled by a weak and indolent king. An official excuse for the invasion was found soon enough: the kingdom was in arrears with its annual tribute and it had annexed a large stretch of land on its southern borders without prior imperial approval. An additional pretence was the personal conflict between Golconda's king, Abdullah Qutub Shah, and his competent but arrogant and all-too-powerful army leader and administrator, a Persian migrant called Mir Jumla. When the latter appealed to the Mughals for protection, when Qutub Shah tried to have him killed, Aurangzeb sent his son Muhammad Sultan (the firstborn of Aurangzeb's second wife, Nawab Bai) with an expeditionary force to the capital Hyderabad, while he himself followed with a large invasion army – even though the hapless king had by then meekly complied with every demand.

The king saved his skin by taking refuge in a nearby fortress and tried to placate Aurangzeb with lavish gifts and promises – and prudently sending an emissary to Dara Shikoh, begging him to plead his case with Shah Jahan. Dara Shikoh, jealous as always of his brother's military success, readily complied, and under his influence, Shah Jahan ordered Aurangzeb to accept the indemnities offered, raise the siege and quit Golconda.

However reluctantly, Aurangzeb complied. But not without substantial compensation: the district of Ramgir (near Golconda) was annexed, the arrears were paid, plus an additional indemnity of ten million rupees. And, last but not the least, one of the king's daughters was given in marriage to Prince Muhammad Sultan. And in a secret understanding with Aurangzeb, he pledged that Muhammad Sultan would be his successor, since he had no male heirs of his own. In June 1656, Mir Jumla entered the Mughal service as prime minister.

***

From Golconda, Aurangzeb's attention turned to his other neighbour: Bijapur. The province had done extremely well since the peace treaty of 1636 under the able guidance of its king, Muhammad Adil Shah. But in November 1656, the good king died, and chaos ensued, with several rebellions breaking out against the new king, Ali Adil Shah II. This was all the pretext that Aurangzeb needed. Anticipating Shah Jahan's permission to annex the entire kingdom – arguing that the new king was not really the son of the deceased sultan, and therefore not a legitimate heir to the throne – he opened hostilities in his own characteristic way, using ruse and trickery: a bribe of two thousand rupees was offered to each Bijapuri officer defecting to the Mughals with one hundred soldiers. On 28 January 1657, when Mir Jumla had arrived with extra reinforcements, he invaded Bijapur. In an unhurried, methodical campaign, he dealt with every resistance, and by July 1657, all the major cities had been taken.

Then, to Aurangzeb's utter frustration, Shah Jahan – most probably under Dara Shikoh's influence – suddenly ordered him to cease operations. A new peace treaty was signed, whereby Bijapur agreed to pay an indemnity of ten million rupees and surrender a number of forts in exchange for the Mughal army's full withdrawal from the country.

Little did Shah Jahan realize that this premature pullback from Bijapur would be his last major decision as emperor. Soon, utter chaos would reign throughout his empire.

War of Succession after Shah Jahan's Illness

On 16 September 1657, the emperor suddenly fell severely ill, with what must have been a case of acute prostatitis and/or kidney inflammation: the symptoms included strangury (the inability to pass urine), high fever, swollen legs and severe abdominal pain. Contemporary gossip attributed the emperor's sudden illness to an overdose of aphrodisiacs – he was reputed to enjoy an extremely active sex life, in spite of being sixty-five years old – but we can, of course, not be sure. All we know is that his condition quickly became critical: unable to eat anything for a week, the monarch seemed to hover on the verge of death.

As wild rumours about the emperor's failing health began to spread like wildfire, chaos and lawlessness erupted in every corner of the empire. The slowly recovering, but still helplessly bedridden emperor now officially appointed Dara Shikoh as ruler ad interim, raising him to the unprecedented rank of sixty thousand and an annual pay of a staggering twenty million rupees. In mid-October 1657, he felt strong enough to travel down the Yamuna in the imperial barge to Agra for a recommended change of air, while Dara Shikoh stayed behind in Delhi.

It was the ideal recipe for civil war: an ailing monarch who had handed over the reins of power; rumours everywhere; a maladroit interim ruler in Delhi, purposely leaving everyone in the dark; and three younger brothers, each of them ambitious *and* fearing for his own life, and each of them left in charge of a substantial army of his own.

***

The first one to move was forty-one-year-old Shah Shuja, then governor of Bengal. He is said to have been a capable and valorous man, but addicted to wine and women, and extremely pretentious – which appears from the grandiose titles he chose for himself: Abu'l Fauz Nasir-ud Din Muhammad, Timur III, Iskandar II, Shah Shuja Bahadur, Padshah Ghazi.[33] Coin having been struck and the *khutba* having been read in his name back in Bengal, he rode out west to claim his throne and prove himself, indeed, a third Timur and a second Alexander the Great. '*Ya takht, ya tabut!*' (the throne, or the tomb!), he is reported to have exclaimed upon leaving his residence. It would presage the fate that would soon befall him and many of his relatives, friends and foes.

Over in Gujarat, at the opposite end of the empire, the youngest of the four, the impetuous thirty-three-year-old Murad Bakhsh, was preparing himself to do the same: seizing whatever money he could get his hands on and declaring himself emperor.

The only one shrewd enough not to make any overt moves yet was Aurangzeb, safely entrenched in the Deccan, well in control of his strong, battle-hardened fighting force, and, at least as importantly: firmly in charge of the revenue collection from wealthy Golconda and Bijapur.

But Dara Shikoh was not fooled. Knowing full well that Aurangzeb was by far the most dangerous of his three adversaries, he made a move to weaken him first, ordering Mir Jumla and his troops back to Delhi. As Mir Jumla's family was living in Delhi, it put him in a rather awkward position, but canny Aurangzeb had his countermove ready. Probably with Mir Jumla's tacit consent, he had him arrested on some fabricated charge and confined to the fortress of Daulatabad, awaiting the moment when they would again be able to work together overtly.

Dara Shikoh's second move was to order Murad Bakhsh to cross the Gujarat border and occupy the province of Berar. Again, it was a smart move: if Murad Bakhsh would have complied, it would have provided a much-needed additional buffer against Aurangzeb; as it happened, however, Murad Bakhsh broke out in open rebellion. He murdered Ali Naqi, Shah Jahan's local finance minister, seized the local treasury and plundered the city of Surat, thus availing himself of the necessary funds to raise a larger army. On 20 November 1657, he declared himself emperor, taking the trouble even of dispatching an official ambassador to Persia to announce his enthronement.

***

This was exactly the kind of imbroglio in which a man like Aurangzeb was like a fish in water. Cautious, he bided his time, engaging in skilful – if utterly devious – diplomacy with the other players.

He felt, as he wrote to Mir Jumla,[34] that he should not launch any campaign for the throne until Shah Jahan's death was confirmed, but he absolutely needed to prevent others – his brothers as well as his own officers – to side with Dara Shikoh. Making sure that he was on excellent terms with his erstwhile adversaries in Golconda and Bijapur, he engaged in secret diplomacy with the two other brothers. He had no other ambition or desire, so he assured Murad Bakhsh, but to live a hermit's life of contemplation and prayer; but he absolutely wanted to prevent an infidel like Dara Shikoh from seizing the throne. He told them that once their common enemy was out of the way, the empire would be shared: Murad Bakhsh would get the Afghan provinces, Kashmir, the Punjab and Sindh and Aurangzeb, the centre and the south. Via speed couriers, the two kept in constant touch with each other and probably also with Shah Shuja, in an attempt to forge a triple alliance against the unholy Dara Shikoh.

Aurangzeb Strikes

But things were moving too fast. They needed to act, or it would be too late, Murad warned Aurangzeb. Dara Shikoh was preparing for war, growing stronger by the day, and Shah Shuja was rapidly advancing against the capital; it was high time Aurangzeb too got involved. After much reflection, Aurangzeb's mind was made up: on 15 February 1658, he set out from what is now Aurangabad (in Maharashtra) to cross the Narmada River and go northwards.

Meanwhile, back in Delhi, Dara Shikoh was ready for war. The main body of his army, under the command of his son Sulaiman Shikoh, together with the Rajput general Jai Singh of Amber, marched eastwards to deal with Shah Shuja, whose forces were closest to the capital. A smaller force under another Rajput general, Jaswant Singh of Marwar, was sent southwards to prevent Murad Bakhsh's and Aurangzeb's armies from joining up. It was a sound, plausible and viable strategy and it very well might have worked, had it not been for a few fatal errors.

***

On 24 February 1658, Sulaiman Shikoh's men scattered Shah Shuja's army in an early morning surprise attack, but then made the grevious mistake of chasing the defeated foe all the way to Monghyr (Munger) in Bihar, a forbidding 1200 km east of Delhi. In mid-May, Sulaiman received an urgent message from his father, ordering him to quickly patch up a peace deal with Shah Shuja and return posthaste to Delhi: In April 1658, Aurangzeb had smashed through Jaswant Singh's blockade near Dharmat (now in Madhya Pradesh), some 600 km south of Agra, joined forces with Murad Bakhsh, and was rapidly advancing northwards.

Realizing that Sulaiman's army would not arrive in time to stop Aurangzeb, Dara Shikoh now hastily scraped together whatever forces he could lay his hands on. He planned to march south to the Chambal River and hold all the crossings until Sulaiman's arrival, but Aurangzeb did not want to play along. Swiftly following the river downstream (south-east), Aurangzeb found an unguarded fordable spot near Bhadaura (in present-day Uttar Pradesh), and crossed over to Dara Shikoh's side of the river. Battle was now inevitable. On 29 May 1658, after a full-day standoff the day before in the sweltering heat of summer, the two armies clashed on the sandy plain of Samugarh, about 15 km east of Agra. In spite of the not so great quality of Dara's army, it was a hotly contested battle, with Dara Shikoh coming extremely close to victory on several occasions and a reckless Murad Bakhsh suffering several arrow wounds. But, in the end, Aurangzeb's and Mir Jumla's level-headedness and superior generalship prevailed. When a disheartened Dara Shikoh panicked and climbed down from the beautifully caparisoned elephant on which he had been riding and mounted a horse to ride away from the battlefield, his army collapsed and fled in disarray.

As fast as he could, he galloped back to Agra, arriving there in the evening. Too ashamed to see his father, he hastily gathered a few belongings – including a train of mules laden with gold coins, compassionately sent to him by his father – and slipped out of the city at about three in the morning the next day, accompanied by his family, a few choice slave girls and a handful of faithful followers. In the following couple of days, however, about five thousand of his troops joined him on the way to Delhi. There still was a glimmer of hope.

***

Soon after Dara Shikoh's headlong flight, squadrons of Aurangzeb's forces blocked all the roads around Agra. Shah Jahan, entrenched in his fort, sent a delegation to Aurangzeb, inviting him to pay him a visit and discuss matters. As a token of goodwill, he added a number of precious gifts, including a famous, bejewelled sword called Alamgir (seizer of the universe) – one notch stronger than Jahangir (seizer of the world).

Aurangzeb must have appreciated the gift and the name, for he would later adopt it as his official title as emperor, but, at that stage, he remained unmoved. He sent his son Muhammad Sultan with the message that he would indeed come and visit Shah Jahan, but only after he (the emperor) had surrendered the fort to his officers. Indignantly, Shah Jahan refused, upon which Aurangzeb, without further ado, laid siege to the fort.

Until then, he had pretended to want nothing but to free his father from the evil clutches of the infidel Dara Shikoh, but now, the mask came off. The emperor, so Aurangzeb claimed, had abdicated in favour of an infidel whose devious plan was to promote idolatry; it was his sacred duty to defend the true faith and safeguard the Mughal throne.

***

An artillery bombardment appeared to have little effect on the massive sandstone walls of the fort. But there was another, more effective way: the fort's water supply from the Yamuna was cut off, and Shah Jahan was now forced to drink the brackish water from the wells inside the walls, which had not been in use for years. This state of affairs was more than what the luxury-loving monarch could take. After three days, he capitulated. Aurangzeb seized the imperial arsenal and treasury, and had his father confined to his private apartments in the harem, with his grandson Muhammad Sultan as guardian and only contact with the outside world.

Three days later, when Aurangzeb was on his way to visit the fort, word reached him that his father had hatched a plan for his assassination; in addition, his men showed him an intercepted letter from Shah Jahan to Dara Shikoh, in which the emperor promised continued support to his eldest son. This was all the evidence Aurangzeb needed: he felt that it was meaningless to invest more time in a stubborn old has-been. He returned to his quarters to prepare for a further campaign against Dara Shikoh. Never would he see his father again; not even would he attend his funeral. From that moment on, contact between them would be limited to a sour, reproachful exchange of correspondence.

***

A few days after Shah Jahan's surrender, Jahanara called on her brother to work out an amicable division of the empire among the four brothers. Aurangzeb would have none of it. In his view, Dara Shikoh was an accursed infidel and needed to be eliminated, for the sake of the common good.

He organized a solemn meeting with the amirs of the empire, appointing imperial officers and, in general, taking full control of the imperial administration – in short, behaving like an emperor without officially declaring himself to be one. Murad Bakhsh, still recovering from his wounds, was nowhere to be seen. That was fine with Aurangzeb: Murad Bakhsh had outlived his usefulness.

Murad Bakhsh's End

On 13 June 1658, Aurangzeb set out northwards towards Delhi, to capture the city and deal with Dara Shikoh. Murad Bakhsh, jealous and sulking, followed him with his own army, but stayed a few kilometres behind. Aurangzeb sensed the menace, and prudently decided not to take on Dara Shikoh before Murad had been dealt with. Moving at an astoundingly leisurely pace – covering a mere 60 km in twelve days – he bided his time, constantly sending Murad Bakhsh all kinds of friendly messages and precious gifts, to woo him and allay his suspicions. Then, on 25 June, near the town of Mathura, like a cobra emerging from hiding, he struck. Murad Bakhsh, returning from a hunting trip nearby Aurangzeb's camp, was persuaded by one of his attendants – presumably bribed by Aurangzeb – to pay his brother a visit. Aurangzeb received him with great cordiality and had a sumptuous feast prepared, with excellent food, buckets of wine and hard liquor. Aurangzeb himself, of course, did not drink any alcohol – he never did. But Murad Bakhsh, much less of a puritan than his brother, gladly hit the bottle. After a while, he found himself dead drunk, and Aurangzeb persuaded him to take a rest and sleep it off; a lovely slave girl was sent in to treat him to a soothing massage. Murad Bakhsh blissfully dozed off, and the girl left; only his eunuch bodyguard Shahbaz, fully armed and alert, remained with him in the tent. But the guard was tricked into leaving the tent – reportedly by Aurangzeb personally, on the pretext that he wanted to ask his opinion on something, and once outside the tent, the poor man was silently strangled by Aurangzeb's henchmen. Without further ado, Murad found himself stripped of his arms and taken prisoner.

The next morning before dawn, four elephants, each bearing a closed howdah, left to the four points of the compass. The one heading north carried the hapless Murad Bakhsh to his prison cell in the fort of Salimgarh, situated on an island in the Yamuna River in Delhi. Aurangzeb clearly did not want to take any chances, but his precautions proved to be redundant: nobody made even the slightest effort to come to poor Murad Bakhsh's rescue; all his officers and troops meekly went over to Aurangzeb.

***

Murad Bakhsh would spend three more years in captivity, until Aurangzeb found an appropriately and conveniently legal way to have him eliminated. The son of Ali Naqi (the Gujarati officer whom Murad Bakhsh had killed back in 1657) was persuaded to file a formal complaint against him and demand justice under Sharia law: blood for blood. Aurangzeb, of course, complied with sanctimonious piety. On 14 December 1661, all the legal proceedings having been meticulously complied with, Shahzada Murad Bakhsh, thirty-seven years of age, was beheaded at Gwalior Fort and buried in what was called the Traitors' Cemetery.

Dara Shikoh's Flight

After Murad Bakhsh's imprisonment, Aurangzeb finally had his hands free to march on to Delhi, which he reached around three weeks later. Then, and only then, on 21 July 1658, a full eight months later than his hotheaded brothers, did he officially proclaim himself emperor. It was but a simple ceremony in a garden outside the city, and he did not even bother to have coin struck and the *khutba* read out in his name: Aurangzeb was interested in true power, not in empty symbols. He was in charge now, but the work was not done. There was still Shah Shuja, defeated but not crushed, lurking in Bengal, waiting for an opportunity to strike again; and also Dara Shikoh, who was quickly gathering new forces, financed with the imperial treasury at Delhi. Both needed to be dealt with, and Dara Shikoh clearly was the first priority.

Dara Shikoh had hoped that his son Sulaiman would join him in Delhi, where they could make a stand against Aurangzeb, but with the latter's rapid advance, there was not enough time. Hence, Dara Shikoh retreated further north to Lahore, destroying the ferries over the Sutlej River behind him. There, he was able to lay his hands on much more additional treasure, plus a large stockpile of weaponry, which Shah

Jahan had been building up, probably to prepare for another campaign against Qandahar. But his hopes of slowing down Aurangzeb's advance soon proved to be idle: three weeks later, Aurangzeb reached the Punjab.

Again, Dara Shikoh did not dare to make a stand: his army, though sizeable in number – 20,000 men – was much too inexperienced against Aurangzeb's ironsides. He fled downriver: to Multan perhaps, or further downstream, to Sindh, where he hoped he would find the necessary reinforcements; failing which, he could always follow in the footsteps of his great-great-grandfather, Humayun, and flee to Persia.

It was a chaotic, panicky retreat, much worsened by Aurangzeb's underhand trickery: forged letters were smuggled into Dara Shikoh's camp, casting doubt on the loyalty of some of his best and bravest officers; others – real ones – promised great rewards to those who would join the imperialists. The resulting mood of mistrust and defeatism predictably resulted in mass desertions. By the time Dara Shikoh reached Multan, his army of 20,000 had shrunk to 14,000 – half of which deserted when he fled further southwards on Aurangzeb's approach.

Shah Shuja's End

Aurangzeb would no doubt have continued the chase to finish off Dara Shikoh in person, but a fresh emergency required his urgent attention: Shah Shuja had left Bengal and was marching west on the tried and eminently convenient pretext of wanting to save his poor, imprisoned father from his brother's evil clutches.

Shah Shuja might indeed have captured Agra, weakly defended as it was in Aurangzeb's absence, had he only moved more quickly. Now, by the time he reached Allahabad, he found his passage to Agra blocked by Aurangzeb's vanguard under Muhammad Sultan, followed soon by the main body of the imperial army, some 90,000 cavalry strong, almost four times the size of Shah Shuja's fighting force.

On 4 January 1659, near Khajuha, close to Allahabad, Aurangzeb confidently encamped his mammoth army within striking distance of Shah Shuja's position, ready to move in for the kill at dawn on the next day. He was in for a nasty surprise: what had promised to be the easiest victory of his career, well-nigh ended in absolute disaster. Before dawn Jaswant Singh, his Rajput general – and erstwhile ally of Dara Shikoh – suddenly turned against him, plundering the camp and arsenal and running off with his elite Rajput contingent of about 14,000 men, cutting down everyone found standing in their way. Utter chaos ensued, with many of Aurangzeb's other soldiers joining in the plundering, or fleeing in panic before what seemed a devastating surprise attack.

Shah Shuja could and should have attacked then and there. In fact, Jaswant Singh had sent him a secret message, informing him about the intended betrayal and inviting him to launch a frontal attack as soon as he would hear about the fracas in the imperial camp. It is a sinister tribute to Aurangzeb's reputation for deceit and trickery that Shah Shuja did not dare to do so, suspecting it to be another one of his brother's ruses.

At that point, Aurangzeb's predicament was bad enough as it was: by the time order was restored, he had lost about half of his army and many weapons and animals. But once again, his personal courage and level-headedness saved the day. When his men brought the disastrous news to him in utter panic, he did not even deign to look up. He calmly finished his pre-dawn prayer, then rose, dismissed the Rajput betrayal as irrelevant and proceeded to prepare for battle.

Still, it was quite a close call. Shah Shuja's was the smaller army, but he did have a number of daunting, heavily armoured war elephants, which he put to use with deadly effect. Aurangzeb's left wing collapsed under the fierce onslaught; the rest began to waver. Undaunted, however, Aurangzeb ordered the legs of his own elephant to be chained together to prevent it from fleeing: he would not yield an inch. The panic in his ranks subsided; a concentrated, massive volley of his powerful artillery and musketeers brought the enemy onslaught to a bloody halt. After that, an all-out counterattack washed over Shah Shuja's outnumbered army like a tidal wave. Shah Shuja barely managed to save his own skin by abandoning his elephant and galloping to safety on horseback; then, like he had done eleven months before, he tried to make his way back to Bengal via the Ganga.

***

Aurangzeb gave him no respite. Muhammad Sultan and Mir Jumla were ordered to take 30,000 men and pursue him until he was captured or killed, while Aurangzeb himself went back westwards to deal with Dara Shikoh. Shah Shuja, still in command of about 10,000 men, did try to make a stand on several occasions; each time, however, he was defeated and driven back.

Then, in a dramatic coup de théâtre, Muhammad Sultan suddenly turned his coat. He had enough of Mir Jumla's overbearingness, and besides, as it turned out, he desperately wanted to marry his uncle's (Shah Shuja's) beautiful daughter, one Gulrukh (flower-faced) Begam. Muhammad Sultan's unexpected treason understandably put Mir Jumla in a tight spot for a moment, but in the end, it did not change anything as far as the military situation was concerned: Mir Jumla kept chasing his adversaries, first to Tanda and then to Dhaka, until, in early May of 1660, some fifteen months after the battle of Khajuha, Shuja and his family escaped by boat to the coast of Arakan (in present-day Myanmar/Burma), where they were offered refuge by Sanda Thudhamma, a local pirate king – by whom, so it is believed, they were all murdered a few months later. One thing is certain: Shuja never gave his brother any more trouble.

***

Muhammad Sultan, incidentally, redefected (without his newfound bride, so it seemed) back to his father, throwing himself at his feet on 20 February 1661. Aurangzeb, however, was unimpressed and unforgiving. Muhammad Sultan was thrown in jail at the Salimgarh Fort in Delhi and then transferred to the Gwalior Fort; he died in hapless captivity on 14 December 1676, fifteen days before his thirty-seventh birthday.

Dara Shikoh's Last Stand

Meanwhile, after 2600 km of headlong flight, Dara Shikoh had finally stopped running. As discussed above, he had fled southwards from Multan; his original plan had been to turn west, into the mountainous, bandit-infested borderlands of Baluchistan and then on to Qandahar and Persia. His family, however, had begged him not to follow that plan. And so, the fugitive – with his pitiful army shrunk to less than 3000 men by now – had continued along the Indus into Sindh. In November 1658, he crossed over to the left bank of the river near Thatta. At that point, preoccupied with Shah Shuja's offensive, Aurangzeb decided to recall the pursuing army: Dara Shikoh, for the time being, was a spent force; Shuja was posing a more immediate threat.

Aurangzeb's decision gave Dara Shikoh a few months of respite. Plodding through the forbidding salt marshes of the Rann of Kutch, he arrived at Ahmedabad, the capital of Gujarat, in January 1659. Surprisingly, the local governor – who was actually Aurangzeb's father-in-law – treated him kindly and actually helped him to recruit and equip a new army. Amidst rumours that Aurangzeb was in trouble in his fight against Shah Shuja, Dara Shikoh was ready to march north again. At this point, the fickle Raja Jaswant Singh of Marwar (who had deserted Dara Shikoh at Samugarh, joined Aurangzeb and then ignobly turned against his new master at the battle of Khajuha), offered to join him with a contingent of 20,000 Rajput troops and march on Agra. Dara Shikoh was elated. This combined army would really have more than a fighting chance. But Aurangzeb, always prepared to put pragmatism ahead of personal feelings, now made diplomatic overtures to the raja: full pardon and new honours if he were loyal; total destruction if not. Sure enough, the fickle raja once again turned his coat. So, Dara Shikoh found himself near Ajmer without the promised Rajput support and Aurangzeb was rapidly approaching from the north. There was no time for an orderly withdrawal back to Gujarat; he would have to make a stand. But he did have time enough to choose the battlefield. Masterfully, he prepared himself a defensive position at Daurai, 7.5 km south of Ajmer, in between two Aravalli hills, his front protected by trenches and his guns skilfully positioned on a hillock dominating the approach.

Aurangzeb along with his army arrived at Daurai on 21 March 1659 and attacked the next morning. It must have been quite frustrating for him to find his huge army unable to use its massive numbers on this narrow battlefield: wave upon wave of his men, laboriously clambering up the slope towards Dara Shikoh's defence lines, were mowed down by his well-placed artillery and musket fire. Then, at nightfall after three full days of bitter fighting, Dara Shikoh's luck finally ran out: Aurangzeb's men had managed to overrun one of his trenches. From then on, Dara Shikoh knew that the battle was inevitably and irreparably lost. Under the cover of darkness, he managed to sneak out unnoticed, with his fifteen-year-old son Sipihr Shikoh and only a handful of men.

After his victory, Aurangzeb left the hunt for the fugitive Dara Shikoh to his officers. He triumphantly returned to Delhi, where, on Thursday, 5 June 1659, he was officially enthroned a second time, as Abu'l Muzaffar Muhyi-ud Din Muhammad Aurangzeb Alamgir.[35] The name Muhyi-ud Din (reviver of religion) was, in fact, a highly significant political statement: Aurangzeb had come to restore the one and only true religion, which, so he claimed, had been imperilled and defiled by his unworthy brother (Dara Shikoh). Equally significant is the Persian verse on his first official coin: '*This coin has been stamped on earth like the shining full moon, by Emperor Aurangzeb Alamgir.*' No

Quranic verses were there, as had appeared on earlier Mughal coins: he did not want them to be defiled by the touch of infidels.

***

Meanwhile, Dara Shikoh found himself in dire straits indeed. Before the battle, he had given orders for his women and their retinue to wait for him, readily mounted on their elephants, by the banks of the Ana Sagar Lake south of Ajmer; but, in his headlong flight, he missed them. Only when they saw the chaos of Dara Shikoh's army in flight around them did they themselves decide to flee as well. They soon found themselves badgered and plundered by their own bodyguards and bands of thieving villagers, but somehow managed to catch up with Dara Shikoh.

With a retinue of some 2000 loyal soldiers who had nobly chosen to rejoin them, they somehow made their way back to Gujarat, where, however, disappointment most bitter awaited them: this time, the gates of Ahmedabad remained ominously closed. There was no alternative, but to head all the way back through the terrible Rann of Kutch, and from there, to traverse Sindh and head for the Bolan Pass and the Persian border.

But fate kept on hounding the hapless fugitives. To Dara Shikoh's utter despair, Nadira Banu Begam, his favourite wife, died of dysentery and exhaustion (in early June 1659). Fulfilling her dying wish, he sent most of the handful of soldiers he had still left to escort her body to Lahore, so that it could find a decent final resting place in Hindustan.

Then, the finishing blow fell. He sought refuge with a local Baluch chieftain, one Malik Jiwan, a man whose life Dara Shikoh had saved some years before, by personally intervening to plead his case when he had been sentenced to be trampled to death by elephants by Shah Jahan. The disloyal Malik Jiwan now returned the favour with a despicable act of treachery: after a few days of hospitality, he had his royal guests seized, and sent word to Aurangzeb.

Soon, Dara Shikoh and Sipihr Shikoh (as well as Malik Jiwan) found themselves as part of a military convoy to Delhi, where, on 29 August 1659, dressed in rags and seated on a small and dirty female elephant, they were paraded through the streets.

Aurangzeb had expected that they would be booed and laughed at by the local populace – mobs do tend to side with the winners – but was much displeased to see how many people openly cried for the hapless prince, who had, in his time, been quite popular. The treacherous

Malik Jiwan even found himself pelted with stones and garbage by the outraged populace.

All of this only strengthened Aurangzeb's resolve: Dara Shikoh had to die, as soon as possible. The usual legal charade was played out in the Diwan-i-Khas: Dara Shikoh was declared an apostate; and the punishment for apostasy under Sharia law – according to the jurists present, anyway[36] – was death.

In a desperate petition, written in prison, Dara Shikoh still attempted to save his life. He had given up all pretence to the throne, he wrote; all he desired was Aurangzeb's permission to retire into a modest home with just one of his servant girls, and he would pray for Aurangzeb's health for the rest of his life.

He could have saved himself the trouble. Aurangzeb had no need for Dara Shikoh's prayers; he wanted him dead. On the margin of Dara Shikoh's petition he wrote in his own hand: '*You first acted as an usurper, and you were a mischief maker.*'[37] There would be no forgiveness, no clemency.

***

In the evening of Tuesday, 30 August 1659, Aurangzeb's henchmen entered Dara Shikoh's place of confinement, and dragged the young prince Sipihr, who was crying and desperately clinging to his father, into another room. Dara Shikoh appealed to the executioners to take another message to Aurangzeb, but they replied that they were no one's messengers and had come to carry out orders. He even then made a pathetic attempt to fend off his assailants with a small dagger he had managed to keep hidden, but was quickly stabbed to death and beheaded, after which the executioners carried the head to Aurangzeb.

Niccolò Manucci provides quite a gruesome account of this incident:

> *When Aurangzeb learned that the head of Dara had arrived, he ordered it to be brought to him in the garden on a dish, with the face cleaned of surface blood and a turban on (the head). He called for lights to be brought so that he might see the mark borne by the Prince on his forehead, and might make sure that it was Dara's head, and not that of another person. After he had satisfied himself he told them to put it on the ground, and gave it three thrusts in the face with the sword he carried by way of his staff, saying: 'Behold, the face of a would-be king and emperor of all the Mughal realms.' He gave secret*

> *orders to place the head in a box, to be sent by runners to the eunuch Itibar Khan, who had charge of Shah Jahan's prison, with orders to deliver it to him when seated at the* [dining] *table.*[38]

More likely than not, Manucci was merely repeating the gory bazaar rumours and old wives' tales that, as usual, had been spreading like wildfire. Aurangzeb certainly was no saint, but senseless acts of cruelty – devoid of any practical purpose or benefit – seemed to be below him: he was much too cool and level-headed a man to lose his self-control and dignified demeanour.

Less spectacular, but probably much closer to the truth is a rivalling contemporary account, which states that when the executioners brought back Dara Shikoh's head, Aurangzeb declared: '*As I did not want to look at this infidel's face during his lifetime, I have no wish to do so now*.'[39] This certainly sounds much more like him.

Dara Shikoh's headless corpse was paraded through Delhi, after which, it received an unceremonious burial in Humayun's tomb. Many more Mughal princes would follow, rightfully earning the monument its sinister nickname: the 'Mughal Dormitory'.

Sulaiman, Sipihr and the Others

It now remains for us to briefly relate the end of Sulaiman Shikoh's sad story. Much to his dismay, he was still 400 km away from Agra when the decisive battle of Samugarh took place (8 June 1658); the sad news of his father's defeat reached him four days later. Abandoned by his generals, he retreated eastwards towards Allahabad. His initial plan had been to head north and, from there, to cross the Sutlej and rejoin Dara Shikoh in the Punjab, but Aurangzeb, an astute tactician, had taken the precaution to block all the ferries. Too weak to fight his way through, the prince had no alternative but to seek asylum in the kingdom of Garhwal (in present-day Uttarakhand), where he stayed for about eighteen months as a guest of the local raja, who even gave him one of his daughters in marriage. But Aurangzeb had not forgotten about him. Late in 1660, he ordered the raja to extradite his young guest; and the poor raja had no alternative but to comply. On Aurangzeb's orders, Sulaiman was imprisoned in the Salimgarh Fort on 14 January 1661 and later transferred to the Gwalior Fort. There, in spite of his desperate plea to grant him a swift and honourable death, he was force-fed every morning with *pousta*, a strong opium-based concoction, which turned him into a witless zombie. He died in May 1662, withered away like a plant in the dark, just twenty-seven years of age. He was Shah Jahan's favourite grandson.

***

In 1662, Sipihr, Dara Shikoh's eighteen-year-old son, found himself treated with much more lenience: unlike his father, his uncles and his elder brother, he had his life spared. And while he did remain imprisoned, Aurangzeb even married him to one of his daughters in 1673, and had suitable living quarters fitted out for the young couple in the Salimgarh island prison fortress. Likewise, another daughter of Aurangzeb was married to one of Murad Bakhsh's sons, residing in the same island prison.

This, too, was Aurangzeb. Where his father would not have hesitated to kill each and every one of his male relatives, Aurangzeb let them live. No doubt, he was a dour and spiteful fundamentalist; no doubt, he was brutally ruthless and capable of whatever ruse or treachery – including perjury – to achieve his goals; but when it came to cold-blooded murder, he at least needed some kind of legal justification. He was a shameless hypocrite, but also, a high principled one.

What If …?

Reams of paper have been used to speculate about what might have become of India had Dara Shikoh prevailed in his struggle against Aurangzeb; after all, it had been an extremely close call. Dara Shikoh's and Aurangzeb's philosophical and political views were so utterly different that the struggle between them seemed like a battle for the soul of India itself.

Dara Shikoh was a proud, haughty man, his attitude towards others varying from condescending kindness to mocking irony. Not surprisingly, he was a consummate courtier, a well-mannered intrigant, but, above all, even more than his great-grandfather Akbar, he was a philosopher and a mystic at heart. While – in spite of Aurangzeb's allegations to the contrary – he always remained a devout Muslim, he was genuinely interested in humankind's other religious traditions.

He studied everything he could get his hands on, including texts on Judaism and Christianity, but his main interest was focused on Islam – the Sufi mystics in particular – and its relationship with Hinduism and the venerable, age-old philosophical insights of the Upanishads. Dara

Shikoh himself translated them from Sanskrit into Persian, with the help of Hindu scholars from Varanasi; he called them 'without doubt or suspicion, the first of all heavenly books in point of time' and 'in conformity with the Holy Quran and even a commentary thereon.'[40] He also composed a treatise entitled *Majma-ul-Bahrain* (the confluence of two oceans), in which he stated that Hinduism and Islam both refer to the same principles of truth and goodness.

Like most broadminded people then and now, he utterly despised bigots and fundamentalists: the orthodox mullahs in general and his own brother Aurangzeb in particular. '*Paradise is there where no mullah exists*,' he once famously wrote. The feeling, alas, was more than mutual. In the eyes of Aurangzeb and the mullahs, he was a despicable heretic, an apostate, and a threat to the true faith, far worse than the worst kind of pagan.

Dara Shikoh was right, of course. There are plenty of arguments from the Holy Quran that show his insights were much closer to the will of the loving, eternal God – if there is one – than the hateful totalitarianism preached and practised by his adversaries, then and now. The Qur'anic verses that appear to justify violence should be understood and read together with those many other, peace-loving verses, which enjoin the believers to be merciful, tolerant, just and kind to others and even to patiently endure injustice and insults from non-believers (for example: Quran: 20:130). And with those other verses – highly relevant in today's context! – which clearly show that religious and cultural diversity, far from being objectionable, are actually *desirable*, a source of enrichment, a state of affairs *wanted* by the Creator Himself:

> *Unto every one of you We have appointed a different law and way of life. Had God so willed, He could have made you one nation, but it is His wish to test you by that which He has bestowed on you.* Vie, then, with each other in good deeds, *for to God you must all return, and He shall make clear to you what you have disagreed about.* (Quran 5:48; see also 11:118-119; 49:13.)[41]

***

Let me digress a bit to make a point. It is a dangerous fallacy – also, and increasingly so, among today's Muslims – to think that 'moderate' Muslims are, in some way, less religious than extremists. On the contrary: a moderate, open and modest attitude is much closer to the true spirit of the Holy Quran than that of misguided extremists, who are doing the cause of their religion a terrible disservice.

There is another, much more impressive, endearing and convincing Islam. That is the fearless and gentle Islam of Khan Abdul Ghaffar Khan (Badshah Khan: 1890–1988), also known by his affectionate nickname, 'the Frontier Gandhi', the Pashtun leader and a deeply devout Muslim, who had no difficulties whatsoever to recognize in his friend Mahatma Gandhi, a practising Hindu, a fellow Muslim in the true, fundamental sense of the word.

***

Let us get back to the main narrative. So, had Dara Shikoh won, would it have made much difference? Possibly. But it needs to be remembered that his ideas of tolerance and friendship have not died with him. Even in defeat, he, and many other people like him, have shaped the Indian soul – more so than the bigots.

The crucial question is: Would he have been able to prevent the ultimate decline and disintegration of the Mughal Empire? We do not know with any certainty, but it seems doubtful. The true causes of that decline – the economic injustice, the bloated and corrupt administration and the disastrous profligacy of the ruling class – most probably would not have gone away. Akbar was a great king who also happened to be interested in philosophy; Dara Shikoh, on the other hand, was a dilettante, a philosopher who wanted to be king. This would, most probably, not have been enough.

As Bamber Gascoigne phrased it eloquently:

> *The Great Mughals had built their astonishing achievement on a combination of talents and sensibilities which … had reached practical fruition in Akbar. The problems besetting an empire which had reached its natural limits of expansion required at least another Akbar to solve them, but his full range of characteristics were now neatly and precisely divided between Dara* [Shikoh] *and Aurangzeb. Dara had inherited the interest in culture, the inquiring mind, the intrinsic tolerance and eclecticism; Aurangzeb had the decisiveness, the physical courage, the ability to inspire and to lead. If Dara had reigned, the family achievement might well have crumbled more pleasantly. Under Aurangzeb's stern hands, it was to grind to its end with blood, toil, tears and sweat.*[42]

Shah Jahan's Wistful End

Shah Jahan would spend the last eight years of his life (1658 to 1666) as an utterly powerless and carefully watched, if relatively well-pampered, prisoner. He was allowed to reside in his white-marble private apartments in the Agra Fort and was free to enjoy the companionship of his *zanana* (his favourite daughter Jahanara, his wives, concubines and personal servants), but any communication with the outside world was strictly controlled. Any personal request had to go through his guard, a mean-minded eunuch named Mutamad. He could not receive any visitors, except with Aurangzeb's permission, and in the presence of his guard, who reported everything he said and did to Aurangzeb. Any attempt to break out of this straitjacket was met with swift reprisals. When he was found sending letters out of the fort in defiance of Aurangzeb's instructions, he was for some time deprived of paper and writing materials.

The early years of the old emperor's captivity were marked by petty conflicts and acrimonious exchanges of correspondence with his rebellious son, with bitter reproaches flowing back and forth. '*How do you still regard the memory of Khusrau and Parvez, whom you did to death before your accession and who had threatened no injury to you*?' Aurangzeb wrote, not without justification, in reply to his father's reproaches. At all times, he stuck to his story: he had never wanted the throne; he had merely defended Islam against an evil infidel's plans. The civil war had never been necessary; it had taken place because Shah Jahan had turned a blind eye to Dara Shikoh's machinations. Besides, Aurangzeb asked: how could he have won without God's approval? Rather than complaining, argued Aurangzeb, Shah Jahan should be grateful to his son for relieving him of the burden of government. '*Submit to the will of God, and your sorrows will turn into peace and contentment*!' was his advice.[43]

Another source of petty conflict was Aurangzeb's sudden interest in his father's personal jewellery, including his diamond thumb ring and his rosary, made of one hundred perfectly matched, magnificent pearls. In the end, Shah Jahan did give up the ring, but stubbornly refused to hand over his pearl rosary; he even threatened to grind it to dust with a pestle and mortar, rather than part with it.

Gradually, the bickering died down; Aurangzeb had other fish to fry and Shah Jahan seemed to have resigned himself to his fate. What else was he to do? He was getting old; most of his male heirs were dead and the rest had spent their entire lives in captivity; there really was no alternative to Aurangzeb.

In those twilight years, Shah Jahan became extremely devout, spending most of his time praying, studying the Quran, and listening to religious discourses. He was ready to meet his Maker.

***

That fateful occasion presented itself a few years later. On 17 January 1666, he suddenly suffered what appears to have been a recurrence of his earlier ailments: the symptoms included strangury and high fever. The end came on Monday, 1 February 1666, fifteen days after the onset of his illness. In between, the old monarch had calmly put his affairs in order. He signed a letter pardoning Aurangzeb, made arrangements for his funeral and consoled his weeping daughter and wives. On the last day, he whispered a last prayer and passed away peacefully in the middle of the night, listening to verses from the Holy Quran. At dawn the next morning, his body, placed in a sandalwood coffin, was carried out of the fortress – through a breach in the wall, as was customary – and taken by boat down the Yamuna to the Taj Mahal, where it was entombed next to his beloved wife.

***

Muslim funerals are never supposed to be ostentatious, but his was embarrassingly humble. No one of note, not one of his descendants, was there to carry the bier. Upon hearing about his father's illness, Aurangzeb had sent his son Muazzam to represent him, but he arrived too late for the funeral.

Aurangzeb had not seen his father for fourteen years, had not cared to visit him during his terminal illness and did not attend his funeral. Only one month later did he deign to travel from Delhi to Agra – but even then, it was to see sister Jahanara. Even though she had sided with Dara Shikoh in the civil war, she had always been his favourite, and he was eager to win her back. She was assigned a grand mansion and elevated to the rank of Padshah Begam (the first lady of the empire); her annual allowance was increased from one million rupees – a staggeringly high amount of money at that time – to an even more extravagant 1.7 million.

Interestingly, Aurangzeb's reconciliation with Jahanara marked the end of the career of her three-year-younger sister and rival, Roshanara.

Throughout the civil war, she had sided with Aurangzeb; after Dara Shikoh's downfall, she had clamoured for his blood; and it is reported how she feasted with her friends when her brother's headless corpse was being paraded through the streets.

Eventually, however, she and Aurangzeb had fallen out with each other. It is said that he deeply resented her libidinous lifestyle; people even whispered that he had her poisoned for that reason. All we know is that she died in obscurity five years later, in September 1671, aged fifty-four. Jahanara passed away ten years later, in September 1681, at sixty-seven years of age. Aurangzeb, who was then on his way to the Deccan, ordered a three-day halt to mourn her death. She was interred – at her own request – in a humble grave near the tomb of Shaykh Nizam-ud Din Auliya in Delhi.

After his meeting with Jahanara, Aurangzeb paid a visit – as conspicuous as it was sanctimonious – to his parents' magnificent mausoleum. Manucci reports that he '*prayed and showed much devoutness, wiping his eyes as if he wept*'.[44] This, too, certainly sounds like him.

CHRONOLOGY

5 January 1592: Birth of Prince Khurram (Shah Jahan).
1 September 1593: Birth of Arjumand Banu Begam (Mumtaz Mahal).
9 October 1610: Khurram marries his first wife, Qandahari Begam.
21 August 1611: Birth of Khurram's first child (to Qandahari Begam): Princess Purhunar.
10 May 1612: Khurram marries Arjumand Banu Begam (Mumtaz Mahal), daughter of Nur Jahan's brother Asaf Khan.
30 March 1613: Birth of Princess Hur-un Nissa to Mumtaz Mahal; dies at three years of age.
1 April 1614: Birth of Princess Jahanara.
28 October 1615: Birth of Dara Shikoh.
23 June 1616: Birth of Shah Shuja.

10 November 1616: Khurram gets the title of Shah Jahan (king of the world).
2 September 1617: Birth of Princess Roshanara.
4 November 1618: Birth of Aurangzeb.
25 June 1619: Birth of Prince Jahan Afroz; dies at the age of two.
16 December 1619: Birth (premature) of Prince Umid Bakhsh; dies at the age of two.
1620: Khurram gets custody of Khusrau.
11 June 1621: Birth of Princess Thurayya (dies at age seven).
January 1622: Death of Khusrau.
June 1622: Qandahar lost to the Persians; Khurram refuses to march against them.
Late 1622: Birth and death of a baby boy (unnamed).
1622–1626: Khurram rebels, but is defeated and retreats to the Deccan, then to Bengal and then to the Deccan again.
8 October1624: Birth of Murad Bakhsh.
March 1626: End of Shah Jahan's rebellion; Dara Shikoh and Aurangzeb sent to court.
4 November 1626: Birth of Prince Lutfallah; dies at the age of one.
8 November 1627: Jahangir dies; war of succession begins. Dawar Bakhsh proclaimed emperor by Asaf Khan.
Late 1627: Asaf Khan defeats, imprisons and blinds Shahryar.
Early 1628: Dawar Bakhsh, Shahryar and other princes executed.
24 January 1628: Shah Jahan formally crowned at Agra.
9 May 1628: Birth of Prince Daulat Afza; dies at the age of one.
Late 1628: Uzbek siege of Kabul.
15 October 1629: Rebellion of Khan Jahan Lodi.
23 April 1630: Birth and death of Princess Husnara.
3 February 1631: Death of Khan Jahan Lodi.
17 June 1631: Birth of Princess Gauharara; Mumtaz Mahal (thirty-eight) dies in childbirth; burial in Burhanpur.
8 January 1632: Mumtaz Mahal's body reinterred in Agra.
26 June 1633: Capture of Daulatabad in the Deccan.
22 March 1635: Inauguration of the Peacock Throne.
September 1635: Shah Jahan leaves Agra on the second Deccan campaign.

6 May 1636: Peace treaty with Bijapur and Golconda.
23 July 1636: Aurangzeb appointed governor of the Deccan.
7 March 1638: Surrender of Qandahar by its Persian governor.
1639: Construction of Shajahanabad (now known as Old Delhi).
1643: Taj Mahal completed.
March 1644: Princess Jahanara critically injured in a fire.
26 February 1645: Aurangzeb appointed governor of Gujarat.
18 December 1645: Death of Nur Jahan.
18 April 1648: Formal inauguration of the Red Fort in Shajahanabad.
23 February 1649: Qandahar captured by the Persian army.
1649–1653: Three failed attempts by Mughals to recover Qandahar; Aurangzeb returns to the Deccan.
15 February 1655: Dara Shikoh reconfirmed as heir-apparent.
7 July 1656: Mir Jumla appointed prime minister.
16 September 1657: Shah Jahan falls critically ill at Shajahanabad.
28 October 1657: Shah Jahan moves back to Agra.
20 November 1657: Murad Bakhsh proclaims himself emperor.
24 February 1658: Sulaiman Shikoh defeats Shah Shuja.
25 April 1658: Aurangzeb and Murad Bakhsh defeat Jaswant Singh at Dharmat.
29 May 1658: Battle of Samugarh: Aurangzeb defeats Dara Shikoh.
19 June 1658: Shah Jahan forced to surrender; then imprisoned.
31 July 1658: First enthronement of Aurangzeb Alamgir.
4 January 1659: Aurangzeb defeats Shah Shuja.
22–24 March 1659: Dara Shikoh defeated at Daurai.
5 June 1659: Second enthronement of Aurangzeb Alamgir.
30 August 1659: Execution of Dara Shikoh at Shajahanabad.
14 January 1661: Sulaiman Shikoh imprisoned in Salimgarh Fort, Delhi.
February 1661 (?): Death of Shah Shuja in northern Burma.
14 December 1661: Execution of Murad Bakhsh at Gwalior.
May 1662: Sulaiman Shikoh dies of chronic opium poisoning.
1 February 1666: Death of Shah Jahan.

Notes and References

1. Abul Muzaffar: father of victory/triumph/conquest. Shihab-ud Din: star/meteor of religion. Shah Jahan: king of the world. Sahib-i-Qirani ath-Thani: lord of the fortuitous conjunction of Jupiter and Venus (one of Timur's titles). Padshah Ghazi: warrior-emperor.
2. Abraham Eraly, *The Mughal Throne: The Saga of India's Great Emperors*, Viking (an imprint of Penguin Books India and Penguin Books UK), New Delhi and London, 1997 and 2000, p. 299.
3. Bamber Gascoigne, *A Brief History of the Great Moguls,* Carroll & Graf *Publishers*, New York, 2002, p. 187.
4. Ibid., p. 188.
5. Eraly op. cit., pp. 313–315; Gascoigne op. cit., 189–191.
6. Giles Tillotson, *Taj Mahal*, Harvard University Press, Cambridge, Massachusetts, USA, 2012.
7. Surah al-Fatiha, the opening chapter of the Quran.
8. W. E. Begley and Z. A. Desai, *Taj Mahal: The Illumined Tomb: An Anthology of Seventeenth-century Mughal and European Documentary Sources*, Seattle, University of Washington Press, 1989, pp. li-lii.
9. The word *urs* literally means marriage, i.e., of the soul of the deceased to God.
10. Fergus Nicoll, *Shah Jahan: The Rise and Fall of the Mughal Empire*, Haus Publishing, London, 2009, pp. 182–183 and the references quoted q.v.
11. Quoted in Diana and Michael Preston, *A Teardrop on the Cheek of Time: The Story of the Taj Mahal*, Doubleday, London, 2007, p. 187.
12. Ebba Koch, *The Complete Taj Mahal and the Riverfront Gardens of Agra*, Thames and Hudson, London, 2006, pp. 152–153, and Tillotson, op. cit., p. 14.
13. Peter Mundy, *The Travels of Peter Mundy in Europe and Asia, 1608–1667*, Bibliolife, Charleston, South Carolina, USA, 2009 edition.
14. Quoted in Begley and Desai, op. cit., pp. 292–293.
15. Koch, op. cit., p. 89, Tillotson, op. cit., pp. 80–84 and Nicoll, op. cit., pp. 183–184.
16. Begley and Desai, op. cit., pp. 261ff.
17. Tillotson, op. cit., pp. 68–73.
18. Quoted in Begley and Desai, op. cit., pp. 291 ff.
19. Ibid., p. 291.
20. Tillotson, op. cit., p. 84.
21. Koch, op. cit., pp. 218–219.
22. The main proponent of this theory was P. N. Oak (a writer), who had made it his mission in life to prove that not only the Taj but also most, if not all, historical structures in India and beyond are, in fact, Hindu. While extremely numerous, his arguments seem only convincing to those who want to be convinced. One example – out of countless many – is that the Taj must have been a temple before it was turned into a tomb, because its typical 'onion

dome' could not possibly be intended to cover a tomb. The dome, he argued, tended to amplify and propagate, rather than muffle, the sounds made inside it. That this kind of dome is typical of Muslim architecture everywhere, inside and outside India, did not seem to bother him too much.

23. Gascoigne, op. cit., p. 178.
24. Nicoll, op. cit., pp. 196–197.
25. Eraly, op. cit., pp. 305–308.
26. Ibid., p. 320.
27. Ibid., p. 318.
28. Sir Jadunath Sarkar (an eminent Mughal historian), quoted, among others, by Eraly, op. cit., p. 324 and R. C. Majumdar (ed.), *The Mughul Empire,* Bharatiya Vidya Bhavan's History and Culture of the Indian People, Vol. VII, Bombay, 1974, p. 205.
29. *O, quam cito transit gloria mundi* is a phrase from the German priest Thomas à Kempis' fifteenth-century work *Imitation of Christ*; the phrase *sic transit gloria mundi* (thus passes the glory of this world) has been used in papal coronation ceremonies for several centuries.
30. The elephant was named Sudhakar, according to the *Padshah Nama*.
31. Also known by her posthumous title: Rabia-ud Daurani.
32. Gascoigne, op. cit., p. 193.
33. Abu'l Fauz: father of triumph; Nasir-ud Din: protector of religion; Iskandar: Alexander (the Great); Shah Shuja: courageous king; Bahadur: brave; Padshah: emperor; and Ghazi: (holy) warrior, 'slayer of the infidel'.
34. Eraly, op. cit., p. 341.
35. Abu'l Muzaffar: father of victory/triumph/conquest. Muhyi-ud Din: reviver of religion (Muhyi means one who gives life; Al-Muhyi, the quickener, is one of the traditional ninety-nine names of God in Islam). Aurangzeb: jewel of the throne. Alamgir: seizer of the universe.
36. Even in the twenty-first century, apostasy is a crime in twenty-three out of forty-nine Muslim-majority countries; in no less than thirteen of them (Mauritania, Nigeria, Somalia, Sudan, Saudi Arabia, Yemen, the UAE, Iran, Qatar, Afghanistan, Pakistan, the Maldives and Malaysia), it is officially subject to the death penalty. The legal basis for such a penalty, however, is highly questionable, as it resides predominantly in the Hadith, and not in the Holy Quran, which famously proclaims that '*there shall be no compulsion in matters of religion*' (2:256).
37. Eraly, op. cit., p. 370.
38. Waldemar Hansen, *The Peacock Throne: The Drama of Mogul India*, Motilal Banarsidass, Delhi, 1986, p. 38.
39. Jadunath Sarkar, *History of Aurangzeb*, Vols. 1 and 2, Orient Longman, Delhi, 1973, p. 341.
40. Eraly, op. cit., p. 335.
41. Quoted from my own work *Paths to Peace: Religion, Ethics and Tolerance in a Globalizing World*, Vakils, Feffer & Simons, Mumbai, 2013.

42. Gascoigne, op. cit., pp. 217–218.
43. Eraly, op. cit., p.378.
44. Begley and Desai, op. cit., p. 311.

Chapter 6
Aurangzeb the Grim

Few characters in Mughal history are as controversial as Aurangzeb. Many Muslims tend to depict him as a misunderstood and tragic hero, a deeply pious man who spent his entire life struggling to further the sacred cause of Islam, while most Hindus, quite understandably, revile him for his bigotry.

As a human being, he was an enigma: treacherous, and at the same time principled, a fascinating mixture of paranoia, fundamentalism, cunning villainy and humble piety. As a ruler, he was a deeply tragic failure. In spite of a long life marked by tireless labour and total dedication, he saw the mighty empire he had inherited crumbling before his very eyes; as a result, he died a sad and deeply disappointed man.

***

With the wisdom of hindsight, one cannot avoid the impression that an equally industrious and disciplined, but wiser, milder and less bigoted king would have been much more successful. No one summarized this impression better than Bamber Gascoigne:

> *To most Hindus Akbar is one of the greatest Muslim emperors of India and Aurangzeb one of the worst; to many Muslims the opposite is the case. To an outsider there can be little doubt that Akbar's way was the right one. One needs perhaps to share Aurangzeb's own strong faith to approve of his policies, and even then it would be hard to admire his character. Akbar disrupted the Muslim community by recognizing that India* [was] *not an Islamic country: Aurangzeb disrupted India by behaving as though it were.*[1]

Aurangzeb's reign is characterized by three disastrous developments: his dogged resolve to impose what he believed was orthodox Islam; his spectacular, but utterly ruinous and largely inconclusive, attempts to annex the entire south of India; and the rise of new, competing powers, both domestic and foreign, that would soon bring about the disintegration of the empire.

Religious Policies

One of Aurangzeb's first measures after his solemn second enthronement (on 5 June 1659) was the appointment of a *muhtasib* (a censor to ensure public decency), whose task included not only the suppression of unIslamic practices such as music, dancing, gambling and the consumption of alcohol but also the prohibition of narcotics, castration and slavery. He also commissioned the Fatwa-e-Alamgiri, a voluminous codification of Sunni Sharia law, principally from the Hanafi school of jurisprudence, which took the legal experts several years to complete. It became an authoritative source of jurisprudence, even in countries far beyond the Mughal borders, including the Ottoman Empire.

There is little doubt that Aurangzeb was sincere in his resolve to rigorously adhere to the precepts of his religion, whatever the consequences, good or bad. Like all fundamentalists, he was strictly legalistic, obsessed with the letter of a law supposedly decreed by God – rather than with goodness, kindness and decency, which should be at the core of any religiousness worthy of that name. A rather ridiculous example of this ill-advised legalism was his insistence on using the (lunar) Islamic calendar for revenue collection from farmers, in spite of the blatantly obvious fact that crops in their ripening cycles are dependent upon the seasons – and, therefore, on the movements of the sun, not the moon. For all its piousness, this kind of fundamentalism is the ultimate blasphemy: to reduce a God – Who, by His own definition is greater than anything conceivable or imaginable – to the smallness of human pettiness, and to a set of arbitrary rules that go against reason. Those who believe in an almighty, all-good God, should realize that reason can never lead to conclusions that are incompatible with divine revelation, for truth cannot contradict truth.[2]

***

Particularly ruinous was Aurangzeb's stubborn insistence on a series of discriminatory measures against his non-Muslim subjects. The first –

which until today has left deep and painful scars on the very soul of India – has been the destruction of a series of Hindu temples. The estimates of the numbers destroyed vary wildly, from a few dozen to a rather fantastical 60,000, but there undeniably was a deliberate, unrelenting policy behind it, starting in earnest when he had been in power for about ten years. As usual, he stuck to the formal rules: the destruction was not wantonly indiscriminate, but directed – at least in principle – against newly built or repaired temples, not against long-standing ones; although there appears to have been considerable ambiguity in the interpretation of that concept. A sad example of this is destruction of the famous Somnath Temple on the western coast of Gujarat, which had been standing for over five hundred years: it had been rebuilt in the twelfth century, after it had been destroyed two centuries before, during one of Mahmud of Ghazni's looting raids.[3] Other extremely important and sacred buildings destroyed on Aurangzeb's orders include the Vishwanath Temple at Varanasi and the Keshav Deo Temple at Mathura in Uttar Pradesh (believed to be birthplace of Lord Krishna) – important places of Hindu worship and learning that, in his thinking, had a bad influence on many of his Muslim subjects.

Even more vexing in the eyes of the common Hindu people of his time must have been the series of discriminatory measures taken against them personally: the tax on Hindu pilgrimages, abolished by Akbar, was reintroduced; endowments enjoyed by Hindu priests and places of worship were abolished; and Hindu merchants were penalized with heavier duties than their Muslim colleagues.[4] The highly symbolic final blow came in 1679, with the reintroduction, in spite of massive protests, of the detested *jizya* (the tax on non-Muslims), assessed at 0.65 per cent of the value of any property. It sent a powerful political message: the Hindus had become second-rate citizens in their own country, tolerated at best, and actively discriminated against wherever possible.

Unsurprisingly, this series of affronts against the majority of his subjects – much aggravated by executions of prominent religious leaders (including the Sikh Guru, Tegh Bahadur, in November 1675) and by the pointless fight he chose to pick with his erstwhile Rajput allies – did not fail to produce dire political consequences: in a few decades' time, Aurangzeb managed to rip apart the very fabric of Mughal society and undermine the legitimacy of his own dynasty. Akbar's spell had been broken; Dara Shikoh's dream had been shattered.

In Search of Glory

The descendants of Timur always had a penchant for grandiose titles, the pomposity of which was, more often than not, inversely proportional to the real power they wielded. And nothing could be more ambitious than the title Alamgir (seizer of the universe); Aurangzeb owed it to himself to grab as much land as possible. The opportunities for glory, however, had been few and far between, and his track record, patchy at best. For instance:

- There had been the north-eastern campaign in 1662, in which Mir Jumla had pushed back an Assamese invasion and added some 500 km of the Brahmaputra Valley to the Mughal territory. The war, however, had been ruinous, with the loss of many men and Mir Jumla dying of consumption on the way back. Barely four years later, the Assamese recovered most of their lost territory.
- There had also been a bloody, if ultimately effective, punitive expedition against the Afghan hill tribes in the north-west; but there were no territorial gains in the area: after the humiliating triple failure under Shah Jahan (in 1649–1653), Aurangzeb never had the guts to take another shot at Qandahar, the most obvious target in the region.
- In 1666, it was proudly announced that the emperor's invincible armies had conquered 'Tibet'; in actual fact, it merely meant that a petty local chief in the stony wastelands of Ladakh had been bullied into building a mosque and minting coin with Aurangzeb's name – hardly worthy of a 'universe-conquering' monarch.

If Aurangzeb wanted military glory, there was only one place where he could find it: in the Deccan. Things had been worsening rapidly down there, with the rise of a defiant and utterly dangerous challenger: Shivaji, the Maratha king. But Aurangzeb found himself having to deal with so much – if partly self-inflicted – trouble in the northern heartlands of his empire that it would take him until late 1681, when he was sixty-three already, before he was able to return to the south, in a grandiose – if ultimately failed – attempt to restore order and establish his authority down there.

Rebellions in the North

The first rebels he had to deal with were the Jats in the Mathura district, some 50 km north-west of Agra. In 1669, a band of Jats defeated the local imperial officer; the prospect of plunder soon inflated the number of insurgents to a daunting 20,000. Aurangzeb himself headed the imperial troops sent out to crush the uprising. Gokula (aka Gokul Singh), the Jat leader who headed the revolt, was captured and publicly executed in 1670, his limbs being hacked off one by one. This gruesome butchery put an end to the unrest, but the Jats remained untamable. In 1691, while on his twenty-six-year-long but ultimately fruitless campaign in the Deccan, Aurangzeb received a report about a most painful affront: at Sikandra, the Agra suburb in the very heartland of Mughal power, Jat plunderers had ransacked his great-grandfather's (Akbar's) tomb. Breaking through the bronze entrance gates, they had torn away the ornaments made of gold, silver and precious stones, and vandalized what they could not carry off. The ultimate outrage had been the desecration of the tomb itself: the mob had dragged out Akbar's bones and thrown them into the fire. Hindus defiling the remains of their erstwhile protector – a sadder symbol for the demise of an empire is hardly imaginable.

The revolt of the Satnami Hindu sect in the Delhi area in mid-1672, while quite worrying at the time, was of less consequence. A swelling bunch of fanatics, reportedly obeying the commands of a toothless old hag, thought themselves invulnerable to Mughal bullets, and indeed, quickly overran several smaller Mughal army units. They were stopped only when Aurangzeb countered their supposed witchcraft with Islamic amulets of his own, embellished with cloth from the Mughal banners. After a series of confrontations, the rebellion was put down.

Far more fateful was the execution in November 1675 of Guru Tegh Bahadur, the ninth Guru of the Sikhs. The Sikh movement had started as a religious movement uniting Muslims and Hindus and preaching universal brotherhood, equality and tolerance – as illustrated in the wonderful words of Guru Nanak (1469–1539), the founder of the movement: *'There is only one God. He is the enemy of no one.'*

Gradually – and not in the least because of Mughal persecution – the movement had evolved into a politico-religious community. In an attempt to extirpate the movement, Aurangzeb had Guru Tegh Bahadur captured and tortured, and, when he refused to convert to Islam, publicly executed in front of the Red Fort in Delhi.

Far from exterminating Sikhism, Aurangzeb had created one of the forces that would ultimately cause the downfall of the Mughal

Empire. Gobind Singh, Guru Tegh Bahadur's young son and successor (born in 1666), created the Khalsa, the Sikh military fraternity, which would become one of India's most redoubtable fighting forces. Guru Gobind Singh (the tenth and last Sikh Guru) also created Sikhism's political structure by declaring that the Guru Granth Sahib (the Sikh holy scripture) was the ultimate spiritual authority, while the temporal authority would be vested in the Sikh nation, the Khalsa Panth. Throughout his life, he remained on the defensive, constantly chased by Aurangzeb's troops; after his death in 1708, however, his political and military successor Banda Singh Bahadur would lay the foundation of what would become the powerful Sikh Empire during the reign of Maharaja Ranjit Singh (1801–1839).

***

Repressing the Sikhs was definitely a strategic mistake, but Aurangzeb would not have to pay the price for it: his successors would. The most damaging strategic error he made during his reign was the pointless and hateful quarrel he picked with his great-grandfather's faithful allies, the Rajputs. The immediate cause was the death of his general Jaswant Singh in December 1678, which left the throne of Marwar (Jodhpur) temporarily vacant. The diplomatic – and morally correct – step for him to have taken was to recognize the claim of Ajit Singh, Jaswant Singh's infant son, born shortly after his death. But Aurangzeb refused to do so and sent in his troops (destroying a good number of temples in the process) to annex the state of Marwar and instal Indra Singh, a highly unpopular nephew of the deceased maharaja, as local governor. The infant Ajit Singh was taken to the imperial harem, on the basis of promises that he would be educated in the imperial household and covered with honours later. The Rajputs were outraged, and a revolt flared up. In a daring and heroic action, the infant prince was smuggled out of the Delhi palace from under Aurangzeb's nose and brought back to his mother in Rajasthan. The lady, who happened to be a royal princess of neighbouring Mewar (Udaipur), now appealed to her family to protect the rights of her son. Aurangzeb found himself at war with two Rajput states. In one ill-advised move, he had managed not only to ruin the work of his ancestors[5] but also, more importantly, to undermine one of the most important pillars of his own military strength and create for himself a dangerous new enemy in the process. This blunder very nearly cost him his throne.

The war quickly evolved into a predictable stalemate – the Mughals occupying the plains and the Rajputs constantly harassing them from the hills and wastelands, but neither of them able to vanquish the other. Such a situation was not at all to the liking of the emperor. In a fit of anger, he demoted Prince Muhammad Akbar (who had been in general charge of the Mewar campaign) and sent him to Marwar. The emperor then ordered a three-pronged advance into the Aravalli hills – Muhammad Akbar was to advance from the west, Muhammad Azam (Aurangzeb's eldest son) from the east and Muhammad Muazzam (later Bahadur Shah I) from the north, but this move failed to produce the desired effect.

Amidst this turmoil, the Rajputs made diplomatic overtures towards Prince Muhammad Akbar: Aurangzeb was ruining Hindustan; what the country needed was a new emperor him on the throne and the Rajputs were prepared to help him capture it.

The offer was a real godsend to the frustrated prince. Aurangzeb was back in Ajmer with only ten thousand men, while he commanded an entire Mughal field army, which would now be supplemented by thirty thousand tough Rajput warriors. He simply could not lose. Besides, he was twenty-three, and Aurangzeb sixty-three. Soon, the time would come that he would have to fight his brothers for the throne, so, why not do it now, given the fact that he had such powerful allies?

Muhammad Akbar issued an edict deposing his father, supported by four ulama who – for a handsome price, no doubt – declared that Aurangzeb had forfeited his right to the throne because of infractions – of all things! – against Islamic law. On 11 January 1681, he declared himself emperor and marched towards Ajmer.

Aurangzeb would not have stood a snowball's chance in hell, had it not been for his son's naiveté and his own deviousness. While Muhammad Akbar should have rushed towards Ajmer, he made it a leisurely excursion, further delayed by his own astrologers (who, most probably, had been bribed by Aurangzeb) advising a slow advance. By the time he reached the Ajmer area, Aurangzeb's army had been sizeably reinforced, not in the least by deserters from Akbar's own army, as well as by the advent of Prince Muazzam. The numbers still favoured the challenger, but Aurangzeb had another trick up his sleeve. Fake letters were smuggled into Akbar's camp, congratulating the prince and thanking him for having enticed the Rajputs to leave the safety of their hills, so that they could now be ambushed and destroyed; the letters were, of course, conveniently allowed to fall in the hands of the Rajput generals. At the same time, another letter was sent to Tahavvur Khan, Akbar's right-hand man, threatening him that his wives and sons would be sold into slavery. That same night, the general sneaked away to Aurangzeb's camp, where, possibly by mistake, he was cut down by Aurangzeb's guards.

***

Meanwhile Durgadas Rathore, the Rajput general, deeply worried by Aurangzeb's fake letter, tried to contact Tahavvur Khan, but finding that he had gone over to Aurangzeb, concluded that the Rajputs were indeed in imminent danger. The entire Rajput army galloped back home, after having sacked and plundered Akbar's camp; and Akbar's remaining Mughal soldiers soon deserted en masse to join Aurangzeb. The next morning, when it was time to give battle, the hapless prince found himself alone with only a handful of faithful followers. He had no alternative but to flee posthaste, with his father's troops in hot pursuit, down to Gujarat and then, further down into the Deccan. There, to Aurangzeb's frustration, in late 1681, he found refuge with an even more implacable and dangerous enemy of the Mughal Empire: the Maratha king Sambhaji, son of the legendary Chhatrapati Shivaji Bhonsle.

This was far too dangerous a development. Later in 1681, Aurangzeb quickly patched up a peace deal with the Rajputs and marched southwards to the Deccan, twenty-three years after he had left it to seize Shah Jahan's throne. Little did he realize that he would spend the remaining twenty-six years of his long life in the Deccan, dragging his mighty army from one Pyrrhic victory to the other, and utterly ruining his empire in the process.

Shivaji and His Marathas

A lot had happened down in the Deccan since Aurangzeb had left it. In the first half of the seventeenth century, there had been two leading actors on the Deccan stage: the Mughal imperialists, eager to push their boundaries southwards, and the local sultanates of Bijapur and Golconda, eager to maintain their independence. A mere supporting role was reserved for the rivalling European powers and their coastal settlements, of no political significance yet, but their excellent gunners were eagerly sought after as allies or mercenaries by the inland powers. Another, even more important source of redoubtable, if not always dependable mercenaries had been the Marathas, the sons of the rugged Western Ghats (mountains) and highlands, feared and respected as a bunch of tough and highly mobile guerilla fighters.

Their military reputation had been established under Shahji Bhonsle, a chieftain from the area of Pune, who had been fighting for the Mughals first, then switched sides to the Nizam Shahi dynasty of Ahmednagar and then entered the service of Bijapur. By the time of his death (in a hunting accident) in January 1664, however, his military reputation had been eclipsed by that of his then rather unruly son Shivaji, who had been carving out a small kingdom for himself by capturing a number of hill forts around Pune.

The authorities in Bijapur did not mind too much, at first: the forts had been held by rivalling Maratha clans, and Shivaji had taken the precaution to write to Sikandar Ali Shah that he was actually taking possession of the fortresses on his behalf.

Shivaji's true intentions became obvious in 1649, when he had a royal seal made and started the construction of a new fort named Raigarh (meaning king's dwelling; in coastal Maharashtra). The sultan was not amused, and even had Shivaji's father arrested and imprisoned for a number of months.

Over the next six years, Shivaji kept relatively quiet – possibly, in order not to provoke any further reprisals against his father; then, in 1656, he resumed his aggressive expansion southwards with the annexation of neighbouring Javli (Jawali), and he did so in truly Machiavellian – or 'Aurangzebian' – style: as the Javli rulers were too strong to be attacked openly, he had the leading members of their family treacherously murdered during a pretended marriage negotiation.

The annexation greatly increased Shivaji's military strength, to the point of making him overconfident: the very same year, he recklessly invaded the Mughal-ruled Deccan. This invasion very nearly brought an untimely end to his career: he was soon crushingly defeated by an army sent by (then) Prince Aurangzeb, who was still governor of the Deccan at that time. Shivaji and the remnants of his army escaped into the mountains; fortunately for them, it was the beginning of the monsoon season and the Mughals did not pursue them. It had been a very hard lesson for Shivaji – one he would never forget. When Bijapur submitted to Aurangzeb, so did he, sending Aurangzeb a letter begging his forgiveness and promising everlasting fealty. Aurangzeb understood full well that the audacious Maratha was lying through his teeth, but with Shah Jahan's suddenly falling seriously ill in September 1657, he had much more pressing things on his mind. Before leaving the Deccan, though, he warned his officers against the 'mountain rat', as he usually called Shivaji.

***

With Aurangzeb gone, Shivaji again had more room to manoeuvre. He cautiously began building himself a power base, i.e., setting up a real, well-administered country with a territory of its own. Soon, the entire northern Konkan – i.e., the Maratha country stretching from Bhiwandi (about 20 km north of Bombay) to the town of Mahad on the Savitri River, some 180 km southwards – was firmly under his rule. Little did Aurangzeb – or Shivaji himself, for that matter – realize that this relatively small stretch of land would turn out to be the birthplace of a great and glorious empire that, before long, would prove to be the Mughal's nemesis. But it was clear to everyone concerned that the Marathas had become much too strong and much too ambitious a regional power.

***

The first one to worry about Shivaji's rising star was Adil Shah, the sultan of Bijapur. He felt that this was no longer a matter to be left to local officers: hence, he sent Afzal Khan, his seniormost general, to deal with Shivaji. The general, at the head of an overwhelming force, soon had him cornered at the hill fort of Pratapgarh (in southern Maharashtra).

The shrewd Maratha again resorted to a ruse: he asked for a meeting with the general, during which he would formally seek forgiveness and pledge allegiance, in exchange for an assurance that he would be left in possession of his forts. Overconfident, Afzal Khan took the bait. On Thursday, 10 November 1659,[6] the two men met in a pavilion erected in a clearing at the foot of a hill, both accompanied by a single bodyguard.

Afzal Khan wore a light tunic, with his sword hanging from his belt. Shivaji, in contrast, was ostensibly unarmed, as it behooved a repentant rebel; in reality, however, he had come more than prepared. He wore body armour underneath his tunic and an iron helmet inside his turban; he had a crooked *bichwah* (scorpion) dagger up his right sleeve, and, last but not the least, concealed inside his clenched left fist, a vicious *vaghnakh* Maratha 'tiger claw': four short, curved, razor-sharp blades attached to a ringed iron finger grip. The 'supplicant' timidly approached his overlord, bowing in his presence. As the Khan, a massive, corpulent giant of a man, rose to magnanimously embrace the humble penitent, Shivaji plunged his claws into his victim's belly, then stabbed him in the chest with his dagger. Afzal Khan's bodyguard, a redoubtable warrior of great repute, jumped to his master's rescue, but was soon killed by Shivaji – who had grabbed his victim's sword – and the Maratha guard. The Khan's bearers tried to carry off their dying master, but were cut down by Maratha warriors waiting in ambush. Then, the signal was given for an all-out attack. The Maratha guerillas fell on the ill-prepared Bijapur camp, killing many men and scattering the rest. Vast amounts of plunder – including many animals – fell into their hands. Significantly, all the Bijapur soldiers who surrendered had their lives spared; many of them entered Shivaji's service.

There is a competing version of this episode, stating that Afzal Khan actually plotted to murder Shivaji – planning to stab him to death while he held him in a bear hug. That may or may not be true: in the past, the Khan certainly had not flinched from using treachery himself. All we know with absolute certainty is that Shivaji got the better of him in a carefully planned surprise attack.

***

Over the next two years, Shivaji launched several devastating raids deep into Bijapur. In 1661, weary of the destructive conflict, the sultan sent Shahji Bhonsle, Shivaji's father, to parley with his recalcitrant rebel son. It was a smart move: Even though father and son had not seen each other in nearly twenty years, filial piety – extremely important in Hindu ethics – prevailed. Shahji was received like a king, and returned, a few weeks later, with Shivaji's solemn promise of undying loyalty to the sultan.

Both the parties kept the peace, for they needed each other's support against a powerful new enemy: the new Mughal governor of the Deccan, Shaista Khan, Aurangzeb's maternal uncle (brother of Shah Jahan's beloved Mumtaz Mahal).

Shaista Khan's mission was to secure all the lands ceded by Bijapur in 1660 – including the Western Ghats, Shivaji's homeland. With overwhelming power, the Mughal army moved into the very heartland of Shivaji's clan. They paid a heavy price for every fort taken, but in the end, the stronger force prevailed: soon, Pune itself fell to the invaders.

But Shivaji, still roaming the mountains with his guerillas, was far from beaten, and he had a spectacular trick up his sleeve.

Shaista Khan had taken up residence in the centre of Pune, in the very home that had once belonged to Shivaji's family. As Pune was an unwalled city, elaborate safety precautions had been put in place: no Maratha horseman was to be recruited to the imperial service and no one, armed or unarmed, was allowed to cross the army lines without a special pass. Yet, Shivaji had a cunning plan prepared, and, in the middle of the night on 15 April 1663, he struck. The date was chosen with judicious care, for it was the month of Ramadan, and the anniversary of Aurangzeb's accession to the throne – the Mughal soldiers would be weakened after a long day of fasting and would be careless after the following feasting and music in the night. On the day of the raid, Maratha soldiers in the Mughal army obtained permission to admit a seemingly harmless marriage party of some two hundred merrymakers into the city; earlier on, another group of Shivaji's men had been dragged into the city as if they were recently captured prisoners of war. Among the infiltrators, reportedly, was Shivaji himself.

Late into the night, the so-called wedding party met up with the would-be prisoners and their guards, discarded their disguise, and stealthily sneaked into the enemy headquarters via a kitchen window. Quickly disposing of the guards, they then broke through a brick wall into the governor's sleeping quarters, where they butchered everyone they could get their hands on. Shaista Khan himself was 'lucky': one of his sons and one of his wives were killed, as well as dozens of his men, and he himself lost a thumb, but in the fracas and under the cover of darkness, a bunch of servants managed to drag him to safety.

Tactically, the raid had been a failure, for the Mughal governor was still alive. From a psychological perspective, however, it had been a terrible humiliation for the Mughals, and a great boost for the Marathas, who now regained the initiative. The very next day, when Mughal forces attacked the fortress of Singhad (meaning the lion's fort), some 30 km south of Pune, the Marathas not only drove them off but also pursued them. And this was only the beginning.

***

Aurangzeb was livid when he heard about the humiliation his army had suffered. Shaista Khan was dishonourably dismissed and transferred to Bengal, and Prince Muazzam appointed in his stead. It was hardly a smart move, for Muazzam, showing even less initiative than his predecessor, comfortably stayed back in Aurangabad, leaving the fighting to his generals.

The Marathas grew bolder by the day. Mughal convoys and possessions were attacked, almost on a daily basis; even ships – including those carrying pilgrims to Mecca – were not safe from their depredations. The ultimate blow to Mughal prestige came in mid-January 1664, when Shivaji boldly invaded Gujarat – a state that had been Mughal territory since the days of Akbar the Great – and sacked the port city of Surat for four full days; the only ones to be wisely left alone during the plunder were the well-armed Europeans in their fortress.

On his return from this spectacular raid, Shivaji learned that his father had died (on 23 January 1664) in a hunting accident in Bijapur. He now took the title of 'raja' and had coins struck in his name. He was a real king now.

***

Later in 1664, deeply frustrated by the state of affairs, Aurangzeb sent another powerful army southwards, led by his ablest general, the sixty-year-old Raja Jai Singh. The old Rajput general succeeded where Muslim commanders had failed: soon, Shivaji found himself on the defensive everywhere. Facing total annihilation by the overwhelming forces of the enemy, he had no alternative but to sue for peace. Jai Singh, a shrewd diplomat and strategist as well as a brilliant general, offered harsh, but mutually advantageous, terms: Shivaji was to surrender two-thirds of his kingdom, i.e., all the territory and forts he had seized in the erstwhile Mughal Deccan. In addition, he would have to send his son Sambhaji to the Mughal court and assist Jai Singh in the war of conquest that the Mughals were about to launch against Bijapur. In return, he was free to keep twelve forts and the Konkan coastal strip which he had taken from Bijapur, plus any Konkan highlands he would manage to conquer.

In November 1665, the Mughal army, assisted by its new ally, attacked Bijapur. To Jai Singh's dismay, however, Bijapur put up a stiff resistance, and the campaign soon faltered, with many a Maratha commander defecting to the enemy. Shrewd as always, Jai Singh now arranged for Shivaji to be formally summoned to the Mughal court. It was a prudent move, for, the war going as badly as it did, it was probably only a matter of time before Shivaji himself would switch sides too, and try to chase the Mughals out with Bijapur's help.

Exactly why Shivaji agreed to venture into the lion's den is not clear. Probably, he saw no alternative; possibly, he had been won over by Jai Singh's suave promises of power, prestige and limitless wealth. He duly consulted his astrologers, set up a chain of command to administer his dominions in his absence and headed to Agra, together with his son Sambhaji and a retinue of about three hundred men, in an impressive cortège of beautifully caparisoned elephants and silver palanquins, all paid for at Aurangzeb's expense.

***

The chilly reception in Agra in May 1666 soon sobered him up. Aurangzeb all but ignored him, and he was given a rank of 'commander of 5000', which would have been prestigious in the days of Akbar the Great, but, by now, was little more than a title for third- or fourth-rate officers. Shivaji's indignant protests were in vain; he was forbidden from attending the court and assigned a comfortable, but well-watched residence, where he stayed in what amounted to house arrest. In vain, he tried every trick in the book to get Aurangzeb to release him: the air and water in Agra did not agree with his constitution; he eagerly desired to return to Bijapur to fight and die in the emperor's service; and he wanted to go Varanasi and spend the rest of his life in prayer as an ash-smeared mendicant. But Aurangzeb would hear none of it. Shivaji was trapped.

Shivaji then planned a cunning escape, which will forever be part of Indian folklore. He first arranged to get most of his men out of Agra back to the Deccan; as expected, Aurangzeb agreed, as this merely weakened Shivaji's position. His next move was to feign a severe, life-threatening illness; during the long process of his 'recovery', true to a pledge he had made to the Goddess Bhavani (an embodiment of power and ferocity), he arranged for money as well as baskets of food and sweetmeats to be distributed on a daily basis among the needy. Initially, each and every basket was inspected with care, but after a few weeks, the guards became negligent. On the evening of 19 August 1666, Shivaji and his son, covered by thick layers of sweetmeats, were carried out of their residence and into safety.

Whether this story is actually true or not, or whether or not, rather more prosaically, Shivaji merely managed to bribe his way out, is not known; but it worked. His escape was discovered only in the early evening of the next day, and by then, he was gone. Not back to the Deccan, as everyone assumed, but northwards, in the exact opposite direction. Disguised as a poor sadhu, his hair and beard shaved off and his body smeared with ashes, he then proceeded east, to the Hindu holy places such as Allahabad and Varanasi. Only then did he head back south-east, through the rough highlands of Bundelkhand,* Gondwana and Golconda, arriving in Raigarh in the month of November 1666.

***

He lay low for a while, well protected in his highland strongholds, using the time to improve his administrative organization. He even entertained a polite exchange of correspondence with Aurangzeb, asking his forgiveness and explaining that he had escaped from Agra out of fear for his life. Aurangzeb graciously – and relieved, most probably – played along, encouraging Shivaji to grab as much Bijapuri land as possible; he even conferred upon Shivaji the title of 'raja'. But in 1670, after a quiet period of about three years, Shivaji boldly resumed the offensive, recapturing several important forts, and, repeating the affront of six years earlier, sacking the Mughal city of Surat a second time with virtual impunity. In June 1674, when he was forty-seven years old, he had himself crowned Chhatrapati, 'emperor', of the Maratha confederation, in a grandiose coronation ceremony featuring ancient Hindu rituals lasting nine days and nine nights. Shortly thereafter, the life-bringing monsoon rains showered the land. The sign was clear: this was a new dynasty, blessed by the gods themselves.

During the remaining six years of his life, he would establish his absolute and unchallenged kingship over a vast area around what is now Mumbai; from there, he would continue raiding the entire Deccan, penetrating as far as the Kaveri River in the south of present-day Tamil Nadu, and frequently bullying the Mughal frontier regions into paying him 'protection money'.

***

Shivaji would have been little more than a marauder, had it not been for his nobility of character and undisputable strategic and political genius. Like Aurangzeb, his formidable opponent, he was a deeply pious man

*Now covering parts of Uttar Pradesh and Madhya Pradesh.

and led an austere personal life; but unlike Aurangzeb, he was not a bigot. He would never vandalize any sacred building or artifact; he had many Muslim soldiers and officers in his employ, for whom he had a mosque built opposite his own palace; wherever he went, he would seek the companionship of Hindu and Muslim holy men. He was ruthless and violent, no doubt; but he was not a savage. He would often hold rich people for ransom, but women and children, be they Hindu or Muslim, were never molested; neither were farmers, crops or animals harmed. He was highly intelligent and an excellent judge of people; and the lands under his direct administration – as opposed to the regions he merely raided – were governed with justice and efficiency.

***

Towards the end of March 1680, he unexpectedly fell gravely ill, with high fever and dysentery; only a few days later, on 3 April, around noon, he passed away; he was then fifty-three years old.

Four months later, after a short but violent power struggle, his elder son Sambhaji Bhonsle, twenty-three years old, ascended the Maratha throne. It was with him that the hapless Prince Muhammad Akbar sought asylum after his escape to the Deccan.

Aurangzeb Strikes Back

Unfortunately for the Marathas, Sambhaji neither had his father's character nor his political or military talent. What could have been the beginning of a grand alliance among Marathas, Rajputs and dissident Mughals quickly got bogged down in a quagmire of internal feuds and rivalries. By the time Aurangzeb himself arrived on the scene in 1681, Maratha power was hopelessly fragmented, and Sambhaji's personal authority all but completely eroded.

Aurangzeb thus had his hands free to concentrate on the important matters first: the final annexation of Bijapur and Golconda. Bijapur fell on 12 September 1686; one year later, it was Golconda's turn. The erstwhile sultans were imprisoned, their lines disinherited and their territories annexed to the Mughal Empire. In despair, the rebellious Prince Muhammad Akbar had fled to Persia earlier in 1686, hoping, quite in vain, that the Shah there would be interested in helping him. He never would see Hindustan again and died in exile in March 1706, one year earlier than his father.

***

With Bijapur and Golconda annexed and with Muhammad Akbar safely out of the country, Aurangzeb could now focus on dealing with the Marathas. Triumph seemed to fall in his lap soon enough: On 11 February 1689, Sambhaji – betrayed, most probably, by a few of his own courtiers – was ambushed and captured while feasting with a bunch of friends in the hill town of Sangameshwar, some 270 km south-southwest of Pune, a region where he thought he would be perfectly safe.

Sambhaji had never been very successful as a ruler; nor was he popular among his subjects, but he did die a hero. Defiantly, he refused to divulge to the Mughals where his family's treasure was hidden or to give them any other information. After weeks of torture, his tongue cut out and his eyes lanced, he was publicly put to death on 11 March 1689, hacked from limb to limb, with piece after piece fed to stray dogs.

***

Aurangzeb's triumph seemed complete. The Mughal borders now extended further south than they ever had or ever again would; his rebel son had fled the country, and the heir of the dreaded Shivaji was dead and gone. In October 1689, imperial troops stormed Shivaji's main fortress Raigarh and seized Sambhaji's family, including his wife and six-year-old son Shahu. They were treated with courtesy, and the young boy was given the title 'raja' and the rank of 7000, two steps higher than what had once been given to his grandfather. All but one member of the Maratha 'royal' family was under Aurangzeb's direct control.

But the Maratha resistance was not over. Shivaji's second son Rajaram Bhonsle was crowned king and smuggled out of the Maratha territory to the heights of Jinji (Gingee), deep in Tamil country; soon after Sambhaji's death, Maratha bands everywhere resumed their raids. The death of Shivaji's heir had perhaps put a temporary end to Maratha kingship, but not to Maratha power, which merely splintered into a multitude of local, often rivalling, groups under separate leaders, with little or no coordination and no central authority.

***

Aurangzeb would waste the rest of his life, trying in vain to kill the many-headed Maratha dragon. His strategy was simple enough: he would capture Rajaram, engage the Marathas wherever he found them and capture all their fortresses and strongholds. That he failed miserably has to do with his own shortsighted stubbornness and his enemy's resourcefulness, but, above all, with the appalling lack of discipline and fighting spirit within his own army.

The 'campaign' against Rajaram was a disgraceful farce. Mughal field commanders tended to drag on their campaigns as long as possible – at court, they were little more than useless lackeys, but in the battle zone, they were like kings – but Zulfiqar Khan, Aurangzeb's field commander, set a new record: the siege lasted for an amazing one hundred months: from October 1689 to January 1698. And when Zulfiqar Khan finally did storm the fortress, after Aurangzeb's umpteenth angry letter, Rajaram – duly forewarned, most probably, by his besieger – comfortably escaped to Satara (in Maharashtra), where he set up court at the hill fortress there. In 1700, that fortress, too, came under siege and eventually surrendered to the Mughals; but Rajaram had meanwhile escaped to Singhad, where he died that same year, most probably of tuberculosis.

***

Meanwhile, in October 1699, Aurangzeb, eighty-one years of age, had taken direct command of the campaign to capture the Maratha fortresses. That, so he figured, quite correctly, was the only way to get things done in the indolent and inherently corrupt Mughal army. Come what may, he had to bring the Marathas to heel: it was his sacred duty; it was jihad against what he considered a bunch of accursed idol worshippers. That he was ruining his entire empire in the process did not seem to enter his mind.

Meanwhile, even though they had no monarch to lead them – after Rajaram's death, his senior widow Tara Bai had barely been able to avert an all-out civil war – the Marathas became stronger and more arrogant by the day. If in the past they had exclusively relied on hit-and-run tactics, they now boldly confronted the Mughal invaders. Powerful Maratha armies scourged the entire southern peninsula. The great city of Hyderabad was twice ransacked: in 1702 and 1704. Even coastal cities on the Bay of Bengal, far away from the Maratha homelands, met with the same fate; and imperial caravans found themselves attacked and plundered with impunity, at barely 20 or 30 km from Aurangzeb's camp. The Mughals had long lost their aura of invincibility: they had become fair game. More often than not, Mughal officers had to play along, meekly paying 'protection money' and/or colluding with the Marathas in plundering the defenceless people of their very own fiefs.

Against his own better judgement, the stubborn old emperor kept muddling through the wild Maratha highlands, with his sluggish, mammoth army of one hundred and fifty thousand soldiers, their cannons and animals, and at least twice as many camp followers. Fortress after fortress surrendered to him – almost invariably through bribery – only to be reoccupied by the Marathas, as soon as he had turned his back.

The ordeal lasted for more than five long years. Finally, in May 1705, after the occupation of yet another petty fortress belonging to an insignificant tribal chief in present-day north-eastern Karnataka, the white-haired, frail and exhausted emperor decided to declare victory – he of course knew better than that – and head back north. Trailed by hordes of triumphant Marathas, like a sick old lion limping away from a pack of hyenas, the 'invincible army' dragged itself back to Ahmednagar.

***

On the way back, in the village of Devapur (now in northern Karnataka) on the Krishna River, the aged emperor fell seriously ill. His condition soon became critical, but then, somehow, he miraculously recovered, and after a six-month recuperation, resumed his journey in end-October. On 31 January 1706, he finally reached Ahmednagar. Twenty-five long years of tireless effort had passed since his arrival in the Deccan, and he had absolutely nothing to show for it. The territories he claimed to have conquered were left behind in ruins, an easy prey for bandits and brigands of all kinds: Marathas as well as former soldiers of the extinct Deccan sultanates. His own great Mughal Empire lay in ruins, its coffers depleted in an unwinnable war, its officers utterly incompetent and corrupt, and its population dirt-poor and discontent. Rebellion was looming everywhere. His own resolve and moral authority still held the empire together, but he realized fully well that it was only a matter of time before it would fall apart like a house of cards. Another ruinous war of succession was just around the corner, and enemies old and new – Marathas, Rajputs, Jats, Sikhs, Persians, Afghans and Europeans – were biding their time.

Back in the days of the civil war, Aurangzeb's earthly success had been, in his own eyes, the clearest proof of divine approval. But now that his empire was falling apart before his very eyes, in spite of so many years of hard and unceasing labour, he no longer knew what to believe. At the age of eighty-nine, he was a feeble old wreck. All his brothers and sisters were gone; some of his own children, and even a few grandchildren, were dead. And there was nothing, absolutely nothing to hope for. Clearly, God was displeased with him. And indeed, had he not laden his immortal soul with sins and stained his hands with the blood of the innocent? What was to become of him? To what punishment would he be doomed?

Aurangzeb's Last Days

Aurangzeb's correspondence during his heydays had always abounded with statements of sanctimonious piousness. The last letters to his sons, however, reveal genuine pangs of conscience and heart-felt personal anguish before God's implacable justice.

The following excerpts from the letters he sent to his sons, shortly before his death, are characteristic of the agony tormenting him. To Prince Azam Shah he wrote:[7]

> *Old age has arrived: weakness subdues me, and strength has forsaken all my members. I came a stranger into this world and a stranger I depart. I know nothing of myself, what I am, or for what I am destined. The instant which has passed in power has left only sorrow behind it. I have not been the guardian and protector of the empire. My valuable time has been passed vainly. I had a patron in my own dwelling (conscience), but his glorious light was unseen by my dim sight. Life is not lasting; there is no vestige of departed breath, and all hopes from futurity are lost. The fever has left me; but nothing remains of me but skin and bone .... The camp and followers, helpless and alarmed, are like myself, full of alarms, restless as quicksilver. Separated from their lord, they know not if they have a master or not. I brought nothing into this world, and, except the infirmities of man, carry nothing out. I have a dread for my salvation, and with what torments I may be punished. Though I have strong reliance on the mercies and bounties of God, yet, regarding my actions, fear will not quit me; but when I am gone reflection will not remain. Come then what may, I have launched my vessel in* [sic] *the waves ...*

To Prince Kam Bakhsh, he expressed his feelings thus:[8]

> *Now I depart a stranger and lament my own insignificance, what does it profit me? I carry with me the fruits of my sins and imperfections. Surprising Providence! I came here alone, and alone I depart. The leader of this caravan has deserted me .... Wherever I look I see nothing but the Divinity. My fears for the camp and followers are great; but, alas! I know not myself. My back is bent with weakness and my feet have lost the power of motion. The breath which rose is gone, and has left not even hope behind it. I have committed numerous crimes, and know not with what punishments I may be seized .... When I was alive, no care was taken; and now I am gone, the consequence may be guessed .... The agonies of death come upon me fast .... No one has seen the departure of his own soul, but I see that mine is departing.*

About these letters, Vincent Smith remarks: '*The sternest critic of the character and deeds of Aurangzeb can hardly refuse to recognize the pathos of those lamentations or to feel some sympathy for the old man on his lonely death-bed.*'[9]

Indeed, even today, Aurangzeb remains an enigma. He was a dour, sanctimonious bigot; his intense paranoia poisoned his entire life and the lives of almost everyone around him; his cold, calculating treacherousness has earned him a place in the ranks of the worst Machiavellians in world history; and in spite of all his hard work, his long reign brought ruin to the empire and its people.

Yet, as Abraham Eraly pertinently remarks,[10] there is another truth about him that is often missed, lost under layer upon layer of his all too well-known misdeeds: that he was, in fact, the mildest and least violent of the Great Mughals. Ironical though it may sound, the decline of Mughal power during his reign was partly brought about by his own lack of firmness: Akbar the Great would never have tolerated the kind of generalized corruption and lack of discipline that became commonplace under Shah Jahan's and Aurangzeb's reign. But there are a few charming anecdotes, showing an unusually kind, modest and tender-hearted Aurangzeb. He, for instance, consoled a terrified eunuch, who had accidentally stumbled against him, knocking him to the floor: '*Why do you fear a created being, one like yourself? Rise and be not afraid.*' Another time, in the twenty-third year of his reign (1681), when he was in Burhanpur and there was a fire near his residence, it was discovered that he had been sleeping above a cellar filled with thirty sacks of gunpowder. This was not a deliberate attempt on his life – the sacks had been left there many years earlier and forgotten – but, nevertheless, a monumental security blunder. Aurangzeb merely reprimanded and demoted the people responsible, wryly remarking that Jahangir would have had them blown up along with the sacks. Another instance of Aurangzeb's fairness was when he found out that a few of his officials had stopped a rivulet flowing from the palace in Lahore, depriving an old man, who ran a watermill downstream, of his livelihood. He had the old man brought to him and paid him a generous compensation, saying: '*You are my neighbour, and my coming here has caused you hardship. Please pardon me.*'

Aurangzeb's unfeigned humility was reflected in his own frugal lifestyle. Behind the conspicuous display of wealth at the Diwan-i-Khas lived an austere man who insisted on paying for his own food and meeting his personal expenses from the sale of his own handicraft: Quranic calligraphy and crocheted Muslim skullcaps. The instructions he left for his own funeral are equally telling: '… [only] four rupees and two annas, out of the price of the caps sewn by me' were to be spent on 'the shroud of this helpless creature'; the rest of his personal savings were to be distributed among the poor. His body was to be committed to earth bareheaded; no dome or canopy was to grace his simple, lowly grave.

The time to obey these instructions came on Thursday, 3 March 1707, at Ahmednagar. In the middle of his morning prayers, fingering the beads of his rosary, he slipped into unconsciousness. Soon after, around 9 a.m., be breathed his last. As he had painfully anticipated during his final, woeful years, his own empire would soon follow him into the abyss, as aptly summarized by S. M. Edwardes and H. L. O. Garrett:[11]

> *With the death of Aurangzeb Mughal rule in India may be said to have ceased to exist as an effective force. None of his successors proved men of any ability. Delhi became a mere cockpit of warring factions and the throne was occupied by a series of* rois fénéants [lazy or good-for-nothing kings] *under whose feeble rule the disintegration of the empire rapidly proceeded. The vultures*[12] *gathered greedily round the prostrate carcass. From the north came Nadir Shah the Persian, and after him the Afghan* [Ahmed Shah Abdali]. *The Sikhs flung off the Mughal yoke and set up their rule in the Punjab. From the south the*

armies of the Maratha confederacy swept unchecked towards Delhi until the field of Panipat ... decided that the throne of Delhi should know no Maratha occupant. From the east came the armies of the* [British] *East India Company, destined in the end to outstrip all its rivals. In just under a century after the death of Aurangzeb, his helpless descendant Shah Alam was taken under British protection, and though a Timurid sat on the throne of Delhi till 1857, it was a mere pensioner of the new rulers of India.*

CHRONOLOGY**

4 November 1618: Birth of Aurangzeb.
1649–1653: Shivaji carves out semi-independent Maratha kingdom.
14 May 1657: Birth of Sambhaji, Shivaji's son.
8 October 1657: Death of Aurangzeb's first wife, Dilras Banu Begam.
10 November 1659: Shivaji kills Afzal Khan, the Bijapur army leader. Battle of Pratapgarh: Shivaji defeats the Bijapur sultanate.
28 December 1659: Battle of Kolhapur: Shivaji again defeats the Bijapur forces.
20 February 1660: Aurangzeb's rebellious son Muhammad Sultan imprisoned for life.
1661: Campaign in Assam under Mir Jumla.
1664: Sacking of Surat by Shivaji.
May–August 1666: Arrest and escape of Shivaji.
1669: Anti-Hindu measures put in place by Aurangzeb; first Jat rebellion.
1670: Major offensive by Shivaji; second sacking of Surat.
September 1671: Death of Roshanara, Aurangzeb's sister.
6 June 1674: Shivaji officially crowned king of the Marathas.

*The Marathas were defeated in the third Battle of Panipat, on 14 January 1761, by Ahmed Shah Abdali.

**The reader should also refer to the Chronology given in Chapter 5 to ensure continuity.

24 September 1674: Second coronation of Shivaji.
1674–1676: Major offensive in the Deccan by Shivaji.
11 November 1675: Execution of the Sikh Guru, Tegh Bahadur.
1679: Reimposition of the *jizya* (the tax on non-Muslims).
3/5 April 1680: Shivaji's final illness and death.
1680–1681: Rajput rebellion; also, rebellion of Prince Muhammad Akbar.
1681: Second Jat rebellion; Aurangzeb goes to the Deccan.
September 1681: Death of Jahanara.
September 1686: Annexation of Bijapur.
September 1687: Annexation of Golconda.
11 March 1689: Execution of Sambhaji; succeeded by his brother Rajaram.
1691: The greatest expansion of the Mughal Empire's southern limits; further inconclusive wars until Aurangzeb's death in 1707.
January 1706: Aurangzeb returns to Ahmednagar.
3 March 1707: Aurangzeb dies.

Notes and References

1. Bamber Gascoigne, *A Brief History of the Great Moguls,* Carroll & Graf Publishers, New York, 2002, p. 223.
2. Dirk Collier, *The Emperor's Writings*, Amaryllis, New Delhi, 2011, the Twenty-ninth Letter.
3. The Somnath Temple was again rebuilt in 1950, after India's independence in August 1947; the mosque standing on its foundations has been moved a few kilometres away.
4. The tax was 5 per cent for Hindu traders and only half as much for Muslim merchants; the latter were completely exempt from the tax two years later (i.e., in 1671).
5. As has been related in Chapter 4, Mewar had been at peace with the Mughal Empire since the treaty of 1615, brought about by Jahangir and Prince Khurram (Shah Jahan).
6. 20 November 1569 as per the present-day (Gregorian) calendar.
7. S. M. Edwardes and H. L. O. Garrett, *Mughal Rule in India*, S. Chand & Co., Delhi, 1956.
8. Ibid., p. 156.
9. Vincent Smith, *Oxford History of India*, Oxford University Press, London, 1981, p. 427.

10. Abraham Eraly, *The Mughal Throne: The Saga of India's Great Emperors*, Viking (an imprint of Penguin Books India and Penguin Books UK), New Delhi and London, 1997 and 2000, pp. 386–387.
11. Edwardes and Garrett, op. cit., p. 157.
12. The word is 'eagles' in the original text.

Chapter 7

The Long, Slow Goodbye: The 'Lesser Mughals'

On Saturday morning, 4 March 1707, the day after Aurangzeb's death, Prince Muhammad Azam conveyed his father's body for burial to Khuldabad, some 30 km north-west of Aurangabad, where it was committed to earth, as per his instructions, in a simple grave near the ancient tombs of venerable Sufi saints.

The tension was palpable: it was only a matter of time before the war of succession would erupt.

Muhammad Azam's Short Reign

Considering that, at the time of Aurangzeb's death, there were no less than seventeen[1] potential pretenders to the throne – sons, grandsons and great-grandsons old enough to rule – the inevitable civil war went off in a quite orderly manner.

There were, in fact, only three official contenders, of whom Prince Muhammad Azam (1653–1707; the elder brother of the disgraced, exiled and meanwhile deceased Prince Muhammad Akbar) clearly had the best credentials. He alone had been born of Aurangzeb's empress-consort, Dilras Banu Begam, herself of royal Safavid (Persian) blood, whereas his two competitors – Muhammad Muazzam, also called Shah Alam, and Kam Bakhsh – were the offspring of lower-ranking Hindu concubines. Moreover, Muhammad Azam had been Aurangzeb's more-or-less official heir-apparent since 1681.

At the time of Aurangzeb's death, Muazzam was in Kabul far away from the scene; Kam Bakhsh was in the southern Deccan, but Muhammad Azam was right at hand near the imperial court. In fact, it was he who had arranged Aurangzeb's funeral.

***

What followed was a race to Agra: whosoever would be able to seize the massive imperial treasure would have a distinct advantage over his rivals. In spite of the forbidding distance, Muazzam made good time. On 10 June 1707, he along with his men reached Jajau, 28 km south of Agra.

In the ensuing battle, Azam and his three sons were defeated and killed; his reign had barely lasted seventy-eight days.

The other contender, Kam Bakhsh, had stayed behind in the Deccan. Almost two years later, on 13 January 1709, he would be defeated and critically injured near Hyderabad in a battle with Muazzam and would die the next day.

'*No sympathy need be wasted,*' affirms Vincent Smith,[2] '*on either Azam or Kam Bakhsh, who were both unfit to rule. The former is described as being "very choleric, a debauchee, rough and discourteous to everybody, also avaricious" .... The latter was a half-insane tyrant, who behaved with "outrageous cruelty", doing acts to his servants, companions, and confidants "such as before eye never saw, nor ear heard".*'

Bahadur Shah I (1643–1712): The Last Effective Mughal Ruler

Muazzam, who, upon his accession had had assumed the rather modest name of Bahadur Shah (the brave king) appears to have been much more of a gentleman. His contemporaries described him as mild-mannered, composed, magnanimous, learned and moderate-minded; and contrary to his father, he was by no means a bigot, but a broad-minded, tolerant Sufi Muslim. As governor of the north-west territories and the Punjab, he greatly relaxed his father's rigorous policies and even maintained a friendly relationship with Guru Gobind Singh, the tenth and last of the great Sikh Gurus and the real founder of Sikh military power, who actually supported him in his fight for the throne. Although he did not re-abolish the *jizya*, the tax was no longer collected; the ban on music was also lifted and not a single temple was destroyed during his reign.

Unfortunately for the empire he inherited, he was, by the time he finally came to power, an old man of 63. He neither had the time nor the stamina nor the military power to fully redress the situation; and he was, alas, succeeded by a series of utterly incompetent nincompoops, who finally brought about the downfall of the empire.

***

Bahadur Shah's only priority was to try and contain the various factionalist hotheads threatening the unity of the empire: the Marathas, the Rajputs and a renegade Sikh rebellion.

He astutely dealt with the Marathas by releasing, in 1707, Shahuji – Sambhaji's son, who had been educated at the Mughal court – and sending him back to the Maratha country, where, predictably, he came into collision with his strong-minded aunt Tara Bai and her son Shivaji II. The resulting internal strife among the Marathas made sure that, for a while at least, they would not pose a threat to the empire.

The relationship with Rajputana was slightly more complex. On Aurangzeb's death in early 1707, Ajit Singh – the rightful heir to the throne of Marwar (Jodhpur), who had been sneaked out of Delhi as an infant and living in hiding throughout Aurangzeb's reign – boldly marched into Jodhpur and expelled the Mughal governor. In 1708, Bahadur Shah briefly managed to retake the city, but when, by the end of that same year, he went down to the Deccan to deal with his rival brother, Kam Bakhsh, the Rajputs came back in force: Ajit Singh and his competent general Durgadas Rathore, in coalition with Jai Singh, the raja of Jaipur/Amber, and Amar Singh of Mewar, effectively kicked the Mughals out of Rajasthan. Bahadur Shah, occupied as he was with the pacification of the Punjab after returning to the Deccan, had no alternative but to confirm the rajas in their respective states.

As far as the Sikhs were concerned: Guru Gobind Singh, who had been a friend and faithful supporter of Bahadur Shah and accompanied him to the Deccan, was assassinated in October 1708 in the city of Nanded (in present-day Maharashtra) by two Afghans upon the instigation of the governor of Sirhind, Wazir Khan, a lifelong enemy of the Sikhs. After the Guru's death, Banda Singh Bahadur (born as Lachman Dev in October 1670), a ferocious Sikh military commander, now wreaked havoc in the region. In the end, Bahadur Shah and his competent general Munim Khan managed to defeat the rebels and drive them into the hills, but Banda Singh Bahadur managed to escape and would continue to cause a great deal of trouble for the Mughals until his capture, in December 1715, along with some seven hundred of his followers. He met his end in June 1716 at Delhi.

Earlier, on 27 February 1712, in his sixty-ninth year, Bahadur Shah had passed away, years too soon to save his ailing and tottering empire. Utter chaos would follow.

Jahandar Shah (1661–1713)

Bahudur Shah's four sons – Khujista Akhtar, Rafi-ush Shan, Azim-ush Shan and Jahandar Shah – immediately became enmeshed in the obligatory war of succession.

The first one to get himself killed – drowned in the Ravi River on 18 March 1712, at forty-seven years of age, after having been defeated by a coalition of his three brothers – was Azim-ush Shan, who had earlier served as governor of Bengal, Bihar and Odisha. He appears to have been a competent man, whose most fateful contribution to Indian history was his 1696 agreement with the British East India Company to build its Fort William (named after King William III) on the eastern banks of the Hooghly River, in what was to become the great city of Calcutta.

The three remaining brothers predictably disagreed about what to do next and quickly fell out with each other. At another battle near Lahore, on 29 March 1712, Jahandar Shah, the last man standing, emerged victorious.

The new emperor, described by contemporary historians as a drunken imbecile, was to 'reign' for eleven months and two weeks, during which period his favourite concubine, a lascivious dancing girl-cum-prostitute named Lal Kunwar, rose to the position of empress-consort.

His lifestyle of shameless debauchery, while quickening the imagination of many, outraged the decent and inspired the ambitious. In early January 1713, his twenty-seven-year-old nephew, Abul Muzaffar Muin-ud Din Muhammad Shah Farrukhsiyar – son of Azim-ush Shan – proclaimed himself emperor and marched from Bihar to the capital. Most of his army having melted away in the face of the enemy, Jahandar Shah found himself defeated, captured, imprisoned, and about one month later, on 11 February, strangled. His body, reportedly, was left to rot outside the Red Fort gate.

Farrukhsiyar (1685–1719)

The usurper, only marginally less debauched but probably more evil even than his predecessor, now established a reign of terror, in which quite a number of high-ranking nobles were executed. Such executions, however, only worsened Farrukhsiyar's fundamental problems: his own indecisiveness, lack of talent and weakness of character, and his heavy reliance on two mighty courtiers and kingmakers, the so-called Sayyid brothers, Sayyid Hasan Ali Khan Barha (1666–1722) and Sayyid Husain

Khan Barha (1668–1720). These two competent, but dangerously ambitious and utterly ruthless men had been governors of Allahabad and Patna, respectively. Their military support had helped Farrukhsiyar gain the throne, as a result of which they had been rewarded with the highest offices, but the king quickly became apprehensive of their power. His treacherous, but ineffective, attempts to get rid of them would ultimately seal his doom.

Apart from his problems with the Sayyid brothers and a failed attempt to enforce the collection of the *jizya*, Farrukhsiyar's reign was marked by a number of important strategic developments, which would ultimately lead to the downfall of the empire: the deepening enmity with the Sikhs and the rise of the Marathas and the British, the powers that would soon come to dominate the entire subcontinent.

The Sikhs

Early in 1715, as mentioned earlier, Mughal troops managed to corner the renegade Sikh leader Banda Singh Bahadur, who, in December that year, after a siege of eight months and much bloodshed, was forced to surrender with seven hundred of his followers. He was put to death in a gruesome manner in June the next year. The Sikhs, however, were far from beaten, and would neither forget nor forgive the outrage committed against them. Soon, they would have their revenge.

The British

Of equal consequence was Farrukhsiyar's imperial *firman* of 1717, granting duty-free trading and territorial rights to the British East India Company – the most broadly based and far-reaching privileges ever granted to a foreign nation. While of little practical use in the beginning – the local governors basically ignored the orders of their sovereign and continued to exact customs duties, anyway – the document was 'the Magna Carta of the company in India', the legal basis for all its subsequent actions. The company was now officially introduced in the Indian power hierarchy – which, a few years later, it was destined to replace.

The Marathas

In an attempt to curb the power of his overbearing protectors, in 1718, Farrukhsiyar sent Husain Khan Barha, the younger of the Sayyid brothers, to the Deccan. At the same time, he issued secret instructions to the governor of Gujarat to intercept and kill him. As it turned out, it was the would-be assassin who was eliminated, and Husain Khan Barha, not surprisingly, was bent on revenge.

As the new Mughal governor of the Deccan, he began far-reaching and fateful negotiations with the Maratha king Shahuji – who had prevailed in the Maratha civil war against his aunt Tara Bai – and the king's highly competent *peshwa* (prime minister) Balaji Vishvanath, the first of a series of powerful Maratha *peshwas*.

Like his illustrious grandfather, the great Chhatrapati Shivaji, Shahuji agreed to accept Mughal overlordship in the Deccan, to pay an annual tribute and to furnish combat troops for the imperial army. In exchange, however, he demanded *swaraj* (home rule/independence) for the Maratha homelands, plus rights to levy the so-called *chauth* and *sardeshmukh* (two important taxes) throughout Gujarat, Malwa and all of the Mughal Deccan.

Farrukhsiyar understandably rejected the demands: he felt that they would, in exchange for very little, effectively end Mughal rule in the entire region. He had had more than enough of the Sayyid brothers, and began actively plotting their downfall. But it soon appeared that he was no match for them. Egged on by his elder brother back in Delhi, the younger Sayyid marched back north, at the head of a powerful combined Mughal–Maratha army. His battle drums sounded the death knell of the emperor, who, on 27 February 1719, was unceremoniously apprehended and thrown in jail. As John Keay wryly remarks,[3] his slow, horrible demise partook of the indecision that had characterized his life, for he was successively starved, blinded, poisoned, and finally, for good measure, strangled and stabbed to death in the night of 27/28 April 1719.

Rafi-ud Darajat (1699–1719) and Rafi-ud Daula, 'Shah Jahan II' (1696–1719)

To consolidate and legitimize their power, the Sayyid brothers urgently needed a new Timurid figurehead on the throne. The choice fell on one of Farrukhsiyar's cousins, one Rafi-ud Darajat, the sickly, teenaged son of Farrukhsiyar's dead uncle Rafi-us Shan. Barely a few months later, on 13 June 1719, the boy died of tuberculosis. But he had served his purpose: before his untimely death, he had, under pressure of the Sayyid brothers, duly ratified the proposed treaty with the Marathas. Appropriately pleased with himself, Peshwa Balaji Vishvanath and his troops returned to the Deccan.

Rafi-ud Darajat's ultra-short 'reign' was troubled by a rival claim to the throne: his great-uncle Nekusiyar Muhammad, a son of the rebel prince Muhammad Akbar, who had spent his entire life in confinement in the Agra harem, was, with the assistance of an overly ambitious local courtier, proclaimed emperor. But since the poor man had never set foot outside the harem and reportedly 'talked like a catamite', his claim was laughingly ignored. The Sayyid brothers quickly retook the Agra Fort and the would-be usurper was unceremoniously thrown in jail at Salimgarh (in Delhi), where he would die in 1723, forty-three years old.

Before dying, young Rafi-ud Darajat had, upon the instigation of the Sayyid brothers, appointed his equally irrelevant elder brother Rafi-ud Daula as his successor. Duly enthroned on 6 June 1719, the young man assumed the preposterous title of 'Shah Jahan II', but was, in spite of his proclaimed overlordship of the entire world, never allowed to set foot outside the imperial court. Unfortunately for the Sayyid brothers, their new protégé fared little better than his predecessor: after a 'reign' of three months and two weeks, he died – states a contemporary chronicler[4] – 'of dysentery and mental disorder', on 19 September 1719.

Muhammad Shah (1702–1748)

For the third time in a single year, the Sayyid brothers found themselves in need of a new emperor. Their choice fell on yet another cousin of the previous three emperors: seventeen-year-old Roshan Akhtar Muhammad, son of Khujista Akhtar (defeated and killed by Jahandar Shah in 1712, together with his two brothers Rafi-ush Shan and Azim-ush Shan). This time, however, the brothers had picked the wrong puppet.

Harnessing the support of a number of disgruntled courtiers – belonging predominantly to the so-called 'Turani' faction (the nobles of Central Asian origin or descent) – the young monarch soon proved to be a consummate intrigant himself. After only a few months, in October 1720, Husain Khan Barha, the younger of the Sayyid brothers, was assassinated by a courtier suitably bribed for the purpose.

Hasan Ali Khan Barha, the elder brother, then on his way to the Deccan, immediately instructed his maternal uncle to put yet another young prince on the throne – one Sultan Muhammad Ibrahim, brother of the late Rafi-ud Darajat and Rafi-ud Daula – and turned back at the head of his army to avenge his brother's death. But he had finally run out of luck. His forces were decisively defeated by the imperial army at Hasanpur (in present-day Haryana, about 115 km south of Delhi); he was captured and thrown in jail. Two years later, in 1722, he was poisoned to death. The would-be rival emperor was sent back to the harem, where he would die of natural causes in 1746.

In marked contrast to the careers of his immediate predecessors, Muhammad Shah's reign was a surprisingly long one: 1719–1748. Long, if tragically inglorious: this indecisive, indolent lover of the arts was forced to witness, as a virtually impotent spectator, the utter humiliation and complete disintegration of his empire. If his rather preposterous pen-name was Sada Rangila, 'ever joyous' or 'ever colourful', his reign most certainly was not, marked as it was by several catastrophic events, notably a wave of Maratha raids on Rajasthan (in 1735), on Delhi (in 1737) and on Bengal and Odisha (in 1740). After the second of these raids came the invasion, bloody massacre and total plunder of Delhi by Nadir Shah of Persia (in 1739), followed, from 1748 onwards, by another wave of invasions by the Afghan Ahmed Shah Abdali (aka Ahmed Shah Durrani). An equally ruinous development was the de facto independence of important provinces including Hyderabad, Oudh, Bihar and Bengal.

The Nizams of Hyderabad

One of Muhammad Shah's main supporters in his struggle against the Sayyid brothers had been the powerful governor of the Deccan, Qamar-ud Din Khan Siddiqi (1671–1748), the so-called Nizam-ul Mulk or 'regulator of the realm'. The grandson of an emigrated nobleman from Bukhara in Central Asia, he had been a successful courtier since the days of Aurangzeb; after the latter's death in 1707, he was first appointed governor of Oudh. He then briefly retired to private life after Bahadur Shah's death, but was later convinced by Farrukhsiyar to take up the governorship of the Deccan, with the lofty title of Nizam-ul Mulk.

After Muhammad Shah's accession to power, the nizam was appointed prime minister of the empire, and given, some years later, the additional title of Asaf Jah (meaning 'as noble and exalted as Asaf, the grand vizier of King Solomon').

Disgusted with the corrupt, back-biting atmosphere at the imperial court, he went back to the Deccan, where – after defeating and killing Mubariz Khan, the previous governor who had been appointed in the days of Farrukhsiyar and now refused to leave his post – he effectively founded an autonomous new clan of his own: the famous nizams of

Hyderabad, also referred to as the Asaf Jahi Dynasty. It should be pointed out, however, that these nizams never declared their formal independence from Delhi: coins continued to be minted in the Mughal emperor's name until 1858, when the very last Timurid had been dethroned and exiled by the British.

***

Similarly, the local nawabs (governors) in Oudh and Bengal became, for all practical purposes, independent rulers, rarely – if ever – sending any tribute payments to Delhi. Vast areas in Rajasthan were ruled by the local dynasties, often in complete defiance of Mughal authority. To the north of the province of Oudh, a clan of Afghan nobles, the Rohillas (mountaineers), had made themselves master of a rich tract of land between the upper Ganges and Nepal, which became an independent dominion known as Rohilkhand. And in the Punjab, bands of warring Sikhs were constantly wreaking havoc.

Meanwhile, says Vincent Smith,[5] '*the capital was the scene of incessant intrigues and treasons, unworthy of record or remembrance*'.

Towards the end of his life, Aurangzeb had reportedly sighed in despair: 'After me, chaos!' He was right. Merely seventeen years after his death in 1707, the great empire that his ancestors and he had fought for and worked for so long and so hard, was falling apart, inexorably, irreparably.

Maratha Power

Meanwhile, Balaji Vishvanath, the first of the famous Maratha *peshwas*, had died in April 1720; his official position had been inherited by his son Baji Rao, a man of extraordinary talent and determination. Under his energetic leadership, the Maratha cavalry swept over the subcontinent, plundering and exacting tribute wherever the hooves of their horses trod. Soon after the Nizam-ul Mulk had left for the Deccan, the Maratha territory expanded up to the Narmada River. In the course of the following years, the Marathas made themselves masters of Gujarat, Malwa and Bundelkhand and even appeared in the suburbs of Delhi in 1737. The Nizam-ul Mulk, who tried to curb their power, was defeated in a brilliant campaign. The appalling weakness of the empire had become painfully evident.

Nadir Shah

Meanwhile, in Persia, the Safavid dynasty had been overthrown in 1736 by Tahmasp Quli Khan (aka Nadir Shah), a Turkic army leader belonging to the Afshar Qizilbash tribe from the northern part of Khorasan (now in north-eastern Iran). He had risen to power during a period of anarchy, in which Iran was all but torn apart by Afghan rebels and Ottoman and Russian invaders. However, in a series of brilliantly fought campaigns, the 'Napoleon of Persia', the 'second Alexander', or 'the greatest warrior Persia has ever produced', as he came to be described later, managed to rally the nation and kick out the invaders. After having deposed his weak and incompetent overlord, he was himself crowned Shah of Iran on 8 March 1736.

Soon after his accession, he was forced to subdue another uprising of Afghan tribesmen, particularly in the border region of Qandahar. He therefore requested Muhammad Shah's assistance to close off the borders around Kabul, in order to make sure that the rebels would not be able to escape. Muhammad Shah did agree in principle, but failed to do anything in practice, partly because his own local officers tended to sympathize with the rebels, who eventually did flee into Mughal territory. Outraged by this development, Nadir Shah sent an ambassador to the Mughal court, formally demanding the extradition of the fugitives. Muhammad Shah, however, chose to bury his head in the sand, keeping the Persian ambassador waiting for a full year. This was all the pretext that Nadir Shah needed to attack his neighbour, whom he knew to be weak, but still tantalizingly wealthy.

In late 1738, Nadir Shah crossed the border into northern Afghanistan, quickly capturing Ghazni, Kabul, Jalalabad and Peshawar and then advancing rapidly through the Punjab. By January 1739, Lahore had fallen, soon followed by Sirhind.

Finally, on 24 February 1739, near the town of Karnal, some 120 km north of Delhi, the imperial army blocked his passage. In spite of its reportedly overwhelming numeric superiority – 200,000 cavalry and 1500 war elephants, according to some accounts, against Nadir Shah's mere 55,000 – the Mughals found themselves decisively beaten in a matter of a few hours, with 20,000 dead on the battlefield against Persian casualties of around 2500. A particularly gruesome detail is the way in which Nadir Shah made short work of the Mughal elephants: camels were yoked together in pairs, laden with baskets full of naphtha-drenched straw and combustibles, driven towards the Mughal lines and set on fire, causing the elephants to panic and wreak havoc in their own ranks.

***

A number of the leading Mughal generals had died on the battlefield. The emperor, Muhammad Shah, who had had no active role in the fighting, was taken prisoner and treated courteously; victor and vanquished entered Delhi together. Everything went well for a few days, when suddenly, the false rumour was spread that the Persian emperor had died. This resulted in riots, whereby several Persian soldiers were killed. Even so, Nadir Shah forbade reprisals.[6] On the morning of 20 March 1739, he rode through the streets of the city to personally assess the situation. When a few Delhiites were reckless enough to throw stones at him, and one even fired a musket, killing a Persian officer right by the Shah's side, his reply was to order a general massacre. The slaughter continued all day long, with thousands of people – most sources estimate the number of slain at about 30,000 – butchered like cattle in their homes and in the streets. In the evening, heeding the Mughal's desperate pleas, the Shah finally ordered the carnage stopped; such was his authority that it ceased instantly.

The next fifty-five days were devoted to the systematic collection of all valuables, private and public – violence and torture being added to other forms of encouragement, as Bamber Gascoigne wryly remarks – until there was absolutely nothing left to plunder. Then, Nadir Shah finally went off, with one thousand elephants laden with treasure of inestimable value, including the famous Peacock Throne (Takht-e-Taus) and the Koh-i-Noor diamond. Of such extravagance was the loot, that the Shah sent home a decree remitting all taxes in Persia for a period of three years. A few hundred of the empire's finest artisans, carpenters and masons accompanied the cortège – a ghastly replay of the 1398 tragedy, when Timur, the Mughal dynasty's murderous ancestor, had similarly ravaged Hindustan.

***

There was nothing to be done, but to bow and accept whatever the Shah ordained. Muhammad Shah's daughter Jahan Afroz Banu Begum was offered in marriage to Nadir Shah's youngest son, and all the territories west of the Indus were annexed to the Persian Empire.

The Mughals would never recover from this deadly blow. In more than one way, the sack of Delhi was the irreparable end of their empire. The country – what was left of it – fragmented and slipped into anarchy. Says Vincent Smith:[7]

> *No central government worthy of the name existed, and if any province enjoyed for a short time the blessing of tolerably good administration, as was the case in Bengal, that was due to the personal character of the noble or adventurer who had secured control over it. Very few indeed of the prominent men of the time possessed any discernible virtues.*

Ahmed Shah Durrani and the Afghans

Meanwhile, over in Persia, the situation had been changing drastically. The conquest of Delhi had been the zenith of Nadir Shah's career, but as his health declined, he became increasingly despotic. More and more revolts broke out, and Nadir Shah repressed them with increasing ruthlessness and cruelty, including the building of towers of skulls, in the tried-and-true Ghengisid–Timurid tradition. Then, on 20 June 1747, while on a campaign against Kurdish rebels in Khorasan, he was assassinated by a group of officers who feared that he was about to have them executed. He was succeeded by his nephew Ali Quli – probably involved in the assassination plot himself – who assumed the imperial title of Adil Shah, or 'the righteous king'. The ensuing civil war between Adil Shah, his brother Ibrahim Shah and Nadir Shah's grandson Shah Rukh resulted in utter chaos, with almost all provincial governors declaring their independence. One of them was Ahmad Shah Durrani, the Afghan leader, who now became India's daunting new western neighbour.

One month before Muhammad Shah's death in April 1748, Durrani invaded India for the first time, sacking Lahore and penetrating as far as Sirhind, where he was repulsed – by chance more by than superior generalship, for the defeat was caused by the explosion of one of his ammunition carts – by a Mughal army under Prince Ahmad Shah, who, as a result of this victory, received the title of Bahadur (brave). However, the Durrani threat remained more than strong enough to exact a tribute from the Punjab. And he would be back for more.

Emperors or Bystanders?

After Nadir Shah's fateful invasion in 1739, the Mughal emperors found themselves reduced to little else – if even that – than kings of Delhi, impotent bystanders of the series of dramatic events that would be shaping the future of India. 'Bystanders' and not even 'onlookers', as a few of them would end their lives as pitiful, blinded prisoners, their eyes gouged out with impunity by their own courtiers.

And yet, there still was a Mughal throne, however shaky and decrepit. As Abraham Eraly remarks in his outstanding study:[8]

> *In a few decades the empire disappeared altogether and the authority of the emperor became confined to the city of Delhi alone. Soon he lost even that petty privilege and became a pensioner, first of the Marathas, then of the British. He was, however, still called the Mughal emperor; others might seize his territory, plunder his treasures, deprive him of power, but none could take away his title or the prestige (however hollow) that went with it. So the Mughal continued to occupy the imperial throne in Delhi for a century and a half after the death of Aurangzeb.*

Most Indian historiographers, when writing about the events after 1739, tend to focus their attention no longer on the Mughal emperors, but on the new main players on the Indian chessboard, such as the Marathas, British, Afghans and Sikhs. This trend is both understandable and justifiable, as the Timurids had indeed been reduced to mere puppet kings without countries, subjects or armies worthy of note. Yet, the tragedy of their personal lives will never fail to fire the imagination.

Ahmad Shah Bahadur (1725–1775)

Emperor Muhammad Shah had always had a rather weak constitution. On 14 April 1748, while sitting in court with his courtiers and attendants, he suffered what appears to have been a massive stroke: he suddenly lost consciousness, and when he recovered, he had lost the power of speech. The next morning, after a long, unhappy reign of almost thirty years, he breathed his last. The crown prince being away from court, the courtiers decided to keep the distressing news a secret: the emperor's body was shrouded in a tablecloth, put into the case of a European clock and buried in the palace garden. On 18 April, Ahmad

Shah Bahadur ascended the throne; the official coronation ceremony was celebrated eleven days later.

According to contemporary chroniclers, the new occupant of the Timurid throne appears to have been a man of little intellect, few talents and even less character. '*He gave himself up entirely to pastime and sports, and bestowed no thought on the weighty affairs of the kingdom*', and in consequence, '*was surrounded by all kinds of youthful pleasures, which every person, seeing the turn of his mind, was anxious to display before him to entice his fancy*'.[9]

The real power behind the throne was the emperor's mother, Qudsia Begam or Udham Bai, who had been introduced to Muhammad Shah's harem as an entertainer/dancing girl and managed to get herself married to him as his third wife. It was widely rumoured that she had an intense love affair – before and after her husband's death – with Nawab Bahadur Javed Khan, the eunuch superintendent of the emperor's *zanana*. In any case, she and her alleged lover became the actual rulers of (what was left of) the empire, until her son's downfall in June 1754.

Civil War in the Deccan – Rivalry between the French and the British

On 1 June 1748, only a few months after Muhammad Shah's death, the seventy-six-year-old nizam of Hyderabad passed away as well. His death led to a war of succession among several claimants, their local allies and two foreign powers, namely, Britain and France.

Early on, the rivalry between French and British settlements in India had remained purely commercial, even when, back in Europe, their respective motherlands were at war. As the colonies grew and prospered, however, hostilities became inevitable. British depredations at sea led to French reprisals on land, including the capture of Madras in 1746. Peace in Europe brought a temporary lull in hostilities and led to the peaceful return of Madras to the British in 1748. However, that same year, the death of the nizam rekindled the rivalry, with each of the European powers backing its own candidate.

In the following decades, the British would prevail, thanks to a combination of factors: superior naval capabilities, personal conflict and jealousy among the French commanders, the tenacity of certain individuals and a more steadfast support by the European homeland. Soon, the British would be asserting their power throughout the subcontinent, while the French settlements, slowly but surely, sank into insignificance.

Continuing Decline

One of Muhammad Shah's very few acts of government was to cede Sindh and the entire Punjab to the Afghan king – not because he wanted to, but because his own local governor had begged him to do so, and there was no alternative; and even this concession was not enough to buy off the cruel Afghan, who would continue to raid Hindustan with impunity. Neither the emperor nor any of the nawabs was any match for him. And as if the Afghan outrage was not enough, the Marathas were now in full expansion mode from the south, annexing both Gujarat in the west and Odisha in the east; it was only a matter of time before Delhi itself and even the Punjab would fall to them. A clash between them and the Afghans was inevitable.

Ghazi-ud Din Feroze Jung, Imad-ul Mulk

Meanwhile, the Mughal dominions – or what was left of them – were plagued by ruinous infighting, the intricacies of which do not warrant a detailed description in a general history overview. Suffice to say that it pitted Safdar Jung (nawab of Oudh and grand vizier of the empire) against Javed Khan, the chief harem eunuch and actual administrator of the empire, and that it ended with the latter's assassination. To counter the skyrocketing influence of the nawab, the emperor appointed young Ghazi-ud Din Khan Feroze Jung, grandson of the deceased nizam of Hyderabad, as Imad-ul Mulk (pillar of the realm) and grand vizier. In the ensuing fight, the nawab was defeated, but graciously allowed to retire to his home base.

However, the emperor soon fell out with his new prime minister, who then entered into an alliance with the Maratha chieftain Sadashiv Rao Bhau. In the resulting clash, the emperor and his vassals were easily defeated, then deposed and imprisoned. On 25 June 1754, he had his eyes gouged out. The hapless, blind emperor spent the remaining twenty-one long years of his life in prison at the Salimgarh Fort (Delhi) and died – of natural causes, so it appears – on 1 January 1775.

Alamgir II (1699–1759)

The new figurehead on the throne in late 1754 was Aziz-ud Din, the second son of Jahandar Shah (and, therefore, grandson of Bahadur Shah I and a great-grandson of Aurangzeb). Out of respect for his great-grandfather, he assumed the imperial title of Alamgir II.

He appears to have been a respectable, kindly and pious man, who never missed any of the daily prayers and occasionally delivered the sermons in the imperial Moti Masjid or Pearl Mosque within the Red Fort. He was a friend and patron of Sufi mystics, and is reputed to have walked calmly through the streets of Delhi to attend prayers at different mosques without adequate security. Nevertheless, at the time of his accession, he was a tired, fifty-five-year-old man, with no experience of either warfare or administration, as he had spent the better part of his life in confinement. Consequently, he was doomed to remain a mere figurehead, with all the real power vested in the hands of his *wazir* and kingmaker, Imad-ul Mulk.

His reign was marked by further dramatic developments, none of which was his doing or his fault, but which, like his predecessors and successors, he was forced to face.

The Third Afghan Invasion

Three years into Alamgir II's reign, the Afghan king Ahmad Shah Durrani invaded India for the third time. Delhi, Agra, Mathura and several other cities were taken, with all the accompanying horrors of wanton bloodshed and pillaging. In the spring of 1757, after taking a daughter of Muhammad Shah in marriage and betrothing his minor son Timur Shah to one of Alamgir II's daughters, he finally returned to Afghanistan, leaving young Timur in charge of the Punjab, Kashmir and the Sirhind district, under the tutelage of one of his generals, Jahan Khan.

On his way back, he attacked and desecrated the Sikh Golden Temple in Amritsar, polluting its pool with the blood of slaughtered cows. It was an outrage that would soon prove to be a major mistake, as it only added to the Sikh resolve to keep fighting the invaders.

Maratha Power at Its Pinnacle

Timur Shah would stay in nominal power for less than a year. Then, the Marathas kicked him out, not only out of Sirhind, but also out of the whole of the Punjab.

Barely had the Afghan king left the scene that a powerful Maratha army, helped by Imad-ul Mulk, occupied the Delhi suburbs and encamped outside the Red Fort. In the ensuing siege, Najib-ud Daula – originally an Afghan but settled in northern Rohilkhand (now in north-western Uttar Pradesh) and Alamgir II's Mir Bakshi or 'paymaster of the empire' – was forced to concede defeat and withdraw to his home base.

Like a tidal wave, the Marathas washed into the Punjab and beyond. It was the absolute zenith of the Maratha Confederacy. By May 1758, their power extended from the Khyber Pass to Bengal and from Kashmir to almost the southernmost tip of the subcontinent. They were about to become the de facto rulers of all of India.

Understandably, the Afghan king did not like this state of affairs one bit. He had been far away from the scene, in Herat, but now returned posthaste to Qandahar, from where he began preparing his next – and most fateful – invasion.

Death of the Emperor

Alamgir II was allowed to occupy the throne for another year, a powerless figurehead at the mercy of his *wazir*, Imad-ul Mulk, and his Maratha allies, until he would have outlived his usefulness. That happened when in the summer of 1759, his heir-apparent, Prince Ali Gauhar, had made a daring escape from Delhi to Bengal, where he began organizing the armed resistance against Delhi and its Maratha allies. The old emperor had become far too dangerous. On 26 November 1759, on his way to meet a holy man who had allegedly come to visit him, he was stabbed to death by assassins sent by Imad-ul Mulk.

A new emperor was put on the throne, Prince Muhi-ul Mulk-ul Millat (1711–1772), grandson of Kam Bakhsh, Aurangzeb's youngest son. The new monarch assumed the ambitious title of Shah Jahan III, but would not occupy the throne for long: in the east, on 24 December 1759, the fugitive Prince Ali Gauhar had himself enthroned as Shah Alam II – with the full support of the Afghans and many a Muslim noble.

The British Make Their Presence Felt

The British, meanwhile, had established much of their power base in the India. In 1755, they had decisively defeated the Maratha naval power in the Bombay area. In July 1756, they sailed from their base in Madras to Bengal, to retake Calcutta, which had been seized by Siraj-ud Daula (lamp of the realm), the local nawab.[10] In the course of the next seven months, the '*famous two hundred days*' as they are called in British historiography, they not only recaptured Calcutta but also took control of the French fort at Chandernagar (about 35 km north of Calcutta) and later decisively defeated the nawab and his French allies at Plassey (Palashi, about 150 km north of Calcutta) on 23 June 1757. The nawab tried to escape, but was assassinated by his treacherous successor, Mir Jafar, who was later (in November 1759) deposed by the British and replaced by an – initially – more obedient figurehead.

The conquest of Bengal in the mid-eighteenth century has – rightly so – been hailed as the cornerstone of the later British Empire in India. Nevertheless, at the Mughal court, it attracted precious little attention at the time. Bengal had long since slipped out of imperial control, and an intra-European quarrel was but small *fait divers* at a time when Delhi itself was being sacked by the Afghan invaders. It would still take a while before people started to realize that the new rulers of Bengal were destined to take control over the entire subcontinent.

The Third Battle of Panipat (14 January 1761) and Its Impact

While Prince Ali Gauhar made his escape from Delhi, the Afghan king (Ahmed Shah Durrani/Abdali) and his local allies prepared themselves for war against the Marathas. Early skirmishes against the relatively small Maratha garrisons in the north-west resulted in victory for the Afghans, who reached Lahore in 1759.

The Marathas took over the city of Delhi on 2 August 1760 and defeated an Afghan garrison of about 15,000 on the western banks of the Yamuna River. However, the Afghan king crossed over to the other side with his main host, placing himself between the Maratha army and its supply base back in Delhi. Contrary to their customary, highly mobile warfare strategy, the Marathas relied on a massive host (estimated at between 45,000 and 60,000), followed by an even larger group of roughly 200,000 non-combatant camp followers. This enormous crowd posed a formidable logistic challenge to the Marathas, who, under the intense pressure of hunger, found themselves caught in dire straits. Abdali imposed a siege (which lasted about two months) against the Marathas. By the end of November 1760, the Afghans had almost cut off food supplies to the Maratha camp based in Panipat (about 80 km north of Delhi). Soldiers began to starve to death. On 13 January 1761, the Maratha chiefs pleaded with their commander, Sadashiv Rao Bhau, to be permitted to die in battle rather than fall victims to famine. Attempts to come to a negotiated settlement having been turned down by the Afghans, the Marathas saw no alternative but to attack at dawn on 14 January. Up to noon, the advantage seemed to rest with them, but a well-timed counteroffensive by the Afghan reserve cavalry caused panic in the Maratha ranks, when seventeen-year-old Vishwas Rao, the *peshwa*'s son and official commander-in-chief of the army, was shot and killed. They suddenly took to flight, pursued by the victors; large-scale slaughter resulted.

It was a disaster for the Marathas. Tens of thousands of their best soldiers and all their leading officers had perished; such was the blow to their fighting spirit and capabilities that it would take them another decade before they made their reappearance in the north. They did manage to recover much of their combined strength and territories, but their confederacy dissolved into five virtually independent states.

***

If the Marathas were the great losers in the third Battle of Panipat – just as decisive in Indian history as the first (Babur's conquest of the Delhi sultanate in 1526) and the second (1556, Akbar's victory over Hemu) Battles of Panipat – the remarkable fact is that there were no clear winners either. One would have expected Ahmed Shah Abdali and his Afghans to run the show, but the very opposite happened: his men rose in mutiny because they had not been paid for two years; as a result, he had no alternative but to head back to Afghanistan. The Mughal emperor, too, had been a nominal winner, but only thanks to the support of the nawab of Oudh, upon whom he now became dependent. The nawab, in turn, would soon be humbled by the British at Buxar (in Bihar) in late October 1764.

The only ones to really benefit in the long term were, in fact, the British. Not because they had sided with any of the parties, but precisely, because they had not. Panipat is where India defeated itself. Now all the British had to do was to pick up the pieces.

What If ...?

With the wisdom of hindsight, it is always tempting to ask oneself: What if the Marathas had won at Panipat? How, in fact, was it possible that they had been defeated in the first place?

The military reasons for the lost battle seem simple: wrong general, wrong strategy and wrong tactics. The actual commander-in-chief of the Maratha army, Raghunath Rao (the *peshwa*'s brother) appears to have been an arrogant, self-satisfied man, deaf to all warnings of his officers and allies. He should have engaged the Afghans with the tried-

and-trusted Maratha tactics of mobile warfare, not with a Mughal-style mammoth host encumbered by hordes of slow-moving, resource-wasting camp followers.

Even more important was the lack of any *political* objective. The Marathas were raiders rather than rulers, with little experience in how a country should be managed to increase the prosperity of its subjects. Let me give a rather provocative comparison: if Geronimo's Chiricahua Apaches had been much more numerous, and if they had by some stroke of good luck been able to conquer Washington D.C., they would not have known what to do with it either, and it is highly unlikely that the rival Native American tribes would have come to assist them – for the simple reason that they hated each others' guts. The same was true of the Marathas: even though their heroic struggle against the Afghans has been interpreted as a war of national liberation, in reality, it was not. The Rajputs did not fight alongside them; neither did the Sikhs. The local (Hindu) peasants flatly refused to help them with their supply problems, and their Jat allies became so irritated with Raghunath Rao's pompous arrogance that they left the battlefield in disgust without firing a single shot.

Shah Alam II (1728–1806)

After the 1761 battle at Panipat, things went back to normal at the Mughal court – to the extent that any such condition was still possible. 'Shah Jahan III', Imad-ul Mulk's figurehead, was duly deposed, and surprisingly, left alive. Imad-ul Mulk himself had wisely made his escape by then, never to be heard of again. Henceforth, Shah Alam II, who had retreated to Allahabad, was the one and only legitimate Mughal emperor – not that such a status meant much.

The new emperor appears to have been endowed with intelligence and stamina, and, in fact, he worked very hard to rebuild and modernize his military power. As Vincent Smith observes, he was the most talented and personable of the later Mughals and, in happier times, he might have had a prosperous reign, but there was little he could do to reverse the situation. He merely was the king of a petty state surrounded by powerful neighbours. More often than not, like his immediate predecessors, he was merely an impotent bystander. And the one major war he did decide to fight, he lost – with dire consequences.

Battle of Buxar: 22 October 1764

As has been recounted earlier, the Battle of Plassey (23 June 1757) had put the British in control of Bengal. After that, Nawab Siraj-ud Daula had been assassinated (in early July 1757) on the orders of his disgruntled general, Mir Jafar, who had colluded with the British and, consequently, was installed as the next nawab. However, the relationship between Mir Jafar and his British overlords quickly deteriorated, as he tried to gain independence from them by associating himself with the Dutch East India Company. The British, however, overran the Dutch forces, and replaced Mir Jafar by his son-in-law, Mir Qasim, in October 1760. The new nawab showered his British protectors with lavish gifts, but then, history started repeating itself. Fed up with British arrogance and their refusal to pay any taxes, he shifted his capital to Munger in Bihar, where he raised an army. Defeated by the British, he fled to Patna, where he killed all the Europeans he could lay his hands on. Pursued by the British, he fled into Oudh, forging an alliance with Nawab Shuja-ud Daula, with the support of the Mughal emperor himself. But in spite of the vastly superior Indian strength and numbers (over 40,000 men, including 5000 battle-hardened Afghan cavalry), the Battle of Buxar was decisively won by Major Hector Munro's well-disciplined force of 7500 – mainly Indian – sepoys.

***

In more ways than one, this victory was more significant even than that at the Battle of Plassey, seven years earlier. Shah Alam was compelled to sign the treaty of Allahabad (on 16 August 1765) with Robert Clive (the British commander-in-chief), securing full '*diwani* rights' (implying that the British were recognized as official Mughal officers, without the need for a local nawab) in Bengal and Bihar, plus the right to collect taxes in what later became Odisha, Bihar, Jharkhand and Uttar Pradesh. With a single stroke, the British had made themselves lord and master over one-eighth of India. The nawab of Oudh was restored to his position, but had to cede the districts of Kora and Allahabad to the Mughal emperor, in addition to paying stiff war indemnities to the East India Company. In exchange for Kora and Allahabad, amazingly, the British discontinued their annual tribute payments of 2.6 million rupees per year. Defeat came at a high price …

Shah Alam's Downfall

The 1765 treaty of Allahabad effectively reduced Shah Alam to the position of king(let) of only Delhi and Allahabad, an easy prey for the much more powerful neighbours surrounding him. This reality became painfully apparent in 1771, when he allowed himself to be persuaded by the Scindia/Shinde Maratha clan to break away from the British and place himself under Maratha protection. The alliance theoretically strengthened both parties, which proceeded to bring Rohilkhand to heel and fought several campaigns against Jat and Sikh rebels. But from a practical point of view, it made the Marathas the effective regents of the state of Delhi, a position they would hold until their defeat in the Second Anglo-Maratha War of 1803.

In spite of the combined Maratha–Mughal strength, northern India in the second half of the eighteenth century was a lawless, dangerous place. The Sikhs raided with virtual impunity – not only the kingdom of Delhi but also Rajputana, Rohilkhand, the lands of the Jats, and even the territory of the dreaded Marathas themselves – until Najaf Khan, the Mughal emperor's highly talented Baluchi general, decisively defeated them in 1777.

Unfortunately, the general passed away on 26 April 1782. Within six years after his death, the Mughal army effectively ceased to exist – because of Shah Alam's bad judgement. He should have appointed the deceased general's nephew, a competent man whose loyalty and valour had been proven on numerous occasions. Instead, he appointed a series of worthless and corrupt, if not outright treasonous individuals, who colluded with the emperor's enemies to reduce the size of his army. Shah Alam thus found himself effectively at the mercy of his ruffian enemies and soon had to bear the consequences. Ghulam Qadir, a half-mad Afghan chief supported by the Sikhs, forced the hapless emperor to appoint him as *wazir* of the empire. In early October 1788, after ravaging the palaces, searching in vain for the Mughal treasure, he flew into a fuming rage, and personally tore the emperor's eyes out with his bare hands. Three servants and two water carriers who tried to help the bleeding emperor were executed on the spot.

After ten horrible weeks, during which the members of the imperial family were humiliated and cruelly maltreated in every imaginable way by this Ghulam Qadir, a group of the emperor's loyalists, supported by the Shinde Marathas, fought their way to Delhi and came to his rescue. Ghulam Qadir somehow managed to escape in the fray, but was soon hunted down and executed by the Marathas in 1789; his eyeballs, nose and ears were sent to Shah Alam. It must have been some kind of consolation.

Blind and utterly powerless, the old emperor had lost everything but his dignity. The mocking contemporary barb – 'the kingdom of Shah Alam is from Delhi to Palam' (Palam being a suburb of Delhi) – really says it all. But his title still carried some weight. Apprehensive of Napoleon Bonaparte's aggressive wars in Europe, the British were more than anxious to regain custody of the aging emperor. On 14 September 1803, British troops occupied Delhi and placed him under their 'protection'. The successor of the all-powerful Akbar the Great had become a pensioner of a foreign trading company – respected but pitied and disregarded, as Vincent Smith wryly summarized the old man's plight.

The British Expansion

Meanwhile, the British had been able to establish their hegemony in most of the subcontinent. The four Anglo–Mysore Wars (1767–1799) had ended with the defeat and the death of Tipu Sultan (on 4 May 1799), a bellicose ally of the French and therefore a mortal enemy of the British. Much of Mysore's territory was annexed by the British, the nizam of Hyderabad and the Marathas. The remaining core around Mysore city was restored to the former ruling dynasty (Wadiyar or Wodeyar) and remained a nominally sovereign Princely State under British suzerainty until August 1947, when it joined the Union of India.

With the fall of Mysore, which had posed a serious threat to British expansion in the south, they turned their attention towards the Marathas.

As has been related earlier, the Maratha Confederacy, after its ruinous defeat at the Third Battle of Panipat (1761), had splintered into five separate, often rivalling powers: the *peshwa* at Pune (the nominal overlord of the Marathas, but by no means the most powerful); the Bhonsles of Nagpur; the Gaekwads of Baroda; and the two strongest, the Scindias/Shindes of Gwalior, and the Holkars of Indore. Feuding between the last two dominant powers led to civil war at the turn of the nineteenth century, with Holkar defeating a combined *peshwa*/Scindia army. This defeat, in turn, led to the *peshwa* seeking refuge with the British and signing the treaty of Bassein (now in north-western Maharashtra) on 31 December 1802, which restored him to his original position, but effectively made him a client of the British, with important territorial concessions and a garrison of 6000 East India Company troops stationed permanently in Pune. The treaty gravely offended the other Maratha leaders, who considered it an insult and an intolerable interference in their internal affairs. Tensions soon mounted when Holkar raided Hyderabad and Scindia formed a military alliance with the raja of Berar – apparently with the intention of ousting the British and/or annexing the nizam's territories. Negotiation attempts failed, and Lord Mornington's (aka Garret Wellesley) younger brother, Major General Arthur Wellesley (the famous Iron Duke of Wellington, who was later to prevail over Napoleon at Waterloo in 1815) declared war on Scindia and the raja of Berar in the latter half of 1803. The capture of Ahmednagar in August 1803, followed by victories of Lord Gerard Lake at Delhi and Wellesley at Assaye (in Maharashtra), seriously weakened the Maratha military capabilities; further British victories at Laswari (near Alwar in Rajasthan) and Adgaon (in northern Maharashtra) resulted in peace treaties with Bhonsle and Scindia, signed on 17 and 30 December 1803, respectively. These victories and treaties gave the British huge territorial gains and made them the dominant power in central India.

***

The last four decades of the eighteenth century marked the rapid transition of the British in India from traders to colonialists. Until the Battles of Plassey and Buxar, they had mainly been out to make profits and keep the French at bay. Now, they wanted real power. Adroitly mixing brute force and suave diplomacy, they had made themselves masters of central India and the entire Gangetic plain. The rest of the subcontinent would follow soon enough.

Akbar II (1760–1837)

The penultimate Mughal emperor of India – and the last one to be buried inside its borders – was born as Prince Mirza Akbar on 22 April 1760, exactly five months after his grandfather's (Alamgir II's) violent murder and some eight months before the Third Battle of Panipat (January 1761) would restore his father (Shah Alam II) to the throne.

He must have had a tolerably pleasant youth, raised as he was in opulence; his political future, however insignificant, seemed ensured when, in May 1781, after the death of his elder brother, he was officially appointed crown prince. Yet, seven years later, he witnessed the lowest ebb of the Mughal Empire, when his father was brutally blinded and he, along with the rest of the imperial family, found himself subject to brutal maltreatment and humiliation – which included being forced to dance before his father's tormentor in exchange for another few hours of life.

Then, after ten horrible weeks, he was liberated, the villain Ghulam Qadir was captured and killed and the guiltless interim puppet emperor, who had been raised to the throne as Jahan Shah IV, duly deposed (and later, undeservedly, killed).[11] Then, with his father's agreement, he had helped him with his duties.

***

It should have come as no surprise to Mirza Akbar that he had little if any power. Yet, with dignified obstinacy, he insisted on maintaining procedures and appearances. Audiences with British officials – including the governor-general himself – were only granted under the strictest rules of protocol ruling the interaction between ruler and subject. It may have helped him to uphold his dignity, but increasingly irritated the British, who had other things to do than seeking the favours of one whom they considered, not without reason, a mere pensioner with no effective influence beyond the walls of the Red Fort in Delhi.

In an attempt to further reduce the emperor's symbolic significance and status, they encouraged the nawab of Oudh and the nizam of Hyderabad to assume full royal titles. The nawab – a mere puppet of the British, anyway – soon complied, but highly significantly, the nizam, out of deference, refused. In spite of his utter lack of power, the Mughal emperor still commanded respect.

But the British were no longer impressed. Towards the end of Akbar Shah's reign, in 1835, they took the final and formal step and simply stopped referring to themselves as official representatives of the emperor. They no longer needed Farrukhsiyar's much-hailed imperial *firman* of 1717, 'the Magna Carta of the company in India', the legal basis for all – or most – of their past actions. They had become legitimate rulers in their own right. Henceforth, they no longer issued coin in the emperor's name; he was now simply referred to as 'king of Delhi', a native kinglet among many others. Simultaneously – and, in hindsight, to the subcontinent's strategic advantage – they began replacing Persian with English as the common language of government.

The great Mughal dynasty was a thing of the past. Nothing of its former splendour remained. '*The great hall of public audience when we saw it*', reports the British bishop, Reginald Heber, who visited the emperor on the last day of 1824, '*was full of lumber of all descriptions, broken palanqueens* [sic] *and empty boxes, and the throne so covered with pigeon's dung that its ornaments were hardly discernable. How little did Shahjehan ... foresee what would be the fate of his descendants ...*'[12]

***

By 1820, the Third Anglo–Maratha War had been fought and won decisively by the British; henceforth, the remaining Maratha leaders, as well as the Rajput rulers in Rajasthan, had to content themselves with the status of Princely States under the tutelage of the British. Except in Assam, Sindh and the Punjab, British supremacy was recognized throughout the subcontinent. The Pax Britannica had begun.[13]

In vain, the old emperor tried to fight the inevitable. Shortly before his death, he requested the well-respected Hindu intellectual and reformer Ram Mohan Roy (1772–1833) from Bengal to plead on his behalf in London. However, as was to be expected, the plea, however eloquently delivered, was to no avail.

As stated earlier, the old emperor was the last one to be laid to rest in his native India. His tomb, along with those of Bahadur Shah I (Shah Alam I) and Shah Alam II, is at Mehrauli, south Delhi, next to the dargah of the thirteenth-century Sufi saint Qutb-ud Din Bakhtiar 'Kaki', to whom, according to some, the Qutub Minar has been dedicated. Whether this is actually correct is far from certain: It seems much more probable that the Qutub Minar has been named after Qutub-ud Din Aibak, the founder of the Delhi Sultanate.

Bahadur Shah II (1775–1862)

It seems appropriate that the last Mughal emperor was the son, albeit not the favourite one, of an emperor called Akbar, albeit, not The Great, and a Rajput Hindu lady. Even more inspiring and encouraging, if deeply tragic, is the thought that this suave, kind-hearted gentleman was a true son of India.

At the time of his enthronement, he was an old man – sixty-one years and eleven months – old enough not to harbour any grandiose ambitions and smart enough to realize the obvious: the sprawling empire of his ancestors was long gone, and it would not be long before he – or at least his family after his death – would be told to move elsewhere. His dynasty had run its course. But he still had a task to fulfil, and did so with dignity, consistency and amiable naiveté.

Much has been written about him – William Dalrymple's authoritative and charmingly well-written study, *The Last Mughal*,* is unlikely to be surpassed any time soon – and much more even about the cataclysmic and highly controversial events that led to his downfall: the Great Uprising or Rebellion of 1857, or as most Indians prefer to call it, India's First War of Independence.

Life at court must not always have been pleasant for Bahadur Shah, or Zafar, as he liked to call himself.[14] Indeed, he was not his father's preferred choice: one of his father's wives, Mumtaz Mahal Begum, had constantly been pestering her husband to declare her own son, Mirza Jahangir, as heir to the throne. Bahadur Shah probably cared very little for power. He harboured no political – let alone, imperial – ambitions and had no inclination towards the affairs of state. He was a highly cultured and devout man, much more preoccupied with literature, poetry, religion and charity than with worldly pursuits.

But fate ordained he should be emperor. His younger brother and would-be rival, Mirza Jahangir, ensured that all by himself by blowing away his own chances. When he heard that Archibald Seton, the British resident at the Red Fort (who had been appointed in 1806), had questioned his father's motives for appointing him as his successor, he first insulted the resident in open court, and a few days later, attempted to kill him, taking a shot at him from one of the palace roofs, which left his intended victim unharmed but did kill his orderly. The British reacted with surprising composure and moderation: the hotheaded young prince was merely exiled to Allahabad, and Zafar (Bahadur Shah) remained the official heir-apparent.

The incident, incidentally, led to a charming folk tradition. The mother of the culprit vowed that if her son was released from Allahabad, she would make offerings at the tomb of Qutb-ud Din Bakhtiar 'Kaki' at Mehrauli (in Delhi). After a couple of years, the culprit was indeed released, and the noble lady lived up to her promise; what followed was seven days of grandiose festivities and merrymaking, in which the entire population of Delhi was free to participate. Such was the success

***The Last Mughal: The Fall of a Dynasty, Delhi 1857*, Bloomsbury, London, 2006.

of the event – called Phool Waalon Ki Sair (the journey/procession of florists) – that it was decided to repeat it annually. The event was celebrated even in 1857, in the middle of the widespread rebellion against the British, and it continues to this day.

***

Bahadur Shah was a skilled calligrapher and an accomplished poet, not only in Urdu and Persian but also in Braj Bhasha (a dialect of Hindi) and Punjabi. His court was home to the most outstanding writers and poets of his time such as Mirza Ghalib and Muhammad Ibrahim Zauq.

Above all, he was the archetype of the amiable, engaging Sufi mystic, profoundly convinced of the unity of God and all people of goodwill who aim to serve Him through goodness and charity. He consciously saw his role as a protector of his Hindu subjects and a moderator of Muslim demands, observes Dalrymple. He never forgot the critical importance of preserving the bond between his Hindu and Muslim subjects, which he always recognized was the central stitching that held his capital city – indeed, India itself, one might add – together. Throughout the 1857 Rebellion, his refusal to alienate his Hindu subjects by subscribing to the demands of the jihadis was probably his single most consistent policy.[15]

That being said, he was also deeply susceptible to the magical and superstitious side of religion. Like many of his followers, he believed that his position gave him tangible healing powers and he entertained a staunch belief in talismans or charms to ward off evil spells. When one of his followers was bitten by a snake, he sent the man a so-called 'seal of Bezoar' (a magical stone antidote against the venom) and some water on which he had breathed. This trait, too, makes him very 'Indian'.

***

Emperor Bahadur Shah is seen as a freedom fighter, since the rebels had made him their commander-in-chief. That is not entirely correct, for as Dalrymple correctly remarks, '*it was with severe misgivings and little choice that he found himself made the nominal leader of an Uprising that he strongly suspected from the start was doomed: a chaotic and officerless army of unpaid peasant soldiers set against the forces of the world's greatest military power ....*'[16] No, a rebel, the old emperor was not. But an Indian patriot, he most certainly was.

The Great Rebellion

The 1857 Gadr or Rebellion (which the British termed a 'mutiny'), a deeply tragic event, which to this day keeps stirring the strongest emotions, has been the subject of numerous books, films and documentaries. Suffice it to state just the most salient facts.

Probably out of ignorance, but clearly out of arrogance as well, the British Army leaders had often displayed a lack of empathy with the Indian soldiers and with their religious and caste sensitivities, which had led to corrosive frictions and grave incidents. Here, the final spark was provided by the ammunition for the new Pattern 1853 Enfield rifle, which used paper cartridges that the soldiers were instructed to tear open with their teeth. Quickly, a rumour spread that the cartridges used a tallow containing cow fat and/or pig fat, which deeply offended both Hindu *and* Muslim religious sensitivities. It was seen by many a high-caste Hindu as a way to irreparably make him lose his caste; it was also seen, by Hindus and Muslims alike, as yet another manoeuvre by the army leadership to forcibly convert the men to Christianity – all the more so, because there were many zealous British officers anxious to preach the Gospel at any opportunity.

In January of the fateful year 1857, a group of Indian soldiers at Calcutta's Dum Dum garrison flatly refused to touch the new rifles and the cartridges, but the revolt was swiftly suppressed. When a similar incident took place in Meerut (in Uttar Pradesh; about 70 km north-east of Delhi), eighty-five soldiers were court-martialled on 9 May. The next day, a rebellion broke out, which spread like wildfire throughout Oudh and the adjoining regions. Luckily for the British, the rebels were ill-organized; and even more luckily, it was not a *generalized* patriotic revolt, as several important regions and Princely States did not join: the major hostilities remained largely confined to the upper Gangetic plain and central India. Still, the rebellion posed a considerable threat to British power, and was contained only with great difficulty. The rebellion ended with the fall of Gwalior in June 1858. Wars tend to be horrible, and this one was no exception, with atrocities on both sides.

On 12 May 1857, when sepoy regiments had seized Delhi, the emperor, Bahadur Shah, reluctantly agreed to give his public support to the rebellion. No later than 16 May, despite his protests, fifty-two Europeans were publicly executed in front of his palace, the avowed aim of the executioners being to make sure that there would be no way for him to back out.

Chaotic times ensued, with precious little civil administration and no military unity of command and coordination at all. It was only a matter of time before the city would fall. When it did, on 14 September 1857, the British victory was accompanied by most brutal, wanton massacre. Bahadur Shah, who had taken refuge at Humayun's tomb, surrendered peacefully on 20 September. Nevertheless, the repression against his family was no less brutal than that against his people. The next day, Major William Hodson, the man who had obtained his surrender, shot the emperor's sons, Mirza Mughal and Mirza Khizr Sultan, and grandson Mirza Abu Bakr, in cold blood and under his own authority, at what came to be called the Khooni Darwaza (bloody gate; about 3 km from the Red Fort), his avowed aim being the 'total extinction' of the dynasty; later on, many other of the emperor's sixteen sons were captured, tried and hung.

***

By the end of March 1858, the British had recaptured most of the rebellious regions. After a forty-day trial, the old emperor was found guilty of treason, assistance to rebellion, and complicity in the murder of forty-nine people. Respecting the guarantee that he had been given upon his surrender, he was not sentenced to death, but exiled to Rangoon, Burma, accompanied into exile by his wife Zeenat Mahal and some of the remaining members of the family. There, he lingered on for another four years, until, on Friday, 7 November 1862, death put him out of his misery. He was buried in Rangoon that same day in an unmarked grave, the exact location of which has only recently been rediscovered.

One may find some solace in the idea that there are believed to be many descendants of Bahadur Shah still living in Burma, India and Pakistan, albeit often in poverty. Even greater solace, however, lies in the knowledge that Bahadur Shah's ideas and ideals will never die.

Notes and References

1. John Keay, *India: A History*, Grove Press, New York, 2000, p. 359.
2. Vincent Smith, *Akbar the Great Mogul 1542–1605*, Clarendon Press, Oxford, UK, 1917; second (revised) edition and third Indian reprint, S. Chand & Co., Delhi, 1966, p. 430.
3. Keay, op. cit., p. 366.
4. Ibid.
5. Smith, op. cit., p. 434.
6. Bamber Gascoigne, *A Brief History of the Great Moguls*, Carroll & Graf *Publishers*, New York, 2002, p. 244.
7. Smith, op. cit., p. 437.
8. Abraham Eraly, *The Mughal World: India's Tainted Paradise*, Weidenfeld & Nicholson, London, 1997 and 2007, p. 379.
9. S. R. Sharma, *Mughal Empire in India: A Systematic Study Including Source Material*, Vol. 3. Atlantic Publishers, Delhi, 1999, p. 666.
10. The loss of Calcutta had involved the death of between forty-one and fifty British nationals, imprisoned, along with a few dozen others, in a hot and much-too-small prison cell, with only two small barred windows to let in a breath of air. The incident, which deeply shocked British public opinion, is referred to as 'The Black Hole of Calcutta'.
11. Jahan Shah IV (Bidar Bakht Mahmud Shah Bahadur, 1749–1790), was the son of the former Mughal emperor Ahmad Shah Bahadur. After his deposition, he was killed in 1790 on the orders of Shah Alam II, even though, reportedly, he had been secretly sending food and water to the imprisoned emperor against Ghulam Qadir's direct orders.
12. Francis Robinson, *The Mughal Emperors and the Islamic Dynasties of India, Iran and Central Asia, 1206-1925,* Thames and Hudson, London, 2007, pp. 177–178.
13. Penderel Moon, *The British Conquest and Dominion of India*, Duckworth, London, 1989, quoted by Keay, op. cit., p. 413.
14. His full name was Abu Zafar Siraj-ud Din Muhammad Bahadur Shah Zafar and he used the word 'Zafar' (victory) as his nom de plume.
15. Keay, op. cit., pp. 446–447.
16. William Dalrymple, *The Last Mughal: The Fall of a Dynasty, Delhi 1857*, Bloomsbury, London, 2006, p. 7.

Epilogue
India's Failed Independence

Yes, the ideal of tolerance and friendship will never perish. People across the subcontinent still share a common culture (languages, food, architecture, movies, etc.). They still admire Gandhi, Kabir, Tagore and the other heroes from their common history. And on an individual level, relations between Indians, Pakistanis and Bangladeshis, at home and abroad, are often quite cordial.

However, we have to be honest with ourselves. Today, that friendship ideal is on the defensive. The united resistance against British colonial rule has not prevented the subcontinent's tragic and disastrous partition; and the voices of bigotry are louder than ever. Why did it go wrong, and where?

India's failed independence is the result of two causes: the political failure of the British empire, and the internal discord among Muslim leaders, deeply divided as they were between 'unionists' and 'separatists'.

A. Failure of the British Empire

It is, of course, quite outside the scope of this book to recount the entire story of the British in India. However, the sequence of events is outlined in the chronology at the end of this chapter.

Suffice it to make a few points about (1) the astonishing story of the British East India Company, and (2) the reasons why its empire ultimately failed.

The Miracle of the British Raj

It is truly amazing that the largest empire in the history of the world was founded, not by a mighty superpower, but by a private corporation that underwent, in just a few decades, '*an astonishing transformation from a trading company of often dubious solvency to a major imperial power with a standing army and territorial possessions far larger than those of the country which gave it birth*', as William Dalrymple aptly phrased it[1].

With the false wisdom of hindsight, we tend to look at that spectacular success as *planned* and *inevitable*, but that was not at all how matters looked in the early days. In fact, British presence in India evolved over several centuries, in five clearly distinct stages.

Stage 1: Securing a Toehold

In the early 1600s, the British had two preoccupations: fending off the Portuguese, and obtaining imperial (i.e., Akbar's and Jahangir's) permission to set up trading posts. The former took them several bloody battles, the latter, years of begging.

Stage 2: Making a Living

Over the next 200 years, that's exactly what the British did: minding their own business and trying to make a profit. Apart from an ill-advised clash with Aurangzeb (1687-1690), nothing spectacular happened. European presence in India in the Shah Jahan/Aurangzeb period was anyway limited to a handful of travellers[2] and a few dozen traders, operating from relatively small 'factories' (trading posts).

Stage 3: Becoming a Regional Power

Of great political consequence was Farrukhsiyar's imperial *Firman* of 1717, granting duty-free trading and territorial rights to the British East India Company — the most broadly based and far-reaching privileges ever granted to a foreign nation. While of little practical use in the beginning, the local governors basically ignored the orders of their sovereign and continued to exact customs duties. The document was 'the Magna Carta of the Company in India', the legal basis for all its subsequent actions. The Company was now officially introduced in the Indian power hierarchy — which, few years later, it was destined to replace.

Stage 4: Getting Rid of the French and Becoming a Nation-Wide Power

With the battles of Plassey (1757) and Buxar (1765), the British became lord and master in Bengal, Bihar and Orissa. After that, their focus was exclusively on their rivalry with the French. The French, who had challenged them in Bengal; the French, who still dominated southern India, directly or via. local allies; the French, who had ousted the British from Madras in 1746; the French, who again laid siege to Madras in 1759, and in 1769, when the city was threatened by their formidable ally, Haidar Ali of Mysore, father of the even more redoubtable Tipu Sultan.

However, in less than 50 years, the Company completely surpassed its adversaries and made itself master of most of India — thanks to the toughness, ambition and military prowess of just a few individuals. Without the adventurous and rapacious Robert Clive, the empire would not have been born; without the competent and energetic administration of Warren Hastings, it would not have survived its infancy; and without the military genius, not to mention the unapologetic imperialism of the two Wellesley brothers (i.e., Richard Colley Wellesley, 1st Marquess Wellesley of Norragh, and his younger brother Arthur, who was to gain immortal fame as the iron Duke of Wellington, Napoleon's nemesis), it would not have reached adulthood. But it did. The erstwhile trading company supplanted the Mughal throne and became the strongest power in India.

It was high time the British authorities got involved. In 1784, the *India Act* brought the Company under direct control of Parliament.

Stage 5: Seizing Absolute Power

With Napoleon decisively defeated in 1815, the British became the strongest military power on earth and built themselves the largest empire in world history.

By 1820, the Third Maratha War had been fought and won. Henceforth, the remaining Maratha leaders, just like the Rajput rulers in Rajasthan, had to content themselves with the status of 'Princely States' under British tutelage. Except in Assam, Sindh and the Punjab, British supremacy was recognized throughout the subcontinent. *Pax Britannica* had begun[3].

In 1835, the Company no longer referred to itself as a representative of the Mughal emperor (henceforth merely referred to as 'King of Delhi'). It issued coins in its own name and replaced Persian with English as the common administrative language.

Then, it conquered the rest of the subcontinent. In 1843, Sindh was added; in 1849, after the second Anglo-Sikh War, the Punjab and the Northwestern Frontier provinces were annexed; the second Anglo-Afghan War (1878-1880) led to the establishment of Afghanistan's western border along the Durand Line[4].

The last Mughal emperor, Bahadurshah Zafar, the unwilling figurehead of the Great Uprising of 1857-1858, was deposed and banished to Burma. He died four years later (7 November 1862) and was buried that same day in an unmarked grave, the exact location of which has only recently been rediscovered.

In 1858, the *Government of India Act*, followed by the *Queen's Proclamation*, put an end to the political anomaly of a commercial corporation owning/controlling a country. From then on, India was directly governed by the British Crown. The East India Company was formally dissolved in 1873 and Queen Victoria officially assumed the title of *Empress of India* on 1 May 1876.

Political Failure of the British Empire

The British empire started as a uniquely successful *colonial* power, but never rose above that level. The British never managed, nor tried to, create a multinational, multi-ethnic country with shared citizenship and equal rights; not even a confederation of nations with some kind of democratic home rule. India and the other colonies were considered, and treated, as mere *possessions*, to be exploited to the sole benefit of Great Britain. The *'natives'* were considered and treated as mere *subjects*, never citizens, not even in their own country.

That, in a nutshell, is the reason why Greater India, from the Khyber Pass to the coasts of Tamil Nadu, finally rose against the British and quite literally told them to *Quit India*. India had been unjustly exploited and impoverished, and its citizens crassly discriminated against.

Exploitation

Quoting from Shashi Tharoor's scathing but extremely well-written and highly persuasive *Inglorious Empire*[5]:

> *At the beginning of the eighteenth century, as the British economic historian Angus Maddison has demonstrated, India's share of the world economy was 23 per cent, as large as all of Europe put together. (It had been 27 per cent in 1700, when the Mughal Emperor Aurangzeb's treasury raked in £100 million in tax revenues alone). By the time the British departed India, it had dropped to just over 3 per cent. The reason was simple: India was governed for the benefit of Britain. Britain's rise for 200 years was financed by its depredations in India.*

Those depredations were based, predominantly, on outrageous taxation and a deliberate policy of *deindustrialization*, reducing India to a mere exporter of raw materials and a massive importer of British products[6].

Apartheid

> *In (the Queen's) celebrated 1858 Proclamation, she expressed her wish that 'our subjects, of whatever race or creed, be freely and impartially admitted to office in our service, the duties of which they may be qualified by their education, ability and integrity duly to discharge'. But what was the reality? In Will Durant's words, it was one of 'political exclusion and social scorn'. In 1857, F. J. Shore, the colonial administrator in Bengal whom I have quoted earlier, testifying before the House of Commons, confessed that 'the Indians have been excluded from every honour, dignity or office which the lowest Englishman could be prevailed upon to accept'. Decades later, Indian graduates from the finest universities of India, Europe and America found that, for the most part, only the lowest places in government service were open to them; according to Durant, just 4 per cent of the 'covenanted' positions in the Indian (initially the 'Imperial') Civil Service, the top cadre, were filled by Indians as late as 1930. ( )*
>
> *Jawaharlal Nehru put it sharply: the Indian Civil Service, he said, was 'neither Indian, nor civil, nor a service'.*[7]

All of the above was based on a self-serving, self-evident feeling of racial and/or civilizational superiority. One Viceroy, Lord Mayo, declared: '*We are all British gentlemen engaged in the magnificent work of governing an inferior race*'.

The British had no illusions about preparing Indians for self-government; their view of Indians was at best paternalist, at worst contemptuous[8]; and never would they accept an Indian in any position which would grant him/her any authority — least of all over British citizens. H. (Harold) Fielding-Hall[9], a relatively moderate British civil servant, who wrote several books about Indian culture, voiced this in no uncertain terms:

> *The Government of India is not Indian, it is English. It is essentially English, the more so and the more necessarily so because it is in India... England has made herself responsible for India, and she cannot shirk or divide this responsibility. ( ) Government must do its work in its own way, and that is the English way. No Indian can tell what this is. ( ) That an Indian should rule Europeans, and that it should be to an Indian they look for the maintenance of peace and order and*

for the administration of justice, criminal and civil, is unthinkable. The stability of the administration is due to its being English, and any threat to that stability would not be borne.

Legal discrimination was mirrored in openly racist social apartheid. In the 1600s and early 1700s, East India Company traders had readily intermarried with Indian women and sometimes even adopted Indian dress.[10] However, then, strict segregation and crass, overt, deeply insulting racism had become the rule. Formal anti-miscegenation laws were promulgated, and Anglo-Indians (or 'Eurasians' as they were called at the time[11]) actively discriminated against. Already in 1786, an order was passed banning the Anglo-Indian orphans of British soldiers from traveling to England to be educated. In 1791, an order was issued that no one what an Indian parent could be employed by the civil, military or marine branches of the Company. In 1795, further legislation was issued, explicitly disqualifying anyone not descended from European parents on both sides from serving in the Company's armies except as pipers, drummers, bandsmen and farriers.[12]

Official dialogue between the British rulers and their Indian subjects remained for a long time limited to 'Councils' without any real authority. Laws, budgets etc. remained firmly under control of the Governor General (Viceroy) and British Parliament.

In their dealings with their Indian subjects, the British quite consciously used 'Divide and Rule-tactics, sabotaging Indian political unity by pitting the various groups (Muslims, Sikhs, Jains, the Hindu casts) against each other. Particularly with regard to the Muslims, every effort was made to highlight differences and to persuade the Muslims that their interests were incompatible with those of the Hindus.

Growing frustration among Indians culminated after World War I, when, in spite of India's huge war effort and over one hundred thousand casualties, Britain broke its promise to grant progressive self-rule to India. Instead, it imposed repressive restrictions on freedom of speech and assembly, and brutally suppressed public protests. The worst incident was the Jallianwala Bagh massacre (13 April 1919), where troops were ordered to shoot unarmed peaceful demonstrators trapped in a walled garden in Amritsar, killing hundreds. That was the point beginning of the end, the final break between the Indians and their European overlords. Nobel Laureate Rabindranath Tagore returned his knighthood in protest; Gandhi and other Indian leaders became firmly convinced that total independence was the only acceptable solution for their country.

It was Gandhi who won the struggle for independence, thanks to his unique, ethics-based resistance against the colonialists. Mohandas Karamchand Gandhi, the Mahatma ('Great Soul'), who coined the term *satyagraha* (literally, *holding on to the Truth*), rejecting any 'untruthful' (unjust, unethical) means. Non-violent resistance and gaining victory, not by inflicting suffering on the opponent, but willingly accepting punishment and suffering. As brilliantly summarized by Tharoor[13]:

> *Where sporadic terrorism and moderate constitutionalism had both proved ineffective, Gandhi took the issue of freedom to the masses as one of simple right and wrong and gave them a technique to which the British had no response. By going beyond the councils and the meeting rooms he seized the public imagination. By abstaining from violence, the Mahatma wrested the moral advantage. By breaking the law non-violently, he showed up the injustice of the law; By accepting the punishments imposed on him he confronted his captors with their own brutalization. By voluntarily imposing suffering upon himself in his hunger strikes he demonstrated the lengths to which he was prepared to go in defence of what he considered to be right.* ***In the end he made the perpetuation of British rule an impossibility***. (emphasis added).

But much to his dismay, he failed to achieve what was nearest and dearest to him: a free and *united* India.

B. Pakistan the Pure: Muslim 'Unionists/Nationalists' vs. 'Separatists/Communalists'[14]

The name 'Pakistan' ('Land of the Pure') itself appears to have been coined in 1933, in a declaration by Choudhary Rahmat Ali, a University of Cambridge graduate. Three years before, in December 1930, the idea of a separate state for India's Muslim population had been formally proposed as a political goal by the acclaimed philosopher, poet and political leader, Sir Muhammad Iqbal, in a speech in December 1930, as the President of the Muslim League. Incidentally and interestingly, the separate state he visualized only included the Punjab, Sindh, the Northwest Frontier Province and Baluchistan, not East Bengal, nor any other of the then Muslim-majority areas, like, for instance, the Hyderabad area in current Andhra Pradesh.

The idea of a separate state for Muslims — which, incidentally, is not the same as an Islamist state as Pakistan was never intended to be one, in the minds of its founding fathers — had been brooding for quite a while. Like all separatist ideologies, it was mainly based on *fear* — fear of privileges lost, fear of discrimination. It should indeed be remembered that the Indian Muslims, though a minority, had for centuries enjoyed a privileged position in most parts of the subcontinent, be it under the Mughal emperors, the sultans of the Deccan or the Nizams of Hyderabad. But if one day those Muslim rulers were to be replaced by a *one man, one vote*, Western-style democracy, the Muslims would suddenly find themselves in a minority in the subcontinent they had been dominating for centuries. Hence, their fear of a 'Hindu Raj' and the growing demand for self-government and self-determination.

In his insightful and well-written book *India*, Stanley Wolpert[15] quotes the following statement, made in a speech at Meerut in 1888, by Sir Sayyid Ahmad Khan (1817- 1898)[16], as 'the earliest public articulation of what would much later be called the "two-nation theory"':

> *Now, suppose that all the English and the whole English army were to leave India, taking with them all their cannon and their splendid weapons and everything, then who would be rulers of India? Is it possible that under these circumstances two nations – the Mahomedans and the Hindus – could sit on the same throne and remain equal in power? Most certainly not. It is necessary that one of them should conquer the other. …*
>
> *Now, suppose that the English are not in India and that one of the nations of India has conquered the other, whether the Hindus the Mahomedans, or the Mahomedans the Hindus. At once some other nation of Europe … will attack India. …*
>
> *Everybody knows something or other about these powerful kingdoms of Europe. … their governments are far worse, nay, beyond comparison worse, than the British Government. It is, therefore, necessary that for the peace of India and for the progress of everything in India the English Government should remain for many years — in fact forever!*

It is interesting to compare this text to the arguments used, many decades later, by Muhammad Ali Jinnah, the leading Muslim politician who was to become Pakistan's *Quaid-e-Azam* (Great Leader):

> *It is extremely difficult to appreciate why our Hindu friends fail to understand the real nature of Islam and Hinduism. They are not religious in the strict sense of the word, but are, in fact, different and distinct social orders, and it is a dream that the Hindus and Muslims can ever evolve a common nationality, and this misconception of one Indian nation has troubled and will lead India to destruction if we fail to revise our notions in time. The Hindus and Muslims belong to two different religious philosophies, social customs, literatures. They neither intermarry nor inter-dine together and, indeed, they belong to two different civilizations which are based mainly on conflicting ideas and conceptions. Their aspect on life and of life are different. It is quite clear that Hindus and Mussalmans derive their inspiration from different sources of history. They have different epics, different heroes, and different episodes. Very often the hero of one is a foe of the other and, likewise, their victories and defeats overlap. To yoke together two such nations under a single state, one as a numerical minority and the other as a majority, must lead to growing discontent and final destruction of any fabric that may be so built for the government of such a state.*[17]

As any history book will tell us, Jinnah's views prevailed in the end. It is important to note, however, that his opinions were by no means shared unanimously. Several highly respected Muslim leaders — Syed Mahmud, Mukhtar Ahmed Ansari, Abbas Tyabi, Hakim Ajmal Khan, Asaf Ali, Saifuddin Kitchlew, Maulana Azad and Khan Abdul Ghaffar Khan, to name a few of the most prominent ones — had been pleading, forcefully and convincingly, for a united India. Saifuddin Kitchlew, for instance, spoke out against partition in public meetings all over the subcontinent, calling it a blatant '*surrender of nationalism for communalism*'.

It is equally important to note here that this intra-Muslim divide (for and against partition) was by no means a divide along *religious* lines. It was not at all comparable to the present-day split between so-called 'fundamentalists' or 'Islamists', against 'moderates' and 'secularists' or whatever they are called or choose to call themselves. On the contrary, many of the most prominent and vociferous pro-Pakistan leaders, including Jinnah himself[18], were convinced secularists, while the ranks of the proponents of Indian national unity included a great number of deeply religious, devout Muslims.

Among the latter, two prominent examples are the great Pashtun leader, Khan Abdul Ghaffar Khan (1890–1988), and Maulana Abul Kalam Azad (1888–1958).

The former, aptly called *Fakhr-e Afghan* ('Pride of the Afghan') and *Badshah Khan* ('King/Emperor of Chiefs') by his many supporters, is still affectionately referred to as the 'Frontier Gandhi' in present-day India. He was at the same time a Pashtun leader, a staunch opponent of British rule in India, a deeply devout Muslim, and a close friend, admirer and follower of Gandhi, as well as a convinced and lifelong pacifist. He strongly and consistently opposed the All-India Muslim League's demand for the partition of India. After the creation of Pakistan, he became a loyal, albeit rather critical citizen of the new country — an attitude which cost him several years of imprisonment and exile.

The latter, a respected religious scholar and one of the most senior Muslim leaders of the Indian independence movement, later became the first minister of education in the Indian government, and was posthumously awarded India's highest civilian award, the Bharat Ratna. He is commonly remembered as Maulana Azad — 'Maulana' referring to his Islamic scholarship, and 'Azad' (free) being the pen name he adopted in the days of the struggle for independence.

As stated above, both Maulana Azad and Badshah Khan (along with other senior Muslim leaders) vehemently opposed the partition of India along religious lines. It is interesting to note, however, the quite *different arguments* they used in doing so.

Maulana Azad opposed partition for two reasons: first, because he thought it was a very bad idea *for the Muslims themselves*. The Muslim community, he argued, would be much more influential, culturally and politically, in a united India than in a partitioned one.

Secondly and more importantly, Azad was opposed to partition because he was profoundly convinced that Indian Muslims and Hindus, after having lived together on the same sacred soil for more than a thousand years, had come to share a common Indian *nationhood*, a common identity that was much more important than any differences between them. And this Indian identity, argued Maulana Azad, absolutely *needed* the Muslim element for India would be incomplete, imperfect, unthinkable without it. *'I am proud of being an Indian'*, Azad declared. *'I am part of the indivisible unity that is Indian nationality. I am indispensable to this noble edifice and without me this splendid structure is incomplete. I am an essential element, which has gone to build India. I can never surrender this claim.'*

Addressing the Indian National Congress, he stated:

> *Full eleven centuries have passed since then (i.e., the advent of Islam on Indian soil). Islam has now as great a claim on the soil of India as Hinduism. If Hinduism has been the religion of the people here for several thousands of years, Islam also has been their religion for a thousand years. Just as a Hindu can say with pride that he is an Indian and follows Hinduism, so also, we can say with equal pride that we are Indians and follow Islam. I shall enlarge this orbit still further. The Indian Christian is equally entitled to say with pride that he is an Indian and is following a religion of India, namely Christianity.*

Of course, Maulana Azad was right. Indian identity could never again be complete without the Muslim element. Indian food, popular music, even the Hindi language itself (the very word 'Hindi' in the first place) would be changed beyond recognition, if one were to 'purge' all Muslim (Persian and Arab) elements from it, just like it would be utterly impossible to 'cleanse' the English language from its 30 per cent Latin and French vocabulary, to go back to its pure Germanic Anglo-Saxon origins. The idiom that would be left, would be impoverished beyond recognition, a mere shadow of the immensely rich and nuanced language it is today. It is impossible — not to mention highly undesirable — to try and erase one thousand years of civilization. In the course of that millennium, Hindus and Muslims have, for all their differences, indeed become *hairs on the same head, eyes in the same face,* as Gandhi once described it. Trying to erase the Indian Muslim element from Indian culture would be like — and would have to include! — demolishing the Taj Mahal. It would, in every sense of the word, be a mortal sin; it would be blasphemy against Mother India herself; and it would rob humankind of one of its richest and most inspiring civilizations — the civilization created by the *meeting of two oceans* (Hinduism and Islam) as Prince Darah Shikoh, emperor Shah Jahan's eldest son, once expressed it so elegantly.

It would, incidentally, be equally disastrous if the Muslim community tried to 'cleanse' itself from its Hindu features as its beautiful culture would be mauled and mutilated beyond recognition.

Quite different from, yet complementary to Azad's practical, political and historical argumentation, was Badshah Khan's sublimely simple and profoundly religious and ethical appeal. When asked why he, a full-blooded Pashtun and a devoted and deeply religious Muslim, had chosen to follow Mahatma Gandhi — a Hindu from faraway Gujarat — Badshah Khan stated:

'Whenever Gandhiji takes an important decision, I instinctively say to myself: This is the decision of one who has surrendered himself to God, and God never guideth ill.'

Indeed, submission to God — the very meaning of the word *Islam* — was Badshah Khan's only criterion:

'I have but one standard of measure, and that is the measure of one's surrender to God.' It is important to note, that Badshah Khan expressed the reasons for his admiration for Gandhi *not in political, but in religious, and more specifically in orthodox Muslim terms*; Gandhi was the best possible leader, because he truly and entirely had surrendered himself to God. And as stated above, that is exactly the definition of Islam: surrender or submission to God. Gandhi, in Badshah Khan's eyes, was a true Muslim, even though he practiced Hinduism. In other words, Badshah Khan judged other people, not by the community in which they happened to have been born or the rituals they observed, but by the extent to which they submitted their lives to truth, justice, compassion and love. This is a profoundly Islamic insight, although it tends to be forgotten much too often these days in so-called 'Islamist' or 'fundamentalist' circles. All creeds have their own rituals and prayers, which may be very different from one tradition to the other. However, at their core and at the core of every ethic worthy of that name lies the same *dīn*, the true spirit of religion, the actual devotion to the deity, or if one prefers to put it in non-confessional terms, the commitment to truth, justice, and love. Only *dīn* matters; for, as Mahatma Gandhi once put it, with provocative simplicity: *God has no religion.*

Badshah Khan never tired of emphasizing that true Islam is a religion of peace and love.

> The Holy Prophet Muhammad came into this world and taught us: That man is a Muslim who never hurts anyone by word or deed, but

> who works for the benefit and happiness of God's creatures. Belief in God is to love one's fellowmen.
>
> *It is my inner most conviction that Islam is* amal, yakeen, muhabat *(work, faith, and love), and without these the name 'Muslim' is sounding brass and tinkling cymbal. The Qur'an makes it absolutely clear that faith in one God without a second, and good works, are enough to secure a man his salvation.*

As we all know, Gandhi's and Badshah Khan's desperate pleas for unity were, most regrettably, of no avail. India was partitioned, most probably never to be reunited again.

As an outsider, it is of course not for me to judge whether or not the creation of Pakistan was necessary. After all, who is to say what would have happened if partition had not taken place? Would there have been less hatred and bloodshed, or more? Admittedly, 'realists' like Jinnah did have a point when they remarked that not all Hindus were as enlightened as Mahatma Gandhi (neither, by the way, were all Muslims as peaceful as Badshah Khan). But it is very well possible that the genies of communal strife would have remained in their bottles, if community leaders had unanimously spoken out for a united India. As a lawyer and a Western European, I'm inclined to believe that concerns about discrimination could have been addressed much more favourably and equitably through a combination of regional and local autonomy, with constitutional guarantees (including so-called blocking minorities, alarm bell procedures and veto rights) for religious and ethnic minorities.

Maybe, just maybe, the partition of India was inevitable. Maybe, as Wolpert phrased it[19], 'there were really too many Indias' to be reconciled between any one constitutional formula. But even if it was inevitable, it cannot be denied that the process has been extremely and unnecessarily painful. Partition has not prevented wholesale bloodshed and suffering — it actually *caused* it. Partition has driven millions of people from ancestral lands where their forefathers had been living for centuries. It has created another Iron Curtain, a grim new border where there never was one and never should have been one. It has compelled two developing nations to waste vast and scarce resources in the defence against people with whom they share a millenary common history and a common culture - people who are really, in every sense of the word, their next of kin.

What is even worse: not only was partition itself painful, *but it has also failed to solve anything, anywhere.*

First, it has not solved anything in what is left of India proper. The Republic of India still has close to 170 million Muslim citizens — one of the largest Muslim populations on the face of the planet. And it has to be said that though the country has had its fair share of violence, and though communal relationships may at times be dangerously tense, India has, by and large, succeeded in maintaining internal peace, law and order.

However, what is much more surprising is the fact that partition has failed to solve anything inside Pakistan. Not only has it not prevented ethnic tensions and rivalry, leading to the violent secession of Bangladesh, it has failed to bring peace and unity to the remaining country of (West) Pakistan as well.

Looking at the current Islamic Republic of Pakistan, it is striking how far it is removed from the vision its founding fathers had for it.

Muhammad Ali Jinnah himself, for instance, repeatedly stressed that Pakistan would be home, not just to Muslims, but to *all* creeds, castes and communities living on its soil.

This is how he expressed his vision, in his policy speech on 11 August 1947, chairing the Constituent Assembly (emphasis added):

> *Now, if we want to make this great State of Pakistan happy and prosperous, we should wholly and solely concentrate on the well-being of the people, and especially of the masses and the poor. If you will work in co-operation, forgetting the past, burying the hatchet, you are bound to succeed. If you change your past and work together in a spirit that every one of you, no matter to what community he belongs, no matter what relations he had with you in the past, no matter what is his colour, caste or creed, is first, second and last a citizen of this State with equal rights, privileges, and obligations, there will be no end to the progress you will make.*
>
> *I cannot emphasize it too much. We should begin to work in that spirit and in course of time all these angularities of the majority and minority communities, the Hindu community and the Muslim community, because even as regards Muslims you have Pathans, Punjabis, Shia's, Sunnis and so on, and among the Hindus you have Brahmins, Vaishnavas, Khatris, also Bengalis, Madrasis and so on, will vanish. Indeed, if you ask me, this has been the biggest hindrance*

in the way of India to attain the freedom and independence and but for this we would have been free people long long ago. No power can hold another nation, and specially a nation of 400 million souls in subjection; nobody could have conquered you, and even if it had happened, nobody could have continued its hold on you for any length of time, but for this. Therefore, we must learn a lesson from this.

You are free; you are free to go to your temples, you are free to go to your mosques or to any other place or worship in this state of Pakistan. You may belong to any religion or caste or creed — that has nothing to do with the business of the state. As you know, history shows that in England, conditions, some time ago, were much worse than those prevailing in India today. The Roman Catholics and the Protestants persecuted each other.

Even now there are some states in existence where there are discriminations made, and bars imposed against a particular class. Thank God, we are not starting in those days. We are starting in the days where there is no discrimination, no distinction between one community and another, no discrimination between one caste or creed and another. We are starting with this fundamental principle that we are all citizens and equal citizens of one state. The people of England in course of time had to face the realities of the situation and had to discharge the responsibilities and burdens placed upon them by the government of their country and they went through that fire step by step. Today, you might say with justice that Roman Catholics and Protestants do not exist; what exists now is that every man is a citizen, an equal citizen of Great Britain and they are all members of the nation.

Now I think we should keep that in front of us as our ideal and you will find that in course of time Hindus would cease to be Hindus and Muslims would cease to be Muslims, not in the religious sense, because that is the personal faith of each individual, but in the political sense as citizens of the state.

Not to say that Jinnah wanted to deny or minimize Pakistan's Islamic heritage; on the contrary. However, it is clear that he wanted all people belonging to religious minorities to have equal rights, as citizens of a tolerant and democratic Pakistan:

The Constitution of Pakistan has yet to be framed by the Pakistan Constituent Assembly. I do not know what the ultimate shape of

> *this Constitution is going to be, but I am sure that it will be of a democratic type, embodying the essential principles of Islam. Today, they are as applicable in actual life as they were 1,300 years ago. Islam and its idealism have taught us democracy. It has taught equality of man, justice and fair play to everybody. We are the inheritors of these glorious traditions and are fully alive to our responsibilities and obligations as framers of the future Constitution of Pakistan. In any case Pakistan is not going to be a theocratic state to be ruled by priests with a divine mission. We have many non-Muslims — Hindus, Christians, and Parsis — but they are all Pakistanis. They will enjoy the same rights and privileges as any other citizens and will play their rightful part in the affairs of Pakistan.*
>
> (Broadcast talk to the people of the United States on Pakistan, recorded February 1948.)

Alas, how sadly mistaken he was. I am sure that he and Iqbal and all the other noble-minded founding fathers of Pakistan would be truly appalled at the current state of affairs in the country they created. Not only have the religious minorities they esteemed and respected all but disappeared. The non-Muslim population has steadily dwindled from 20 to 30 per cent back in 1947, to less than 3 per cent today. That in itself is sad enough; but it is even more frustrating to see, that this 'religious cleansing' has failed to bring any peace to the rest of the population. On the contrary, sectarian hatred and violence today is as bad as it has ever been. Not only is there the painful Sunni-Shia divide; not only is there the violence and discrimination against the remaining non-Muslims (including Christians, Hindus, the adherents of the Baha'i faith and the so-called Ahmadiyya Muslims, who are officially considered non-Muslims by virtue of a 1974 constitutional amendment), the mainstream Sunni Muslim community finds itself increasingly divided as well, up to and including terrorist attacks on health workers and on venerable Sufi shrines and festivals, which have enriched Indian Muslim spiritual life, not to mention world culture - for centuries.

Let me end this paragraph on Indian partition with a quote from Mahatma Gandhi[20] speech on Indian Independence Day, 26 January 1948, four days before his violent death at the hands of a misguided young Hindu extremist:

> *Before leaving this topic of the day, let us permit ourselves to hope that though geographically and politically India is divided in two, at heart we shall ever be friends and brothers helping and respecting one another and be one for the outside world.*

Indeed, as a Western European, I can testify to the immense power of peace. Never in the history of our continent have we enjoyed such safety and prosperity as since the day the two former archenemies, Germany and France, decided they would never fight again. One can only hope that someday, Indians, Pakistanis, Bangladeshis, Nepalese, Bhutanese and Sri Lankans will be united as members of a diverse, free, strong, peaceful and prosperous South Asian Union, following that same European model.

After all, the subcontinent is home to over 1.6 billion people — roughly one billion Hindus, 500 million Muslims, and 100 million Buddhists, Jains, Sikhs, Parsis, Jews and Christians. They cannot possibly hope to convert, assimilate, separate from or eliminate each other. It is their destiny — as well as their sacred duty — to enrich and inspire each other and the rest of humankind with the incomparable wealth and wisdom of their respective traditions. To do this, they do not at all need to relinquish their identity, nor their sovereignty. What their distant European cousins have been able to do, after so many centuries of ruinous wars, they can too.

Notes and References:

1. William Dalrymple, White Mughals, Penguin Books, New Delhi, 2002: p. 7; also quoted by Peggy Mohan, Wanderers, Kings, Merchants: The Story of India through its Languages, Penguin Random House, India, 2021, page 229.
2. Including Joannes de Laet (1581-1649), Sebastião Manrique (c. 1590-1669), François Pelsaert (c. 1595-1630), Peter Mundy (1597-1667), Jean-Baptiste Tavernier (1605-1689), François Bernier (1620-1688), Jean de Thévenot (1633-1667), Niccolao Manucci (1638-1717), and Giovanni Francesco Gemelli Careri (1648-1724).
3. Penderel Moon, quoted by John Keay (op.cit., page 413).
4. On 12 November 1893; confirmed in the Anglo-Afghan Treaty of Rawalpindi of August 1919, after the Third Anglo-Afghan War.
5. Shashi Tharoor, Inglorious Empire: What the British Did to India, Penguin Random House, New Delhi, 2017, pp. 2-3.
6. Ibid, pp. 1-35.

7. Ibid, pp. 50-51 ff.
8. Ibid, p. 57.
9. Ibid, pp. 58-59.
10. William Dalrymple, White Mughals, Love and Betrayal in Eighteenth-Century India, HarperCollins Publishers, India, 2002.
11. Shashi Tharoor: Inglorious Empire: What the British Did to India, Penguin Random House, New Delhi, 2017, page 70.
12. William Dalrymple, op. cit., pp. 50-51.
13. op.cit.,pp. 123-124.
14. This paragraph is based on my 2013 essay 'Paths to Peace', pp. 8-23.
15. Stanley Wolpert, India, third edition, University of California Press, Berkeley, 2005.
16. Ibid, pp.59-60.
17. Excerpt from the Presidential Address delivered by Quaid-e-Azam at Lahore, 22-23 March, 1940 (http:/ / www. nazariapak. info/ data/quaid/ statements/ two-nation. asp), Nazariapak.info
18. Who, incidentally, readily drank alcohol, ate non-halal foods, and wore Western-style suits for most of his life.
19. Stanley Wolpert: India, third edition, University of California Press, Berkeley, 2005, page 66.
20. Mohandas Karamchand Gandhi; Selected Writings, Dover Publications, 2012, page 211.

CHRONOLOGY
THE BRITISH IN INDIA

First Phase: *The East India Company*

1588: England defeats the Spanish Armada; first British attempts to get involved in the Americas and in the lucrative spice trade in Asia.

1592: Sir Walter Raleigh conquers the Portuguese carrack *Madre de Deus* and its huge treasure (3 August 1592). At least equally valuable is the ship's rutter, containing vital information on trade with India, China and Japan.

1599: Incorporation of the *East India Company.*

1600: Elisabeth I of England grants the Royal Charter to East India Company (31 December).

1609-1611: Captain William Hawkins at Jahangir's court. Conflicts with the Portuguese.

1611: The East India Company sets up its first factory in India, but *outside* of the Mughal empire, at Masulipatam/Machilipatnam, near the estuary of the Krishna River on the East coast of India, a major trading centre for luxury textiles.

1612: A British fleet under Captain Thomas Best arrives near Surat. Late October, it successfully repulses an attack by a much more numerous Portuguese battle fleet in the Battle of Swally (Suvali, near Surat).

1615: A Company fleet under Nicholas Downton is attacked near Surat by the entire Goan fleet, led by the Portuguese Viceroy, João de Azevedo, personally. The English fleet takes a defensive position amongst the sandbanks, with the *Merchant's Hope* blocking the entrance, neutralizing to some extent the vast numerical superiority of the Portuguese. Portuguese attempts to conquer the *Merchant's Hope* by boarding and fire ships are beaten off with great loss of life to the attackers. The fighting goes on for three weeks, but in the end, on 13 February, the Portuguese withdraw, the English defensive position being too strong for them to break. Portuguese losses in killed, burnt and drowned are said to amount to nearly 500 men, against only four Englishmen killed in action. The victory greatly increases the English' reputation and influence. Henceforth, the Portuguese no longer rule the waves in the Indian Ocean.

February 2: Sir Thomas Roe, special envoy of King James I, embarks with 15 followers on the *Lion*, part of a four-ship fleet commanded by William Keeling. Uneventful six months' voyage to Surat, via the Cape, the Comoros, and Socotra.

1616: Roe presents himself at Jahangir's court on 10 January. He will remain at court until September 1618. Throughout his stay, on a personal level, Jahangir remains kind and courteous. However, the emperor's personal esteem and vivid interest in European art and other *curiosities* is combined with a total indifference to the objects of Roe's mission, as well as a principled unwillingness to sign a treaty on equal terms with the king of so small a nation. In Jahangir's eyes, only the Shah of Persia and the Ottoman Sultan could to a certain extent claim to be his equals.

1618: While unsuccessful in his attempts to secure a formal treaty, Roe does return to England with a written confirmation of England's trading rights:

> *Upon which assurance of your royal love I have given my general command to all the kingdoms and ports of my dominions to receive all the merchants of the English nation as the subjects of my friend; that in what place soever they choose to live, they may have free liberty without any restraint; and at what port soever they shall arrive, that neither Portugal nor any other shall dare to molest their quiet; and in what city soever they shall have residence, I have commanded all my governors and captains to give them freedom answerable to their own desires; to sell, buy, and to transport into their country at their pleasure. For confirmation of our love and friendship, I desire your Majesty to command your merchants to bring in their ships of all sorts of rarities and rich goods fit for my palace; and that you be pleased to send me your royal letters by every opportunity, that I may rejoice in your health and prosperous affairs; that our friendship may be interchanged and eternal.*

Note: British historians — rightly and understandably so — consider this letter to be a major step in the process that would ultimately lead to the British Raj. However, we should not forget that, at the time, the whole matter was a mere detail in Jahangir's eyes. It is quite telling that Ambassador Roe's stay is not mentioned even once in Jahangir's voluminous and detailed memoirs.

1625: The East India Company sets up factories on the eastern coast of India.

1687: Failed attempt by the East India Company to seize the port of Chittagong.

The Company transfers its west Indian headquarters from Surat to Bombay.

1688: Conflict with Aurangzeb. The East India Company is expelled from Bengal; the French are allowed to establish a settlement at Chandernagore (on the Hugli/Hooghly River).

1689: Aurangzeb's forces capture Bombay.

1690: The East India Company seeks Aurangzeb's pardon. In exchange for a sizeable indemnity, Bombay is restored to them, and they are allowed to resume trade in Bengal. Job Charnock founds Fort Williams (and the future city of Calcutta).

1717: Firman of Farrukhsiyar, granting toll-free trade and territorial rights to the East India Company — the broadest and most far-reaching rights ever granted to a foreign nation. While of no practical importance at first, this document became the *Magna Charta* of the Company in India, the legal basis of all its subsequent initiatives, for by virtue of that edict, the Company had become officially part of the Mughal Empire's administrative hierarchy — a hierarchy it was destined to replace a few decades later.

1751: Hostilities between the British and French in South India.

1756-57: Fall and recapture of Calcutta.

23 June 1757: Battle of Plassey (Palashi): the British defeat the Nawab of Bengal and his French allies. The trading company has become a *political* power.

22 October 1764: Battle of Buxar (Baksar): the British defeat the united army of the Nawabs of Bengal and Awadh and the imperial army of Shah Alam II.

16 August 1765: Shah Alam II is compelled to sign the Treaty of Allahabad, granting full *diwani* rights to the British, meaning they are recognized as Mughal officers, with rights to act in their own name (i.e., without the local Nawabs) in Bengal and Bihar. In addition, they acquire the right to levy taxes in Orissa, Bihar, Jharkhand and Uttar Pradesh. In one swoop, the East India Company has become lord and master of more than one-eighth of India's territory; the Mughal emperor has become a powerless pensioner of the British.

1784: The *India Act* brings the East India Company under direct control of Parliament.

4 May 1799: The Fourth Mysore War ends with the death of Tipu Sultan, the '*Tiger of Mysore*', an ally of the French.

1775-1818: In three wars (1775-1782, 1803-1805) the British put an end to the military power of the Marathas. Henceforth, the Maratha leaders — just like the Rajput kings of Rajasthan — will have to content themselves with the status of *Princely States* under British tutelage. With the exception of Assam, Sindh the Punjab (which will follow later), British supremacy is established throughout the subcontinent. The *Pax Britannica* has begun.

1835: Appearances are no longer kept up. Henceforth, the British rule in their own name. They no longer position themselves as representatives of the Mughal emperor, who is referred to as 'king of Delhi'. Persian is replaced by English as administrative language of the empire — an administrative measure with far-reaching geopolitical consequences to this day.

1843: Conquest of Sindh.

1845-1849: Defeat of the Sikhs in two short wars (1845-1846 and 1848-1849); the Company rules in the Punjab.

1852: Second Burmese War: annexation of northern Burma (Myanmar).

1857-58: Bloody repression of '*Great Mutiny*'. The last Mughal Emperor, Bahadur Shah Zafar is banished to Burma, where he expires four years later. His body is buried in an anonymous grave.

Second Phase: *The British Raj*

1858: *Government of India Act*, followed by the *Queen's Proclamation*: India is henceforth governed directly by the British Crown. The East India Company is formally dissolved in 1873.

1861-1941: Lifetime of Rabindranath Tagore, the famous Nobel Prize-winning Bengali poet, writer and social reformer.

1869-1948: Lifetime of Mohandas Karamchand Gandhi, the Mahatma ('Great Soul'), the charismatic Indian nationalist who commanded the admiration of friend and foe with his tactics of nonviolent resistance.

1873: The British East India Company is formally dissolved.

1876: British occupation of the Afghan city of Quetta (in present-day western Pakistan).

1876: Queen Victoria is proclaimed *Empress of India.*

1876-77: Famine, badly mishandled by Viceroy Lord Lytton.

1876-1948: Lifetime of Muhammad Ali Jinnah, founder of Pakistan.

1878-80: The Second Afghan War leads (in 1893) to the establishment of the *Durand Line*, Pakistan's current western border with Afghanistan. The border is drawn arbitrarily, based on geopolitical military considerations at the time; it runs through the homelands of Pashtun people on both sides of the border.

1885: A group of intellectuals establishes the *Indian National Congress*, aiming to represent Indian public opinion to the British authorities.

1893: Establishment of the Durand Line (12 November).

1889-1964: Lifetime of Jawaharlal Nehru.

1891-1956: Lifetime of Bhimrao Ramji Ambedkar, lifelong champion of the casteless 'Untouchables', designer of the Indian Constitution and India's first minister of justice after independence.

1896: Indian nationalist Bal Gangadhar Tilak demands *purna swaraj* (independence, literally 'complete self-government').

1905: Partition of Bengal leads to violent protests and boycott of British goods; the decision is reversed in 1911.

1906: Establishment of the *Muslim League* (Muslim political party).

1914-1918: World War I. Indian troops are deployed *en masse*, with heavy casualties.

1919: Jallianwala Bagh massacre (13 April), with troops ordered to shoot unarmed peaceful demonstrators trapped in a walled garden in Amritsar, killing hundreds. Gandhi is now firmly convinced that total independence is the only acceptable solution for his country.

1919: The Third Anglo-Afghan war ends with the Treaty of Rawalpindi, signed on the 9 August, confirming the Durand Line as Afghanistan's western border.

1920: Gandhi formulates his *satyagraha* strategy (literally, *holding on to the Truth*), i.e. non-violent resistance and refusal to cooperate with the colonial power.

Muslims launch the pan-Islamist *Khilafat* movement.

1922: *Chauri Chaura* massacre, in which troops open fire on unarmed demonstrators, upon which protesters set fire to a police station, killing all the occupants; harsh repression by the British.

1930: The Indian National Congress issues a Declaration of Independence (*Purna Swaraj*) on 26 January. Nehru becomes leader of the Indian Congress Party. Mahatma Gandhi leads the legendary 'Salt March'.

1937: Burma (Myanmar) becomes a separate British colony.

1937: Provincial autonomy. The unitary Congress Party convincingly wins the elections — also with the Muslim electorate.

1939: Beginning of World War II. Strong Indian protest against the Indian declaration of war by the Viceroy, without consultation with the Indian representatives. Congress Party members resign *en masse.*

1940: Lahore Resolution: resolution of the *Muslim League* for the creation of the State of Pakistan.

1942: *Quit India Movement. Cripps Mission* (British attempt to secure full Indian cooperation in the war effort in exchange for home rule after the war) fails; Congress Party leadership imprisoned for the duration of the war.

1945: Failure of the Simla Conference, chaired by Lord Wavell:

Muslim League refuses to accept any Muslim representatives appointed by the Congress Party.

The British elections are won by the Labour Party, which supports Indian independence.

1946: National elections in India; this time, the Muslim League wins the majority of the Muslim votes. Sectarian violence in Calcutta and other parts of the country.

1947: King George VI appoints Admiral Lord Louis Mountbatten as Viceroy of India, with the task of guiding British India's transition to independence (20 February). Mountbatten tries to preserve the unity of the country, but Muhammad Ali Jinnah remains unyielding.

On 15 August 1947, India and Pakistan gain their independence. The hastily drawn border between the two cuts right across the Punjab and Bengal, with some 14 million people suddenly finding themselves living on the 'wrong" side of the border. Chaotic mass migration with terrible bloodshed.

Britain exits India.

Mountbatten remains in Delhi until June 1948, as India's first *Governor General.*

1971: Bangladesh (East Pakistan) gains independence.

India's traumatic mutilation has failed to solve anything. Lingering issues such as sovereignty over Kashmir have led to four wars (in 1947, 1965, 1971 and 1999) and countless border clashes, terrorist attacks and sectarian violence.

The voices of fundamentalist bigotry are louder than ever; yet Greater India's common heritage remains alive in the hearts of many.

Appendix
Genealogical Chart*

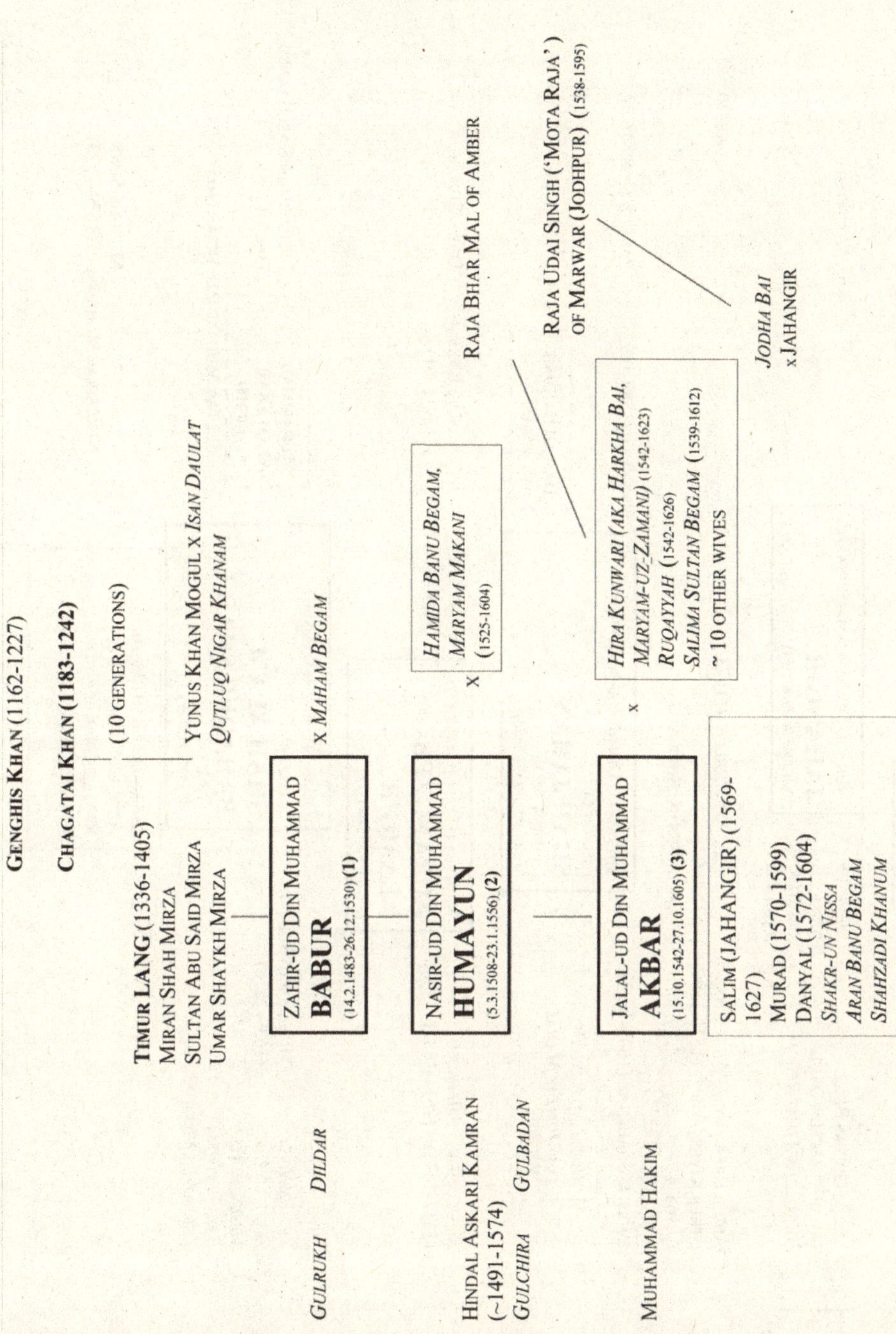

*The names of women apear in *italics*.

AKBAR

MIRZA GHIYAS BEG (AKA I'TIMAD-UD DAULA: (D. 1622) X *ASMAT BEGAM*

*MEHR-UN NISSA AKA **NUR JAHAN'*** (1577-1645)

NUR-UD DIN MUHAMMAD SALIM
JAHANGIR
(30.8.1569-28.10.1627) **(4)**

ABU'L HASAN (AKA 'ASAF KHAN') (D.1641)

OTHER WIVES (1570-1599) (1572-1602)

X *JODHA BAI* (1573-1619)

X ~ 20

MEHR-UN NISSA X 'SHER AFGAN'

LADLI X SHAHRYAR (1605-1627)

*ARJUMAND BANU BEGAM AKA **MUMTAZ MAHAL'*** (1593-1631) X

SHIHAB-UD DIN MUHAMMAD KHURRAM
SHAH JAHAN
(5.1.1592-1.2.1666)
(R. 24.1.1628-19.6.1658) **(6)**

KHUSRAU (1587-1622)

DAWAR BAKHSH (1603-1628) **(5)**

PARVEZ (1589-1626)

ROSHANARA (1617-1671)

JAHANARA (1614-1681)

MUHYI-UD DIN MUHAMMAD
AURANGZEB ALAMGIR
(4.11.1618-3.3.1707) **(7)**

SHAH SHUJA (1616-1661?)

MURAD BAKHSH (1624-1661)

DARA SHIKOH (1615-1659)

ZEB-UN NISSA
ZINAT-UN NISSA
MEHR-UN NISSA
BADR-UN NISSA
ZUBDAT-UN NISSA

MUHAMMAD SULTAN (1639-1676)

QUTB-UD DIN MUHAMMAD MUAZZAM
SHAH ALAM BAHADUR SHAH I
(14.10.1643-27.2.1712)
(R. 1707-1712) **(9)**

MUHAMMAD AZAM SHAH (1653-1707) **(8)**

MUHAMMAD KAM BAKHSH (1667-1709)

SULTAN MUHAMMAD AKBAR (1657-1706)

JAHANDAR SHAH (1661-1713)
AZIM-US-SHAN (1664-1712)
RAFI-US-SHAN (1671-1712)
KHUJISTA AKHTAR (1673-1712)

MUHI-US-SUNNAT

NEKUSIYAR MUHAMMAD (1679-1723)

contd ...

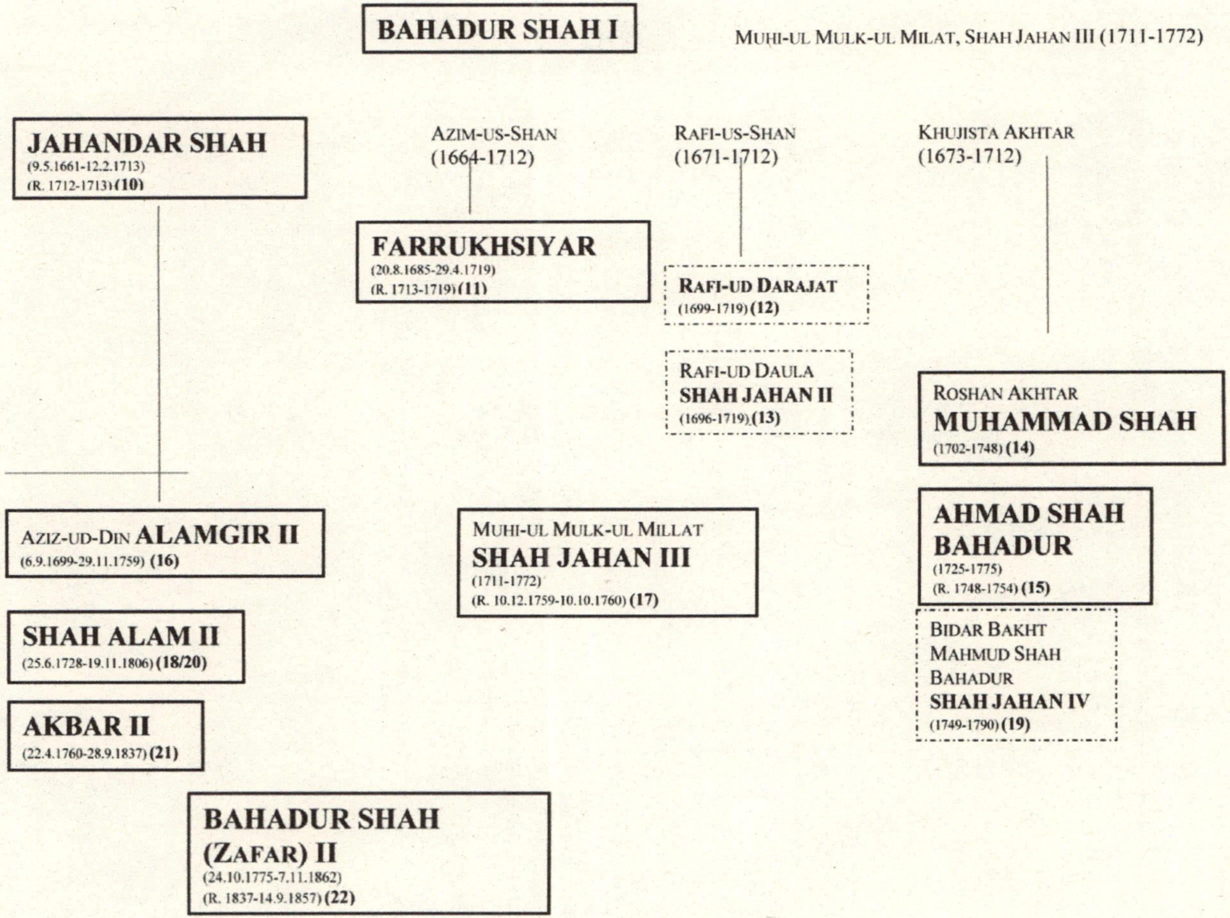
BAHADUR SHAH I
MUHI-UL MULK-UL MILAT, SHAH JAHAN III (1711-1772)
JAHANDAR SHAH
(9.5.1661-12.2.1713)
(R. 1712-1713) (10)
AZIZ-UD-DIN ALAMGIR II
(6.9.1699-29.11.1759) (16)
SHAH ALAM II
(25.6.1728-19.11.1806) (18/20)
AKBAR II
(22.4.1760-28.9.1837) (21)
BAHADUR SHAH
(ZAFAR) II
(24.10.1775-7.11.1862)
(R. 1837-14.9.1857) (22)
AZIM-US-SHAN
(1664-1712)
FARRUKHSIYAR
(20.8.1685-29.4.1719)
(R. 1713-1719) (11)
MUHI-UL MULK-UL MILLAT
SHAH JAHAN III
(1711-1772)
(R. 10.12.1759-10.10.1760) (17)
RAFI-US-SHAN
(1671-1712)
RAFI-UD DARAJAT
(1699-1719) (12)
RAFI-UD DAULA
SHAH JAHAN II
(1696-1719) (13)
KHUJISTA AKHTAR
(1673-1712)
ROSHAN AKHTAR
MUHAMMAD SHAH
(1702-1748) (14)
AHMAD SHAH
BAHADUR
(1725-1775)
(R. 1748-1754) (15)
BIDAR BAKHT
MAHMUD SHAH
BAHADUR
SHAH JAHAN IV
(1749-1790) (19)

Bibliography

It will be clear that any secondary-source historiography in the genre of *The Great Mughals and Their India* cannot be written without extensive reference to, and indeed, borrowing from, the work of others. Even when referring to primary sources (e.g., the *Baburnama*, *Jahangirnama*, Abu'l Fazl's *Akbarnama*, and so on), the new work necessarily relies on earlier translations and comments by professional linguists and historians. The publications to which this book is most indebted to are shown in bold typeface.

This book does not lay claim to any truly novel historical discoveries or insights; its sole ambition is to offer the reader as objective a synthesis as possible, indicating, wherever needed, which subjects tend to be controversial. For it is, alas, rather typical of Indian historiography in general, and of the Mughal Empire in particular, that its true story is often clouded by a mist of urban legends and confabulations; and this situation is much worsened by a regrettable, but growing, tendency among many, to reinterpret history on the basis of present-day communal and political affiliations. Against this tendency, the avowed aim of this book is to remind its readers of Oscar Wilde's famous bon mot that the pure and simple truth is rarely pure and never simple.

Primary Sources

- **Abu'l Fazl Allamī, *The Ā'in-ī-Akbarī* (institutions of Akbar), three volumes in Persian. The first volume translated by H. Blochmann (1873) and revised by D. C. Phillott (1927). The second and third volumes translated by H. S. Jarrett (1893–1896) and revised by Jadunath Sarkar (1949), *Bibliotheca Indica*, No. 61, reprinted Delhi, 1988.**
- **Abu'l Fazl Allamī, *The Akbar Nāmā*, translated from the Persian by H. Beveridge (1902–1939; in three volumes) Low Price Publications, Delhi, reprinted 1989 (ISBN 81-85395-03-9).**
- **Bābur, Emperor of Hindustan, *The Baburnama: Memoirs of Babur, Prince and Emperor*; translated, edited and annotated by Wheeler M. Thackston. Introduction by Salman Rushdie, Random House, New York, 1996–2006 (ISBN 0-375-76137-3).**
- Badauni (Mulla Abdul-Kadir Muluk Shah of Badaun), *Tarikh-i-Badauni (Muntakhabut Tawarikh)*, in *The History of India: As Told by Its Own Historians: The Muhammadan Period,* the posthumous papers of the late Sir H. M. Elliot, edited by Professor John Dowson, Susil Gupta Publisher,

Calcutta, 1875, third reprint, 1961. Available online via https://archive.org/details/cu31924024066593.

- **W. E. BEGLEY AND Z. A. DESAI, *Taj Mahal: The Illumined Tomb: An Anthology of Seventeenth-century Mughal and European Documentary Sources*, Cambridge (Massachusetts, USA), Seattle (University of Washington Press, USA) and London, 1989 (ISBN 0-295-96945-8).**
- **MILO CLEVELAND AND EBBA KOCH, *King of the World: The Padshahnama*, an imperial Mughal manuscript from the Royal Library, Windsor Castle, UK, with new translations by WHEELER M. THACKSTON, Thames and Hudson, New York, 1997 (ISBN 0-500-974489).**
- **FATHER FERNÃO GUERREIRO, S. J., *Jahangir and the Jesuits, with an Account of the Travels of Benedict Goes and the Mission to Peru*, translated by C. H. PAYNE, London, 1930; Munshiram Manoharlal Publishers, New Delhi, 1997 edition (ISBN 81-215-0769-3).**
- **JAHĀNGĪR, *The Jahangirnama: Memoirs of Jahangir, Emperor of India*, translated, edited, and annotated by WHEELER M. THACKSTON, Oxford University Press, New York, 1999 (ISBN 0-19-512718-8).**
- **FATHER PIERRE DU JARRIC, S. J., *Akbar and the Jesuits: An Account of the Jesuit Missions to the Court of Akbar*, Gorgias Press, Piscataway Township, New Jersey, USA, 2008 edition. Translated with an introduction and notes by C. H. PAYNE, London, 1926 and New Delhi, 1999 (ISBN 81-7536-162-X).**
- ***Letters from the Mughal Court, The First Jesuit Mission to Akbar (1580–1583)*, edited and with an introduction by JOHN CORREIA-AFONSO and a foreword by S. NURUL HASAN, published for the Heras Institute of Indian History and Culture, Bombay, by the Gujarat Sahitya Prakash, Anand, 1980.**
- JOSEPH A. KECHICHIAN and R. HRAIR DEKMEJIAN, *The Just Prince: A Manual of Leadership, Including Sulwan al-Muta' Fi 'Udwan al-Atba'* (consolation for the ruler during the hostility of subjects) by MUHAMMAD IBN ZAFAR AL-SIQILLI, Horizon Books, Singapore and Kuala Lumpur, 2003 (ISBN 981-05-1948-6).
- MUHAMMAD BĀQIR NAJM-I-SĀNĪ, *Advice on the Art of Governance (Mauizah-i-Jahāngīrī): An Indo-Islamic Mirror for Princes*, Persian text with introduction, translation and notes by SAJIDA SULTANA ALVI, State University of New York Press, New York, 1989 (ISBN 0-88706-918-5).
- R. NATH, *India as Seen by Babur (A.D. 1504–1530)*, MD Publications, Delhi, 1996 (ISBN 81-7533-000-7).

Political, Cultural, Religious and Military History Sources

- FRANCO ADRAVANTI, *Tamerlano: La stirpe del Gran Mogol*, Bompiani (Publishers), Milano, Italy, 2003 (ISBN 88-452-9221-5).
- BIANCA MARIA ALFIERI, *Islamic Architecture of the Indian Subcontinent*, Laurence King Publishing, London, 2000 (ISBN 1-85669-189-6).

- MUZAFFAR ALAM AND SANJAY SUBRAHMANYAM (EDS.), *The Mughal State 1526–1707,* in *Oxford's India Readings, Themes in Indian History*, Oxford University Press, New Delhi, 1998 (ISBN 019-565-225-8).
- **M. ATHAR ALI, *Mughal India: Studies in Polity, Ideas, Society, and Culture*, with a preface by IRFAN HABIB, Oxford University Press, New Delhi, 2006 (ISBN 0-19-564860-7).**
- M. ATHAR ALI, *The Mughal Nobility under Aurangzeb*, Asia Publishing House, Bombay, 1968 (ISBN 0-210-31247-5).
- CATHERINE B. ASHER, *The Cambridge History of India*, Vol. I.4, *Architecture of Mughal India*, Cambridge University Press, UK, 1992 (ISBN 0-521-26728-5).
- ANTÓNIO BAIÃO, *A Inquisição de Goa: Tentativa de Historia da sua Origem, Estabelecimento, Evolução e Extinção (Introdução á Correspondência dos Inquisidores da India 1569–1630)*, Vol. I, Academia das Ciências, Lisboa (Lisbon), 1945; and Vol. II, Coimbra, Imprensa da Universidade, 1930 (Vol. II was published before Vol. I).
- S. R. BAKSHI AND S. K. SHARMA (EDS.), *Akbar the Great Moghul*, Deep and Deep Publications, New Delhi, 2000 (ISBN 81-7629-163-3).
- S. R. BAKSHI AND S. K. SHARMA (EDS.), *Humayun the Great Moghul*, Deep and Deep Publications, New Delhi, 2000 (ISBN 81-7629-162-5).
- S. R. BAKSHI AND S. K. SHARMA (EDS.), *Jahangir the Great Moghul*, Deep and Deep Publications New Delhi, 2000 (ISBN 81-7629-164-1).
- SUCHISMITA BANERJEE ET AL (EDS.), *Great Monuments of India*, DK Publishers, London, 2009 (ISBN 978-1-40534-173-8).
- DOUGLAS BARRETT AND BASIL GRAY, *Treasures of Asia: Painting of India*, The World Publishing Company, Cleveland, Ohio, USA, 1963.
- A. L. BASHAM (ED.), *A Cultural History of India*, Oxford University Press, Oxford, UK, 1975 (ISBN 019-563921-9).
- VALÉRIE BERINSTAIN, *Mughal India, Splendours of the Peacock Throne* (translated from the French in 1997), Thames and Hudson, London, 1998 (ISBN 0-500-30083-6). Also published as *India and the Mughal Dynasty*, Thames and Hudson, New York, 2001 (ISBN 0-8109-2856-6).
- MICHELE BERNARDINI, *Il mondo iranico e turco*, in *Storia del mondo islamico (VII-XVI secolo)*, volume secondo, Giulio Einaudi (Publisher), Torino, Italy, 2003 (ISBN 88-06-16833-9).
- WILFRID BLUNT, *Splendours of Islam*, Angus and Robertson, London, 1976 (ISBN 0-207-95682-0).
- PERCY BROWN, *Indian Architecture* (*Islamic Period*), D. B. Taraporevala Sons and Co., Bombay, 1956 (ISBN 88-06-16833-9).
- **DAVID CARROLL, *The Taj Mahal*, Newsweek Book Division, New York, 1972 (ISBN 0-88225-024-8).**
- **DIRK COLLIER, *The Emperor's Writings: Memories of Akbar the Great*, Amaryllis, New Delhi, 2011 (ISBN 978-81-910673-6-1).**
- **DIRK COLLIER, *Paths to Peace: Religion, Ethics and Tolerance in a Globalizing World*, with a foreword by HERMAN VAN ROMPUY, honorary**

president of the European Council, Vakils, Feffer & Simons, Mumbai, 2013 (ISBN 978-81-8462-075-7).

- STEPHAN CONERMANN, *Das Mogulreich, Geschichte und Kultur des muslimischen Indien*, C. H. Beck (Publishers), München (Munich), 2006 (ISBN 3-406-53603-4).
- **WILLIAM DALRYMPLE, *The Last Mughal. The Fall of a Dynasty: Delhi 1857*, Bloomsbury, London, 2006, and New York, 2007 (ISBN 978-1-4000-4310-1).**
- FREDERICK CHARLES DANVERS, *The Portuguese in India, Being a History of the Rise and Decline of Their Eastern Empire*, in two volumes, Asian Educational Services, New Delhi and Madras, 1992 (ISBN 81-206-0391-5).
- ASOK KUMAR DAS, *Dawn of Mughal Painting*, Vakils, Feffer & Simons, Bombay, 1982.
- ASOK KUMAR DAS, *Splendour of Mughal Painting*, Vakils, Feffer & Simons, Bombay, 1986.
- LEO DE HARTOG, *Genghis Khan, Conqueror of the World*, Tauris Parke Paperbacks, London and New York, 1989 and 2004 (ISBN 1-86064-972-6).
- M. S. DIMAND, *Handbook of Muhammadan Art*, Hartsdale House, New York, 1947.
- **RICHARD M. EATON, *The Rise of Islam and the Bengal Frontier 1204-1760*, University of California Press, Berkeley, USA, 1993 (ISBN 0-520-20507-3).**
- S. M. EDWARDES AND H. L. O. GARRETT, Mughal Rule in India, S. Chand & Co., Delhi, 1956.
- **ABRAHAM ERALY, *The Mughal Throne: The Saga of India's Great Emperors*, Viking (an imprint of Penguin Books India and Penguin Books UK), New Delhi and London, 1997 and 2000 (ISBN 1-84212-723-3).**
- ABRAHAM ERALY, *The Mughal World: India's Tainted Paradise*, Weidenfeld & Nicholson, London, 2007 (ISBN 978-0-297-85209-4); originally published as *The Last Spring: The Lives and Times of the Great Mughals*, Viking (an imprint of Penguin Books India and Penguin Books UK), New Delhi, 1997.
- CARTER VAUGHN FINDLEY, *The Turks in World History*, Oxford University Press, New York, USA, 2005 (ISBN 0-19-517726-6).
- JORGE FLORES AND NUNO VASSALLO E SILVA (EDS.), *Goa and the Great Mughal*, Calouste Gulbenkian Museum, Lisbon, and Scala Publishers, London, 2004 (ISBN 972-8848-05-6).
- ***www.fourmilab.ch.*** The free *calendar convertor*, which can be found on this highly interesting website under the section 'Astronomy and Space', has proven extremely useful for the conversion of Muslim and Persian dates into Julian and Gregorian (Common Era) calendar dates and vice versa.
- ROBERT FREDERICK, *The Time Chart History of India: An Illustrated Chronological Chart of the History of India from the Paleolithic Age to Present Times*, self-published, Bath, UK, 2005 (ISBN 0-7554-5162-7).
- **BAMBER GASCOIGNE, *A Brief History of the Great Moguls*, Carroll & Graf Publishers, New York, 2002 (ISBN 0-7867-1040-3).**

- R. C. Gaur, *Excavations at Fatehpur Sikri* (a national project), Aryan Books International, New Delhi, 2000 (ISBN 81-7305-178-X).
- Rumer Godden, *Gulbadan: Portrait of a Rose Princess at the Mughal Court*, Viking Press, New York, 1980 (ISBN 0-670-35756-1).
- **Jos Gommans, *Mughal Warfare: Indian Frontiers and High Roads to Empire, 1500–1700*, Routledge, London and New York, 2002 (ISBN 0-415-23989-3).**
- Professor Dr Olivinho J. F. Gomes, *The Religious Orders in Goa (XVI–XVII Centuries)*, Goa Books, Chandor, Goa, 2003.
- Gulbadan, *Humāyūn Nāmā: The History of Humāyūn*, translated by Annette S. Beveridge, Munshiram Manoharlal Publishers, Delhi, 2001 edition (ISBN 81-87570-99-7).
- **Irfan Habib, *An Atlas of the Mughal Empire: Political and Economic Maps with Detailed Notes, Bibliography and Index*, Oxford University Press, New Delhi, 1982–1986 (ISBN 19-560379-6).**
- **Irfan Habib (ed.), *Akbar and His India*, Oxford University Press, New Delhi, 1997 (ISBN 019-564-6320-0).**
- Gavin Hambly, 'Asia Central', in *Historia Universal Siglo Veintiuno*, Volumen 16, Madrid, 1972 (ISBN 84-323-0068-3).
- J. C. Harle, 'The Art and Architecture of the Indian Subcontinent' in *The Pelican History of Art*, Penguin Books, London, 1986-1987 (ISBN 0-14-0561-49-8).
- Ibn Hasan, *The Central Structure of the Mughal Empire and Its Practical Working up to the Year 1657*, Oxford University Press, London, 1933; reprint Karachi, 1967.
- Robert Hillenbrand, *Islamic Art and Architecture*, Thames and Hudson, London, 1999 (ISBN 0-500-20305-9).
- **Dilip Hiro, *History of India, Rough Guide Chronicle*, Penguin Books, London, 2002 (ISBN 1-85828-842-8).**
- **H. Hosten S. J., 'List of Jesuit Missionaries in "Mogor" (1580–1803)', *Journal of the Asiatic Society of Bengal*, Vol. VI, No. 10, 1910, pp. 527–541.**
- Lawrence James, *The Rise and Fall of the British Empire*, Little Brown, London, 1994 and 1998 (ISBN 0-349-10667-3).
- Takeo Kamiya, *The Guide to the Architecture of the Indian Subcontinent*, translated by Geetha Parameswaran. Annabel Lopez and Bevinda Collaco (eds.), Aatsushli Saito Publishers, Tokyo, 1996, and Architecture Anonymous, Bardes, Goa, 2003-2004.
- **John Keay, *India: a History*, Grove Press, New York, 2000 (ISBN 0-00-638784-5).**
- A. Khoshkish, *Fársi Robáiyáte Omar Xayyám; Omar Khayyam*, in English by Edward J. Fitzgerald, en Français par J. B. Nicolas ou C. Grolleau, Ketab Corp., Los Angeles, 1977 (ISBN 1-883819-15-6).
- Ebba Koch, *Mughal Architecture: An Outline of Its History and Development (1526–1858)*, Prestel (Publishers) Munich, 1991 (ISBN 3-7913-1070-4).

- **EBBA KOCH, *The Complete Taj Mahal and the Riverfront Gardens of Agra*, Thames and Hudson, London, 2006 (ISBN 0-500-34209-1).**
- RUBY LAL, *Domesticity and Power in the Early Mughal World*, Cambridge University Press, Cambridge, UK, and New York, 2005 (ISBN 0-521-61534-8).
- A. K. S. LAMBTON, *Persian Vocabulary*, Cambridge University Press, Cambridge, UK, 1954 (ISBN 521-09154-3).
- STANLEY EDWARD LANE-POOLE, *History of India* (in nine volumes), Doubleday, Page and Company, New York, 1906–2008 (ISBN 978-1-60520-496-3).
- IRA M. LAPIDUS, *A History of Islamic Societies*, Cambridge University Press, Cambridge, UK, 1988 (ISBN 0-521-29549-1).
- ELIAS LIPINER, *Osbaptizadosempé, Estudosacerca da origem e da luta dos Cristãos-Novosem Portugal*, Vega Publishers, Lisboa (Lisbon), 1998 (ISBN 972-699-592-2).
- **R. C. MAJUMDAR (ED.), *The Mughul Empire*, Bharatiya Vidya Bhavan's History and Culture of the Indian People, Vol. VII, Bombay, 1974.**
- E. D. MACLAGAN, 'Jesuit Missions to the Emperor Akbar', *Journal of the Asiatic Society of Bengal*, Vol. LXV, 1896, pp. 38–113.
- G. B. MALLESON, *Akbar and the Rise of the Mughal Empire*, WILLIAM WILSON HUNTER (ED.), Rupa Publications, New Delhi, 2005 (ISBN 81-291-0697-3).
- JUSTIN MAROZZI, *Tamerlane: Sword of Islam, Conqueror of the World*, HarperCollins, London, 2004 (ISBN 0-00-711612-8).
- K. S. MATHEW, TEOTONIO R. DE SOUZA AND PIUS MALEKANDATHIL, *The Portuguese and the Socio-cultural Changes in India, 1500–1800*, Institute for Research in Social Sciences and Humanities, Meshar, Tellicherry, Kerala, 2001 (ISBN 81-900166-6-0).
- GEORGE MICHELL (ED.), *Architecture of the Islamic World, Its History and Social Meaning*, Thames and Hudson, London, 1978, 1995 and 2009 (ISBN 978-0-500-27847-5).
- GEORGE MICHELL AND MUMTAZ CURRIM, *The Majesty of Mughal Decoration: The Art and Architecture of Islamic India*, Thames and Hudson, New York, 2007 (ISBN 978-0-500-51377-4).
- **ANTONI DE MONTSERRAT AND JOSEP LLUÍS ALAY, *Embajadoren la corte del Gran Mogol, Viajes de un Jesuita Catalán del siglo XVI por la India, Paquistán, Afganistán y el Himalaya*, translated from Catalan (Barcelona, 2002), Milenio, Lleida, 2006 (ISBN 84-9743-175-8)**
- HARBANS MUKHIA, *The Mughals of India*, Blackwell Publishers, Oxford, UK, 2004 (ISBN 1-4051-3318-X).
- R. NATH, *Jharoka: An Illustrated Glossary of Indo-Muslim Architecture*, Historical Research Documentation Programme, Jaipur, 1986.
- R. NATH, *Private Life of the Mughals of India (1526–1803 A.D.)*, Historical Research Documentation Programme, Jaipur, 1994 (ISBN 81-85105-20-0).
- **FERGUS NICOLL, *Shah Jahan: The Rise and Fall of the Mughal Emperor*, Haus Publishing, London, 2009 (ISBN 978-1-906598-18-1).**

- DAVID NICOLLE AND ANGUS MCBRIDE, *Mughul India 1504–1761*, Men-at-Arms Series 263; LEE JOHNSON (ED.), Osprey Publishing, Oxford, UK, 1993 (ISBN 1-85532-344-3).
- KONSTANTIN S. NOSSOV AND BRIAN DELF, *Indian Castles 1206–1526: The Rise and Fall of the Delhi Sultanate*, Osprey Publishing, Oxford, UK, 2006 (ISBN 1-84603-065-X).
- AMINA OKADA, *Indian Miniatures of the Mughal Court*, H. N. Abrams (Publishers), New York, 1992 (ISBN 0-8109-3461-2).
- AMINA OKADA AND M. C. JOSHI (photography by JEAN-LOUIS NOU), *Taj Mahal*, Abbeville Press, New York and London, 1993 (ISBN 1-55859-617-8).
- E. JAIWANT PAUL, *Baji Rao: The Warrior Peshwa*, Roli Books, New Delhi, 2000 (ISBN 81-7436-129-4).
- ISAÍAS ROSA PEREIRA, *A inquisiçãoem Portugal, Séculos XVI–XVII, Período Filipino*, Vega Publishers, Lisboa (Lisbon), 1993 (ISBN 972-699-384-9).
- DIANA PRESTON AND MICHAEL PRESTON, *A Teardrop on the Cheek of Time: The Story of the Taj Mahal*, Doubleday, London, 2007 (ISBN 978-0-385-60947-0).
- DIANA PRESTON AND MICHAEL PRESTON, *Taj Mahal: Passion and Genius at the Heart of the Mughal Empire*, Walker Books, New York, 2007 (ISBN 0-8027-1511-7).
- AHSAN JAN QAISAR, *Building Construction in Mughal India: The Evidence from Painting*, Oxford University Press, New Delhi, 1988 (ISBN 19-562260-X).
- MUHAMMAD QAMARUDDIN, *A Politico-Cultural Study of the Great Mughals (1526–1707)*, Adam Publishers and Distributors, New Delhi, 2004 (ISBN 81-7435-386-0).
- *Religion at Akbar's Court, www.columbia.edu/itc/mealac/pritchett/00islamlinks/ikram/part2_12.html.*
- **RAGHU RAI AND USHA RAI, *Taj Mahal*, Times Editions, Singapore, 1986-1987 (ISBN 981-204-608-9).**
- MOHINDER SINGH RANDHAWA AND JOHN KENNETH GALBRAITH, *Indian Painting: The Scene, Themes and Legends*, Vakils, Feffer & Simons, Bombay, 1980.
- FRANCIS ROBINSON, *Atlas of the Islamic World since 1500*, Phaidon Press, Oxford, UK, 1982–1991 (ISBN 0-7054-0860-4).
- **FRANCIS ROBINSON, *The Mughal Emperors and the Islamic Dynasties of India, Iran and Central Asia, 1206–1925*, Thames and Hudson, London, 2007 (ISBN 978-0-500-25134-8).**
- **ROWENA ROBINSON AND SATHIANATHAN CLARKE (EDS.), *Religious Conversion in India: Modes, Motivations, and Meanings*, Oxford University Press, Delhi, 2003 (ISBN 019-566329-2), in particular the papers on pp. 23–28 (by Rowena Robinson); pp. 54–74 (by Stephen F. Dale); and pp. 75–97 (by Richard Eaton).**
- MALISE RUTHVEN WITH AZIM NANJI, *Historical Atlas of the Islamic World*, Oxford University Press, Oxford and New York, 2004 (ISBN 0-19-860997-3).

- J. J. Saunders, *The History of the Mongol Conquests*, University of Pennsylvania Press, Philadelphia, USA, 1971 and 2001 (ISBN 0-8122-1766-7).
- Annemarie Schimmel, *As Through a Veil: Mystical Poetry in Islam*, Oneworld Publishers, Oxford, 1982 and 2001 (ISBN 1-85168-274-0).
- Annemarie Schimmel, *Islamic Names*, Edinburgh University Press, Edinburgh, 1989 (ISBN 0-85224-563-7).
- Annemarie Schimmel, *Mystische Dimensionen des Islam: Die Geschichte des Sufismus*, Eugen Diederichs (Publishers), München (Munich), Germany, 1992 (ISBN 3-424-1116-9).
- **Annemarie Schimmel, *The Empire of the Great Mughals: History, Art and Culture*, with a foreword by Francis Robinson, Reaktion Books, London, 2004, and Oxford University Press, New Delhi, 2005 (ISBN 019-567334-4), translated from the German.**
- Robert Sigaléa, *La Médecine traditionnelle de l'Inde: Doctrines prévédique, védique, âyurvédique, yogique et tantrique; Les Empereurs Mogols, leurs maladies et leurs médecins*, Olizane (Publisher), Genève (Geneva), 1995 (ISBN 2-88086-179-9).
- Chob Singh Verma, *Mughal Romance*, Prakash Books, New Delhi, 2004 (ISBN 81-7234-080-X).
- Som Prakash Verma, *Art and Material Culture in the Paintings of Akbar's Court*, Vikas Publishing House, New Delhi, 1978 (ISBN 0-7069-0595-4).
- **Vincent A. Smith, *Akbar the Great Mogul 1542–1605*, Clarendon Press, Oxford, UK, 1917; second (revised) edition and third Indian reprint, S. Chand & Co., Delhi, 1966.**
- **Vincent A. Smith, *Oxford History of India*, Oxford University Press, London, 1981 (ISBN 10: 0195612973).**
- Percival Spear, *A History of India*, Vol. 2, Penguin Books, Harmondsworth, 1965 and 1970 (ISBN 0-14-02-0770-8).
- Henri Stierlin, *L'Art de l'Islamen Orient d'Ispahan au Taj Mahal*, Gründ (Publisher), Paris, 2002 (ISBN 2-7000-2156-8).
- **Giles Tillotson, *Taj Mahal*, Harvard University Press, Cambridge, Massachusetts, USA, 2012 (ISBN 9780674066281).**
- **G. H. R. Tillotson, *Architectural Guides for Travellers: Mughal India*, Viking Books, London, 1990 (ISBN 0-670-82642-1).**
- S. A. I. Tirmizi, *Mughal Documents* (*1526–1627*), Manohar Books, New Delhi, 1989 (ISBN 81-85054-71-3).
- Roberto Tottoli, *Vita di Gesù secondo le tradizioni islamiche*, Sellerio (Publisher) Palermo, Italy, 2000 (ISBN 88-389-1587-3).
- Joseph Velinkar, S. J., *India and the West: The First Encounters: A Historical Study of the Early Indo-Portuguese Cultural Encounters in Goa*, Heras Institute of Indian History and Culture, St. Xavier's College, Bombay, 1998.
- Richard von Garbe, *Akbar, Emperor of India: A Picture of Life and Customs from the Sixteenth Century*, translated from the German by Lydia G. Robinson, The Open Court Publishing Company, Chicago, 1909 reprint (ISBN 1-43251927-1).

- FRANCIS WATSON, *A Concise History of India*, Thames and Hudson, London, 1974.
- STUART CARY WELCH, ANNEMARIE SCHIMMEL, MARIE L. SWIETOCHOWSKI AND WHEELER M. THACKSTON, *The Emperor's Album. Images of Mughal India* (published by) the Metropolitan Museum of Art, New York, 1987 (ISBN 0-8109-0886-7).
- ANDREW WHEATCROFT, *Infidels: A History of the Conflict between Christendom and Islam*, Random House, New York, 2005 (ISBN 0-8129-7239-2).
- **STANLEY WOLPERT, *India*, third edition, University of California Press, Berkeley, USA, 2005 (ISBN 0-520-24696-9).**
- MICHAEL WOOD, *The Story of India*, BBC Books, London, 2007 (ISBN 978-0-56-353915-5).
- World of Islam Festival Publishing Company, *Paintings from the Muslim Courts of India*, London, 1976 (ISBN 0-905035-10-0).
- ZEENUT ZIAD (ED.), *The Magnificent Mughals*, Oxford University Press, Karachi, 2002 (ISBN 0-19-579444-3).

Index